Madeleine's Children

MADELEINE'S CHILDREN

Family, Freedom, Secrets, and Lies in
France's Indian Ocean Colonies

SUE PEABODY

OXFORD
UNIVERSITY PRESS

OXFORD
UNIVERSITY PRESS

Oxford University Press is a department of the University of Oxford. It furthers
the University's objective of excellence in research, scholarship, and education
by publishing worldwide. Oxford is a registered trade mark of Oxford University
Press in the UK and certain other countries.

Published in the United States of America by Oxford University Press
198 Madison Avenue, New York, NY 10016, United States of America.

CIP data is on file at the Library of Congress
ISBN 978–0–19–023388–4

1 3 5 7 9 8 6 4 2
Printed by Sheridan Books, Inc., United States of America

Contents

Acknowledgments   vii

Note on Currency, Measurements, and Place Names   xiii

Introduction: I Am Furcy   1

1   Madeleine: A Child Slave in Precolonial India   11

2   Crossings: Oceans, Islands, Race, and Free Soil   27

3   Family Secrets: Maurice, Constance, and Furcy   49

4   The Revolution: Emancipation without Freedom   66

5   The Limits of Law: Madeleine's Betrayal   87

6   A Perfect Storm   101

7   Incendiary Arguments, Justice Suspended   118

8   English Liberties   136

9   Freedom Papers Hidden in His Shoe   157

10 Damages and Interest   175

    Afterword: Remembering Furcy   195

Abbreviations   201

Notes   203

Index   309

Acknowledgments

HISTORIANS HAVE A STRANGE relationship with the truth. We try to tease it out of scraps of paper, landscapes, tombstones, and the stories that were produced at particular moments in the past. Each carries testimony forward from generation to generation, but all are shaped by the embellishments or omissions crafted for a particular audience's needs.

Paper is especially seductive to historians. Imprinted at a unique moment in time, its words remain more or less unchanging—confined to a folder, box, or a register, preserved in an attic, cabinet or archive—until discovered or called upon to divulge its story at a later date. We search for these papers, with the assistance of the often tedious and uncelebrated labors of librarians, archivists, and catalogers, and today code programmers and photographers. We interrogate the documents, reading them for what their authors intended for us to know, but also against the grain and between the lines, for what the words unintentionally reveal or what the original writer never realized.

This project has taught me more deeply than I ever realized before how vast is the slippage between written evidence and historical truth. So many things have happened that were never recorded on paper. So many written records bend the truth for posterity.

A BOOK SO MANY years in the writing depends a great deal on the kindness of strangers, friends, and strangers who become friends. From the kernel of an idea to its final realization, it has been both an intellectual and a personal adventure. I am inexpressibly grateful to those who have shared their expertise, their time, and their hard-won documents with me.

My own travel to the archives and the opportunity to present my work was greatly facilitated by numerous institutions and individuals over the course of a decade, and it is a great pleasure to recognize them here. At the beginning, when the book was just a new idea, Évelyne Combeau-Mari dared to express encouragement and invited me, with the support of Prosper Ève, then president of the Association Historique Internationale de l'Océan Indien (AHIOI) and Yvan Combeau, director of the the Centre de Recherches sur les Societes de l'Océan Indien (CRESOI), to begin my archival research at the Archives départementales de La Réunion. Subsequent archival research was funded by Washington State University Vancouver, a Washington State University Edward G. Meyer Professorship, and an American Council of Learned Societies Fellowship.

Fellow researchers have been incredibly generous, pointing me toward sources overlooked and sharing photographs or transcriptions of sources that might shed light on the lives of Madeleine and her children and the broader history of Réunion, Mauritius, and France. I am deeply indebted to Danna Agmon, Richard B. Allen, Jean-Michel André, Annie Blayo, Pierre H. Boulle, Jérémy Boutier, Patrick Boutier, Marina Carter, Adrian Carton, Amitava Chowdhury, Gwyn Campbell, Patrick Drack, Nicholas Draper, Edward Duyker, Gilles Gérard, Hubert Gerbeau, Mélanie Lamotte, Nathan Marvin, Chantal Plévert, Lorelle Semley, and Elke E. Stockreiter. Researchers took valuable time away from their own projects to help me fill the gaps at a distance, including John Boonstra, Dwight Carey, Arad Gigi, Miles Hewitt, Mélanie Mezzapesa, Raphael Mezzapesa, Preston Perluss, and Rob Shafer. I especially wish to thank Les Amis du Service Historique de la Défense à Lorient (ASHDL), under the direction of René Estienne, for helping me to locate key documents concerning Madeleine's early life.

Opportunities to present my work in progress helped to sustain and sharpen my project. These were supported by (in chronological order): Centre d'Études nord-américaines, École des Hautes Études en Sciences Sociales; Gilder Lehrman Center for the Study of Slavery, Resistance and Abolition, Yale University; Association des Historiens de l'Océan Indien (AHIOI), Centre de Recherches sur les Sociétes de l'Océan Indien (CRESOI); Universidade Federal do Estado do Rio de Janeiro and Universidade Severino Sombra (Vassouras), Brazil; University of Pittsburgh, Department of History Colloquium; Faculdade de Direito, Universidade Nova de Lisboa; Black Atlantic Seminar of the Robert Penn Warren Center for the Humanities, Vanderbilt University; French Atlantic History Group, McGill University; McNeill Center for Early American Studies, University of Pennsylvania; Obermann Center for Advanced Studies, University of Iowa; Queens University Department of History; Paul E. Beik Memorial Lecture, Swarthmore College; Indian Ocean World Centre, McGill University; Centre d'Histoire de l'Université des Sciences Politiques; Asia Research Centre, Australia Research Council Linkage Grant, Murdoch University, and the Indian Ocean World Centre, Major Collaborative Research Initiative, McGill University; Eurasia in the Modern

Period: Towards a New World History and the Institute for Advanced Studies on Asia, Tokyo University; L'Institut d'Histoire de la Révolution Française, Université de Paris I–Sorbonne; University of California, Berkeley; Le Morne Heritage Trust Fund, the Ministry of Arts and Culture Centre for Research on Slavery and Indenture, University of Mauritius, Le Centre Nelson Mandela pour la Culture Africaine, IMAF; Omohundro Institute; Institut national de recherches archéologiques préventives, and the French Colonial Historical Society.

Writing is hard; revision is much more pleasurable, especially thanks to these historians who invited me to attend their workshops or generously took time to read and comment on emerging chapters: Ned Alpers, Gwyn Campbell, Amitava Chowdhury, Jennifer N. Heuer, Mélanie Lamotte, Colette Le Chartier, Nathan Marvin, Joseph C. Miller, Vickram Mugon, Jennifer Palmer, Rebecca Rogers, Dominique Rogers, Brett Rushforth, Rebecca Hartkopf Schloss, Aditi Sen, Alyssa Sepinwall, Jennifer Sessions, Jeyaseela Stephen, Vijaya Teelock, Thomas Vernet, Cécile Vidale, François Weil, and Sophie White. Students in my classes enthusiastically dug into each chapter and helped me to see the story from their point of view. Likewise, the camaraderie and insights of the Portland French History Research Group both improved the work and made it a lot more fun: Mary Ashburn Miller (Reed College), Michael Breen (Reed College), Thomas Luckett (Portland State University), Barbara Traver (Washington State University Vancouver), Patricia Goldsworthy Bishop (Western Oregon University), Edward Timke (University of Michigan), Kate Bredeson (Reed College), and John Ott (Portland State University). In the camaraderie department, I'd also like to thank my dear friends and colleagues in the Washington State University Libraries, the history and English departments, and the Collective for Social and Environmental Justice for making daily life bearable—you know who you are!

I'm especially grateful to the five colleagues who patiently read and commented upon the full manuscript in one of its drafts from beginning to end. Their suggestions were invaluable in tightening and polishing the final version. Terisa J. Rond was the first person to read the entire manuscript from cover to cover; her readerly observations vastly improved the story's liveliness and flow. Mid-project, Pierre H. Boulle, fellow traveler and co-conspirator, invited me to join him in researching the nineteenth-century evolution of the Free Soil principle—I'm so glad that he did! Later he read the manuscript cover to cover; the book would be significantly less accurate and less consistent in style without his eagle eye. Sophie White has shared with me many an adventure in her homeland and abroad; her generous reading helped keep the wind in my sails when the coastline seemed very far away. Brett Rushforth saw through to the heart of the work and held it to his own high standards; the final version owes a great deal to his insight and perceptive creativity. Finally, my editor, Susan Ferber, believed in the project from the get-go and patiently brought it to fruition; *Madeleine's Children* bears the mark of her dedication to scholarly editing.

I like to say that Réunion and Mauritius are about as far away as you can get from my home in Vancouver, Washington, in the United States. Draw a line through the center of the globe and it will emerge a few hundred miles south of Réunion in the middle of the Indian Ocean. To travel there via Paris takes a full twenty-four hours of flight, and when you arrive, daytime has become night, winter is summer, the sun passes in the north, and all the stars are unfamiliar. That is why I am so very grateful to the handful of individuals who showed me kindness during my research and made me feel welcome there.

My husband, Scott Hewitt, and I met Mélanie and Raphael Mezzapesa as the managers of the simple *auberge* where we stayed while we hunted in the archives. They brought us into their family more than once, and Mélanie became my essential photographer of many of the historical censuses. She even accompanied me to a *kabar* when I was unsure how to get there. This book would not exist without her efforts on my behalf. Prosper Ève encouraged my naïve inquiry into his field of expertise, even when others would have made of us competitors. I relied heavily on his deeply researched books, and we shared a few meals together. I'm grateful for his spirit of collegiality with a foreign interloper. Gilles Dégras, originally of Martinique, now community organizer and poetic spirit of Réunion, invited me into the world of Liber Nout Furcy. I hope that this book does not paint too disappointing a picture of his hero. Let us all find freedom in community. Anthropologist Gilles Gérard encouraged me to dig more deeply into the memory of slavery and freedom that lingers in Réunion today. He introduced me to Madeleine's descendants and, through his scrupulous research, helped me to find the ending of Furcy's story. I owe an eternal debt to his scholarly generosity.

Furcy's family took me away from my own for the better part of a decade, sometimes literally, oftentimes in the scholarly absentmindedness of the obsessed. It takes a special kind of love to tolerate the endless ruminating and to share the joy of discovery. I'd like to thank my extended family for helping us hold down the fort and sharing in the adventure: Craig Erken, Helen Hewitt, Judy Peabody, Llyn Peabody and Chris Burns, and Jennie, Kris, and Jesse Rhoads. Two of us didn't make it through to the end: Robert Peabody and Richard Hewitt. I'm so sad that my father and my father-in-law aren't here to hold the finished book in their hands; each of them encouraged me to become a historian and helped me believe in this project. In the end, the three who have most deeply sustained me through all of this are my husband, Scott Hewitt, and my children, Miles and Louise. All of us have lived with Madeleine and Furcy for a long time. I'm so grateful for your laughter and your hugs; you are my sunshine in this drizzly gray forest.

Note on Currency, Measurements, and Place Names

WHILE THE LIVRE (BEFORE 1795) and the franc (after 1795) were the main units of currency in France, European commerce in the Indian Ocean was conducted primarily in the piaster (in French *piastre*), a gold coin equivalent to the Maria Theresa dollar ($) and the United States dollar (after 1774), and worth about six livres or five francs.[1] In order to find the approximate equivalent in contemporary currency, I converted the historical currency into U.S. dollars of the period, and then used the website *Measuring Worth* to calculate 2015 purchasing power, based on the consumer price index.[2]

Land in the Mascarene Islands was measured in *gaulettes* (a measurement unique to Isle Bourbon) and *arpents*, even after the introduction of the French metric system during the Revolution, and well into the twentieth century. The *gaulette* could indicate either length or area. Within the parish of Sainte Marie, the *gaulette* was equal to twelve *pieds*, but throughout the rest of the island it equaled fifteen *pieds*. The French *pied* (literally, "foot") of the Old Regime was equivalent to about 12.8 American or British inches.

Consistency in spelling or the naming of places is not prevalent before the middle of the nineteenth century, but it can be useful to present readers. In general, the historical place names have been retained as they would have been given in eighteenth- and nineteenth-century French, so, for example: Chandernagor for Chandan nagar, Saint-Denis, and so on.

The two islands at the heart of the story underwent multiple name changes over the centuries. The island that the French call Réunion today was originally called Mascarene Island in the seventeenth century, then Isle Bourbon (or sometimes "Isle de Bourbon")[3] until the French Revolution, when it was renamed Réunion (1794–1806), then, briefly (1806–1810), Isle Bonaparte until British conquest. The name Isle Bourbon was restored until the Revolution of 1848, when it became once again Réunion. Likewise, the island called Mauritius today was originally called Dina Harobi by Arab cartographers, renamed Maurits by the Dutch in 1598, and then renamed Isle de France under French rule (1715–1810). The British restored the name Mauritius after they occupied the island in 1810; it achieved independence as the Republic of Mauritius in 1968. In general, I have used the official name used by contemporaries in each successive era, signaling these changes as they first appear in the text.

Madeleine's Children

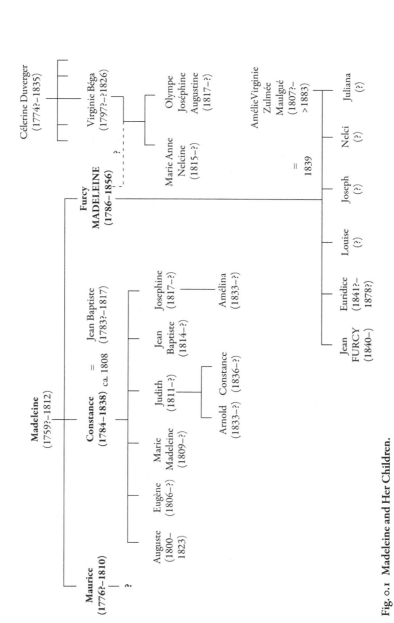

Célerine Duverger
(1774?–1835)

Virginie Béga
(1797?–?1826)

Olympe
Joséphine
Augustine
(1817–?)

Marie Anne
Nelcine
(1815–?)

Furcy
**MADELEINE
(1786–1856)**

?

Madeleine
(1759?–1812)

Constance = Jean Baptiste
(1784–1838) ca. 1808 (1783?–1817)

Auguste   Eugène   Marie   Judith   Jean   Josephine
(1800–   (1806–?) Madeleine   (1811–?) Baptiste   (1817–?)
1823)   (1809–?)   (1814–?)

           Arnold   Constance   Amélina
           (1833–?) (1836–?)   (1833–?)

**Maurice
(1776?–1810)**

?

AmélieVirginie
Zulmée
Maulgué
(1807?–
>1883)

=
1839

Jean   Euridice   Louise   Joseph   Nelci   Juliana
FURCY   (1841?–   (?)   (?)   (?)   (?)
(1840–)   1878?)

Fig. 0.1 **Madeleine and Her Children.**

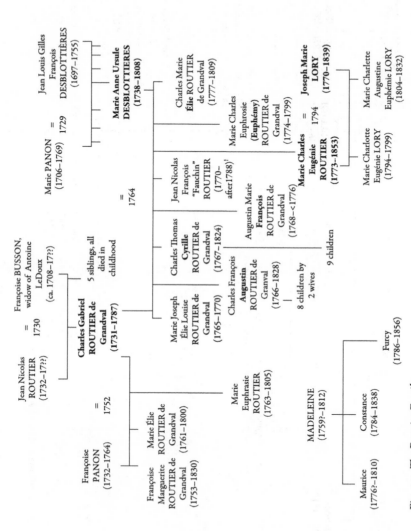

Fig. o.2 The Routier Family.

Introduction

I AM FURCY

I am Furcy. I was born free in the Routier house, to the free Indian woman Madeleine, then in the service of this family. I have been held as a slave by Monsieur Lory, son-in-law of Madame Routier. I claim my freedom. Here are my papers.[1]

WITH THESE WORDS, FURCY declared himself free on 21 November 1817 in Isle Bourbon, France's colony in the southwestern Indian Ocean. Thus began three decades of legal struggle as Furcy repeatedly challenged his putative master, Joseph Lory, in French and British courts while attempting to forge a new life for himself as a free man.

Today Furcy's legal struggle is well known in the islands where he lived: Réunion, an overseas *département*, or state, of France (formerly Isle Bourbon) and the independent Republic of Mauritius (formerly Isle de France), thanks to popular dramatizations of his story. At least two plays, a novel, and a song depict Furcy as the hero of an epic story to free himself from unjust slavery.[2] As dramatic as fictional accounts are, the real-life story of Furcy's determined persistence and ultimate success in winning his freedom makes more sense set in relief against the legal structures of slavery and freedom in France's overseas empire before France abolished slavery in 1848. Through detective work, this book traces the actual lives of Furcy and his family members through archives in France (including Réunion), Mauritius, and the United Kingdom. What it reveals is the gulf between the letter of the law and the lived experiences of people under slavery and freedom, and the too common chasm between law and justice.

It is no wonder that artists have embraced Furcy's life as the stuff of fiction. His mother, Madeleine, was sold into slavery as a child in Chandernagor, France's trading enclave in northeastern India, in the 1760s. Her French mistress brought Madeleine to France for a brief visit in 1772 and then gave Madeleine as a lady's maid to a colonial couple, the Routiers, who brought her as a domestic servant to their estate in Isle Bourbon. Within the Routier household, Madeleine gave birth to three children of her own: Maurice, Constance, and Furcy. Following the master's death in 1786, Madeleine's mistress filed manumission papers, freeing her in 1789, but she kept Madeleine's free status a secret from her—at least according to her children's later testimony—and retained her as a servant for another two decades. When the widow Routier died in 1808, Madeleine's youngest child, Furcy, became the slave of Madame Routier's son-in-law, Joseph Lory.

French law prohibited whites from giving bequests to people of color, whether during their lifetimes or in their testaments. So, in a legal sleight-of-hand, the widow Routier arranged her affairs so as to leave her loyal servant Madeleine a pension that was only revealed to Madeleine at the widow's death. This sum should have been sufficient to purchase Furcy's freedom, which Madeleine tried to negotiate with Joseph Lory. But Lory, in collusion with local notary officials, tricked the illiterate Madeleine into orally affirming (because she could not sign) a receipt for a pension that she never actually received. When Madeleine tried to press Lory to liberate her son—as she had understood the deal—the master showed her the notarized paperwork and denied that he owed her anything.

Therefore, when Furcy asserted his freedom from Lory on November 21, 1817, he understood his right to liberty in purely personal terms: he believed himself entitled to his freedom – perhaps even to have been promised it by Madeleine's deceased mistress – and wanted redress for Joseph Lory's deceit of his mother. The lawyers and judges who assisted Furcy in court realized, however, that since the receipt was technically legitimate, they could not try his case on those grounds. Instead, they introduced a host of legal arguments to justify Furcy's freedom under French law, most of them deriving from Furcy's relationship to his mother. Since Madeleine was born in India, rather than Africa, lawyers argued that South Asian Indians could not be legally enslaved under French law. Because Madeleine had had a brief sojourn in France as a teenager, they insisted that she was the beneficiary of France's Free Soil principle, whereby any slave who set foot on French soil instantly became free. Laws prohibited the sale or gifting of slaves in the continental kingdom, or metropole, so they argued that Madeleine's transfer to new masters in 1772 was illegal and void. Because Furcy was so young, "barely weaned from his mother's breast,"[3] at the time of her manumission in 1789, they pointed to later legislation that freed children under the age of seven along with their mothers.

None of these arguments found traction in Isle Bourbon's colonial courts, which were controlled by the creole (island-born) planter elite.[4] When France's highest court of appeal, the Royal Court of Paris, ultimately affirmed

Furcy's freedom in 1843, only five years before the declaration of general emancipation throughout the French empire, Furcy was fifty-seven years old, an old man by the standards of the time.

I Have Been Held a Slave

MADELEINE'S CHILDREN IS THE first full-length biographical history to explore what it meant to be a slave and to become free in France's Indian Ocean colonies.[5] Despite the parallel histories of plantation slavery and abolition in the French and British empires,[6] no slave autobiographies were published in the French language before 1848.[7] Slave narratives appeared in English with increasingly regularity in the late eighteenth and early nineteenth centuries, a powerful form of propaganda to draw readers to the antislavery movement.[8] Yet no equivalent to *Equiano's Travels, Incidents in the Life of a Slave Girl*, or *Narrative of the Life of Frederick Douglass* exists for the million or so men and women enslaved in France's Atlantic slave colonies of the seventeenth to nineteenth centuries: Martinique, Guadeloupe, Saint-Domingue, Guiana, or Louisiana, let alone those of the more distant Indian Ocean colonies of Isle Bourbon or Isle de France.[9]

The absence of historical French slave narratives was no accident. While British and American antislavery activists seized upon the older genre of the captivity narrative to recount the passage from slavery to freedom, France was lurching from Old Regime, to Revolution, to Empire, to Restoration, to constitutional monarchy and republic. The essentially Protestant narrative of subjection (to sin) and redemption (as salvation) did not resonate with contemporary French political struggles.[10] Instead, France's internal political upheavals drew attention away from the suffering of a few hundred thousand colonial slaves in the distant colonies, especially when they took up arms and liberated themselves, founding the independent nation of Haiti in 1804 and signaling the end of France's first global empire, which had once included much of Canada, the Mississippi Valley, and fortified trading posts in Madagascar and India. French censorship largely restricted the publication of politically charged content from the Ancien Régime to the mid-nineteenth century. Thus, there was no real audience for slave narratives in France.

This is not to say that French slaves were silent about their lives and conditions. French slaves gave spoken and written testimony in letters, newspapers, and legal forums but did not pen book-length autobiographical accounts.[11] Likewise, a handful of French writers and artists created fictional narratives of slaves' lives in short stories, novels, plays, and, more recently, film.[12] The most famous of these is Claire de Duras's 1820 book, *Ourika*.[13] This novella by a French noblewoman was based on the life of a real Senegalese girl, brought to France by her master in 1786, despite a French ban on the introduction of blacks to the metropole.[14] In this and other fictional accounts, lettered French men and women deployed the conventions of sentimental literature to give voices to their subjects and to highlight the injustice of racism.[15] Yet true life stories of plantation slaves never became part of the French canon.

This microhistory of Furcy and his family is not merely a unique family saga. It uses Furcy, Madeleine, and their extended family as a case study to probe the lived experiences of slavery and freedom in French and world history. Their individual histories illuminate the complex, varied, and locally particular manifestations of Indian Ocean slavery, derived from older systems in Africa and Asia, and show how this slavery changed radically through the introduction of the Atlantic plantation system, especially as sugar monoculture transformed the economies of Isle Bourbon and Mauritius.[16] Furcy's story showcases the many kinds of labor performed by enslaved people as well as the nuances of family relationships. While laws dictated that slaves and their free descendants owed "respect" to their masters, their daily gestures, conversations, and interactions operated quite independently of state regulation. Careful attention to Furcy's legal battles reveals the hypocrisy, contradictions, and outright fabrications deployed by planters, colonial legal officials, and metropolitan authorities to maintain slavery, as well as idealists' efforts to reform corruption and exploitation. The recovery of hidden genealogies shows how official tripartite categories of race ("white," "black," and "free people of color"), born of Atlantic systems of settlement, were in tension with the diverse populations in slavery and in freedom in France's Indian Ocean colonies. In other words, Madeleine and her children inhabited a microcosm of the wider changes transforming the French global empire, from its pinnacle in the middle of the eighteenth century through three revolutions (1789, 1830, and 1848) and its entry into the modern era.

Born Free in the Routier House

THIS BOOK ACCORDS CONSIDERABLE attention to the men and women who claimed Furcy as their slave: the Routier and Lory families. Furcy's history cannot be understood without careful attention to the lives of his masters, with whom his life was inextricably linked.

As wealthy free people, Furcy's masters appear frequently in a variety of historical records. The selection and preservation of papers produced by the master class make it possible to reconstruct the genealogy, land transactions, slaveholding patterns, and daily life of France's Indian Ocean colonial plantocracy. The French government kept scrupulous records of its subjects for tax purposes, while the Catholic Church (and, following the Revolution, the French state) maintained records of the sacramental milestones in the lives of the faithful: baptisms, marriages, and deaths. Notaries—private officials charged with drawing up and retaining the proper paperwork for all kinds of transactions, including sales, deeds, proxies, marriage contracts, manumissions, and wills—sat at the juncture of personal and commercial life in France and its colonies. Madeleine and Furcy, along with his siblings Maurice and Constance, are also noted in official records, but with much less frequency, since they were of marginal interest to the official record keepers except insofar as they were property or owners of property. Given that these records form the foundation of historical research, it is inevitable that the masters' lives constitute a large part of what can be known with certainty about Madeleine and her children.

While Furcy's masters were not exactly typical of the French slaveholding class in the Indian Ocean colonies—they were wealthier than most—their experiences shed light on the wider patterns of colonization, family formation, and transfer of property between generations. Many historians have explored how the colonial state's regulation of sex and the family undergirded racial and gender hierarchies in the colonies and in Europe and in economies founded in slavery.[17] Understanding this social fabric helps to illuminate what "freedom" meant in this particular context and the life as a free man to which Furcy aspired.

The specific and limited meanings of freedom are another key theme explored in this book. In French and American culture, freedom—*liberté*—is generally imagined in binary opposition to slavery. Nevertheless, French and American conceptions of freedom diverge in important ways. In French republican ideology, liberty is counterbalanced by equality (*egalité*) and brotherhood (*fraternité*), while Americans cherish personal freedoms, such as speech and religion. The celebration of freedom as an abstraction therefore can mask the very specific nature of rights and liberties enjoyed by the "free" in a particular society. Some kinds of freedom are recognized and enforced by the state. Other experiences of freedom are, by their very nature, performed in opposition to or outside the law.

Sociologist Orlando Patterson famously defined slavery as "social death," the violent stripping of the social ties that bind individuals to their identity within community.[18] Freedom, Patterson observes, is a composite concept, derived from at least three strands: personal freedom, "the condition of not being coerced by another person . . . the conviction that one can do as one pleases"; organic freedom, based in privileges or liberties accorded by those with more power in opposition to those with less; and civic freedom, "the capacity of all adult members (usually men) to participate equally in the social and political life of their natal community."[19] This framework illuminates some of the contradictions within the single term. The latter two qualities—organic and civil freedom—imply hierarchical social structures, in which some are free and some are not. All three of these meanings of freedom were at work in Furcy's life, whether in the assumptions and actions of his masters or in some of his actions as a free man.

Historians of slavery in Africa have posited the converse: that freedom consists in belonging—to family networks, to a community, to a polity. As Igor Kopytoff and Suzanne Miers put it in their seminal work, "'Freedom' [lies] not in a withdrawal into a meaningless and dangerous autonomy, but in attachment to a kin group, a patron, to power. . . . Here the antithesis of 'slavery' is not 'freedom' qua autonomy but rather 'belonging.'"[20] The irony, of course, is that "belonging" is exactly what a slave does to his or her master. The social ties that protect a vulnerable individual from arbitrary exploitation can also be construed as the natural authority of patriarchs or masters over their subordinate family members or slaves. This crucial dynamic is essential to understanding why, in societies where power operates through legalized hierarchies of family or patronage, some people prefer to remain in slavery or subordination, rather than resisting individually or through collective action. Some find safety or stability in protection, but the danger, of course, of belonging in this sense is that a patron may not protect forever. Death or departure can leave the weaker partner defenseless, needing to construct new communities of belonging and security. So, as Madeleine and her children pursued freedom, this condition meant different things in particular contexts and changed over time.

There is another reason why the Routier and Lory master families feature prominently in this book. Furcy belonged to this family not only as a slave but also as a son. Furcy insisted as much when he wrote to his legal ally Louis Gilbert Boucher in 1826, "I was born a French colonist, and I am the son of a Frenchman by birth."[21] Although no definitive proof has yet come forth, all circumstances suggest that Furcy's master, Charles Routier, was also his father. This means that Jean Routier was Furcy's grandfather, and Augustin, Cyrille, Eugénie, and the rest of Charles Routier's children were Furcy's half-siblings. Joseph Lory was Furcy's half-brother-in-law. Thus their relationships across slavery and freedom are integral to understanding the lives of Madeleine and her children.

To the Free Indian Woman, Madeleine

MADELEINE'S CHILDREN ALSO REVEALS the historical complexities of race.[22] When Furcy initially declared himself free in 1817, his legal champions built his case around the assertion that the Indians of South Asia were not subject to slavery under French law.[23] Local colonial authorities deemed this idea seditious, tantamount to inciting thousands of Indian-descended slaves to revolt. Yet the idea was hardly new. In sixteenth-century Spanish America, before Asia and the Americas were fully disambiguated in European minds, Bartholomé de las Casas famously urged the Spanish crown to ban "Indian" slavery in favor of importing slaves from Africa. In the eighteenth century, both French and British American colonies moved to outlaw "Indian" slavery, by which they meant the capture and sale of indigenous Americans. In 1759, a French lawyer argued that this ban also applied to slaves from India. These legal discourses were no doubt on Furcy's lawyers' minds.

While France's early history of colonial slavery in the Americas produced the racial categories of black (*nègre* or *noir*) and white (*blanc*) in the seventeenth and eighteenth centuries, its subsequent history of race relations diverged in important ways from Louisiana and the Antilles, especially in the Indian Ocean sphere, where place of origin persisted as the dominant label of identity through the eighteenth century.[24] French colonial censuses recorded the birthplace of each resident of the Indian Ocean colonies. They used the term *créole* to mean "born in the colony" for both slaves and free people, regardless of color. Creoles could be fully descended from European ancestors ("white" in modern parlance) or those from any other region of the world. Thus the census label *créole* makes it difficult to reconstruct the colonies' racial makeup. In fact, the term *blanc* ("white") is better understood as a synonym for "freeborn" than as a racial descriptor, since many such individuals descended from Asian and African, as well as European, ancestors.

Originally there was little legal discrimination on the basis of race in French law, but this changed rapidly over the course of the eighteenth century. As slavery expanded in the Atlantic and the Indian Ocean colonies,

French culture and law gradually overrode the 1685 edict granting former slaves "the same rights, privileges, and immunities as are enjoyed by freeborn persons."[25] By 1777, racial thinking was so ingrained in French policymakers that the government barred the entry of all "blacks, mulattoes, and other people of color" to the continental kingdom of France, regardless of whether they were enslaved or free. However, during the Revolution (1789–1799) and again in the Restoration (1814–1830) and July Monarchies (1830–1848) of the early nineteenth century, the French government turned away from formal legal discrimination on the basis of racial categories (though, to be sure, informal racism persisted in many interactions, especially in the colonies). Class and gender redefined French citizens' experience of political and civil rights during the Revolution and again as Napoleon's Civil Code (1804) re-centered society around the bourgeois patriarch.

Yet, even as early as the seventeenth and eighteenth centuries, the Atlantic racial categories of "black" and "white" did not map easily onto the binary legal statuses of slavery and freedom in France's Indian Ocean colonies. This was not merely due to the racial mixing of white masters and black slaves. Many of the original settlers to Isle Bourbon and Isle de France were free immigrants from Madagascar and India, so that by the middle of the eighteenth century a large proportion of the "creole" (island-born) colonists, although inscribed as "white" in colonial censuses (meaning "free"), were descended from free African and/or Asian parents and grandparents.[26]

Thus, when France's administrators in Paris and the Caribbean colonies issued a series of laws that increasingly restricted free people on the basis of color, a gulf emerged between those race-based restrictions emerging from the French Atlantic and the diverse and hybrid communities half a world away in Isle Bourbon and Isle de France. Local practices tended to ignore the inconvenient Atlantic categories of race until they became a useful means to assert power by later immigrants and the islands' wealthiest families, most of whom—thanks to France's land tenure and marriage policies—could trace their ancestry back to their French mothers and the handful of European women who had settled in the Indian Ocean colonies.

Here Are My Papers

ALTHOUGH I FIRST STUMBLED upon Furcy's legal brief (*factum*)[27] in the National Library of France in 1990, I did not return to his story until 2007, when, inspired by other historians' biographies of slaves in the Atlantic world, I realized that a biographical project was possible.[28] Even as I began to tease out clues to Furcy's life from this document, other historians were publishing on the history of French colonial slavery in the first half of the nineteenth century, offering new insights into the context in which he lived.[29]

Thus began a decade-long quest to archives in Réunion, Mauritius, Paris, Aix-en-Provence, and London to identify Furcy's ancestors and to understand his legal struggle for freedom. Because Furcy tangled in the courts of two empires (France and Britain) over three decades, his life is unusually well preserved in the historical record, perhaps better than any other slave in French history, with the exception of Toussaint Louverture.[30] Furcy's lawsuit, ascending through multiple levels of appeal over nearly three decades, produced literally hundreds, if not thousands, of pages of documents in varying degrees of legibility and conventional forms. The archives of Réunion and London hold a handful of his letters to legal officials, rare evidence of Furcy's voice, though mediated by a professional letter writer.[31] Clearly, Furcy belonged to an elite category of privileged slaves. As such, his experience cannot be taken as typical, but it does shed light on the more common practices and conditions of enslaved people in France's Indian Ocean empire.

By contrast, the rest of Furcy's family members have left a lighter impression on the historical record. Madeleine, Maurice, and Constance appear primarily in terse administrative inventories—censuses, parish records, manumission documents, the notariat, and the *état civil*—which offer considerably less insight into their internal lives or how they would narrate their own experiences. Yet as I began to write Furcy's story, I was drawn again and again to the other members of his family, especially his mother and his sister. Even here Furcy's lawsuit is critical in establishing some of the basic facts of their lives. Constance, a free woman of color when her younger brother Furcy embarked on his legal battle in 1817, offered important testimony, especially regarding her mother and her older brother, Maurice. However, some of the most detailed accounts of Madeleine's early life do not enter the public record until 1837 in the midst of Furcy's appeal, several decades after her death.[32] Like so much of the paper trail left by Furcy's struggles with Joseph Lory, the reported details of Madeleine's origins and childhood are therefore problematic; since they bore directly on the lawsuit and were recorded decades after the events transpired, many "facts" are the product of faulty memory and even deception.

The chasm between the written documents and the lived experience of slavery and freedom is the most persistent theme of this book. At each critical juncture of the story—Madeleine's childhood, the births of her children, Constance's and Madeleine's manumissions, the death of Madame Routier, Furcy's legal wrangling for freedom and reparations—significant discrepancies arise between how legal papers were designed to function and how they were deployed by the master class to different, even opposite, ends. Over and over, Madeleine, Constance, and Furcy faced colonial elites who patently manipulated the legal system and the historical record to serve their own purposes. Furcy sought, and sometimes obtained, assistance from other powerful patrons who also used the law, but in the course of litigation, his allies likewise fabricated arguments and evidence to fight fundamental injustices.

Madeleine's Children aims to untangle the truth from these knotty sources and to understand what slavery and freedom meant within each particular context. Here, family is key. Old Regime colonial law denied enslaved men and women formal recognition of lineage and ancestry. They bore no last names and were denied the capacity to pass an inheritance along to their children. Conversely, free people in France's plantation colonies—even those who were born into slavery and were eventually freed—invested in slaves, which often constituted the greater part of the property that they purchased, saved, and deeded to their heirs. Thus, it is not surprising that Furcy's struggle for freedom—waged over the better part of three decades—manifested itself as a struggle to assert himself as a father and husband in an increasingly bourgeois colonial society. Freedom meant belonging to family, acknowledging the debt to ancestors, and preparing a legacy for generations yet to come.

I

Madeleine

A CHILD SLAVE IN PRECOLONIAL INDIA

IN 1837, A WEALTHY colonial merchant, Joseph Lory, brought papers before the judge of a lower court in the French Indian Ocean colony of Isle Bourbon. He was accompanied by Jules Mourgue, a known slave smuggler, identified as "sworn interpreter in the languages of English and Spanish, living in Saint-Denis," deemed a suitable translator of Portuguese.[1] Two original receipts recorded in fading script on yellowing paper testified to the sale of a girl slave by two Portuguese slave traders in India:

> I, Sabino de Gomes, certify to have sold to Mr. Faustino Santiago, a young girl [*bicha*[2]] ... by the name of Badale, for the sum of 28 rupees,[3] under the condition that at any time, if any persons reclaimed the said young Indian girl, I would respond for the sale that I have made ... and finally I sign the present with witnesses, 9 December 1762.
>
> (signed) Sabino de Gomes

> I, Faustino de St. Yago, certify to have sold a *bicha* ... named Madeleine, age thirteen,[4] for the sum of 55 Arcot[5] rupees. I made the said sale to Mademoiselle Despense under the condition that if someone reclaims the said young Indian girl, I will commit to respond to the said sale, in faith of which I have signed the present witnessed act.
>
> Chandernagor, 8 October, 1768
> (signed) Faustino de St. Yago[6]

These two fragile papers are the sole surviving evidence of the early life of Madeleine, who lived most of her life as a slave to French Indian Ocean colonists. They are also very possibly forgeries.

What is certain is that a baby girl was born around 1759 on the Indian subcontinent, probably in the northeastern province of Bengal.[7] Calcutta, the region's capital, had grown rapidly from a small fishing village of less than 12,000 in 1710 to about 125,000 residents in the mid-eighteenth century but was dwarfed by the capital city of Dacca, some two hundred miles to the northeast, where Mughal rule had attracted almost a million people. The vast majority of Bengali inhabitants were peasants, subsisting on crops farmed in the fertile soil of the Ganges River delta. Through diplomacy, Europeans—first the Portuguese, but since the seventeenth century Dutch, French, and English traders too—had established trading enclaves in Bengal, paying significant rental fees to local rulers to take advantage of the region's many commercial products, especially high-quality cotton and silk textiles, to trade them at a profit in the world markets of Africa, Asia, and Europe. One such enclave was the French "factory," or trading post, of Chandernagor, on the Hoogly River, some 22 miles north of Calcutta, where Madeleine's mistress, Mademoiselle Despense, resided.

Customarily, masters chose new names for their slaves, whether at the baptism or simply when accounting for them on census returns. According to the second receipt, a Catholic master selected the name Madeleine for the Bengali girl, and probably arranged for her baptism, though no such record has been found in the parish records of Chandernagor.[8] In selecting these new slaves' names, slave owners not only eradicated the former identity of their new "property" but also made it almost impossible to trace these slaves' family lineages.[9] Madeleine's original name and those of her parents are probably lost forever.

The most detailed testimony regarding Madeleine's origins, these two bills of sale, first arose in the decades following her death, in legal disputes. The origin and timing of these documents cast doubt on their accuracy. The first, a transcription of the "original" 1768 Portuguese bill of sale between Faustino de St. Iago and Mademoiselle Despense, was offered in 1821 as evidence by Commissioner General Philippe Panon Desbassayns, the highest civil officer of Isle Bourbon, as part of an effort to smear a political enemy.[10] Later, Furcy's putative master, Joseph Lory, entered both bills as evidence of Madeleine's enslavement when Furcy undertook his appeal in Paris in 1837.[11] Both documents are highly suspect, but since the two receipts offer the most detailed evidence of Madeleine's early life, their historical plausibility must be analyzed.

Slavery in Eighteenth-Century India

MADELEINE EITHER BEGAN HER life as the daughter of an enslaved woman or, more likely, was pawned by her family into debt bondage at a moment of severe economic crisis.[12] Children were in high demand in eighteenth-century India and in the expanding Indian Ocean slave trade.[13] For the price of purchase and the little food and clothing they needed, masters could control children with affection, force and neglect; children also learned languages and tasks relatively easily. Although the practices and regulations regarding the enslavement and trade in children in India varied among the region's many peoples, religious traditions, rulers, and regimes, the British tried to pin down local customs into consistent, codified practices in the second half of the eighteenth century.[14] For example, British judges in Patna, Bengal, observed:

> We find that there are two kinds of slaves in this Province— Mussalman & Hindoo—the former are properly called *Moolazadeh* and the latter *Kahaar*. Slaves of either denomination are considered in the same light as any other property & are transferrable by the owner or descend at his demise to his heirs. They date the rise of the Custom of *Kahaar* Slaves from the first incursions of the Mahomedans when the Captives were distributed by the general among the officers of his army to whose posterity they remained. All other slaves have become so by occasional purchase as in cases of famine &ca.[15]

Thus, the British colonizers distinguished between an indigenous system of slavery, debt bondage—whereby poor people ransomed their children into temporary local enslavement as a means to survive a bad harvest—and captivity through military conquest, attributed to the arrival of Muslim invaders during the eleventh through the sixteenth centuries.

A wide range of social positions in precolonial India have been translated into Western languages as "slave".[16] Classical Hindu legal authorities variously recognized seven or fifteen different varieties of bondage—which was not the same as caste status—while Islamic law in Mughal India distinguished between three distinct categories of slave.[17] Although some slaves were put to work in agriculture and others were employed in skilled trades, the vast majority were employed in domestic or skilled household service.[18] This alone marks a significant difference between Atlantic and Indian Ocean slave systems in the seventeenth and eighteenth centuries.[19] To be sure, enslaved people in the Americas occupied a wide range of positions, from miner and herder to nanny and messenger. But from the middle of the sixteenth century, the vast majority of chattel slaves in the Americas were men imported from West and Central Africa to engage in plantation labor.[20] In India, slaves were typically local women and children from nearby rural peasant communities.[21]

Within a couple of decades of Madeleine's birth, British authorities examined Indians' complaints that their children were being stolen and sold into slavery. Portuguese and French traders were especially noted for their purveyance of child slaves across the Indian Ocean to colonies like Isle Bourbon (Réunion), Isle de France (Mauritius), and the Cape of Good Hope, and also into the Atlantic system.[22] As a result, in 1774 the British East India Company issued a law requiring that European slave traders follow

> the ancient law of the country . . . [which] requires that no slave shall be sold without a *Cawbowla* or Deed attested by the *Cauzee* [*qazi*, Muslim judge][23] signifying the place of the Child's abode & if, in the first purchase, its parents names, names of the seller & purchaser & minute description of the persons of both.[24]

The use of written deeds of sale (known as *cawbowla* or *kabolah*) therefore preceded the intrusion of the European slave trade in precolonial India, but whether they were required in every transaction is unclear. British judges further described "traditional" practices regarding the deeds of sale: "The *Kabolah* must be signed by the Mother or Grand Mother and not by the father."[25] Presumably this stipulation was designed to safeguard against child trafficking, to prevent men from kidnapping children and pretending to be the father at the point of sale. However, this custom does not appear in other Muslim slave regulations, and it seems to have been a local practice.[26] In any event, the receipts furnished for Madeleine in the nineteenth century do not list her parents' names.

Other Bengali practices applied specifically to female slaves. As in most slave systems, "children . . . born of Slaves are the property of the owner of the woman, tho' married to a slave of a different family."[27] This ensured that a slaveholder retained ownership of all children produced by his or her female slaves at a time when paternity was difficult to prove. According to British authorities, many Indian families relied heavily on female domestic slaves:

> The female slaves, we are told, are of more use in families[,] none being without them. It is urged that a condition of this kind is consistant [*sic*] with the manner of a country where women are kept in continued retirement & such privacy observed in regard to them as would be much affected by a frequent change of servants.[28]

The Muslim practice of purdah required that every elite household maintain a significant number of female domestic servants, since the ritual purity of elite women depended on culturally debased female servants moving between household seclusion and the streets.

France in India and the Town of Chandernagor

INTO THIS WORLD OF overlapping local customs entered an array of Europeans with their own understandings of what it meant to be servants and slaves. France belatedly followed Portugal, the Netherlands, and Britain into the Indian Ocean world trading networks, with a handful of ships passing there in the sixteenth and early seventeenth centuries.[29] At first, European traders sought spices—cloves, nutmeg, mace, and pepper. Medieval and early modern cookbooks and medical tracts show that these spices were valued for their "hot" and "dry" qualities and were prescribed by apothecaries to treat "phlegmatic" diseases.[30] The French government chartered a series of trading companies allowing them to engage in exclusive trade in particular regions, including in the Indian Ocean.[31]

The French East India Company, founded in 1664 with a fifty-year monopoly on French Indian Ocean trade, was modeled on the Dutch and British joint stock companies and promoted by the king's principal minister and the architect of his colonial empire, Jean Baptiste Colbert. However, while Paris merchants comprised the initial investors and directors of the Company, Louis XIV was the primary stockholder.[32] The Sun King's original charter essentially granted the Company feudal lordship over French establishments in the Indian Ocean, including judicial authority and the power to grant land concessions in Madagascar and neighboring islands, with the obligation to propagate Christianity.[33] Foreigners could naturalize as Frenchmen by donating 3,000 livres to the Company treasury; even larger sums (10,000–20,000 livres) could buy the right to participate in the general assembly, while sums greater than 20,000 livres purchased a seat on the board of directors.[34] The Company was entirely dependent on commercial and diplomatic relations with the Mughal emperor and local authorities at each site where it hoped to trade. Indian rulers, in turn, saw French merchants as pawns to be played to advantage against their Dutch and English counterparts. Gradually the French Company established trading posts (*comptoirs*) at coastal sites throughout the Indian subcontinent.[35]

Madeleine's early life after her sale to Mademoiselle Despense took place in Chandernagor, France's trading center in Bengal from 1690.[36] There the French purchased agricultural products (sugar, indigo, cane), minerals (iron, steel, lead, tin), and animal byproducts (silk, wax), but from the end of the seventeenth century, the highest demand was for manufactured goods: cotton and silk textiles.[37] The French recruited weavers and dyers to Chandernagor to produce colorful silks and cotton prints that their ships carried west across the Indian Ocean. Europeans were not the only, or even necessarily the primary, consumers of these fine fabrics. African elites demanded only the best textiles from Bengal and Gujarat in exchange for ivory and slaves.[38] To purchase these wares, the French imported items from Europe and other ports in the Indian Ocean sphere: high demand spices—pepper, coffee, cloves, cardamom—and the all-important specie, silver.[39]

The French India Company foundered by the end of Louis XIV's reign and in 1719 merged with Law's Company of the West (*Compagnie d'Occident*) as the India Company (*Compagnie des Indes*), ultimately achieving a global network extending from the Americas to China.[40] In the 1730s the French trade of rice, muslins, and opium in Bengal, organized around the small settlement in Chandernagor, expanded in exchange for silk, porcelain, tea, and lacquerware from China, piasters (silver currency) from Manila, spices from Achin (in Malacca), teak from Burma, cowries from the Maldives, and coffee from Mocha (Yemen).[41] As landlord of Chandernagor, the Company drew 3,500 livres annually and housed local weavers who produced raw silk for trade.[42]

By 1757, Chandernagor was a thriving town of sixty thousand, spreading out from the riverfront fort housing the administrative buildings and governor's residence. Fort d'Orléans, a massive structure, had been built on the river front a half- century earlier.[43] Arriving by boat one ascended the stairs beside the fort to find the market stalls and a building called the Dutch Octagon at the center of a little public square. On either side, upstream and downstream, were the private houses of Europeans, on streets set at right angles to one another. An outpost to the west guarded the inland approach to the city.[44] Two neighboring villages, Boroquichempour (population about fifteen thousand) and Choknossirabat (population eleven thousand), likewise grew larger in the 1750s, spurred by the French commercial activity.[45]

The 725 residents of the French center of Chandernagor were thus vastly outnumbered by their Indian neighbors; this figure included 329 "servants and slaves," constituting about 45 percent of the urban resident population. Domestic servants were clearly an essential aspect of early modern life in India, as they were in pre-revolutionary France. Intermarriage between French men and local women was common, as elsewhere in the French empire, provided that both partners were of the same social standing. Indeed, marriage to local elites was an important way to solidify networks for trade and diplomacy.[46] In the middle of the eighteenth century, some 79 percent of the male residents of Chandernagor were whites born in Europe or other French colonies, but 67 percent of their wives were local women of Eurasian or Asian descent.[47]

Madeleine's mistress, Anne Despense de la Loge, was an unusual resident of this enclave. Probably the younger daughter of a nobleman from a village midway between Paris and Dijon, she was born sometime between 1712 and 1731.[48] In 1755, Mademoiselle Despense accompanied the daughter of a Company artillery officer from a convent in Paris to Chandernagor so that the girl could rejoin her parents there.[49] These two unmarried women, along with a third, a "Mademoiselle La Saurée, requested in marriage by Sr. Isac, employee," arrived in Pondichéry in June 1755, before continuing on to Bengal.[50] Despense received 5,400 livres upon her arrival, worth about $27,000 in today's currency, enough to purchase as many as seven slaves if she were so inclined, though whether this was an advance on a letter of credit or payment for services rendered is unclear. In 1739 Governor Dupleix had complained, "No European women come here to us, except those not wanted in Pondicherry."[51] Perhaps Despense had arrived as a potential bride for one of the elite Frenchmen of Chandernagor, but the wedding never occurred, whether because of her insubstantial dowry, appearance, or demeanor. Instead, Despense moved into a house "to the west of the [Company]," where she lived for more than a decade.[52]

Despense, and later Madeleine, probably attended one of the two Catholic churches that served the community of Chandernagor.[53] According to Lory's evidence, Madeleine was baptized before she became the slave of "une demoiselle Dispense."[54] In the mid-eighteenth century, poor people from any religion could become slaves in a household practicing another religion, but Hindus typically owned only Hindu slaves, while Muslim and Christian masters expected their household slaves to convert to their own religions.[55]

In Hindu households, caste was an important factor in determining who could or could not be enslaved to whom, and for what purposes.[56] Higher caste individuals, such as Brahmans (priests and religious teachers), Kshatriyas (warriors), or Vaishyas (farmers or traders), were unlikely to become enslaved and could not legally be enslaved to anyone of a lower caste. Membership in a lower caste (e.g., Sudras, the artisans and laborers) or exclusion as an "untouchable" did not imply slave status, though members of these castes were more likely to become enslaved through debt. Hindu notions of ritual purity meant that society was divided into "pure" and "impure" castes. People belonging to the former, who might come into close contact with the master's

family, were more frequently employed as household servants or water bearers, whereas the latter were assigned tasks that might bring them into contact
with impurities—such as launderers or palanquin bearers who carried the
ornate cabinets suspended between two shafts on their shoulders and walked
barefoot in the streets.[57]

Unfortunately, the Chandernagor census of 1768 does not list the names of
the enslaved or free servants living in European households, so it is unknown
how many of them had been baptized into the Christian faith. Likewise,
the parish records for the churches of Chandernagor do not include non-
Europeans; no record for Madeleine's baptism can be found.[58] Nevertheless,
by all accounts, Madeleine's mistress was a devout Catholic, so she doubt-
less preferred Christian servants. The claim that Madeleine was baptized—
whether prior to entering Despense's service or afterward—is therefore highly
plausible.

War, Famine, and Bondage

RIVALRY WITH THE BRITISH East India Company generated armed
conflict at intervals in the eighteenth century, increasing in 1744–1754
and culminating in the Seven Years' War (1756–1763). Despite protection
from the Bengali nawab Siraj ud-Daulah, Chandernagor was the first French
enclave to fall to Robert Clive, in 1757.[59] By the 1763 Treaty of Paris, France
ceded Canada, Louisiana, and recent conquests in the Deccan interior of
India, a substantial defeat that marked the beginning of the British imperial
ascendency and France's waning global power. The treaty permitted France to
retain five trading posts in India—Pondichéry, Karikal, Mahé, Yanoan, and
Chandernagor—but the Company was barred from fortifying these posts or
maintaining anything more than a basic military presence there.

In the 1760s, the French quickly recovered commercially from their
defeat. The "surpassing" quality of Chandernagor was remarked upon by
a British traveler in 1768, despite the recent destruction of the old French
fort.[60] However, Governor Chevalier wrote to the directors general of the
French Company in 1768 and 1769 that the situation of the French in
Chandernagor was becoming increasingly desperate, as the British sought to
choke the French off from supplies of saltpeter, salt, and arrack, the preferred
alcoholic beverage. Likewise, they interfered with the cotton supply chain,
both at the source and by luring weavers away from the French.[61]

Madeleine almost certainly became a slave of the French as a result of a
regional famine. British conquerors in the second half of the eighteenth

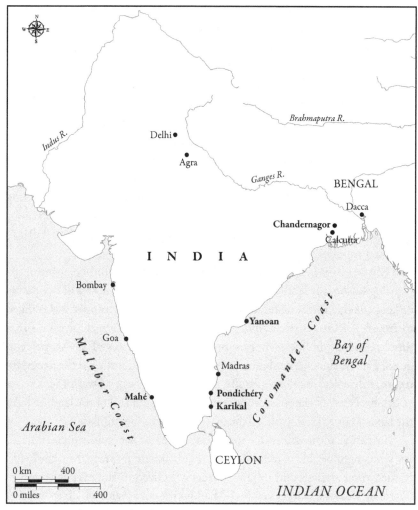

Fig. 1.1 Map of French India after the 1763 Treaty of Paris. France's Indian trading posts are indicated in boldface.

century witnessed and commented on the frequency of famine in India, especially Bengal, and how it drove poorer families to mortgage their children into debt bondage. Historians debate the degree to which these famines were inevitable natural phenomena caused solely by drought or flood, as opposed to social crises caused by human reactions to "acts of God."[62] Environmental factors—insufficient or excessive rainfall—certainly precipitated scarcity and inflated prices for food, but social responses could exacerbate or moderate the impact. Of course, famine was not unfamiliar to Frenchmen in the eighteenth century; indeed, France saw periodic bread riots as scarcity and economic policy triggered inflation, pricing the staple food of Parisians beyond the reach of the vast urban poor. These crises were interpreted by contemporaries as "famine plots," orchestrated by the king or his ministers, not acts of God.[63]

Bengal was economically dependent on monsoons—seasonal reversals of prevailing winds bringing powerful rainstorms—which affected both crops and the ships that entered and exited the ports. Rains normally arrived from the southwest in June or July to fill the streams and rivers over their banks, inundating the flood plain and depositing rich fertile soil. They departed in September and returned again from the northeast in mid- to late October. Too little rain meant drought; too much could drench the soils, drowning the cash crops of cotton, betel, tobacco, lentils, and rice, but also the poor people's staple, taro. Both drought and excessive flooding threatened drinking water supplies.[64]

Debt bondage in India grew out of sharecropping. At the beginning of the planting season, the landlord (*giri*) would supply a fixed amount of rice paddy or land (*bhuta*) to the sharecropper (*adhiar*). The sharecropper was obliged to return the interest-free *bhuta* at the end of the season. However, other supplies—seeds, bullock—were supplied at interest rates of 25–50 percent, due at harvest time. If the sharecropper's plantings did not yield the necessary return, he carried the debt into the next planting season. Over time, a series of bad harvests left the sharecropper in the virtual control of the landlord. All the labor went to paying off a debt that could never be fulfilled.[65]

The people most vulnerable to famines were not necessarily peasant farmers, who might be able to make do with their animals or forage from the fields. Rather, rural artisans and urban workers who lived in the cash economy— boatmen, weavers, market vendors—had no resources with which to weather an extreme crisis.[66] Grain dealers profiteered by purchasing and holding surplus grain, then selling it at inflated prices to those who could afford it.[67] The children of these families were presumably the first to succumb to starvation and disease.

Records suggest that significant droughts affected Bengal in 1711, 1718, 1727, 1728, 1732, and 1734; then the region entered a period of excessive flooding in 1737, 1741, 1742, 1752–1753, 1755, 1763, and 1767. A severe drought in 1761 caused an inflationary spike.[68] It was likely one of these last crises that drove an impoverished family to pawn their daughter into the bondage that ultimately led her to the household of Mademoiselle Despense.

While social mechanisms such as debt bondage worked to establish reciprocal relationships and obligations in Indian society, European traders initiated a transoceanic slave trade in Indian slaves similar to the Atlantic trade in West Africans, if on a much smaller scale. In the seventeenth and especially the eighteenth centuries, Dutch, British, and French were increasingly accused of kidnapping free people—both children and adults—and forcing them onto ships bound for Jakarta, Burma, Sri Lanka, and the French plantation colonies of Isle Bourbon and Isle de France.[69]

The Chandernagor Census and French Deeds of Sale

THE NINETEENTH-CENTURY BILL OF sale testifying to Madeleine's slave status gave her family name as "Badale." Today Badale is a prominent name in Maharashtra, in western India, which is geographically and culturally very distant from Chandernagor in the northeast. Unfortunately, while the census tables for Chandernagor list the surnames of Europeans, they do not list the names or households of Indians in its "black town" or the two neighboring villages, Boroquichempour and Choknossirabat, leaving no independent confirmation of a slave girl or family by the name of Badale in the region.[70] On the other hand, the censuses of Boroquichempour and Choknossirabat categorize the Indian residents into dozens of categories, giving some insight into the composition of these Indian villages. Here the census takers use the notion of caste and occupation more or less interchangeably.[71] For example, they categorize residents by recognizable caste terms (e.g., Brahmans, Rajputs, Barbirs, Haris, Pariahs), ethnicities or nationalities (Tamils and the Euro-Indian Christians known as "Topas"), and occupation groups (writers, carpenters, blacksmiths).[72] The name Badale does not appear within these categories.

Presumably, most of the deeds for the sale of slaves in eighteenth-century India have long since become dust, but a handful of these acts survive from two eighteenth-century French settlements in India, Karikal and Mahé.[73] As a small but quantifiable sample, they can be compared to Madeleine's receipts to see whether her alleged sales were typical. While these fifty-two acts of sale hardly constitute a full measure of the scope or frequency of slave sales in French India between 1766 and 1792, they represent a small sampling of a much wider trade that is documented in other sources, such as shipping, importation, and legal records in the metropole or in the importing plantation colonies.[74]

The fifty-two surviving deeds from Karikal and Mahé make it clear that traffic in children was pervasive. All of the acts record slaves between the ages of two and seventeen, for a mean age of 7.7, with boys and girls sold in roughly equal numbers. Many were of lower caste, and some bore Christian names.[75] Thus the young ages claimed for Madeleine's sales (three and nine) would have been fairly common in French India.[76]

It would have been easy for Lory to manufacture salient details for the deed of sale he offered as evidence of Madeleine's early enslavement. Based on the contemporaneous deeds of sale, Lory's reported prices for Madeleine in the 1760s—twenty-eight rupees ($14,000) at the age of three and fifty-five rupees ($27,500) at the age of nine—are quite high. The Karikal deeds reveal that the going price for child slaves in the 1760s and 1770s was typically three pagodas (a gold coin worth roughly $1,300 in today's currency, so about $3,900), a little less than the average price of an adult African slave in this era in Isle Bourbon.[77] Teenage slaves were considerably more valuable: the oldest slave in the collection of deeds brought sixteen pagodas ($20,800), and one, a Christian slave baptized as Antoine, sold for ten ($13,000). Perhaps Lory's higher prices were closer to the going rates in 1821 and 1837 when Lory submitted the receipts as evidence of Madeleine's original sales.[78]

The evidence from the surviving deeds from Mahé and Karikal of the 1770s also suggests that Lory's claim that Madeleine's parents sold their daughter into slavery is not farfetched. The vast majority of the sellers mentioned in the deeds, thirty-four of fifty-two, had Indian names; the remainder were French or possibly Portuguese. About a third of the Indian sellers are noted as the father, mother, or both parents, especially in the earlier records. (Apparently, the practice observed elsewhere by the British, of requiring the signature of the mother or grandmother on the deed, was not customary here.) Some records mention both relationship and caste, as in: "Nagatta, of the Vellaja [landlord] caste, sold her daughter Camalahi."[79] When the parents' names are not specified, their castes (e.g., "Paria" in six deeds, or "Bayadère," professional dancer, in one) convey that the seller is a parent fallen on especially hard times.

On the other hand, perhaps Madeleine was stolen. The Indian merchant and diarist Anandaranga Pillai, writing in 1743, a little over a decade before Madeleine's birth, describes an instance of the common practice of abduction into slavery near Pondichéry:

Mr. Soude, who serves under Mr. Cornet, the keeper of the warehouse of the port, commissioned Paramanandan to bring him slaves, and gave him a certain sum of money for that purpose. Paramanandan sent out his men to collect these; they purchased some and inveigled others into their clutches. They either mixed some deleterious material in the lime which the victims used with their betel and nut, or placed them under a spell by means of the magic paint, which they carried in a box in their hands. And then overpowering them, reduced them to slavery. . . . It further transpired that these kidnappers possessed a house in a village near Tranquebar and that they were in the habit of alluring there the people living in the hamlets to the west of that place. Batches of fifty or a hundred individuals were imprisoned at one time in the building. They were conveyed during the night, in a boat to Ariyankuppam, where they were confined in a house belonging to Paramanandan. Here their heads were shaved, black cloths were given them to wear and each individual had a fetter placed on one leg. During the night, they were removed again and brought to the house of Mr. Soude, when they were put into the slave prison until a vessel came to take them away, when it arrived they were placed in boats and carried on board.[80]

It is clear, then, that enslavement in India did not necessarily differ significantly from practices encouraged by European traders in Africa or Southeast Asia, although the use of poisons or "magic" was not typical elsewhere. It is, however, similar to impressment, a method used by many European navies to recruit sailors in this era; the Dutch were particularly renowned for incapacitating landlubbers with liquor and carrying them unconscious to ships, where they woke up to new, arduous lives as seamen.[81]

Impoverished Indian parents, while willing to place their children in peonage, nevertheless feared that the master might sell their children to foreign traders, an irreversible loss. One contemporaneous record, not an act of sale, shows how a father deliberately introduced language into the contract seeking to prevent the permanent enslavement of his child:

> Comarin, of the Vellaja caste, restored his son, age twelve, to Appu, charging him with raising him and furnishing all of his needs, without being able to sell him as a slave. The father received three and a half pagodas [about $4,500] for the transfer of his son.[82]

Perhaps Madeleine was the victim of a similar arrangement gone awry.

The Portuguese names specified in Joseph Lory's receipts, Sabino de Gomes and Faustino Santiago, are highly plausible but ultimately unverifiable. The majority of slave purchasers in these Mahé and Karikal transactions (62 percent) had French or Portuguese names. Some were agents for East India company employees in Pondichéry, the capital of French India. Several seem to be regular traders, their names appearing three or four times in the fifty-two deeds.[83] One of these, an Alexandre de Rosaire, was a member of the Topas, a hybrid Euro-Indian Catholic community living in coastal India.[84] According to the 1753 Mahé census, among the hundreds of members of the Topas community, many of whom had Portuguese names and some of whom were wealthy enough to own several slaves, are several men with the surname Gomes.[85]

Therefore, the Portuguese surnames of Madeleine's putative slave traders are certainly credible. Either man could have belonged to the Portuguese or Topas communities of the Indian subcontinent. However, neither of the specific names Sabino de Gomes or Faustino Santiago appear in the Chandernagor census of 1768, which lists all the Europeans. Nor do they appear in any of the indexes to the inventories of the archives from eighteenth-century French India.[86] Of course, absence of evidence is not evidence of absence. It is possible that the traders were not themselves residents of a French enclave. They might have lived among the hundreds of Topas in the neighboring villages of Boroquichempour and Choknossirabat, classified by caste but not enumerated by name.[87] Perhaps their names could be found through careful combing of eighteenth-century Portuguese archives. However, without confirming evidence of their presence, we must also consider the possibility that Furcy's master, Joseph Lory, invented these names and, with the help of his cronies, forged the two receipts to support his case much later, using plausible details to anchor his story in documentary evidence.

Madeleine and Her Mistress

AS PART OF FURCY'S initial colonial lawsuit for freedom in 1817, his elder sister Constance testified that Madeleine was "placed by her parents at a young age in the care of the *demoiselle* Dispense, then a nun in Chandernagor."[88] This woman, Anne Despense de la Loge, appears in the Chandernagor census of 1768 (no age listed, but probably between 38 and 56), one of only sixty-eight white women in the town and one of only fourteen born in France.[89] Instead of appearing among the male heads of household in the far left column of the census, she is listed at the beginning of some twenty women whose husbands were absent or dead. Despense was, quite unusually, a single French noble woman in Bengal who was not a widow.[90] It is not clear whether the census grouping reflects its own internal principle of organization (masterless women) or whether they lived together in some kind of community under the protection of the Company. Did Mademoiselle Despense belong to an uncloistered religious community in Chandernagor? The Ursuline community established in Pondichéry decades earlier had fallen victim to jurisdictional disputes between the Jesuits and the Capuchins in 1739.[91] There is no confirmation of a formal religious house for women in Chandernagor, though the presence of all these women living together in the census is certainly suggestive.[92]

Though Madeleine is not named in the census, she perfectly matches the demographic profile of enslaved servants in Chandernagor in 1768. Females were preferred to males by almost two to one, and more than four-fifths of these servants were enslaved.[93] Anne Despense de la Loge employed six servants: one free male, three free females, one male slave, and one female slave. Clearly she was a woman of means. Could the female slave be Madeleine?

Given the young age at which Madeleine entered slavery, it is unlikely that she retained many memories of her birth family as she grew up, though her experience in this regard was far from unique. In a rare eighteenth-century slave autobiography from the Muslim world, Miskīn, a Turkish boy sold to a Muslim master in Panjab, Afghanistan, reflected:

> I do not remember what name I had been given. I have also forgotten the names of my parents. . . . As I was separated from my parents during my childhood, I remember neither my origins nor my community.[94]

Likewise, Madeleine's parents and birthplace have been erased from the record.[95] But her origins in India remained important enough to share later with her children.

Miskīn's autobiography continues: "I was undiscerning, illiterate and innocent. . . . From conversations of the knowledgeable, and the company of [learned people], I could derive good examples. . . . I stored in my heart the pearls of knowledge gathered from reading books on ancient and later histories."[96] As a girl and the dependent of an eighteenth-century French woman, Madeleine was never taught to read or write. This was not because she was enslaved but because literacy was not deemed necessary or useful to most French girls of the time.[97] Madeleine's lack of basic literacy skills would much later prove catastrophic for her and Furcy.

The two fading, torn receipts produced by Joseph Lory to lay claim to Madeleine's future son Furcy reside in the Departmental Archives of Réunion. To prove definitively whether these are later forgeries or genuine receipts for Madeleine's early sales would be difficult, but the question must be posed: Are they genuine, or did Lory manufacture them to retain control of Furcy?

If the two Portuguese slave traders really existed and samples of their handwriting could be found, one could compare these documents to confirm the receipts' legitimacy, but to date no Sabino de Gomes or Faustino de St. Yago has been found in the archival record. If they never existed, there are no signatures or handwriting to compare, so forgery can't be proven this way either.

What about the receipts' paper and ink? Experts pay attention to unique watermarks embedded in historical papers to date their manufacture. Paper dating later than the 1760s would be proof that the receipts were created after the fact. Can the chemical composition of the paper, which is markedly darker than the papers surrounding the receipts, suggest anything certain about its age? Forgers have been known to dip paper in a coffee solution to suggest aging, and coffee was certainly available to Lory in Isle Bourbon.[98] The chemical composition of the ink might be tested to determine whether it was the same ink that produced the writing that supposedly dated from the 1760s and that of 1837. However, the Departmental Archives of Réunion does not have the time or resources for such an investigation.[99]

It seems entirely possible that the first receipt, from 1762, which does not mention the name of Madeleine or Mademoiselle Despense, is an authentic bill of sale from that year, perhaps drawn from some ancient folder by Jules Mourgue or his brother-in-law, Isle Bourbon's commissioner, Philippe Panon Desbassayns, to support his position to the king's minister in the political feud catalyzed by Furcy's lawsuit. The second, the first to bear the names of Madeleine and Mademoiselle Despense, did not appear in the historical record until 1837, as Furcy appealed his case to Paris. It seems likely that it was manufactured on a scrap of eighteenth-century paper to "prove" the legal transfer of Madeleine to Despense in 1768. The signatures of witnesses on each document are quite varied, which suggests either a superb forger or collusion between several individuals. But a definitive answer as to whether Joseph Lory or his allies forged the papers is not possible without expert investigation by professional conservators.

While Madeleine's true origins are obscure, her experience as a child slave in India was likely typical. Whether pawned by her parents during famine or kidnapped by a slave trader, she ended up the Catholic servant of a Catholic mistress in a French trading post. Her position there, in the thriving commercial hub of Chandernagor, allowed Madeleine to learn French language and customs in the service of a wealthy French woman. Such training at a young age would afford her a relatively privileged position in slavery. Thoroughly accustomed to language, religion, and subservience, Madeleine's childhood prepared her for the intimate role of personal servant to French masters. For her part, Mademoiselle Despense was beginning to tire of colonial exile, which would effectively change Madeleine's life forever.

2

Crossings

OCEANS, ISLANDS, RACE, AND FREE SOIL

SADLY, THERE ARE NO surviving portraits of Madeleine, her children, or any of the people in their immediate circle. Therefore, Madeleine's appearance must be imagined on the basis of a few scant clues. While most bureaucratic documents categorize Madeleine as *Indienne*, a few described her as a *négresse*, suggesting that her skin was fairly dark.[1] Her hair could have been curly or straight, her eyes hazel or brown, her face round or thin. Likewise, the appearance of her mistress, Mademoiselle Despense, is completely unknown.

European ideas about color and status, what we call "race" today, were undergoing dynamic change in the eighteenth century. Like their English and Dutch counterparts, the French used the terms "black" (*noir*) or "negro" (*nègre*) informally to designate Indian servants as well as Africans in the Indian Ocean sphere.[2] The words *nègre* (male) and *négresse* (female) typically connoted slave status, though they could also refer to free blacks, especially as derogatory terms. Borrowed from the Italian term *raza*, the French term *race* referred first to breeds of animals and then to people.[3] The seventeenth-century French traveler to India François Bernier was the first writer to systematically divide the world into four races on the basis of color, but he did not try to explain the causes of these differences.[4] Older explanations held that blackness was the result of "maternal imagination," whereby a pregnant woman could gaze upon a black man, a portrait of one, or even a dark object and thereby color her growing fetus, or of the curse of Ham, considered retribution for when Noah's errant son looked upon his father's nakedness.[5] By the middle of the eighteenth century, Enlightenment scientists debated whether skin color was inherited or the result of prolonged exposure to intense sunlight near the equator, but few doubted that such physical traits were intrinsically linked to moral attributes.[6]

Madeleine's travel between the Indian Ocean world and Europe caused her to be inscribed as a racialized subject in passenger lists and later censuses. In Bengal, Madeleine might be described by a host of different status markers—her original caste, her slave status, her religion. By transiting the oceans on a French ship, she acquired the label *négresse*, which emphasized her slave status. Slave or free, black or Indian, Madeleine's status had legal ramifications as well.

Departure

IN 1770, MADEMOISELLE DESPENSE decided that it was time to leave Chandernagor and return to France. As a mere girl of eleven or twelve, Madeleine had no alternative but to follow her mistress. Where could she escape to? Who would take in such a runaway? Would the conditions necessarily be better than her current situation?

The long ocean voyage to France would take Madeleine from the semi-cloistered space she had inhabited in Chandernagor into the masculine worlds of ships and port towns. Her brief residence in France would be pivotal in future legal debates about her son's freedom. Thus, Madeleine's ocean crossing was not merely a physical or geographical relocation. Her passage, occurring at a time when French naval forces were gathering in the Indian Ocean for war, marked a significant rupture between her childhood and her adulthood, full of lingering and unforeseen consequences.

Two crises at the end of the 1760s probably drove Mademoiselle Despense to leave India after sixteen years' residence there. First, the October monsoon of 1769 never arrived, and Bengal began to suffer a severe, unprecedented drought, "insomuch as the oldest inhabitants never remember anything like it."[7] The famine of 1770–1771 was one of the worst of the century, with up to half of all crops lost and the peasantry suffering massive dislocation and death.[8] Second, rumors reached the English in Bengal that French troops were amassing in the island colony of Isle de France, suggesting an imminent threat of attack on the British Company forces nearby at Fort William in Calcutta.[9] The unfortified city of Chandernagor was a poor place for a middle-aged spinster to wait out a retaliatory or even preemptive British attack. Mademoiselle Despense determined to pack up and live out the rest of her days in France.[10]

As she made her arrangements to depart, Despense decided to bring three servants, all listed in passenger records as "*noirs*" to serve her during the long crossing, which typically lasted seventeen to twenty months. For passengers of elevated status and officers of the navy, a retinue of two to three attendants was not unusual. From among her six servants, Despense selected Madeleine, as well as Cécile and Janot, the last of whom was about sixteen. Passenger records offer the first definitive, named evidence of Madeleine in the historical record, confirming that she did travel with Mademoiselle Despense from India to France in 1771–1772.[11]

Travel across the Indian Ocean took advantage of seasonal winds and currents. From November to March, the monsoon winds blow from the northeast, facilitating westward travel. Late in December, Madeleine and her mistress boarded the *Hector*, a ship carrying 148 crewmen, and the ship weighed anchor on 11 January 1771.[12] As the boat slipped southward over the equator, the North Star and all the familiar constellations of Madeleine's childhood disappeared, to be replaced by unfamiliar points and patterns of light. Neither Madeleine nor Mademoiselle Despense would ever return to India.

Perhaps Madeleine felt terrified and despairing, as did the thirteen-year-old servant boy Munnoo who accompanied his master, William Hickey, from Calcutta to England. Hickey locked "the wretched boy" in the ship's cabin, as

> [Munnoo] fixed himself at the quarter gallery window where he sat looking the very image of despair. . . . There he remained as long as the vessel that was rapidly conveying his old friends from him was discernible, leaving the poor fellow in the midst of strangers and in a scene as uncouth as it was novel to him.[13]

Cécile, Janot, and Mademoiselle Despense were not the only souls who would share Madeleine's fear, excitement, seasickness, and tedium during the ocean crossing. Four French and English women passengers, several French children, and a handful of Frenchmen, including the captain, Augustin Louis Desblottières, all brought servants, most of whom were variously described as *noir* or *nègre*. These people waited on their wealthy masters and mistresses at meals, tidied their cabins, washed their laundry, held their basins, and emptied their slop buckets. If Madeleine was among the youngest of these servants, at least there were several women and the children of Madame Ogerdias to keep her company. Within a few days, Madeleine probably made contact with the other young people and found ways to pass the time in games or storytelling in between the chores she, Cécile, and Janot performed for Mademoiselle Despense. In this way, at least, Madeleine's ocean journey differed radically from the voyages of millions of African slaves transported in cargo holds, chained and forced to sleep in their own waste.

While there is no day-by-day record of Madeleine's voyage, a particularly eloquent traveler had penned his observations aboard an East India Company vessel in the Indian Ocean just three years earlier. Bernardin de Saint-Pierre's

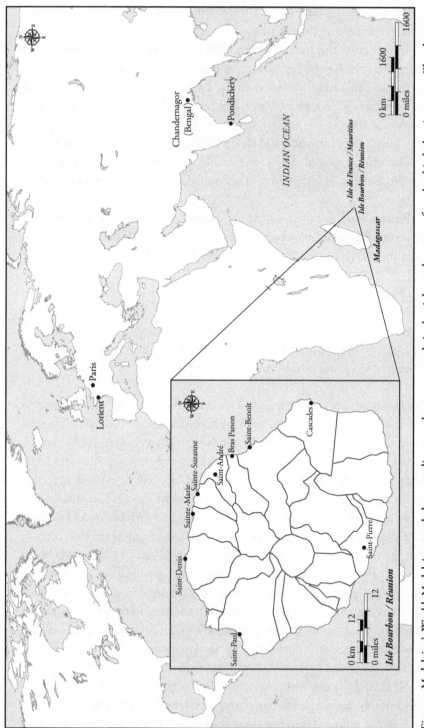

Fig. 2.1 Madeleine's World. Madeleine traveled greater distances than most people in the eighteenth century, from her birthplace in or near Chandernagor to Lorient, France, to Isle Bourbon (today Réunion Island).

sentimental story of star-crossed lovers in Mauritius, *Paul and Virginia*, would become one of the most popular novels of the late eighteenth and nineteenth centuries, but his *Voyage à l'Ile de France*, describing his 1768 journey, is full of trenchant commentary and vivid descriptions of the clouds, the storms, the sun, the waves, the fish, the birds, thirst, and scurvy. Regarding their human companions, Bernardin notes that although French sailors were essentially "frank, generous, brave, and above all good husbands," they could be "in general, taciturn and somber," and prone to "drunkenness."[14] He watched one sailor steal from another while he slept.[15]

Land and Sea

SIX MONTHS INTO THE voyage, in June 1771, the *Hector* made landfall on the island of Isle de France, located about six hundred miles east of Madagascar, where it docked for four months, picking up water, supplies, and passengers, and waited for the seasonal winds that would facilitate travel around the Cape of Good Hope.[16] Madeleine observed the island with curiosity as the *Hector* approached its sloping, low, forested mountain ranges, the remnants of the extinct volcano that had once pushed the island from the ocean floor.[17]

The *Hector* probably docked in Port Louis, the newer deepwater port on the island's northwest coast. Madeleine would have found herself jostling among the thousands of Indian and African laborers imported there some decades earlier by the island's enterprising governor, Mahé de la Bourdonnais—some under contract, some purchased as slaves, and some kidnapped—to construct the new port in a district to the south of the city.[18] Along the wharves and in the fort, some ten thousand soldiers and sailors had recently arrived, sent there by Louis XV in anticipation of a new naval war with Britain.[19] These military men overwhelmed the island's resident population of 3,163 Europeans and 587 free residents from the Indian Ocean basin (mostly from India and Madagascar, the latter known as "Malagasy"). All of these inhabitants depended on the 15,027 Indian, Malagasy, and African slaves who fed, housed, and cared for them. Isle de France's earliest permanent communities were the maroons—former slaves and their descendants brought by the Dutch in the seventeenth century who escaped and continued to live in the island's interior and along the remote shorelines where the French had not yet established control. Indeed, France's colonists were relatively recent arrivals, having only begun to settle Isle de France two generations earlier, in 1721 after the Dutch abandoned the colony in 1710.[20]

Thus, in 1771, men dramatically outnumbered the few women brought to Isle de France as domestic servants, slaves and, more rarely, wives. Madeleine would have sensed this gender imbalance, probably staying close to her mistress when they left the ship. It was no place for a woman or girl to walk alone, day or night. The port was full of seamen on leave and hard-scrabble opportunists who came into town from the plantations; they were unlikely to find Madeleine's position as the maid of a French traveler an impediment to their flirtation or harassment. After the ship took on fresh water and supplies, Madeleine and her companions were probably relieved to leave behind the Isle de France but also fearful of the second half of their journey through treacherous waters along the African coast.

As the *Hector* departed on October 18, it carried away thirty-two new passengers: thirty-one men and one woman.[21] Some of them were Company officers, others were skilled masters of their trade—a surgeon and his assistant, a mason—but most were soldiers and apprentices, like the rifleman Louis Rousseau, nicknamed "Franchise," the drummer Jean Roussette, and Antoine Piccart, a soldier released from duty on the Isle de France. The ship also carried a couple of colonists from the island and its neighboring island colony, Isle Bourbon. Virtually all French travelers passing between the Indian Ocean and France boarded at Isle de France, because Isle Bourbon lacked a protected harbor and facilities to repair ocean-going ships.[22] The *Hector* replenished water and food supplies again at the Cape of Good Hope a few weeks later. Captain Desblottières may have looked the other way while twelve stowaways (men with names like "Jean" or "Louis," with Dutch, English, or French surnames) hid onboard the ship. These men were of working age, between sixteen and forty; Desblottières could force them to work to earn their keep.[23]

The presence of so many more soldiers and sailors on the ship may have left Madeleine vulnerable to sexual predation on the voyage.[24] Would the presumably devout Mademoiselle Despense have offered any protection—implicit or explicit—to Madeleine in Port Louis or at sea? It seems likely that Madeleine enjoyed some shelter on this outbound voyage for several reasons. The captain, seeking to prevent jealousies and fights with so few women on board, had strong motivation to run a tight ship. Mademoiselle Despense's high status, too, may have given sailors second thoughts about molesting a girl in her entourage. They would know that Madeleine's sexual purity was valuable to Mademoiselle Despense, both symbolically and potentially economically in any future sale, and might therefore have respected her property to avoid her wrath. Yet the adolescent Madeleine remained vulnerable in isolated corners of the ship.

Free Soil and Indian Blackness

ON 22 MAY 1772, sixteen and half months after departing Bengal, the *Hector* docked in France's Atlantic port city of Lorient.[25] Bernardin de Saint-Pierre, who had passed through the city four years earlier, described this booming commercial center, then very much under construction:

> Lorient is a little city in Brittany, thriving more and more due to trade with the Indies. It is, like all the new cities, regular, aligned, and imperfect: its fortifications are mediocre. There one can discern some beautiful shops; the auction house, which is not yet finished; a tower for exploration; some quays begun; and some large lots where nothing is yet built. It is situated at the base of a bay where the rivers of Blavet and Ponscorf empty, which deposit a lot of silt in the port. This bay or harbor is defended at its entry, which is straight, by [the city of] Port Louis . . . [by contrast,] an old and deserted village. It's like an old gentleman living next door to a financier. The nobility lives at Port Louis, but the merchants, the chiffons, the silks, the gold, the pretty women are found at Lorient. . . . The carpenters' clatter, the caulkers' racket, the foreigners' affluence, the rowboats' perpetual movement in the harbor inspire I don't know what drunkenness.[26]

Bernardin perfectly captured the growing social divisions between France's older, waning nobility and the emergent merchant class. Here Mademoiselle Despense and her three servants, no doubt woozy from their months at sea, descended to terra firma, the "free" soil of France.

Since at least the middle of the sixteenth century, French law recognized a fundamental maxim of Free Soil: any slave setting foot within the continental kingdom thereby became free.[27] Over the course of the eighteenth century, hundreds of slaves achieved their freedom in this way, especially in Paris, where magistrates continued to grant liberty over the objections of royal functionaries until the Admiralty Court was dismantled during the Revolution.[28] Yet the maxim was interpreted differently over time and in different locations. Isle Bourbon slaves who traveled to France from the Indian Ocean knew that arriving there made them free but, according to one observer in 1714, creole slaves believed that their birth in France's colonies should free them as well, since the colonies were part of "France":

> [The slaves] who are creole say that their father and mother [i.e., those born in Africa or Asia] were in truth slaves. But that they themselves, having been born in France [i.e., the French empire], where there are no slaves, in good justice, they should not be. They also say that that they do not carry the title of "slave" and that [slavery] has no effect. By this principle, they want to be the first and similar to the mulattoes. The truth is that they are much better blacks than the others and that their masters have much regard for them and that they consider them more like their children than their slaves.[29]

In other words, in the early eighteenth century, at least some of the creole children of the slaves imported across the oceans to France's colonies believed that they were entitled to their freedom for having been born in French territory.

At this early date, a good decade before the dramatic commercial expansion of the Indian Ocean slave trade, slaves comprised less than half of Isle Bourbon's total population of about a thousand residents.[30] In this context, creole slaves, some of whom were no doubt the children and grandchildren of the island's free male European, Malagasy, and Indian immigrants, were claiming a privileged status over the newer arrivals. While royal authorities in Versailles never embraced the idea that Free Soil extended to the island colonies, in practice, it remained relatively easy for masters to liberate and recognize their enslaved children, adding to the free, propertied population of color on the island. The same report continued:

> The other blacks that want to prevail are the Indians, which, by an Indian vanity, say that they are born of free fathers and mothers, [and] that if they are slaves, it is only because someone took them or fooled them and sold them without their consent.[31]

Here is early evidence that a significant population of Indians had been lured or kidnapped by European traders to work in Isle Bourbon, only to find themselves stranded there and impressed into slavery. Similar tactics could have been employed in Madagascar or the African mainland, so claims on the basis of Indian origins may be beside the point. Yet this passage make clear that early in the period of Isle Bourbon settlement two vague ideas—French Free Soil and Indian Freedom—were already joined in the popular imagination.

As France established slaveholding in its overseas colonies in the Atlantic world—the Caribbean islands of Martinique, Guadeloupe, and Saint-Domingue (later, Haiti), along with Louisiana, Guiana, and Senegal—colonial elites lobbied the royal government to be able to bring their slaves to France as domestic servants and status symbols without fear of losing control over them by virtue of the Free Soil principle.[32] Writing for Louis XIV, the minister of the navy, Jérôme Phélypeaux, comte de Pontchartrain, clarified in 1707: "The intention of his majesty is that the Negroes who have been brought into the kingdom by the inhabitants of the islands, who refuse to return there, may not be constrained to do so . . . [by virtue of] . . . the privilege of the soil of France."[33] French colonists rallied and, following the king's death, successfully lobbied for a new law, the Edict of October 1716, which suspended the Free Soil principle if masters fulfilled certain conditions. Masters were to obtain permission from royal officials and pay a large deposit before they left the colonies with their slaves as security against their eventual return. The Declaration of 15 December 1738 closed several loopholes in the 1716 edict, requiring all masters bringing their "enslaved negroes" (*nègres esclaves*) into France to register them with port officials upon arrival or risk having them confiscated and sent back to the colonies as the king's property, where they would be put to work by the colonial government or resold for profit.

Strangely, Mademoiselle Despense never registered Madeleine as her slave upon reaching Lorient.[34] If we assume that the pious spinster was aware of and intended to follow French law, this could mean that Madeleine was not, in fact, her slave. Perhaps Madeleine, along with Cécile and Janot, were three of the four free servants tallied in Mademoiselle Despense's census record in Chandernagor. If so, what happened to her next in France was nothing short of enslavement—the inverse of the Free Soil principle. On the other hand, it seems more likely that Madeleine was indeed her mistress's slave, but Despense convinced herself that registering Madeleine was not necessary, since Indians were not, in the words of the law, *nègres*, and thus not subject to registration upon entry.[35] Such an interpretation was slippery at best, especially since Madeleine had been labeled a "*négresse*" in the passenger list.

The meanings of the words *nègre* and *noir* were in flux in the middle of the eighteenth century. In the wake of the Seven Years' War, French administrators in the Caribbean colonies and in the metropole were increasingly issuing new laws to reinforce hierarchy based on ancestry and appearance.[36] Both scientific and administrative proto-racialist discourse had begun to make fundamental distinctions between "*Indiens*" and "*Noirs*," suggesting that, unlike black Africans, Indians were not naturally subject to slavery.[37] An obscure 1727 French East India Company regulation had banned the export of (presumably Indian) slaves from Chandernagor and Pondichéry but made no mention of other French Company sites in India (for example, Mahé or Karikal), nor did it prohibit slavery within the continent, so it was not a complete ban on Indian slavery.[38] In any event, the 1727 regulation had been forgotten as little as three decades later and was omitted from an important 1759 legal decision by the Parlement of Paris, which found an Indian slave, Francisque, to be free. His lawyers had argued for his freedom on the basis of both Free Soil and his Indian origins, but the ultimate grounds for the French high court's affirmation of his freedom were never specified.[39] Responding to complaints that North American and Carib Indians were being illegally enslaved in Martinique, Louis XV issued an ordinance in March 1739 reiterating the ban of trading in "Caribs and Indians."[40] A 1767 directive issued by the French minister of the navy ordained that "Indians" were not to be considered eligible for enslavement, but he did not specify whether by "Indians" he meant only those from North America or also those from South Asia:

> His Majesty has always recognized, and he wishes his Superior Councils [i.e., colonial legislative and judicial bodies] to recognize an essential difference between Indians [*Indiens*] and Negroes [*Nègres*]; the reason for this difference derives from the fact that Indians are born free, and have always retained the advantage of liberty in the colonies, while the Negroes were only introduced there to live in a state of slavery.[41]

In either case, while mid-eighteenth-century French policy was clearly preoccupied with distinguishing between Indians and Africans, the enslavement of Asian Indians was a common practice in the Indian Ocean.

So, while Mademoiselle Despense almost certainly considered Madeleine her slave, the ambiguity of her status as an Indian allowed the mistress to feel no compunction in neglecting to register Madeleine with port authorities; indeed, masters' noncompliance with the registration formality was common in French ports. At the same time, she would not have feared Madeleine's escape to France's free soil, since she would not have expected a girl to survive alone in this foreign land. As in Chandernagor, Madeleine's only alternative would have been to flee her mistress and to bind herself in service to some other adult. Would the possible benefits of such an escape outweigh the evident risks of starvation, exposure, maltreatment in the hands of another master, or arrest?

While Madeleine made no move to escape her mistress, Mademoiselle Despense had no further use for her in France. French servants were relatively easy to hire and, unlike Madeleine, posed no ambiguity as to their legal status in the metropole. Indeed, from the outset of her voyage Mademoiselle Despense probably planned to dispose of Madeleine, knowing that a trained colonial servant would be valuable to a French mistress returning to the colonies. Probably through the *Hector*'s captain, Augustin Louis Desblottières, Mademoiselle Despense made the acquaintance in Lorient of a French colonist, Marie Anne Ursule Desblottières Routier, age thirty-four, who had arrived in France from her natal Isle Bourbon with her husband and children a couple of years earlier.[42] Her husband, Charles Gabriel Routier de Granval, forty-one, a wealthy plantation owner and former officer in the French East India Company, was searching for a female servant to attend to his pregnant wife on their return voyage. Introductions were made, and Charles and his wife selected Madeleine to accompany them back home.

Madeleine's legal status at this moment was highly ambiguous. If Madeleine was somehow understood as Mademoiselle Despense's free servant until this point (a possibility, though unlikely), it was the transaction with the Routiers that ultimately transformed Madeleine into a slave. Any recorded contract of her gift or sale between Mademoiselle Despense and the Routiers (for example, by a notary in Lorient) apparently did not survive, since neither Furcy nor his adversaries furnished a copy in later legal proceedings. It seems more likely that both parties understood that the dubious transaction was better left unrecorded, since French law prohibited the sale or gifting of slaves in the metropole.[43] The first evidence of this transaction in the archival record appears almost two decades later, when Madame Routier filed a manumission petition to formally declare Madeleine free in Isle Bourbon. When she did so, Madame Routier declared that she was freeing Madeleine "to fulfill the obligation that she had contracted in France to procure the liberty of the said Madeleine, who had only [been] given to her upon this condition."[44] This statement makes clear that Mademoiselle Despense had intended that Madeleine should eventually be free. Whether written or verbal, however, the contract between Despense and the Routiers was vague as to exactly when and where Madeleine would achieve her liberty. The manumission declaration would eventually become pivotal evidence in Furcy's freedom suit.

Given France's patriarchal social structure, by which all dependents (wives, children, and servants) were under the authority of a single head of household, both Mademoiselle Despense and Charles Routier presumed that Madeleine was such a dependent whose condition was subject to their negotiation. Emancipation from their authority would only come when Madeleine was older and could either marry—and thus come under the authority of her husband—or when she was formally manumitted and could seek a position as a paid servant. Such "freedom" was thus embedded within the gendered hierarchical social structure. Eighteenth-century residents of France—and India, for that matter—could not imagine Madeleine ever enjoying a freedom like that of the aristocratic spinster Mademoiselle Despense.

The Routier Family

CHARLES ROUTIER AND HIS new wife suddenly became the most powerful people in Madeleine's world. If Madeleine's ancestry cannot be traced in extant archives, Charles's family tree is amply preserved in church and state records.[45]

Charles was a child of empire, crossing the Indian and Atlantic Oceans six times during his life. His father, Jean Nicholas Routier, a native of a village in northern France, enlisted as a soldier in the French East India Company at the age of twenty-three.[46] He arrived in Isle de France in 1730, only nine years after the French began to settle there and two years after the first French women were imported by the government to help establish the colony.[47] Within months of his arrival, Jean married Françoise Busson, one of the few French women on the island who, at age twenty, was already the widow of another colonist.[48] Dangers inherent in transoceanic crossings and high mortality rates in the colonies meant that widowhood and remarriage were frequent throughout France's empire.[49] The couple's first son, Charles Gabriel, was born a year later and would be the only one of their six children to survive infancy.[50]

The East India Company granted parcels of land, known as concessions, to colonists, who were bound to repay the Company, in cash or more often with whatever they grew on them.[51] At first, Jean Routier attempted to farm near Grand Port, in the island's southeast, but he soon negotiated for a new concession in the Plaines de Wilhelm, a fertile inland region closer to the colony's burgeoning new commercial and political center in Port Louis.[52] By 1738, Jean Routier was one of only 101 colonists to own concessions on the island; together, these men owned 672 slaves.[53] When he became an officer in the Company, Routier adopted the sobriquet "de Grandvalle" ("of the large valley," later spelled de Granval) to add luster to his standing.[54]

Jean's son, Charles, must have traveled to France for an education as a young man, then responded to a wartime proclamation like that of 1745 to recruit "everyone, European or creole, who desires to acquire honor, glory and profit."[55] In 1746, he is rostered as a chestnut-haired fifteen-year-old volunteer, receiving military wages aboard the *Brilliant*, traveling from Lorient to Isle de France.[56] Father and son fought the English together in Pondichéry, India, in 1747, then returned to Isle de France, where the elder Routier obtained yet another concession, this time a plantation called Consistance in Moka, a west-central district of the island.[57]

In 1752, Charles Routier, age twenty-two, married Françoise Panon, granddaughter of the founder of a major dynasty on France's other Indian Ocean island, Isle Bourbon.[58] Charles must have seemed a good bet for the Company and the Panon clan, for he soon received a Company concession of about 264 acres of prime real estate adjoining his father's land, which he doubled in size through purchase the following year.[59]

But times were difficult for Charles and his new wife, and for the Isle de France more generally. Charles probably left his wife and their first child, a daughter, while he served in the Seven Years' War, for they had no recorded children between 1753 and 1761. A smallpox epidemic struck the island in 1757, taking the lives of colonists and slaves alike. This was followed by famine, as colonial slaveholders sought to profit by pulling their slaves from farming and renting them out for the many building projects initiated around Port Louis.[60] Meanwhile, thousands of soldiers and sailors temporarily stationed on the island consumed its stores, but did not contribute to food production, a perennial problem for Isle de France.[61] Following the French defeat in 1763, the Company collapsed in debt, and the crown had to rescue it with loans.[62]

Charles and Françoise's second and third daughters, Marie Élie and Marie Euphrasie, were born toward the end of the war in 1761 and 1763, but this last birth was likely the cause of Françoise's death.[63] A young widower with three young daughters, Charles—or possibly his father, Jean—entered into negotiations with the Panon family to find him a new wife. A suitable cousin was found: another of Augustin Panon's grandchildren, an heiress to prime land and slaves in Isle Bourbon.[64] Charles immediately boarded a ship bound for France, and on 8 February 1764 he married his second wife, the Isle Bourbon creole Marie Anne Ursule Desblottières.[65]

Routier's two marriages to the grandchildren of Augustin Panon were strategic. By wedding the granddaughters of one of the earliest French women to migrate to Isle Bourbon, Routier perpetuated both the family's ties to France

and the property consolidation of the colonial creole elite. The original patriarch, Augustin Panon, was not a wealthy or noble man but a carpenter who
had migrated to the colony from Toulon in 1689. There he met his Parisian
wife, Françoise Chatelain, one of two survivors of a disastrous effort to supply
the colony with French women in 1673; she was, by the time Panon arrived,
a wealthy widow.[66] Fortune smiled upon the couple, or they had strong genes,
for all five of their children survived to adulthood and married. Their prog-
eny eventually included 36 grandchildren, 87 great-grandchildren, and 213
descendants in the fifth generation, most of whom continued to live in Isle
Bourbon or Isle de France, and a few who would eventually navigate to the
highest echelons of colonial administration and the French government. These
men would support Joseph Lory as he fought to retain Furcy as his slave.

The colonial elite's capacity to invoke both male and female lineages
through naming practices contrasted markedly with the invisibility of ancestry inherent in French Indian Ocean naming practices for slaves. While the
names of Madeleine's parents are long forgotten, the island's French creole families could trace their genealogy back to European parish registers.
Though many came from humble origins, like Augustin Panon, these early
colonists began to style themselves as a landed aristocracy, adding honorifics to their surnames after features of their colonial estates. Access to fresh
water for irrigation was desirable, so Augustin Panon's second son Joseph
affected the name Panon-Lamare (*mare* meaning "pool"), while his grandson became known as Henri Paulin Panon Desbassayns ("of the ponds").
A granddaughter would marry Nicholas Pierre Gillot de l'Étang ("of the
swamp").[67]

While Isle Bourbon's elites assumed quasi-aristocratic surnames, the given
names they bequeathed to their children were also strategic. Families recycled
the same given names endlessly in a constant reinforcement of the familial
networks that bound them through both blood and spiritual kin. Custom
dictated that children were often baptized with the first name of a relative of
the same sex or of their godmother or godfather. So Charles Routier's first
child by his first wife, Françoise Marguerite, shared her first name with her
mother, her grandmother, and her great-great-grandmother, the original
female immigrant from France. Five of the seven children of Charles's second
marriage to Marie Anne Ursule Desblottières—boys and girls alike—were
named Marie, tying them to both their mother, Marie Anne, and their grandmother, Marie Panon.[68] Likewise, Charles Routier gave his first name to five
of his children by his second wife.[69] Versions of these names (Marie Charlotte,
Marie Charlette) were passed along into the next generation. Since the

multiplication of Charleses and Maries was confusing, most of the Routiers eventually were known by a distinct given name—Augustin, Cyrille, Éugénie, or Élie—and these, as opposed to their baptismal names, are sometimes used exclusively in the census records.

Stepmothers, Wet Nurses, and Widows

ON 14 NOVEMBER 1764, eight years before they met Madeleine, Charles, together with his new wife, Marie Anne, and his eldest daughter from his first marriage, Françoise Marguerite, traveled from Lorient, France, to Isle de France, where their family rapidly increased.[70] Marie Anne assumed the role of stepmother to all three children from her husband's first marriage. There is no record of her relationship with these children, but she may have not had much time for them. Together the couple produced babies annually for the first four years of their wedded life: a daughter, Élie Louise, and three sons, Augustin, Cyrille, and François.[71]

Marie Anne's fertility, however, underscores the importance of wet-nursing for elite families. By relegating the breastfeeding of her babies to another woman, Marie Anne was able to give birth more rapidly to a series of heirs. This practice was not unique to the colonies or the French-speaking world.[72] For centuries women in powerful families had freed themselves of the burdens of caring for infants while entrusting their children to other women who could provide milk and childcare.[73] The wet nurses became available either when their own infant died or because they had arranged for yet another woman, usually lower in status, to take their baby so that they could use their milk to earn wages in service to the wealthiest families. Colonial slavery allowed for this practice to continue, but the baby did not need to be sent from the city to a peasant family, since the wet nurse could be brought within the household service staff. In spite of a concerted eighteenth-century campaign to persuade wealthy and middle-class women to breastfeed their own children, French mothers did not abandon the use of wet nurses until much later in the nineteenth century.[74] In Isle de France and Isle Bourbon, colonists frequently turned to enslaved women to feed and raise their babies.

It is not clear whether the Routiers, like residents of Florence, Paris, or the Spanish empire, believed that sharing a wet nurse between two babies was unhealthy for the employer's child.[75] Bernardin de Saint-Pierre suggested otherwise in his ebullient description of two French women of Isle de France breastfeeding each other's children in one of the most widely read romantic novels of the eighteenth century, *Paul et Virginie* (*Paul and Virginia*):

> Their mutual friendship was intensified by the sight of their children.... They took pleasure in washing them together in the same bath, putting them to sleep in the same cradle. They each often suckled the other's baby.[76]

The scene celebrates the mothers' mutual nursing as a positive act of maternal friendship, but perhaps the tone would be otherwise if one of the mothers had been a slave. By the eighteenth century, some Louisiana Frenchmen criticized the use of black wet nurses, whose milk, they claimed, would corrupt the children.[77] If local custom held that nursing two babies was inappropriate or unhealthy, the wet nurse who had recently given birth herself was required to give up her own baby (assuming it had survived) to another nursing mother, which could be life-threatening for the wet nurse's newborn, or wean her baby.[78] Even so, colonial wet-nursing created important, reciprocal bonds between the master's family and the women who gave their bodies for the survival of the master's children. Complex feelings developed between the creole sons and daughters and the enslaved women who sustained them. While some colonial mistresses no doubt felt warmth, perhaps even gratitude, to these surrogates, such feelings might be tinged with mistrust, guilt, or resentment.[79]

Charles, Marie Anne, and the Routier children continued to live in Isle de France until 1768, when the family moved to the nearby island, Isle Bourbon, probably so that Marie Anne could be near her aging mother as she approached the end of her life. A year later, on 7 November 1769, Charles Routier's mother-in-law, Marie Panon Desblottières, was given the last rites and died at home.[80] Immediately upon her death, two court officers walked through the house, making a careful inventory of every belonging, and then locked the house with a red wax seal to ensure that nothing was pilfered before her belongings could be distributed to her heirs. One week later, five men representing the widow's heirs gathered to witness the "lifting of the seals," a ritual revealing of the deceased's property before its distribution.

Each of the men surveying the widow's lifetime accumulation bore a military title marking the Company service by which they had earned their land concessions in the quasi-feudal system, several of them now officers in the recently established Bourbon militia.[81] Marie Anne Ursule Desblottières Routier was not there; her husband, Charles, represented the family.

The inventory of the dead woman's property reveals its relative simplicity in terms of material possessions; she was wealthy by colonial standards, but her home and furnishings were not especially lavish. The four-room city bungalow held furnishings suitable for entertaining, including "two end tables, twelve armchairs, four chairs, three sofas, two mirrors, three tables, eleven curtains, two silver candelabras," and a handful of utilitarian or ornamental items of lesser value, including a coffee maker (*cafetière*), eight pots, and a silver salad bowl. The bedroom on the first floor held a bed surrounded by four comfortable chairs, two tables, a mirror, and the symbol of her Catholic faith, "a Christ."[82] The attic was empty.

Despite the officers' careful documentation of the widow's belongings, they were strangely casual about the widow's real wealth: the land and slaves of her rural property by the Rivière des Pluies.[83] These would be apportioned to her heirs, including Marie Anne Routier. They took at face value the testimony of the caretaker, Antoine La Salle, that the plantation

> consists of the slaves that the deceased listed on her census, the tools necessary for the exploitation of the plantation, food for the blacks, . . . two thousand [unspecified unit] of coffee in casks, the wheat harvest is currently underway, and there are several furnishings, like the chair, always attached to the plantation house.[84]

The owner of ninety-four slaves in 1760, Marie Anne's mother was, at her death, one of the wealthiest planters in the island.[85] Assuming her slaves averaged in value the going rate of 750 livres apiece, they were collectively worth 70,500 livres, about $365,000 in today's money.[86] The original concession, known as La Mare, extended from the coastline to the summit of the mountains between the Rivière des Pluies and the Ravine des Figuiers in the Sainte-Marie district.[87] Already subdivided over three generations, the widow Desblottières's property (including land and slaves) was distributed amongst her heirs, who, by law, had to each receive an equal share of her estate, unless she made prior provisions through gifts.[88] Unless any of the heirs was wealthy enough to buy out the others' shares, the only way that the property could be equally distributed was to split up the land and slaves into equivalent, but much smaller, portions. One of the dangers of this Parisian policy of equal distribution was that, over generations, the original colonial concessions would gradually become subdivided into smaller and smaller parcels. In this case, Charles' wealth allowed the family to preserve the Desblottières lands intact. Charles apparently sold off some of his property in Isle de France and bought out the other heirs; both the plantation and townhouse passed whole to Charles Routier via his wife Marie Anne.[89] It was on these two properties that Madeleine and Furcy would live much of their lives.

A Meeting in France

IN JANUARY 1770, ABOUT two months after the widow Desblottières's death, Charles and Marie Anne sent their eldest son, four-year-old Augustin, to France accompanied by a French servant. They followed two months later with their other two children, Élie (or Marie) Louise and Cyrille, along with their domestic slaves, Jeannot and Jeanneton, leaving behind Charles's daughters from his first marriage.[90] No doubt the timing of the voyage was related to the transfer of the estate and perhaps the impending naval muster. The couple also decided that it was a good time for their children to begin their education in France, so that they could speak, read, and write at a level appropriate to their station.

The eighteenth-century traveler Bernardin de Saint-Pierre noted that this "finishing" in France was typical of families of rising fortune in Isle Bourbon, a custom he frowned upon. An avid fan of Jean Jacques Rousseau's honest and simple virtues, Bernardin noted approvingly that the older colonists of Isle Bourbon, presumably the widow Desblottières's generation, lived with "very simple manners":

> The greater part of the houses did not close up; even a lock was a curiosity. Some of them put their money in a tortoise shell beneath their door. They went barefoot, wearing blue cloth, and lived on rice and coffee; they took almost nothing from Europe, content in a life without luxury, so long as they lived without needs. They combined with this moderation the virtues as follows: good faith in commerce and nobility in manners.[91]

However, he continued, critically:

> The last India war [i.e. the Seven Years' War] has altered these customs a little. The volunteers of Bourbon distinguished themselves there by their bravery. But the textiles of Asia and the military distinctions of France entered their island. The children, richer than their parents, wanted to be more highly esteemed. They . . . went to Europe to seek out pleasures and honors in exchange for the union of families and

the repose of the bucolic life. As the fathers' attention fell primarily on their sons, they arranged for their passage to France, whence they rarely returned. And so it came to pass that some five hundred daughters aged in the island without finding a husband.[92]

Bernardin was exaggerating the numbers, but the increasing gender imbalance of colonial creoles was real. In 1752, Isle Bourbon's 697 free men outnumbered the 549 free women, and their 967 sons had a slight edge over the 921 daughters.[93] By 1788, the island's adult male colonists numbered 1,472, while the women had grown to 1,615; this gender reversal occurred both within the population considered "white" as well as those labeled "libres"—with 135 freedwomen for 116 freedmen.[94] Whether this was due, as Bernardin claimed, to men's preference for returning to Europe or the prevalence of colonial widowhood remains to be explored. But the reality was that by the eve of the Revolution, free women outnumbered free men in Isle Bourbon. The reverse was true of the enslaved population, which swelled in the late eighteenth century as a result of the slave trade: by 1788, 17,322 men outnumbered 11,496 women, who were raising only 9,256 enslaved children.[95]

While colonial elites could expect to traverse the oceans more than once in a lifetime, the journeys were always fraught with danger. The Routiers' second passage to France brought tragedy when their oldest daughter, Élie Louise, died at sea, somewhere off the coast of Africa, on 26 April 1770—whether by illness, accident, or a rogue wave is unknown.[96] At the time, Marie Anne was pregnant. In France she gave birth to another son, named for his grandfather, Jean Nicholas François Routier, on 25 November 1770.[97]

The Routiers' manifestly pro-natal strategy, facilitated by their wet nurses, was not unusual for its time. Death could come at any moment in a world so closely dependent on sufficient food and without reliable medical interventions. Having lots of children—or dependents like slaves—was a way to hedge one's bets, to draw from their labor and resources and to ensure comfort and survival. In most pre-modern societies, these relationships were figured as reciprocal: not patriarchy but paternalism. Protection was theoretically exchanged for labor. However, while militarized global trading companies created opportunities for a handful of families to raise their status and their standard of living, imperial capitalism also introduced new instabilities of boom and bust, already visible in the few short years since the French colonized Isle de France. The fluctuating economic cycles would only continue as French and foreign colonists arrived in greater numbers, importing ever-greater numbers of slaves to try to extract maximum profit from their trading enterprises.

Madeleine the Midwife

IN JULY OR AUGUST of 1772, while living in France, Madame Routier realized with certainty that she was again with child.[98] Charles and Marie Anne must have been delighted to find Madeleine available as a servant for the ocean voyage on their return home, and they reached an agreement with Mademoiselle Despense.

Family lore and later legal arguments held that Mademoiselle Despense entered a convent, before or after Madeleine's departure, but documentary evidence does not support this. Furcy would later insist that his mother had entered the convent too, which is where Despense and Madeleine supposedly met Madame Routier,[99] but that, too, seems unlikely. His lawyer suggested in 1838 that

> Mademoiselle Despense, a nun by profession, whose sentiments of piety taught her that in the eyes of religion and evangelical morality, all men are equal, had no other means by which to give Madeleine her freedom immediately [in France, since this was forbidden by the 1738 law] but to confer her to an honorable person, so that she could be freed upon arrival in Isle Bourbon.[100]

Setting aside the lawyer's anachronistic references to "evangelical morality" and the "equality of all men" as products of nineteenth-century antislavery discourse, other facts suggest that Mademoiselle Despense never entered a cloistered community, with or without Madeleine.

After Despense gave Madeleine to the Routiers, her male servant Janot remained in her service for three more years.[101] (The fate of her third Indian servant, Cécile, is unknown.) Despense's decision to retain Janot and send Madeleine back to the colonies is consistent with the gendered pattern of black migration in France's eighteenth-century empire. When the government ordered all blacks in the kingdom to report their whereabouts to authorities in 1777—the notorious law known as the *Police des Noirs* (Policing of the Blacks)—71 percent of the 1,735 nonwhites registered in 1777 were male, most of them servants in their late teens and twenties.[102] At this time, Janot declared himself to authorities at Eu-et-Tréport, a port town on the English Channel about seven miles from Auberville-sur-Yères, the town where a "noble and virtuous" woman surnamed "Despence de la Loge" had served as godmother to a French girl born in 1773.[103] It seems unlikely that Mademoiselle Despense ever entered a convent in Morbihan, where male servants would not be welcome; this was just a story that Madeleine and the Routiers told. If Despense did eventually enter a cloistered religious community, it would have to have been several years after Madeleine (and Janot) left her service.[104]

The Routier adults—grandfather Jean, Charles, and Marie Anne—departed Lorient on board the *Brune* on 12 September 1772, along with a detachment of the legion of Isle de France, accompanied by two male French servants and Madeleine, "*negresse domestique de Mad. Routtier* [*sic*]" (Negro servant of Madame Routier).[105] As Madame Routier's only servant—indeed, the only female servant on the ship—Madeleine was responsible for caring for her mistress, who was entering the last trimester of her pregnancy. This selection of Madeleine from among what must have been other options in the busy port town of Lorient raises many questions.

Had Madeleine—by most accounts about thirteen years old, but possibly a few years older[106]—somehow become pregnant herself, whether on the ship or in France, thus making her a possible candidate to become Madame Routier's wet nurse when she gave birth at sea in early December? This scenario seems unlikely; the precise timing of the two pregnancies for wet-nursing would have been an extraordinary coincidence. Instead, Charles and Marie Anne Routier probably selected Madeleine for her health—she had already survived the long ocean voyage to France—and her virtue, making her a suitable lady's maid for Marie Anne, who was already an experienced mother.

But did Madeleine's shipboard duties also include serving Monsieur Routier? In most slaveholding cultures, one of the master's essential prerogatives was sexual access to his female servants and slaves (not to mention his wife).[107] By custom, Marie Anne Routier would not have been sexually available to her husband once her pregnancy was confirmed. So it is quite like that the young Madeleine was selected precisely to attend to his sexual urges, perhaps even because she was a virgin, and therefore not a carrier of venereal disease. It is impossible to know how Charles might have initiated their first encounter. The unequal power in the relationship between masters and enslaved women means that the latter never gave their consent as a peer, but at least in British North America, masters sometimes deployed rituals of wooing.[108] They ordered women to work in places that isolated them from others, where it would be difficult to resist, and demanded repeatedly, over their objections, that the women submit. As far as we know, Madeleine did not become pregnant on either voyage, to or from France. However, if such a child died or was sold outside of the

Routier household, and Madeleine did not tell her later children, there would be no paper record of her loss.

Somewhere off the coast of Africa, on 27 February 1773, Marie Anne Routier felt the pangs of labor, and Madeleine (perhaps assisted by the ship's surgeon, Haudressy) helped catch her baby girl, Eugénie. As Madeleine's previous mistress, Despense, had had no children, the experience was likely unfamiliar—even frightening—to Madeleine. The surgeon performed a preliminary baptism, but the family waited until a year after their arrival to baptize their daughter Eugénie in the church of Sainte-Marie in Isle Bourbon.[109] The fates of Madeleine and Eugénie would be entangled for the rest of their lives.

As a child, Madeleine had already traveled much further than most people in the world. When Mademoiselle Despense chose her to accompany her across the seas to France, Madeleine was separated from all that she had known. This isolation and alienation was repeated when Madeleine passed to the Routier family, who took her to an unfamiliar island in the Indian Ocean, where she would be again surrounded by strangers.[110] By contrast, the many passages that the Routier family undertook between France and the colonies bound them within family networks, rather than separating them from family and community. Through these voyages, the Routier sons learned to know themselves as "free" and French from an early age and could expect that, upon reaching adulthood, they would assume direction of their own lives as heads of families. For wealthy French daughters like Eugénie, adulthood would bring an arranged marriage and motherhood, or—if family resources fell short of the bar—spinsterhood. Following Bernardin de Saint-Pierre's dictum, Eugénie would never leave her island home. One of the marks of freedom, then, in France's oceanic empire was the capacity to travel freely to the place that one desired, though always navigating state regulations and the all-encompassing patriarchal family.

3

Family Secrets

MAURICE, CONSTANCE, AND FURCY

AS THE SHIP BEARING Madeleine, the Routiers, and Charles Routier's enslaved manservant Jeannot sailed from France south along the African coast, past the Cape of Good Hope and deep into the Indian Ocean, they probably saw a flock of *pailles en queue* ("straws in tail"), white seabirds with black markings and long, elegant tails—the first hints of Madeleine's future home—gracefully spiraling and dipping over the sea. The ship landed in Port Louis, Isle de France, on 21 March 1773, where the deepwater port received the largest ships.[1] From there the family and their attendants took a smaller vessel to Isle Bourbon, 140 miles to the west and south. As they approached, the illusion of three distant little islands resolved into the single land form of Isle Bourbon itself, with its three volcanic peaks.[2]

The unique geography of Isle Bourbon shaped its slow settlement as a French colony in the seventeenth and eighteenth centuries. While Isle de France, with its reef-protected coves and harbors, was quickly overrun and exploited by colonists and smugglers from many nations, Isle Bourbon's dangerous shoreline and paucity of natural ports limited regular contact with outsiders, eventually creating a more provincial, inward-turning culture. The French discovered that Isle Bourbon's hillsides were good for growing coffee, while its higher altitudes and sloping coastal plain supported staple crops native to Europe and the Americas: wheat, corn (*maïs*), and potatoes, as well as the African root staple manioc and, in a few marshy places, rice. Isle Bourbon's multiethnic families, their slaves, and their descendants initially concentrated on growing food for personal consumption, then turned toward producing surplus to supply ships trading throughout the Indian Ocean.

To appreciate Madeleine's life within the Routier family, it is helpful to understand the evolving legal and social categories in France's overseas colonies. As colonists populated Isle Bourbon, French authorities issued laws to define and regulate their relationships. In France, laws and customs distinguished between "legitimate" Catholic families and illegitimate "natural" children (bastards). In the Atlantic colonies of the Caribbean, Canada, and Louisiana, these civil law categories, together with France's colonial

slave codes and regulations, over the eighteenth century eventually produced four legal categories of race: Indian, black, white, and "free people
of color" (*libres de couleur*)—the last a generic label for people of mixed
ancestry. However, these increasingly fixed Atlantic racial categories could
not adequately encompass the diverse populations of France's Indian Ocean
colonies, as the unique ethnic descriptors in the local laws of Isle Bourbon
and Isle de France attest. In these eastern colonies, eighteenth-century censuses recorded free and enslaved peoples' place of birth—for example, a village in France, the island of Madagascar, Africa, India, or specific regions
in each (e.g. Mozimbique, Bengal, Malabar), and *créole* (born in the colonies)—rather than recording their color or race. Even as French officials
struggled to categorize and control the diversity of the colonies' populations, royal law cast a veil over the paternity of slaves. Except in the increasingly rare cases when slaves married one another within the church, their
babies were baptized, and thus legally known, only as their mothers' children, while their fathers—of any origin—were rendered anonymous in the
historical record.

An Eden of Sorts

UNTIL THE MIDDLE OF the seventeenth century, no people lived on the
island that became Isle Bourbon. Although it rose out of the ocean as a result
of the same tectonic and volcanic processes that created Isle de France, Isle
Bourbon's geological age is considerably younger, and it remains volcanically
active. As a result, Isle Bourbon hosted a wide variety of microclimates, from
tropical near the shoreline to alpine in the higher elevations, each home to
unique plants and animals.

Isle Bourbon's first permanent human settlers were not slaves but two
French convicts and ten Malagasies, including three women, exiled to
the island in 1662 for staging a revolt against the governor of the nascent
French colony in Madagascar. That enormous island off the southeast coast
of Africa—larger than the states of North and South Carolina, Georgia,
and Florida combined—held numerous distinct societies and communities organized under a variety of political, ethnic, and lineage alliances.[3] The
Malagasy's ancient ancestors were both Africans and explorers from Indonesia
(and possibly India), leading the French to describe them later in the nineteenth century as *rougeâtre* (reddish), rather than *noir* (black).[4] These few
Malagasy women founded the first families of Isle Bourbon with the French
and Malagasy men.[5]

Instead of suffering in penal misery, Isle Bourbon's founding settlers thrived on the fertile island, eating from the indigenous fruit trees and hunting the tortoises, birds, fish, and feral European livestock deposited there earlier for provisioning by passing Portuguese and Dutch ships. In 1664, King Louis XIV authorized the establishment and monopoly of the French East India Company for all French Indian Ocean trade. When the French colony in Madagascar failed the same year, the king sanctioned the complete relocation of the Indian Ocean relay post to Isle Bourbon, including additional Malagasy women. From the beginning, then, the island was settled by diverse and hybrid families, already in political tension with one another. The first few decades were punctuated by conflicts between independent-minded colonists and the colonial administrators sent to coerce their productivity to benefit the Company stockholders in France.[6]

The Company declared the purpose of the Isle Bourbon colony was to grow provisioning crops—wheat, corn, manioc, and rice—for the Company's trading vessels, so that ships could restock at the midway point between the Cape of Good Hope and trading posts in Asia.[7] This project began to alter the island's ecology, especially at the northern shoreline, as colonists cleared land for farming and introduced new animals, domesticated and otherwise. Horses and cattle depended on cleared pastureland, while the omnivorous pigs foraged deep into the forest, feasting on fruits, lizards, and sand-nested eggs of birds and turtles. Even more destructive was the unintended invasive species: the ship-borne rat, which devoured Isle Bourbon's native birds' eggs and hatchlings. Chickens and pigeons competed with indigenous species for insects and seeds.[8]

The multiethnic composition of the island's initial founding members was consistent with French patterns of colonization elsewhere during the seventeenth century. In North America, Senegal, Madagascar, or India, the French modus operandi—modeled on two centuries of successful Portuguese precedent—was to form alliances with local women, who became wives but also business partners, with access to clans and commercial networks in the colonized territory. Time and again, Frenchmen who arrived in foreign lands bargained with local elites to marry women with connections to local lineages of power.[9] On a previously unpopulated island like Isle Bourbon (or France's Caribbean islands, where most of the indigenous people were decimated by disease or displaced through warfare), the early settlement patterns allowed for a new colonial aristocracy to emerge.

Between 1663 and 1673, Louis XIV's minister and architect of the expanding French empire, Jean-Baptiste Colbert, began to experiment systematically with sending French women as wives to colonies across the globe.[10] In 1673 he sent sixteen orphan girls from the general hospital in Paris to Isle Bourbon under the supervision of a nun of the Saint-Joseph order. Following a disastrous stop in Madagascar, where half of the French colony was massacred, only two girls ultimately arrived in Isle Bourbon. One of these was Marie Anne Routier's grandmother, Françoise Chatelain, who, together with her husband, the carpenter Augustin Panon, founded one of the dynastic families of the island.[11]

By 1690, Isle Bourbon's censused population consisted of only 290 people grouped in 46 families.[12] These included 10 "French" families, 12 "Portuguese"[13] families (headed by men with French or Portuguese surnames but with Eurasian wives), 14 Franco-Malagasy families, 8 Malagasy families, 2 Dutch families, and 30 *noirs* from either Madagascar or India.[14] The "blacks" were servants or, more probably, slaves, and in most cases the census returns omitted their family ties.[15] Therefore, only 30 percent of the island's residents, most of them French fathers, could be considered "white," in the sense of having two European parents.[16] In fact, of the 77 free women living in Isle Bourbon, only 16 (20 percent) would be considered "white" by that definition.[17]

Racial terms like "black" and "white" obscure an important point: in Isle Bourbon's early years of colonization, the colonists of various hues were largely united by Catholic culture, sanctioned by the French state. Since 1664, Colbert's reforms had encouraged marriages between French subjects and indigenous women (*femmes du pays*, i.e. Malagasy, Indian, and so forth) in the Indian Ocean and New France, provided they were Catholic.[18] French settlers to Isle Bourbon learned their catechism at home in the parishes of their birth, but they could recite the rosary with fellow Catholics born and raised in India and Madagascar, thanks to earlier conversions by sixteenth- and seventeenth-century missionaries from Europe who established Catholic congregations throughout the Indian Ocean world.[19] When censuses later began to use the term "white," all descendants of the earliest free settlers—regardless of hue or origin—claimed this designation. "White" meant "free" and was not reserved solely for the descendants of Europeans.

Enter the Slave Trade

TO ASSURE ISLE BOURBON'S productivity, the French East India Company recruited both voluntary and involuntary colonists. The free included Frenchmen and other Europeans, but also skilled workers (smiths, masons, bricklayers, carpenters, lascars [sailors], and even peons) from India, with salaries equivalent to their European counterparts.[20] The Company's increasing need for laborers to grow grain on Isle Bourbon led to the acceleration of the Indian Ocean slave trade, which in turn dramatically altered the composition of Isle Bourbon society across the eighteenth century (see Table 3.1). By 1713, slaves outnumbered the island's free population.[21] Following the Seven Years' War, free trade only intensified the scale of the slave trade, such that by 1776 slaves outnumbered the free by four to one.[22] Over time, Isle Bourbon's rain patterns and fertile soil channeled settlement from the northwest, at the island's one natural harbor, eastward along the coastal districts named for Catholic saints: Saint-Paul, Saint-Denis, Sainte-Marie, Sainte-Suzanne, Saint-André, and Saint-Benoît. Other settlers planted corn or turned to husbandry, herding goats, sheep, and cows in the drier parishes to the west, but the lower and less reliable rainfall rendered the western coastline mostly unsuitable for large-scale plantations.

The legal categories "slave" and "free" mask vital cultural diversity within each. While the words "European" and "white" began to creep into administrative and parish records by the middle of the eighteenth century, these glossed over the many regional, linguistic, and national variations (e.g., Breton, Basque, Sicilian, Londoner, Dutch), not to mention religious affiliations, of this increasingly diverse society.[23] By the second generation, their varied ancestral origins and ethnic heritages merged within the label *créole*, which meant "born in the colonies," or *de Mascarin*, "of Mascarin

Table 3.1 Population of Isle Bourbon, 1686–1804[i]

	Slave	Free	Total	Slave ratio[ii]
1686[iii]	28	241	269	0.1
1709	378	516	894	0.7
1719	773	443	1,216	1.7
1733	6,441	1,630	8,071	4.0
1752	13,390	3,134	16,524	4.3
1763[iv]	15,419	4,267	19,686	3.6
1776	26,175	6,340	32,515	4.1
1787	37,265	8,752	46,017	4.3
1804[v]	50,350	14,762	65,112	3.4

i. Several historians have undertaken the demographic analysis of the population of Isle Bourbon, most notably J. V. Payet, *Histoire de l'esclavage à l'Île Bourbon* (Paris: L'Harmattan, 1990); Ève, *Naître et mourir à l'Île Bourbon*; and Michèle Dion, *Quand La Réunion s'appelait Bourbon* (Paris: L'Harmattan, 2006). Here, with the exceptions of 1686, 1763, and 1804, I use Dion's figures from p. 23. Census figures certainly undercount the island's actual population.

ii. The number of slaves for each free person.

iii. Guët, *Les origines de l'île Bourbon*, 141.

iv. André Scherer, *Histoire de la Réunion*, Que Sais Je? (Paris: Presses Universitaires de la France, 1965), 62–66.

v. Scherer, *Histoire de la Réunion*, 62–66.

Island," the original name the French gave Isle Bourbon.²⁴ Creoles could be any color, whether within the free population (sometimes labeled "white," regardless of ancestry) or among the enslaved (which included some descendants of French men and African or Asian women).²⁵ While the church's parish records kept track of Catholic families, especially those owning land and slaves who needed records to prove legitimate descent in order to pass property to their children, other free creole people and their family ties remained undocumented in these registers, obscuring their diverse origins. In other words, the familiar and emerging racial categories of the French Atlantic—*blanc, mulâtre, noir, de couleur*—were not applied with precisely the same meanings in seventeenth- and eighteenth-century Isle Bourbon.

Among the privileges accorded by the French king to the East India Company in 1698 and renewed thereafter until 1720 was a provision that encouraged Catholic marriages between French subjects and foreigners, awarding the spouses and their children with French citizenship and the capacity to inherit:

> Those of our subjects who pass into the countries conceded to the [East India] Company preserve their rights, as if they would live in our king-dom, and those who will be born of them and of people of countries with whom they will contract marriages, will be censused and reputed subjects [*Régnicoles*] and of French origin [*naturels français*], provided that they always profess the Catholic Apostolic and Roman religion.²⁶

This provision permitted families of mixed ancestry to be classified within the populations labeled "French" and "creole" in Isle Bourbon censuses. Only the few manumitted slaves unrelated to these French families were distinguished from the rest of the colonial population by the label "free people" (*libres*), and some freedwomen who married Frenchmen eventually merged into the general "creole" category over time. The number of censused *libres* remained very low (around forty) until 1767, when the crown took over direct administration of the colony.²⁷ According to travelers, hostility between free people of various hues was less pronounced in Isle Bourbon than in France's Caribbean colonies, at least in part because so many creoles descended from a mix of European, African, and Asian ancestors.²⁸

While the earliest captives brought to Isle Bourbon had come from Madagascar or India, the need for more labor drove the French East India Company to send slave-trading vessels to the coast and offshore islands of

East Africa, where they competed with Portuguese and Omani Arab slave traders. There the French borrowed the Arabic word *kaffir*, meaning "pagan," and labeled these African slaves *caffres* or sometimes *mozambiques*.[29] Thus, Isle Bourbon's standard census categories for slaves—*Indien/Malabar, Malgache, Caffre/Mozambique*, and *Créole*—flattened important distinctions that these people would have perceived among themselves: their particular tribes, villages, lineages, kingdoms, languages, castes, and religions.[30] As with the free population, the census requirement to designate on the basis of origin— essentially birthplace, in the broadest sense—means that the category "creole" hid their ethnic differences and admixture in subsequent generations born on the island.

Religious and ethnic diversity in Isle Bourbon and Isle de France directly affected royal laws regulating slavery and freedom. For example, the comprehensive "Letters patent in the form of edict" of December 1723 for France's Indian Ocean colonies omitted the provisions imposing Catholic faith on all colonists and slaves that had opened the 1685 edict for France's Caribbean colonies.[31] A 1730 injunction barred the sale of Christian slaves to "a gentile or Muslim."[32] A 1767 ordinance prohibited "all lascars, Malabars, Indians and other blacks [from] dancing and playing their tom-toms [after] eleven p.m."[33] By the 1760s, the French ministry went so far as to direct Indian Ocean administrators to permit Muslim worship in the Indian Ocean colonies.[34] Thus, by the middle of the eighteenth century, just as French administrators in the Atlantic world were beginning to standardize the triad of racial categories (white, black, and "people of color") as the basis of legislated hierarchy, local administrators in the Indian Ocean were specifying the greater ethnic and religious diversity of both the enslaved and the free populations of Isle Bourbon and Isle de France in their local laws.

The bundle of regulations issued by Louis XV in 1723 to manage the enslaved and free populations of Isle Bourbon and Isle de France (only two years after the latter came under French jurisdiction) mark an important transition in French management of colonial populations. Historians of the French Atlantic have long compared the 1724 Louisiana Code Noir with its Caribbean predecessor, the royal edict of March 1685, both of which eventually came to be known as the Code Noir (Black Code).[35] The Louisiana code is accurately recognized as embodying a more racially segregated approach to colonial law.[36] However, Louisiana's ban on interracial marriages was present in nearly identical language a year earlier in the comprehensive Indian Ocean Letters patent of December 1723, issued for Isle Bourbon and Isle de France. By article 5 of the 1723 Code Noir for the

Indian Ocean islands the king prohibited "whites subjects of either sex to contract marriage with blacks under penalty of punishment and an arbitrary fine. . . . We also prohibit our white subjects, as well as freed or freeborn blacks, to live in concubinage with slaves." The law set penalties for all men—regardless of color—who violated this injunction and sired children with their female slaves. "However," the king added, "We do not intend the present article to apply when a free or freed black man who was not married during his concubinage with his slave shall marry the said slave in the forms prescribed by the church; [in such instances] the said female slave will be freed by this means and the children rendered free and legitimate."[37] In this way, royal policy in the Indian Ocean plantation colonies attempted to prevent future mixing between "white" men and women of color, regardless of whether the latter were free or enslaved.

No such ban on interracial marriages would ever be issued by the king for the Caribbean colonies of Martinique, Guadeloupe, or Saint-Domingue,[38] but Isle Bourbon's prohibition of mixed marriages was reiterated in nearly identical terms for the newer colonies Louisiana in 1724 and French Guiana in 1741.[39] In fact, the Louisiana interracial marriage ban really only makes sense in light of its Indian Ocean precedent. In contrast to Isle Bourbon, Louisiana did not have a significant population of free people of mixed European and African ancestry at the time that the 1724 edict was issued (though admixture with Native Americans was common) as it transitioned from a frontier colony with slaves to a full-blown plantation society. The French crown aimed to nip mixture between Frenchmen and African women in the bud there and in Isle de France, only recently claimed for France in 1721.[40]

The 1723 ban on interracial marriages was not the first attempt to limit miscegenation on Isle Bourbon and can best be explained by the larger presence of nonwhite free people (i.e., free immigrants from Madagascar and India) and their descendants as heads of family in Isle Bourbon. As early as 1674, the viceroy of the Indies had prohibited Frenchmen in Isle Bourbon from marrying "negresses" under any conditions.[41] This pronouncement differed starkly from the subsequent 1685 Caribbean edict, which had actually provided incentives for single masters, including whites, to legitimize relationships with their enslaved concubines and children in Catholic marriages; such marriages automatically freed the master's wife and children.[42] The Isle Bourbon interracial marriage ban was reiterated in subsequent instructions to the island's governors in 1689, 1701, and 1710, and again in 1767 legislation.[43]

Despite these repeated injunctions, Isle Bourbon's ban on interracial marriages was rarely followed, especially since the East India Company privileges granted the status of French subject (*régnicole*) to a person of either sex who married a French subject.[44] Moreover, since racial descriptors only began to be applied regularly in parish records during the second half of the eighteenth century, many of Isle Bourbon's marriages of free people included individuals of mixed European and Malagasy, Indian, or African ancestry. Although not stated explicitly, an essential function of the ban on interracial marriages was to restrict the inheritance of colonial real estate to the legitimate descendants of the earliest generations of settlers, especially those descending from white French women. In this way, French law designed for Isle Bourbon was instrumental in producing a privileged racial category of whiteness, founded upon the very limited presence of white women in the Indian Ocean colonies, and from there it passed more widely into French colonial law.

Other provisions of Indian Ocean slave law that would have a direct effect on Madeleine and her children were those regulating the transition from slavery to freedom and the rights of free people of color. While the Indian Ocean slave code specifically prohibited the breaking up of enslaved families through seizure and sale for debt, at least until the children reached puberty, it did not explicitly state that children would be freed when masters freed their mothers (except in cases of free black men marrying the women they manumitted through marriage as specified in article 5).[45] Although both Caribbean and Indian Ocean slave codes decreed that freed slaves and their descendants would be on equal footing with naturalized subjects of the French king, over the course of the eighteenth and nineteenth centuries other articles, as well as local and royal legislation, introduced a variety of liabilities for free people based in race, thus undermining the equality projected in the original slave codes.[46] Most especially, the 1723 Mascarene code declared free blacks (*nègres*) "incapable of receiving from whites any donation *inter vivos* [a bequest], by reason of death or otherwise," thereby prohibiting mixed-race children from inheriting from their white fathers or, unthinkably, white mothers.[47] Yet, if children of mixed ancestry were formally inscribed as *blanc* in parish or census records, as most were in Isle Bourbon, there was nothing to stop them from inheriting their father's property. As in colonial Saint-Domingue, officials were content to overlook the letter of the law when it came to upholding the wishes of the deceased.[48]

The Routier Plantation

MADELEINE ARRIVED IN THIS rapidly growing colony with her master and mistress and their baby, Eugénie, sometime in 1773.[49] Thanks to the slave trade and burgeoning immigration from Europe, Isle Bourbon had 32,515 residents, with the 26,175 slaves outnumbering 6,340 free colonists (*habitants*).[50] In the intervening decades, the settlers had spread from the original hamlets in and around Saint-Paul, at the island's northwestern coastline, to the lush eastern farming parishes and southward into the drier ranchland.

Disembarkation at Isle Bourbon was difficult and dangerous. Unsteady from their voyage, members of the Routier family carefully made their way across the drawbridge held up by iron chains, extending eighty feet out into the sea, and down the rope ladder to land. This was better than the alternative, as described by one contemporary: "Throughout the rest of the island, one can only make landfall by throwing oneself in the water."[51] Luggage followed via ropes and pulleys. Then they traveled, either by horse-drawn carriage or held aloft by slave porters in palanquins, through the streets of the capital city, Saint-Denis, and over muddy roads to the family's plantation in the rural parish of Sainte-Marie, about six miles to the southeast. Male slaves followed, hauling the Routiers' luggage on their backs.

The Routiers were among the island's wealthiest planter families, with almost 175 acres of prime land in three parcels in Sainte-Marie and a smaller plot in the Saint-André parish further to the east.[52] While most of the Routiers' neighbors planted some manioc to feed their slaves, the Routiers' overseer ordered the slaves to plant commodities for the Indian Ocean market: 120,000 *pieds* in corn, 73,000 in wheat, 12,000 in vegetables or beans (*legumes*), and 5,000 in rice , but also 10,000 feet in coffee at the higher elevations. Likewise, their 131 slaves—67 men, 39 women, and 25 children—tended the Routiers' 80 pigs, 64 cattle, and 40 goats—supplemented, no doubt, by numerous chickens and pigeons, not counted on the census.[53]

Madeleine probably moved into the Routiers' wooden house, sleeping at the foot of her mistress's bed, or in an antechamber to her bedroom, or in one of the plantation's nearby slave huts: impermanent, airy, thatched dwellings so insubstantial that they were not listed among the Routiers' structures on the census forms. In her new home, Madeleine busied herself catering to her mistress's needs, as well as those of Madame Routier's children, occasionally running errands to the fireproof kitchen outbuilding, which was built by slaves from local volcanic stone.[54] A granary and storehouse, made of wood and clapboard, completed the plantation's structures.[55]

The seasonal rhythms that Madeleine had known in the northern hemisphere were reversed in Isle Bourbon. Corn (grown to feed the island's slaves) and wheat and rice (destined for their masters' tables) were planted at the outset of the rainy season in December. The first coffee harvest began in March, with three subsequent collections through July.[56] Thus began Madeleine's life as a plantation slave.

Nanny and Mother

THE RHYTHMS OF MADELEINE'S life in Isle Bourbon continued to be intimately intertwined with Madame Routier's fertility. Within a year of their arrival, her mistress gave birth to another daughter, Euphémie, born 24 June 1774; Euphémie and her sister, Eugénie, were baptized a few weeks later by the missionary priest in a double ceremony in the parish church of Sainte-Marie.[57] A little brother, Élie, would be born a few years later on 24 May 1777, recycling the name of his sister who had died en route to France.[58] Meanwhile, grandfather Jean Routier returned to Europe with his grandson, Fauchin, on his ship *La Brune*—another example of the increasing feminization of the colony and the importance placed by the elites on a French education for their sons.[59] Altogether, Charles Routier fathered eleven children (three with his first wife and eight with his second) while rising in the ranks of the Isle Bourbon militia. In 1780, he was promoted to major.[60]

Sometime between 1775 and 1777 Madeleine became a mother herself. Her eldest child was a boy named Maurice, but despite being firstborn, he is the least visible of her children to posterity.[61] By the middle of the eighteenth century, Isle Bourbon masters arranged for their slaves' baptisms less and less frequently, and there is no extant record of Maurice's baptism, which may suggest that his relationship to the Routier family was relatively unimportant.[62] Whether formally baptized or not, slaves generally received their names from their masters. Maurice's shared a first name with the Routier's overseer, Maurice Coëffard, a Breton from Sarzeau, but that may be a coincidence.[63] In France, law and custom denied illegitimate children the right to use their father's surname unless the father recognized the child through a formal practice known as naturalization.[64] In the French Caribbean colonies, free people of color were forbidden to use surnames belonging to whites, but this prohibition was never formally extended to Isle Bourbon, and some freedmen and women, some presumably the masters' offspring, publicly adopted their masters' surnames.[65] Throughout the French empire, custom dictated that slaves received no surname at all, and if a sexual union was not formalized through Christian marriage, the father's name was omitted from the baptism record.

The identity of Maurice's father is thus hidden from the historical record. In 1776, Madeleine would have been about seventeen years old, ripe for sexual activity with any of the men, slave or free, who surrounded her.[66]

The proximity of Maurice's birth to that of Élie Routier—in May 1777—is interesting. Perhaps Madeleine was re-enlisted as Charles Routier's sexual partner during his wife's confinement. However, other signs point to the possibility that Maurice's father was another man on the plantation, outside the Routier clan, perhaps another slave. Unlike the voluminous archival references to her later children, Maurice is only known to be Madeleine's first child due to a passing reference in Constance's much later testimony.[67] Second, Madeleine is incorrectly labeled as an African woman (*cafrine*) in the 1780 census, suggesting ignorance of, or lack of interest in, her Indian origins on the part of whoever tallied the census.[68] Her misdesignation as African underscores that her skin was dark; it could hint that Maurice's father was an African man or that she was relegated to fieldwork. Finally, Maurice reappeared in subsequent censuses with generalized (rather than precise) ages (1780: "Morice, *créol*, 5," and 1787, "Maurice, *créol*, 10"), another sign of his relative unimportance within the household.[69] On the other hand, Maurice was eventually groomed for domestic service, so he did receive some favor within the Routier family. In any event, the timing of Maurice's birth made Madeleine an excellent potential wet nurse for Marie Anne Routier's youngest son, Élie.

Tempests and Fortunes

DAILY LIFE—EVEN SURVIVAL—FOR MADELEINE and the Routiers was profoundly influenced by the weather. Between 1656 and 1850, some 64 cyclones—the tropical storms known as "typhoons" in the Pacific and "hurricanes" in the Atlantic—hit Isle Bourbon or Isle de France during a period that saw some of the most destructive storms in the islands' history.[70] Though deadly, these storms typically did not kill many people on impact; their few unfortunate victims typically died when their houses collapsed or through drowning in flooded rivers or ravines.[71] The cyclones' arrival along the Indian coastlines could be devastating due to dense human settlement and a broad, shallow bay, which made villages vulnerable to the devastation of storm surges and flooding.[72] By contrast, the deep ocean drop-off of Isle Bourbon allowed the storm surges to flow around the island; there the most deadly effects of severe weather were felt not immediately but in the destruction of seed intended for sowing or already in the ground and the resultant famines in subsequent months.[73] Cyclones alternated with periods of drought, when the winds carried rainfall to other parts of the Indian Ocean, leaving Isle Bourbon's soil parched, hard, and cracked. In these times, only the seeds planted in low-lying basins would germinate, and even then, the seedlings might wither in days of endless sunshine.

The Routiers' youngest child was born in 1777, just as a severe drought took hold of Isle Bourbon, lasting into the following year.[74] The northeastern parish of Sainte-Suzanne, bordering Sainte-Marie, ran out of food, necessitating the importation of corn and rice to feed the poorer inhabitants and slaves. The drought was followed by a series of powerful storms, threatening the lives of everyone on the island. Several windstorms were followed by the cyclone of January 1779.[75] Then came an extreme drought in the south, which drove down food production to dangerously low levels. In November 1779 another major cyclone whipped the island. The powerful cyclone of 1780 further devastated half the corn plantations and one-quarter of the rice harvest. Cyclones hit yet again in January and February 1781, depressing corn and rice production still further.[76]

The impact of these storms on the Routiers' slaves can be deduced in aggregate losses; of the 131 slaves that Madeleine met upon arrival, only 114 remained in 1784.[77] Yet the reality is more complicated than these raw numbers suggest. Already by 1780, the Routiers' slaves were aging, with over half of the slaves older than thirty years old and twelve of them functionally retired from the workforce.[78] Since none of the enslaved children enumerated in 1780 were under the age of three, it is likely that the poor harvests had lowered fertility and/or increased child mortality on the Routier plantations.[79] Meanwhile, the presence of nine children born in Madagascar indicates that the Routiers had replaced some of their slaves with fresh laborers from the transoceanic trade.[80] By 1784, the Routiers had lost eight male field hands, possibly through sale to raise cash. At the same time, they added four creole girls through birth or purchase. Together with the aging of other girls into puberty, these dynamics helped to bring better balance to the sex ratio on the plantation. It seems likely that the Routiers deliberately replaced males with females with an eye to improving the fertility of their slave population and the hope of eventually increasing their workforce through reproduction.

A Daughter, Constance

IN FEBRUARY 1784, CHARLES Routier filled out the census form on behalf of his 77-year-old father in France.[81] Charles's eldest sons, Augustin (18), Cyrille (17), and "Fauchin" (14), had returned to the island from France, and the two daughters, Eugénie (11) and Euphémie (10), along with the youngest boy, Élie (7), completed the family.

Months after the census form was filed, Madeleine gave birth to her second child, a girl named Constance. This time Charles Routier arranged for the baby to be baptized in April 1784.[82] Because Madeleine was not married to Constance's father, his name does not appear in the baptismal record. By the second half of the eighteenth century, births outside of wedlock were common in Isle Bourbon; fewer than twenty-five percent of the slaves baptized in Saint-Denis were born to married parents.[83] In fact, even for whites, about a fifth of the children baptized in the capital city of Saint-Denis in the 1780s were designated *enfants naturels*, that is, born to unmarried parents.[84] On the other hand, the selection of white godparents for Constance—in this case the master and his daughter Euphémie—was much less common by the late eighteenth century, with more than half of godparents being other slaves.[85] In fact, even when the Routiers baptized other slave children, they typically selected slaves or unrelated whites as godparents.[86] Constance was special.

Within days of Constance's baptism, Charles Routier took a six-month trip to Isle de France, returning in November 1784.[87] Was this voyage purely business, or did Constance's birth provoke tension between Charles and his wife or a local scandal? Somehow during Charles's absence, the baby Constance became the property of Matthieu Vetter, a twenty-seven-year-old cooper arrived in Isle Bourbon only two years earlier from Alsace.[88] The following September, Vetter filed a request to manumit Constance, only one and a half years old. The liberation of children was not particularly unusual; slaveholders freed many more children than adults in late eighteenth- and early nineteenth-century Isle Bourbon, as elsewhere in the French empire.[89] But Constance's manumission, approved by colonial administrators on 13 January 1786, put her in a very elite group of former slaves and their descendants designated as "free people of color" (*libres de couleur*) in Isle Bourbon. These constituted only 11 percent of the free population and about 2 percent of the overall population of the island.[90] The manumission document states that Constance was freed "upon the offer of making her [Constance] a gift of *la nommée* Suzanne, an Indian woman, age thirty, and to have care of her for all time so that she will never be a burden to the colony."[91] The expression "le/la nommé(e)," ("the one known as,") designated someone of low social status (e.g., a servant or laborer), ineligible for the honorifics *monsieur, madame,* or *mademoiselle.* The manumission's latter clause, about not depending on colonial charity, is formulaic in all such acts. But actually freeing a baby and then giving the child her own thirty-year-old slave ("the one called Suzanne") as a gift was unusual—even startling.

Who was Constance's father? A much later account, generated during Furcy's freedom suit, names Matthieu Vetter.[92] This is certainly a possibility, but it seems more likely that Charles Routier paid Vetter to act as a surrogate—to pretend to be Constance's owner (and father) so that Routier could discreetly manumit her by proxy. In other words, Charles Routier himself—or possibly one of his adult sons, Augustin (19) or Cyrille (18)—is a more likely candidate. Any of these men would have had access to Madeleine and possessed the power to coerce sex with the family slave.[93]

A very similar incident had taken place just three years earlier in Isle de France. In 1781 a prominent white man tried to hire a lower-status white family to adopt and conceal his illegitimate child through the actions of an intermediary. The go-between approached Matthieu des Landes, manager of a plantation, with a proposal to "make his fortune," saying:

> You saw that small girl who was dining at the table; she is the illegitimate child of M. Leroux Kermorseven and Demoiselle Dupont. I know that your wife gave birth to a baby on board the ship that brought you here from France some four years ago. That child is now dead; M. Leroux Kermorseven's daughter is about the same age. What you need to do, my dear des Landes, is to declare yourself the father of the girl, who we will pretend is the very same child that your wife gave birth to on board the ship. In order to execute this in the utmost secrecy, we will go to the parish of Moka to baptize her. I will be the godfather and my daughter the godmother.[94]

Des Landes negotiated a fee of 12,000 livres (about $60,500 today) for the favor, which hints at the degree of shame and possible punishment that he faced, but his wife objected to the scheme, and it erupted into a public scandal. In the case of Constance, within two weeks of her manumission, on 30 January 1786, Vetter married Félicité Constance Douyère, a creole girl ten years his junior who would eventually bear him six children.[95] It is easy to imagine that Routier, wishing to manumit Madeleine's illegitimate daughter, Constance, paid Vetter a substantial sum for the subterfuge; perhaps this was the very capital Vetter needed to embark upon married life.

Several clues and later developments tend to support the idea that Madeleine may have negotiated Constance's freedom in exchange for her own ongoing companionship with the Routier patriarch. The first clue is the choice of the daughter's name, Constance, no doubt selected by Charles Routier to denote Madeleine's constant loyalty to him or the family more generally. Second, later censuses show that neither Constance nor the mysterious slave woman Suzanne remained in the Vetter household.[96] Changes in the number, age, and origins of Vetter's slaves over the next few years suggest that he was a minor slave speculator, purchasing younger slaves, fresh from Madagascar and the East African coast, and then reselling or trading them at a profit.[97]

If Constance was not living with Vetter, where was she? She is not listed within the Routier household in 1787 and does not reappear on the censuses until 1796.[98] Her whereabouts during her childhood are therefore hidden. As neither a recognized member of a white family nor a (taxable) slave, she slipped outside the administrative system of surveillance. However, her childhood was apparently put to good use. Later evidence makes it clear that Constance was taught to read and write, probably at a young age.[99] Given the preferential treatment of Constance, it seems logical to conclude that she was Charles Routier's daughter with Madeleine.

Furcy

FROM 1785 TO 1788, Isle Bourbon's southern districts suffered a long period of drought, which once again devastated wheat production.[100] In 1785, an anonymous writer complained that "two thirds of slaves are not fed by their masters," resulting in slaves' escapes, thefts, and even violent crimes.[101] During this period, Charles Routier and several of his adult sons, the latter employed as volunteers in the merchant marine, traveled back and forth between Isle Bourbon and Isle de France, perhaps seeking to procure food or purchase more slaves.[102] In October 1786, Charles' father, Jean Nicholas, died in France, though his heirs would not learn the news until months later.[103]

On October 7, 1786, only a month after Constance's manumission papers were filed, Madeleine gave birth to her third child, a boy baptized "Fursi."[104] The close timing of Constance's manumission suggests that her freedom may have been predicated on Madeleine's giving birth to another slave for the Routier family, as a replacement for the one that they freed. As before, Fursi, or as all subsequent documents would spell it, Furcy, was listed as "the illegitimate son [*fils naturel*]" of Madeleine, without naming the father.[105] Through the selection of his godparents, Furcy was assigned to the spiritual supervision of two slaves belonging to other masters: Pierre, belonging to a "Monsieur Silve," and Anne, slave of "Monsieur Vernon," but neither master appears in the Saint-Denis censuses, suggesting possible further subterfuge on the part of Charles Routier.[106]

The given name Furcy is unusual in French-speaking societies, but not unheard of.[107] An Irish Saint Fursey helped to spread Christianity to the British Isles during the seventh century, but his feast day is January 16, making this an improbable source for the name of Madeleine's son.[108] In the early nineteenth century, a schooner named *Furcy* appears frequently in the pages of the *Gazette de Maurice*, the newspaper of Isle de France, and the name seems to have been relatively common for both slaves and free people there.[109] Most curiously, several names chosen by the Routier family for their own children or their slaves—Eugénie, Constant (the masculine form of Constance), and Furcy—appear among the names of the children of Perrine Jeanne Lory, the elder sister of Furcy's future master, Joseph Lory, suggesting a long-established relationship between the two families.[110] Or maybe the name was just in the air, enjoying a brief spell of popularity. Whatever the origin, the baby, like all slaves and many free people of color throughout the French empire, received no surname. Until much later in life, he bore only his given name: Furcy.

When Furcy was an adult, a Parisian journalist would describe him as having a "mulatto tint, but with very regular features and black hair, altogether similar to that of many Europeans . . . a color which perhaps notes that there was an alliance, on the part of his mother, with a negro."[111] The reporter here assumes that Furcy's Indian mother was light-skinned, with features like Europeans. Yet Madeleine was sometimes designated as a "négresse," and even an African (*cafrine*), indicating her darker skin. So while Furcy's father could conceivably have been a dark-skinned slave or free man of color, it is equally possible—even likely—that Furcy's "mulatto tint" and "regular features" were the legacy of a white father, the partner of his darker Indian mother, Madeleine.

Furcy himself claimed a French father. Years later, when trying to muster support for his liberation, Furcy would insist, "I was born a French colonist and I am the son of a Frenchman by birth."[112] He wrote this in a letter; it was never declared in legal proceedings and could have no bearing on his legal grounds for freedom. Additional circumstantial evidence suggests that Furcy's father, like that of his sister Constance, was Charles Routier. As Furcy grew up, he received special attention and training within the Routier household as the head butler (*maître d'hôtel*) and learned to speak in the idiom of the planter class.[113] If Charles Routier was indeed Constance's father, it seems entirely plausible that he continued his relationship with Madeleine, as his wife Marie Anne was forty-eight and likely beyond childbearing years.

4

The Revolution

EMANCIPATION WITHOUT FREEDOM

MADELEINE'S YOUNGEST SON, FURCY, was one of nine children born to enslaved mothers on the Routiers' Sainte-Marie plantation between 1784 and 1787.[1] Unlike the previous decade, these years, with regular but not excessive rainfall, allowed for economic expansion. The Routiers purchased nine boys via the flourishing transoceanic slave trade, five from the African mainland, three from Madagascar, and one from India, increasing the total workforce to 131 slaves.[2] While these field hands (*pioches*) harvested the Routiers' coffee, corn, wheat, wheat, rice, and vegetables, Madame Routier, probably assisted by Madeleine, raised her six children, aged nine to nineteen. As one contemporary observed, "Old age does not arrive in [Isle Bourbon] much more rapidly than in our temperate climates. In general, the white women preserve quite well; there are some of them who astonish by their beauty. They stay out of the sun more than the men."[3]

If the Sainte-Marie plantation was thriving, however, its master was not. In 1787, a year after Furcy's birth, the patriarch, Charles Gabriel Routier de Granval, died at the age of 56.[4] French death records from this period do not state cause of death, but 56 was relatively young for such a wealthy man. His substantial estate passed to his 49-year-old widow, Marie Anne Ursule, née Desblottières. The widow Routier's eldest son, Augustin, took over his father's business trips to Isle de France.[5] Cyrille (19), Fauchin (18), Eugénie (14), Euphémie (12), and Charles (9) pursued their educations at home.[6] Madeleine (*indienne*, age 29) was listed among the widow's slaves, as were her two sons, Maurice (*créol*, 10) and "Furci" (*créol*, 1), but not her free three-year-old daughter, Constance, nor Constance's slave, Suzanne.[7] Constance probably continued to live with her mother in the Routier household but was undeclared in the census. Since the form demanded only the declaration of legitimate family members and slaves, Constance's embarrassing presence within the family could remain officially unacknowledged. The fate of Constance's slave Suzanne—if she ever truly existed—is a mystery.

This chapter follows Madeleine and her children through the years of the French Revolution, considering how this cataclysmic upheaval in world history impacted the slaves in Isle Bourbon. At its heart is another historical puzzle. On 3 July 1789, less than a fortnight before Parisians stormed the Bastille, the widow Routier filed papers with colonial administrators to free Madeleine, a manumission ratified by them three days later. Under law, Madeleine was therefore undisputedly free from that day forward. Moreover, her free status should have been doubly secured in 1794 when the revolutionary government in Paris declared the abolition of slavery throughout the French empire. However, despite these two forms of liberation—one personal, at the behest of Madeleine's owner, the second by the revolutionary state—in 1796 the widow Routier once more declared Madeleine as her slave on her census return. If Madeleine had been legally freed twice over, why did her mistress claim her as a slave? To understand Madeleine's ambiguous status—on paper and in life—is to glimpse the instability of revolution and freedom and to consider how people tried to navigate these seismic social changes in daily life.

The Indian Ocean Difference

THE DAILY LIFE OF slavery in Isle Bourbon responded to the seasonal rhythms of planting and reaping, the milestones and demands of family life, sickness, and burials. Each event was interpreted through the languages and cultures of Africans, Malagasy, and Indians, which merged and overlapped in plantation life. As a resident workforce, slaves shared common elements in their lives: rising at dawn and moving to the fields to undertake the essential agricultural tasks for the season. Annual grains like wheat and corn demanded plowing, sowing, and weeding, followed by reaping, threshing, and hauling, while perennials like coffee needed weeding, harvesting, and fertilizing. Manioc (cassava, yuca), an essential component of the workers' diet, also required a great deal of labor preparing the ground, planting the stalks, and harvesting the roots. To supplement the bland starches, slaves maintained their own garden plots, raising poultry on their own time. In times of extremity, they also stole chickens or even larger animals, like the cow belonging to the farmer François Grosset in October 1779.[8] A minority of slaves working as domestic servants rose before dawn to prepare the more varied food of the masters—wheat bread and rice, meat and fish, fruits and vegetables—clean the house, maintain the gardens, and occasionally visit the markets to buy supplies in town.[9]

Less well documented but easy to imagine are the daily gestures of deference and authority that distinguished slavery from freedom. Masters looked
directly at anyone they chose and casually deployed their voices to command,
issuing orders directly to slaves, or, more frequently, to their overseers, who
deployed switches or canes to ensure obedience. Likewise, slaves were expected
to lower their eyes before their masters and commanders and received orders
without question or were subjected to corporal discipline. At a time in history
where social hierarchies were the norm, slaves rarely responded to indigni-
ties with organized violence in Isle Bourbon, and slave revolts were relatively
rare.[10] Instead, when the master's or overseer's treatment became unbearable,
slaves removed themselves to secret hiding places in the hills or the shelter of
friends and family on another plantation for days or weeks. Although they
faced punishment upon return, they used the temporary respite to make their
value known to the master; perhaps he would think twice about the behavior
that prompted the flight. Others fled permanently to the mountainous inte-
riors and created new lives and communities as maroons—self-liberated men
and women.[11]

Key to the transformation of the conditions of slavery in the Indian
Ocean was the introduction of sugar. Already by the 1780s, planters in
France's neighboring colony, Isle de France, were beginning to replace their
food crops with lucrative sugar cane.[12] The tall grass withstood hurricanes
better than other staple or export crops, but it also forced a more rigorous
labor regime than other tropical commodities. When the rapidly growing
cane, rich in sucrose, ripened, it needed to be processed immediately or the
sweet juice would rot within the stalks. Slaves harvested the tall grasses with
machetes and then hauled them on their backs or with animal-drawn carts
to the sugar factory (*sucrerie*), where they fed the grasses between enormous,
powerful rollers, which squeezed the juice from the cane. In the sugar factory the cane juice went through several stages of condensation, as slaves
strained the crushed cane from its juices into successively smaller cauldrons
to boil off the moisture, leaving crystalline brown sugar, which was sold in
that form or sent to European refineries to be purified into refined white
sugar. Hot and dangerous, the sugar factory had all the hallmarks of modern industrial labor: specialized, repetitive tasks, relentless hours of production, and human labor organized to maximize the efficiency of the machines.
Injuries were common from the swinging machetes, the sharp cane stalks
under bare feet, the crushing rollers, and the burning cauldrons. Sugar production was most efficient on large estates with workforces of at least one
hundred slaves.[13]

While the labor of hoeing, planting, weeding, and harvesting the essential grains in Isle Bourbon was also seasonal and often arduous, it was never driven by the furious deadlines of the cane harvest, when workers, rushing against the breakdown of sucrose in the cane, had to labor night and day in the boiling house in the tropical summer heat. At least in comparison to slavery in the United States and the Caribbean, including Saint-Domingue, direct brute force (whippings, staking in the sun, torture) was apparently less common in pre-revolutionary Isle Bourbon.[14] Isle Bourbon law permitted masters to punish their slaves with force, including whipping to thirty lashes, but mutilation and execution were reserved as a prerogative of the colonial state.[15] It is hard to know whether the supposedly benign treatment of slaves in eighteenth-century Isle Bourbon was because of a shared culture of hierarchy and deference, the relatively small social distance between masters and slaves, or the familiar rhythms of producing staple foods for local consumption, on whose survival everyone depended. These conditions would change with the introduction of the proto-industrial regime of sugar cultivation and processing after the Revolution. On the other hand, suicide was all too common, reflecting a pervasive state of misery and hopelessness.[16]

All of this raises the question of how Madeleine, Maurice, Constance, and Furcy were treated by the Routier family. There is no explicit archival evidence for the early years of their lives. Nevertheless, it seems likely that as both Madeleine and eventually Furcy were trained for domestic service, they learned to monitor their masters' moods closely and to anticipate their needs. Fluent in French from an early age and attendant on the desires of the master and mistress, they observed and participated in the Routiers' most intimate moments: ongoing tensions and squabbles, vulnerability in sickness and grief, rituals of lovemaking, joy in celebrations. Madeleine and her children were extensions of the family, but not legally recognized as such except as slaves and servants. Later evidence makes it clear that Madeleine was truly valued by her mistress and loved by her own children. On the eve of the Revolution, she was at the heart of the Routier family and all its branches, surrounded by Maurice (about 11), Constance (3), and the infant Furcy.

Madeleine's Manumission

ON 3 JULY 1789, when Furcy was "barely weaned from his mother's breast,"[17] the widow Routier petitioned the colony's administrators asking to free three slaves, including Madeleine and Jeannot, *creole*, 37, the enslaved domestic servant who had traveled with the Routiers to and from France, arriving in Isle Bourbon on the same ship as Madeleine in 1773.[18] Like the other two slaves manumitted by the widow in 1789, Madeleine, *indienne*, age thirty, was to be liberated in the formulaic language, "in recognition of the good services that she has rendered her [mistress]," but also "to fulfill the contract that [Madame Routier] had made in France to procure the liberty of the said Magdelaine [*sic*], who was only given to her under this condition."[19] This phrase would later be cited as evidence of Madeleine's residence in France and proof that an illegal gift or sale had been contracted between Mademoiselle Despense and Madame Routier. The manumission document concluded by noting that, as a free woman, Madeleine would be able to "enjoy and use the rights, privileges, and prerogatives of persons born in the condition of freedom without being troubled or bothered by anyone." According to later copies of the document, Madeleine, like Jeannot, would receive an annual pension of 600 livres plus living expenses. The administrators swiftly granted all three requests on 6 July 1789.

Madeleine's manumission was a relatively rare act in Isle Bourbon at this time. On the eve of the Revolution, manumission rates for the entire colony hovered at about one hundred per year, out of a total slave population of approximately 37,500 in 1787–1788.[20] Indeed, the censused free (*libre*) population of the island in 1788 included only 116 men, 135 women, and 778 children.[21] Yet some free people of color—like Constance—simply fell off the censuses, especially if they did not own property that could be taxed. Neither the people themselves, nor their wealthier neighbors, nor the government had any incentive to report them in the official tax records. If the former slaves entered into marriages with free people, they or their children might eventually pass into the general population category of "creole," without racial designations.

In recalling Madeleine's manumission to Furcy's legal counsel decades later, Constance insisted, despite the official act recorded in the colony's register, that:

> it was not until shortly before [Madame Routier's] death, [which] occurred in October 1808, nineteen years after her manumission, that Madeleine was informed of her condition [i.e., her freedom]. During this long interval, her status was hidden from her.[22]

In other words, the widow Routier never told Madeleine she was free. If Constance was correct, Madeleine continued to live in the Routier household, ignorant of her newly acquired paper "liberty."[23]

Why would Madame Routier free Madeleine and then not bother to tell her? The widow was very wealthy; savings in the annual head tax on slaves was not her reason for freeing the three slaves. Perhaps Madame Routier was fulfilling a promise made to her husband. If Charles was Constance and Furcy's father, it is easy to imagine that the widow Routier had a complicated relationship with Madeleine. By freeing her, the widow fulfilled the obligation to her husband, perhaps a deathbed wish, but by not informing Madeleine of the act, the widow continued to enjoy the benefits of her service. On the other hand, perhaps Constance's 1817 claim that her mother had never been notified of her free status was simply wrong. It is possible that Madeleine had negotiated her freedom with her mistress and was fully aware of her status as a free woman but continued to work for the Routier household out of loyalty and to be near her daughter, Constance, who remained in the widow's Saint-Denis household. It is even possible that the widow entered into a verbal agreement with Madeleine: If you continue to work for me until my death, I will leave you enough money that you will be able to purchase your sons' freedom. The fact that the widow eventually filed a new version of the manumission act with the newly added clause specifying Madeleine's pension of 600 livres per annum months before her death in 1808 makes this scenario quite plausible.[24]

Revolution at a Distance

THE FRENCH REVOLUTION ESTABLISHED a powerful universalist discourse when the Declaration of the Rights of Man and Citizen, drafted in 1789, guaranteed all French men "equality, liberty, security, and property."[25] This clause also created insurmountable conundrums for colonial slavery: Did the Revolution make free people of color, now legislated into subordinate status in the colonies, "equal" to whites? Did "liberty" apply to France's colonial slaves? If so, how could the "security" and "property" of the colonial masters be assured?

In August 1791, slaves in France's largest and wealthiest Caribbean colony, Saint-Domingue, set fire to the cane fields and brandished machetes against their masters, catalyzing the largest and most successful slave revolt in world history, the Haitian Revolution.[26] Two-thirds of the colony's slaves had been born in West and Central Africa and were taken prisoner in wars stimulated by the unquenchable Atlantic slave trade.[27] Using their military prowess, former slaves and free people of color pressured the vulnerable republican colonial leadership to abolish slavery, first in Saint-Domingue in 1793 and then throughout the French empire on 4 February 1794.

As liberals and then radicals in Paris began to imagine the French nation anew, they experimented with innovative political, legal, and cultural forms, designed to make a clean break with the past. First, a series of new constitutions offered new rights, new definitions of citizenship, contested ideas about race, and radical reformations of family law.[28] Second, in an effort to release France from the constraints of Catholic institutions and personnel, the revolutionaries abolished religious orders and convents and required priests to swear loyalty to the French nation. Among the many ritual changes they introduced were a new calendar with a ten-day week and the more enduring metric system; the Revolution redefined time and space as decimal systems.[29] Finally, with slavery abolished, the French Revolution imagined—but never effectively implemented—a new relationship between the metropole and the colonies, all to be administered under one universal system of law.[30]

Isle Bourbon was buffered from some of the most radical shifts of the French Revolution by its sheer distance from Europe, but, following the 1793 execution of King Louis XVI of the Bourbon dynasty, Jacobins bent on obliterating any memory of the monarchy renamed the colony La Réunion in 1794. News traveling from Paris took half a year to arrive, giving colonists the ability to cherry-pick the innovations that benefitted them. Male property holders took advantage of expanded rights of self-governance, and, after 1792, unhappy spouses could divorce; from 1793, illegitimate children recognized by their fathers were newly permitted to inherit from them.[31] Ships arrived daily bearing black sailors and radical republicans who spread rumors of developments in the rest of the French empire, but Isle Bourbon continued to see little armed resistance on the part of slaves.

The foremost historian of the revolutionary period in Isle Bourbon, Claude Wanquet, credits even-handed leadership by colonial authorities for the lack of serious slave revolts there.[32] However, scholarship from the French Caribbean colonies suggests other possible explanations for slaves' organized violence, or lack thereof, which might be assessed for Isle Bourbon as well. As in Saint-Domingue and Guadeloupe, escape to the mountainous interior was a constant factor in Isle Bourbon before and during the Revolution.[33] If flight—or *marronage*, as it was called—presented a "safety valve" for slaves prone to resistance in Caribbean colonies, at least prior to the major revolt of 1791, then access to remote volcanic highlands functioned similarly in Isle Bourbon, even to the point of tempering masters' treatment of their slaves, who otherwise might become fugitives.[34] Indian Ocean slave traders made a point of selecting children and teenagers to import from Madagascar, India, and the East African mainland;[35] weak and vulnerable from famine and trauma, they would not have had the opportunity to gather the strength or the unity to organize militarily against their masters. It is also significant that sugar cultivation did not reach Isle Bourbon until after the Revolution; the rhythms and practices of farming staples for the subsistence of the entire population were likely not as brutal as the relentless production of sugar for export.[36] If the Saint-Domingue slave revolt drove Parisian revolutionaries to seek free men of color as their allies and eventually the abolition of slavery in France's most important Caribbean colony, the French and Haitian Revolutions also accelerated Atlantic-style slavery in France's Indian Ocean island colonies as Atlantic sugar production collapsed and the Isle Bourbon planter elite anxiously tried to retain their control over both slaves and free people of color.

Three Weddings, a Divorce, and Several Funerals

MADELEINE AND HER CHILDREN experienced significant upheaval in Isle Bourbon during the period of the French Revolution, but not because of the changes emanating from Paris or the Caribbean. Shortly after Madame Routier filed manumission papers for Madeleine, the widow began to arrange the marriages of her four adult children, hinting at yet another element in the timing of Madeleine's paper freedom: the need to remove her and Jeannot from the estate before she began to distribute wedding gifts. Charles's death in 1787—likely unexpected—had put the widow in a difficult situation with regard to her property. How should the land and slaves be divided among her children? If she waited until her own death, the customary law of Paris that regulated the colonies would distribute everything equally among them, forcing the division of the landed property into ever smaller portions in the process.

Centuries of evolving legal practice in France nevertheless offered the widow a strategy for maintaining the Routiers' key properties in Sainte-Marie and Saint-Denis intact. She could convert the property she inherited (the *propres*, as distinct from the *acquêts*, property acquired during her marriage) into gifts and distribute them to her younger children as wedding dowries; by custom on such occasions the heirs renounced their right to an inheritance.[37] If Madame Routier wanted to keep the Sainte-Marie plantation and its labor force intact, she needed to select her children's mates and design the marriage contracts carefully.

In 1790, Marie Anne Routier contracted the marriages of her eldest sons, Augustin (24) and Cyrille (23), to two sisters, Thérèse Agnès and Anne Adélaïde Rathier-Duvergé, daughters of Isle Bourbon's commissioner general, the highest ranking civil official, with previous posts in New Orleans, Isle de France, and Pondichéry.[38] By pairing two sets of siblings, the widow hedged her bets; should any member of the two couples predecease the others without heirs, the family lands could be passed intact to the next generation. Augustin remained on the family's hilly plantation in Sainte-Marie, where he farmed coffee and goats, with the six slaves received from his mother.[39]

Yet Marie Anne Routier's optimistic arrangement soon went awry, at least for Augustin. After the birth of four children, one of them stillborn, his wife, Thérèse Agnes, demanded a divorce for reasons of "incompatibility and character" in 1795.[40] Augustin took a new wife, the daughter of a ship captain and a distant relative in the Panon family, in the church of Sainte-Marie on 10 June 1800. They continued to live on the plantation in Sainte-Marie with the eldest of his children by his first wife, Charles.[41] Meanwhile, Cyrille took up residence in Sainte-Suzanne, further to the east, where he farmed coffee and cloves and raised goats and pigs.[42] His wife, Adélaïde, eventually bore him nine children.[43] Madeleine's eldest son, Maurice, eventually joined them there, though not until after the Revolution.[44]

More important for Madeleine, Constance, and Furcy was the wedding of the widow's eldest daughter, Eugénie, whose birth Madeleine had attended at sea two decades earlier. The widow used Eugénie as the bait to trap an enterprising young merchant, Joseph Lory, whose business acumen and ambition must already have been evident.

Joseph Lory: Isle de France Creole

JOSEPH LORY WAS BORN in 1770 on his father's plantation in Montagne Longue, Isle de France, inland from the government center of Port Louis.[45] His father, André Lory,[46] had arrived from Nantes earlier that year, probably with his wife, Jeanne Perrine Bertin, and two older children, Perrine Jeanne and André.[47] As was customary, Joseph traveled to France as a young man, probably for schooling; he must have witnessed the outbreak of the Revolution there.[48] Having returned to Isle de France in 1792, the following year Joseph moved permanently to Isle Bourbon, arriving on board the ship *Le Volcan*.[49] The youngest of three children of a successful planter who stood to inherit the value of one-third of a large plantation in Isle de France, Joseph Lory must have looked like a promising prospect for twenty-one-year-old Eugénie.[50] Their nuptials took place on 7 April 1794 in Saint-Denis and were attended by many of the island's prominent citizens.[51] A scant nine months later, Eugénie gave birth to a daughter, Marie Charlotte Eugénie Lory.[52]

In contrast to her fertile mother, however, Eugénie had no more children with Joseph Lory until a second daughter, Euphémie, arrived a decade later in 1804.[53] Did Eugénie's first pregnancy compromise her health? Did a series of miscarriages bring heartache but leave no record? Does the long period between births bespeak marital discord between husband and wife? Or did Joseph Lory practice a more bourgeois notion of family planning, deliberately limiting their number of children so as not to divide up the estate? Unfortunately, no decisive documentary evidence exists to answer any of these questions.

The year 1799, when Napoléon staged his coup over the Directory in France, brought tragedy to the extended Routier family. First, the island suffered an intense drought, severely diminishing the wheat harvest.[54] Perhaps these disruptions fostered a contagion that led to the death of Eugénie and Joseph Lory's four-year-old daughter at the home of her grandmother on January 16.[55] Within three weeks, the family also had to bury her maiden aunt, Euphémie, who died at age twenty-five at the widow Routier's home.[56] The couple's second daughter, Marie Charlette Augustine Euphémie Lory, named after both her dead sister and her aunt, was baptized on 8 January 1804.[57] Euphémie, as she was called, would be the Lory's only child to grow to adulthood, but, like her namesakes, she would die unmarried, at the age of twenty-eight, survived by both of her parents.[58]

Although Lory and his wife did not produce a large family, there is no immediate indication that Lory turned to his enslaved women for sex. Based on the racial inscriptions applied to slaves in Isle Bourbon census records in the 1840s, none of the children born to women enslaved in the Lory household before 1812 were identified as mulatto.[59] In this regard, Lory apparently behaved more like a bourgeois merchant than his father-in-law with aristocratic pretentions, Charles Routier, whose wealth and career as a military officer may have normalized sexual access to his subordinates.

On the other hand, Lory may have found a sexual outlet with the slaves on his father's estate in Isle de France. A much later census lists a family of three mulatto siblings who stand out among the largely black workforce, each holding a privileged position on the plantation and bearing the surname "Eraste": Benoît, the overseer (born in 1794); Perrine, seamstress (b. 1801); and Eugène, domestic (b. 1814).[60] The surname—Erastes in English—suggests a dark sense of humor or spite, for it is the Greek term for a pedophile, the elder male lover of a youth, usually an adolescent boy.[61] In combination with the designation of "mulatto," the name implies a white father who had seduced a much younger slave. Perrine Eraste was apparently named after Joseph Lory's mother or sister, and Eugène is the masculine form of Joseph Lory's wife's name, only compounding the mystery of their parentage. Was it Joseph; his brother the ship captain, André; or another white man who began this family on the eve of Joseph's departure for Isle Bourbon and his arranged marriage with Eugénie? Was Joseph Lory practicing for his marriage bed?

Hunger and Freedom in the Mascarenes

THESE IMPORTANT SHIFTS IN the relationships between the two intersecting families, Madame Routier's and Madeleine's, played out against the backdrop of the French Revolution, at once very distant and in other ways immediate. How did the Revolution affect the daily lives of slaves?

The primary effects were economic, as planters' fortunes rose and fell through hoarding and profiteering or mounting debt, each of which might contribute to slaves' deprivation and hunger. At the same time, the new experiment in popular sovereignty gave rise to competing factions in the legislature who loudly debated local policies from the left and right, including policies affecting slaves. Over the revolutionary decade, Isle Bourbon's colonial assembly temporarily outlawed the importation of slaves, while alternately expanding and limiting opportunities for manumission. Paris's 1794 declaration of general emancipation induced acute anxiety in slaveholders, resulting in hypervigilant policing and punishment of slaves.

The Revolution transpired rather differently in France's Indian Ocean colonies than in the Atlantic. Unlike in the Caribbean, where British and Spanish armies invaded and occupied Martinique, Guadeloupe, and Saint-Domingue for periods of the Revolution, direct combat was not a part of the Mascarene experience until the British occupation in 1810, during the Napoleonic era. As a result, slaves experienced revolutionary warfare only indirectly, through the stationing of French troops and their impact on the local economy. Whereas previous food shortages in both islands had previously resulted from the natural disasters of cyclones and droughts, it was the presence of French soldiers and sailors that effected a series of revolutionary crises that directly affected slaves' well-being.[62] In December 1789, a dramatic increase in the cost of wheat (though not of corn, the slaves' staple) strained the budgets of white colonists.[63] On 4 July 1791, a major eruption of the volcano La Fournaise may have precipitated a new economic crisis as grain prices rose rapidly in February-March 1792.[64] The colonial assembly responded with a measure requiring masters to feed their slaves adequately, implying that masters had reduced their slaves' food allocations in response to rising costs.[65] A corn crisis in January 1793 further disrupted the food supply, especially for slaves.[66] The assembly renewed its directives toward feeding slaves on 14 June 1793 and 18 August 1794, imposing severe penalties for noncompliance.[67] With the exception of the 1791 eruption (which may or may not have affected the harvest), each of these inflationary crises had resulted from increased demand caused by human, especially the need to provision French naval ships stationed in the Mascarenes to stave off British invasion, rather than natural events.[68]

In 1792, the Legislative Assembly in Paris decided to withdraw governmental subsidies of the slave trade as "contrary to the principles of liberty."[69] The following year, the colonial assembly of Pondichéry passed a series of decrees banning the slave trade but allowing masters already in possession of slaves to dispose of them as they wished.[70] In 1794, the colonial assemblies of Isle de France and Réunion (Isle Bourbon having been renamed that year) decided that suspending the slave trade was pragmatic for a variety of reasons, though ideological grounds were also invoked. In Isle de France, the ban was initiated at the behest of a group of sans-culottes, the radical vanguard of republican politics, ostensibly because of a shortage of foodstuffs there, while in Réunion colonists suspended the trade for fear of disease contagion and slave resistance.[71] By 1796, some colonists expressed concern that abolitionist propaganda coming from Isle de France might have infiltrated the slave population in Réunion.[72] While voices in the legislature continued to demand enforcement of the ban, the illicit trade persisted— even flourished—during the Revolution, with authorities only enforcing the prohibition intermittently until it was lifted in 1802. Before the Revolution, some 38,074 slaves were declared on census forms; by 1804, this number had risen to 50,350.[73]

During the Revolution, Isle Bourbon masters and the colonial assembly fluctuated wildly in their propensity to free individual slaves. In August 1791, the colonial assembly of Isle Bourbon suspended all manumissions in the colony. However, in May 1793 it reversed this policy, prompting many masters to free their slaves in a flurry between 1793 and 1794.[74] In August 1794, the assembly passed significant new restrictions on manumissions, fixing the minimum age at thirty years for women and thirty-five years for men.[75] By April 1795, it resumed a more liberal policy, triggering another flood of manumissions, especially of women and children, bringing the manumission rate up to almost one percent of the slave population.[76] Then, in 1799, as part of an overall series of repressive measures, the colonial authorities began challenging manumissions that appeared spurious.[77]

Although the earliest economic crises of the revolutionary decade in Isle Bourbon were human-caused, renewed bad weather hit in 1795, including a severe cyclone at the end of January, which ruined much of the corn. This was followed by cyclones on March 13 and April 9–10 that completely ravaged both Réunion and Isle de France. These storms were followed by drought, further undermining corn and rice production.[78]

The economic disruption of 1795 prompted several transactions in the widow's family that show how lenders could use someone else's debt to enrich themselves. On January 26, Madame Routier's new son-in-law, Joseph Lory, purchased the mortgage debt of 22,500 livres (a little less than $400,000 in today's money) owed by the merchant Claude François for the first payment on real estate he had previously purchased from another merchant in the Sainte-Suzanne district.[79] By extending credit to François, Lory stood to profit in one of two ways: either by collecting on the interest when François repaid the loan six months later or by foreclosing on the property when the loan came due on 30 June 1795. Lory must have passed the tip to his mother-in-law, for two weeks later she made a similar transaction: she purchased Claude François's debt of 22,500 livres for the second and final payment, due six months after the first, on 1 January 1796.[80] Finally, on 13 February 1795, the widow took out a loan from "Citizen Fortin," currently in France, for 25,043 livres, payable in three installments on 10 February 1796, 1797, and 1798; as security she offered the mortgage to all her property—movables and real estate.[81] Thus, the widow was banking on the fact that she would be able to collect from Claude François in time to pay off Fortin. Is this how the widow acquired the land in Sainte-Suzanne for her son Cyrille? At a minimum, these financial transactions suggest how both Joseph Lory and the widow Routier speculated in the lending and mortgage markets of Réunion during the economic upheaval of the revolutionary decade.

Emancipation Suspended

WHILE THE POLITICAL AND economic upheavals of the revolutionary decade exacerbated the uncertainties of daily life, Madeleine continued to live with the widow Routier in her townhouse in Saint-Denis. The most important events to shape Madeleine's legal relationship to her mistress following her manumission in 1789 were triggered at a distance by the Revolution in France and its Atlantic colonies. On 15 May 1791, the National Assembly in Paris had authorized voting rights for freeborn people of color in France's colonies worldwide. The following August, the slaves on the northern plains of Saint-Domingue began their insurrection, which forced the republican colonial officers to seek military and political assistance from free men of color in the colony. In February and March 1793, following Louis XVI's execution, France added Britain and Spain to the growing list of nations against which it had declared war, and several leaders of the Saint-Domingue slave revolt, including the future general Toussaint Louverture, joined the Spanish army in the eastern half of the island as officers fighting the French.[82] Thus on 20 June 1793, the desperate French republican commissioners in Saint-Domingue, Leger Félicité Sonthonax and Etienne Polverel, besieged by General Galbaud, the ally of the royalist planters, offered freedom to any slaves who would fight on behalf of the republic.[83] When this did not attract the fighting force they needed, Sonthonax, a liberal republican, eventually decreed the abolition of slavery throughout Saint-Domingue.[84]

When the "tricolor" Saint-Domingue delegation bearing this news reached the National Convention, radicals enthusiastically declared general emancipation throughout the French empire on 4 February 1794 (16 Pluviôse Year II). The text of the abolition decree is brief, suspending the details of implementation for an unspecified date in the future:

> The National Convention declares that slavery of the Negroes in all the colonies is abolished. In consequence it decrees that the men living in the colonies, without distinction of color, are French citizens and will enjoy all the rights assured by the constitution. It returns [the action] to the Committee for Public Safety to quickly make a report on the measures to take to assure the execution of the present decree.[85]

Word of the Parisian emancipation decree reached Réunion ahead of official instructions. By 6 September 1794 colonists had learned the news, which spread quickly through the enslaved population, despite administrators' efforts to quarantine these potentially dangerous tidings.[86]

Within a week, a group of slaves in the parish of Sainte-Marie went on strike, but not to demand immediate abolition. Nine blacks belonging to Louis Ricquebourg, led by the 22-year-old African-born overseer Honoré, left the plantation en masse to ask their former master, Dufresne, to buy them back because of Ricquebourg's ill treatment, citing his "continuous threats . . . ,

the little time that he allowed them to take their meals, [and] the poor treatment experienced by his former slaves," who had been beaten by hand, foot,
and hookah pipe (*chabouc*). They complained that Ricquebourg made them
carry loads weighing a hundred pounds and threatened them to beat them
with a hundred lashes or to sell them to other masters, "who would give them
neither holidays nor Sundays." The assembly turned a deaf ear to the men's
protest, ordering them returned to their new master, with the exception of
their spokesman, Honoré, who was to be punished by the municipal authorities "according to the wishes of his master."[87]

At least one slave dared to speak up for emancipation. In September 1794,
Manuel, a Catholic creole slave of Saint-Paul, challenged two men in the road,
asking one of them why the colonial assemblies were meeting, and then allegedly stating: "It is time that [slavery] ends, that it is only us who suffers, because
we are owed our liberty." However, upon questioning, Manuel denied these
accusations, saying "that he believed that the blacks are free after they have been
in the land" (presumably the free soil of France).[88] Despite his backtracking to
a safer assertion (the National Constituent Assembly in Paris had declared on
28 September 1791 that slaves arriving in the metropole were thereby freed),
Manuel, like so many others convicted of spreading sedition (*mal propos*), was
sent into exile.[89] Upon arrival in Madagascar, the republican officer protested
his relocation, stating that authorities had no way to manage him there except to
sell him back to colonists in Isle de France or Réunion. The assembly eventually
allowed Manuel to return to Réunion, where he disappears from the records.

Others, inspired by the Saint-Domingue slave revolt, threatened direct violence against the master class. Witnesses claimed that Jean Pierre, a free man
of color working on his father's plantation, spoke frequently of slave revolt.
He allegedly stated to a Malagasy freeman, Zaïre, "that if he was punished . . . ,
he would do as had been done to the whites in America, that their throats
would be slit."[90] Like Manuel, he was sentenced to deportation. Another son
of a slaveholder, Pierre Louis, still enslaved, was accused of hosting gatherings
attended by slaves from other plantations, who "danced to the sound of his
drum in his cabin until dawn." He was overheard to proclaim that "if the war
comes here, he would be the first to cut the throat of whites."[91] A special tribunal sentenced Pierre Louis to death by hanging, after which his head was to be
placed on a pike by the road to his master's plantation. However, the colonial
assembly, noting procedural irregularities in the trial, overrode the sentence,
imprisoning Pierre Louis until he was re-sentenced, this time to be marched
through the streets (presumably in chains) on the second anniversary of the

emancipation decree (15 Pluviôse 1796), after which he was immediately sent into exile.[92] As this example suggests, from the informal rumor of the abolition decree in September 1794 until early 1796, when colonial authorities received official notification that specific instructions for its implementation would soon arrive, the colonial assembly tended to act with moderation when faced with slaveholders' anxiety over signs of resistance or verbal complaint by slaves or free people of color.[93]

On 7 February 1796, realizing that the Parisian directive to liberate slaves was imminent, the Réunion colonial assembly passed a resolution that the general emancipation decree, "an act of ruin and death for the colonies," was "inadmissible in the island"; the colonial decree was emulated a few weeks later by the Isle de France assembly.[94] Réunion's new attorney general, Levillan-Desrabines, fanned planter anxiety, encouraging denunciations of potential disorder, including any republican or abolitionist sentiment on the part of slaves, free people of color, or colonists. In February 1796, a black man wearing the uniform of the national guard brandished a pistol and declared loudly in public, "Liberty! Liberty! Live free or die.'" Slaves and free blacks displaying republican insignia of any kind were now subject to arrest. In this climate of intense instability, new reports emerged of masters and mistresses using extreme force (such as chains or brutal beatings) to instill fear in their slaves.[95]

On 18 June 1796, the long-awaited ship bearing the Parisian commissioners, René Gaston Baco and Etienne Burnel, arrived in Port Louis, Isle de France, with instructions for implementing the abolition decree. However, the two bearers of general emancipation would never make it to Réunion. They arrived on a "Décadi," the revolutionary day of rest, and most of the colonists were in the countryside with their families. The local authorities did not want to let the commissioners land but decided that they could not in good conscience turn away the long-distance travelers (the ship had already lost some forty sailors to scurvy during the voyage). Eventually the colonists permitted the commissioners to disembark and address the island's colonial assembly. Meanwhile, legislators spread word to the plantations to send armed men to Port Louis. Rumors also brought families of landowners seeking protection "in the fear of seeing themselves exposed to the murders and disasters that had taken place in the western colonies" of the Caribbean.[96] By the third day, June 21, the crowd in the streets had grown enormous and volatile:

The fence around the government building was surrounded by the mob in the middle of a thunder of cries: "Leave! leave!" To these cries, which repeated in the echoes of the mountains surrounding the port, some bands of armed national guards surrounded the barracks and would not allow a single soldier to leave. The commissioners were told to take their uniforms under their arms, which were held as national rags, and in this sad outfit, they were conducted to the port in the middle of cries repeated thousands of times, "Leave, leave!"[97]

The crowd, waving sabers and guns, drove the commissioners to a skiff waiting to transport them back to the ship. The two men were lucky to escape with their lives. Instead of trying their luck at Réunion, which, after all, had initiated the rejection of the abolition decree, the commissioners returned to Madagascar to pick up supplies, then slowly made their way back to France, having failed in their mission to abolish slavery in France's Indian Ocean colonies.[98]

In this way, the colonists of both islands used the revolutionary fervor emanating from Paris to consolidate their self-rule. This autonomy and their distance from the metropole allowed them to reject the abolition of slavery precipitated by the Saint-Domingue slaves' revolt and imperial warfare. How did Madeleine and her children experience the distant declaration of emancipation and its rejection by the colonists of Isle Bourbon and Isle de France? Archival sources suggest that Madeleine's freedom was full of ambiguities and contradictions.

Madeleine: Neither Slave nor Free

IN THE MIDST OF these volatile years, having married off her adult children, the widow Routier moved from her plantation to Isle Bourbon's capital city of Saint-Denis, whose streets were filled with soldiers anticipating renewed naval warfare with Britain. Her 1796 census form (Fig. 4.1) shows "Citizenness" (*Citoyenne*) Desblottières, widow Routier, living in her town home in Saint-Denis, with Madeleine and another slave, an aged Malagasy man named Maque, 61.[99] Madeleine's daughter, Constance, appears for the first time in the Routier census as "free" (*libre*)," age thirteen.[100] Presumably Constance had been living with the widow and Madeleine all along, but undeclared in earlier censuses as neither a slave nor a (recognized) family member. On the verge of young adulthood, Constance needed to be accounted for in the census return.

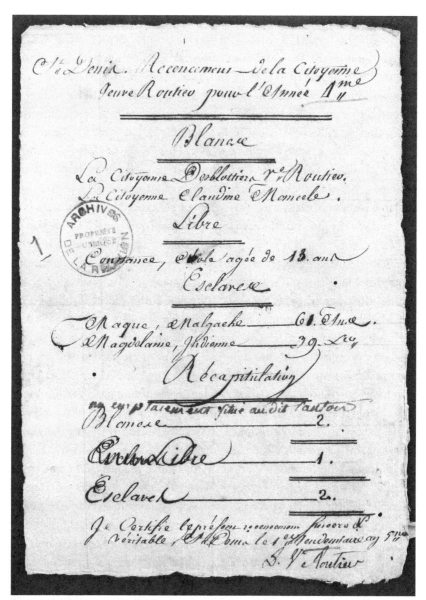

Fig. 4.1 The Widow's Census. The Year IV (1796) Saint-Denis census return for *Citoyenne Veuve Routier* (Citizenness Widow Routier) shows Madeleine as her slave and Constance as free (ADR L 142/1).

The widow's 1796 census return contains two anomalies that suggest how fragile the condition of freedom was for people of color in the wake of the expulsion of the Parisian commissioners. The first anomaly was probably just a mistake made in haste. Constance had been freed as an infant in 1787, and the widow correctly characterized her as free in the first lines of the current census. However, when it came time to tally up the number of free and enslaved people living in her household, she wrote: "Whites: 2," then accidentally skipped over the category "Free People of Color," and wrote "Slaves." Realizing her mistake, the widow then crossed out the term "Slaves," and replaced it with the term, "Free," counting Constance as "1." Apparently Madame Routier initially forgot to include Constance in the final tally, perhaps because the girl's position as a free nonwhite teenager was so awkward.

The second anomaly is far more serious. Despite having filed manumission papers for Madeleine in 1789 (and consistent with Constance's later testimony that Madeleine did not know she was free), in 1796 the widow listed Madeleine, *indienne*, 39, as her slave. Why would the widow Routier—who gave Madeleine her freedom in 1789—claim her as a slave in 1796?

The social and political upheaval surrounding the abolition of slavery created opportunities but also danger for slaves of elevated status (such as tradespeople and domestic servants) and for free people of color. Other historians have shown how, after slavery was legally abolished in Saint-Domingue (1793) and Guadeloupe (1794) until the formal reimposition of slave law in 1802, Caribbean masters continued to draft legal documents of individual emancipation to establish or secure the freedom of their former slaves.[101] These notarial inventions, modeled on the older manumission acts, were intended to protect the people that masters had already manumitted from re-enslavement in the event that a new pro-slavery government came to power (whether foreign, such as the British or Spanish, or French, should the monarchy be restored), or if the people in question became refugees beyond the French colonies. Such freedom papers—although technically redundant in light of the general emancipation decree—functioned as talismans of liberty that could be produced for anyone who might challenge a person's freedom on the basis of their color. Even so, many people of color, including the free-born or those freed before 1794, who fled the French Caribbean colonies during revolutionary warfare as refugees—especially women—were vulnerable to enslavement in places where slavery was all too prevalent, including Cuba and the United States.[102] These women's darker skin, gender, and lack of a community that recognized and could protect their free status made it possible for unscrupulous whites to claim them as slaves.

The timing of the widow's census statement was crucial: she signed it on 22 September 1796 (1 Vendémiaire Year V), just three months after the commissioners bearing Parisian instructions for the implementation of the emancipation decree had been driven from the Isle de France.[103] At this point, the widow could not have known whether Parisian officials would return and try to impose abolition on Réunion's slaveholders. In the meantime, she completed her census form, claiming Madeleine as her slave. When she filed the censuses of 1799, 1800, 1801, 1806, and 1808, she restored Madeleine's free status.[104] The 1796 declaration was thus an exception.

The widow's intentions or motivations are difficult to reconstruct. In 1796, at a time of so much uncertainty about whether the emancipation decree would be enforced, perhaps she labeled Madeleine as her slave in order to bind her to the household. In this case, she may have rationalized her decision as a form of protective paternalism. Then, in 1799, when the Mascarenes' rejection of the Pluviôse emancipation decree was firm, the widow may have felt that it was safe to restore Madeleine's paper freedom in the census. On the other hand, perhaps the widow wavered in her decision to free Madeleine in 1796, fearing that her loyal servant might leave her if the emancipation decree was somehow forced upon the colonists. The census declaration would give the widow Routier written evidence of her ownership of Madeleine as her slave. If so, the census declaration represents the widow's intention to renege on the 1789 manumission. Both hypotheses, benevolent and controlling, are consistent with Constance's later testimony that Madeleine did not know she had been freed in 1789. In filing the incongruous census return, Madame Routier probably reasoned that "what she doesn't know won't hurt her." On the other hand, if Madeleine enjoyed a tacit, verbal understanding with her mistress that she was free and chose to continue to serve the widow voluntarily, the 1796 census represents a dangerous moment when Madeleine could have lost her paper freedom.

Free Women, Enslaved Men

THE MANUMISSIONS OF CONSTANCE and Madeleine, daughter and mother, are consistent with manumission patterns throughout the world. In patriarchal societies from Bengal to the Swahili Coast of Africa to Brazil and the southern United States, women and children tended to be manumitted far more frequently than adult men, but not necessarily because of their intimate relationships with their male masters. Many colonial widows owned female slaves in Atlantic port cities where they could be rented out or put to productive labor. Slaves who worked near the docks as market women, laundresses, or prostitutes, if permitted to retain a portion of their earnings, might amass a nest egg in the cash economy, even to the point of purchasing their own freedom, or that of family members, with their savings.[105] Masters of both sexes, however, tended to retain their adult male slaves in favor of freeing females and children. The men's physical strength in frontier economies, in addition to their symbolic value as subordinate men, was more valuable in slavery than in freedom, at least in France and in the areas where European men established colonies.[106]

What became of Madeleine's two sons, Maurice and Furcy, during the Revolution? With no surviving census records for Sainte-Marie in the 1790s, it is difficult to say for sure. Maurice next appears in 1805 as a domestic servant among the 67 slaves on the widow's Sainte-Marie plantation, managed by her eldest son, Augustin, and again in 1806 at the widow's Saint-Denis residence, so he remained unambiguously enslaved to the widow Routier for the duration of the Revolution.[107]

Furcy's residence throughout the Revolution and the subsequent years of his youth remains a mystery. He does not appear on the censuses in any of the Routier family households until 1806, when Joseph Lory filled out the paperwork for his mother-in-law, the widow Routier, and claimed Furcy, creole, nineteen, as one of the widow's five domestic slaves at the townhouse in Saint-Denis.[108] Furcy's absence from the Routier censuses (including those of Augustin and Cyrille) during the Revolution begs explanation. Given his youth, it is possible that Madame Routier understood him to be freed in 1789, along with his mother, and simply omitted him thereafter from her census returns, as she had with Constance before the girl turned thirteen. Furcy may have spent his youth on one of the Routiers' Sainte-Marie plantations, tending Augustin's goats or, more likely, performing small tasks like gardening and training to support himself as a servant, until Madeleine could arrange for his freedom to be formally declared. But if the shared understanding between Madeleine and the widow Routier was that Furcy was already free, the lack of formal paperwork made him especially vulnerable to re-enslavement.

5

The Limits of Law

MADELEINE'S BETRAYAL

THE NAPOLEONIC ERA THAT transformed Europe in the first decades of the nineteenth century also brought anguish and upheaval to Madeleine and her children. As Bonaparte came to power in 1799, a rumor spread through Réunion that the government planned to enforce France's 1794 emancipation act, renewing panic among planters and their representatives in the colonial assembly.[1] A severe drought further heightened colonial anxieties, prompting colonists to increase violence against their slaves and authorities to intensify surveillance and arrests of both slaves and free people of color.[2] In June 1800, the assemblies of Isle de France and Réunion suspended all manumissions.[3] During this period, neither the widow Routier's sons nor her son-in-law, Joseph Lory, played significant roles in island politics. Perhaps they were among those suffering from the "culpable apathy" lamented by Isle Bourbon's colonial assembly when it chastised the island's citizens for not participating in district assembly meetings in March 1800.[4]

The 1802 Treaty of Amiens brought a brief lull in warfare between France and Britain, during which Bonaparte officially restored slavery to the colonies that had never actually abolished it in 1794. These included Réunion and Isle de France, but also Martinique, spared general emancipation by English occupation.[5] Needless to say, the French government's resurrection of the pre-revolutionary colonial slave laws for these islands was received warmly by Réunion planters, but it also fed into worries about armed maroons—those escaped slaves dwelling in the mountains—joining forces with the planters' slaves to attack French plantations and the unfortified cities near the coastline. Meanwhile, Bonaparte appointed a special committee of legal experts and charged them with reforming French civil law into a unified code, eventually known as the Napoleonic Civil Code, issued in 1804. The Civil Code consolidated patriarchal authority over married women and their children.[6] It also limited the capacity of illegitimate children and their mothers to name natural fathers over the men's objections.[7]

The Code Decaen

SHORTLY AFTER RESTORING THE legal framework for slavery in 1802, Napoleon appointed Charles Decaen as captain general of France's Indian Ocean colonies.[8] Decaen arrived in Isle de France on 16 August 1803 and ruled that island, as well as Réunion and French India, from there. On 26 September 1806 he renamed Réunion "Isle Bonaparte" in homage to the newly crowned emperor.[9] Aware of Napoleon's plans to modernize and rationalize French law in Europe, Decaen set about regularizing the legal regimes of the Mascarenes with a series of laws that eventually became known as the Code Decaen.

Implemented during a period of active naval conflict with Britain in the Indian Ocean theater, the Code Decaen increasingly restricted the rights of free people of color and asserted greater control over slaves, including Madeleine and her children. Anxious to suppress slave resistance and escape, Decaen issued a comprehensive fugitive slave law in January 1804 with a new policing system and a bureaucracy to pay for it. Slaves convicted of escape faced a year in chains, longer for repeat offenses.[10] For the first time in the Isle Bourbon's history, official birth, marriage, and death records (the *état civil*) segregated whites and free people of color into distinct registers.[11] Soon thereafter, Decaen resurrected the prohibition against people of color inheriting from whites, whether or not their fathers recognized them, a marked deviation from the Civil Code in France.[12] Two successive decrees in October 1804 and June 1805 imposed new, precise requirements for masters who wished to manumit their slaves.[13] For example, while the 1723 Code Noir had allowed slaves to save up cash or other belongings (like chickens or pigs) as private savings (a peculium), the new decrees expressly forbade them from using this nest egg to purchase their own freedom.[14] Slaves could not be freed until they had served for a minimum of five years unless they had performed a "significant service" to their master or the colony. The manumission process itself was made impossibly bureaucratic, requiring three public announcements of the intention to free (much like the posting of marriage banns) and the appointment of a third party guardian (*patron*) to act legally on behalf of the slave or freedman during and after manumission. Masters were required to deposit enough money to support their slaves for six months (as opposed to the lifetime annuity guaranteed under the Old Regime legislation), which made it cheaper for masters to free their slaves but also left freed men and women at the mercy of the wage market. The sum would be held by the Bureau of Charity, and the guardians were to ensure that the freedmen received these funds on a monthly basis or in a lump sum after three months if they could prove that they would use the money to purchase slaves or land.[15]

Not all provisions of these laws restricted freedom; when mothers were freed, the Code Decaen stated explicitly for the first time that their children under the age of seven would automatically be freed as well.[16] However, while this new provision might seem to be congruent with France's valorization of family ties, in practice it could put a damper on manumissions. Any master who wished to free his illegitimate children, as had happened frequently in the past, would also have to free his enslaved concubine, a more expensive proposition. Moreover, the required public declarations in advance of the emancipation would subject his extramarital relationship to scrutiny and scandal.

Cyclones and Drought

CONSTANCE CONTINUED TO LIVE with Madeleine and the widow in the Saint-Denis townhouse.[17] By the age of fifteen, Constance had become sexually active. In September 1800, she gave birth to an illegitimate son, Auguste, and in 1806 to another, Eugène.[18] The names selected for Constance's children, echoing imperfectly those of the widow's own adult children (Augustin and Eugénie), subtly honored the family ties to what were probably the deceased Charles Routier's unacknowledged grandchildren. As Constance was unmarried, the father or fathers of her sons are not named, but Auguste's father may have been Constance's future husband, a free man of color and farmer named Jean Baptiste Euphémie, about the same age, who later recognized and legitimated him, but not Eugène, at the time of their marriage.[19]

Meanwhile, operations on the Routiers' plantations continued under their new heads of household. The widow, together with her sons, Augustin and Cyrille, collectively owned about 266 acres of farmland in the Sainte-Marie and Sainte-Suzanne districts.[20] Joseph and Eugénie Lory did not own land, but lived for a time with their fifteen slaves in Sainte-Marie, probably on the widow's property.[21] About a third of the 131 slaves that the widow had owned in 1787 continued to live on her Sainte-Marie plantation, La Mare.[22] The widow had transferred eighteen (mostly middle-aged or elderly) slaves to her sons and son-in-law during the Revolution, probably as wedding gifts.[23] The Routiers' pro-natal strategy of populating the workforce through reproduction, evident in the 1784 census, was clearly paying off; fully 30 percent of the widow's 63 remaining slaves in 1805 had been born on her land within the last two decades.[24] By contrast, Augustin and Cyrille had purchased (possibly illegally during the Revolution) imported African and Malagasy slaves to farm their coffee, wheat, and corn plantations.[25]

Extreme weather in 1806–1807 provoked one of the most severe economic and demographic crises in the history of the two islands.[26] Two successive cyclones of 21 February and 11 March 1806 destroyed two-thirds of the harvested crops, hitting the easternmost districts—Sainte-Suzanne, Saint-André, Bras Panon, and Saint-Benoît—especially hard. The crisis prompted Decaen to order colonists to plant sufficient food to feed their slaves. The subsequent months of drought created a food crisis of near-famine proportions, as speculators in Réunion continued to sell their grain to Isle de France at exorbitant prices.[27]

Joseph Lory may have taken advantage of this crisis to cheat a free woman of color out of the legal title to her property. The notarial transaction is complex but is worth considering for its insights into Lory's business acumen. In 1792, a man named Montendre Adam Jams had arranged to buy land in Bras Panon, in the Saint-Benoît district, from Anne Luce, a free woman of color, for 5,600 livres (about $22,300 in today's money). In 1806, in the wake of the two hurricanes, Jams could not pay the balance of 5,200 livres (now about $15,000, thanks to currency fluctuations) due on the property, but on April 2 of that year, Lory signed papers agreeing to pay off the balance of Jams's debt. This meant that Lory became the lender on a long-term mortgage for Montendre Adam Jams and would collect future payments or the land itself if Jams went into default. A formulaic note stated that Lory had paid the woman Luce the sum by proxy, "out of sight of the notaries."[28] However, given later transactions between Lory and other free people of color, it seems reasonable to wonder whether Anne Luce ever saw the cash.

Two back-to-back cyclones, each lasting more than ten days, flooded Isle Bourbon in December 1806 and January 1807, eroding so much topsoil that the sea turned yellow.[29] In their wake, the island faced real starvation, prompting the police commissioner to propose a tax on foodstuffs and the city of Saint-Paul to consider a series of measures prohibiting the exportation of grain, collecting a reserve of seed grain, and encouraging wheat production. In March 1807, the mayor of Sainte-Suzanne, the district where Cyrille Routier lived with his wife and growing family, lamented:

The 600 individuals of the white and free population and 1,500 of the blacks are reduced to famine. This lack of food causes daily desertions and abuses [*dilapidations*], even the deaths of many blacks killed by guards, and the difficulties of service in a time when it is most needed and the despair of landholders.[30]

The lack of food was causing social unrest and increased violence toward the "blacks." Another cyclone slammed the island in March 1807, and the succeeding dry season returned the island to the extreme drought conditions of the previous year. A measure of the extremity of the crisis is that wheat, normally reserved solely for whites, was used to feed slaves because the corn and manioc crops were completely lost. By June, the price of corn had risen sixfold in three years, and the governor prohibited the export of all foodstuffs from the colony. Farmers on the western slopes replaced some coffee trees, destroyed by recent natural disasters, with corn.[31] While the capital district of Saint-Denis did not suffer immediately from the crisis, the death rate in the Routiers' plantation district, Sainte-Marie, increased by 72 percent and Sainte-Suzanne by 130 percent in 1807.[32] Famine finally reached Saint-Denis in 1809.[33]

The effect of the crisis of 1806–1807 on the Routier family can be seen in their census returns. In 1780, the Routiers' manager had instructed their slaves to diversify the planting of their Sainte-Marie properties in coffee, manioc, wheat, rice, corn, and vegetables. By 1804, the family owned more land and slaves, but they concentrated on planting wheat and corn, letting some 20 percent go to pasture or woods, while the second son, Cyrille, conducted an experiment in sugar, planting a small patch; it must have failed, for he did not turn to sugar again for more than a decade. The coffee trees produced minimal harvests in 1806 and 1807 (Augustin writes "superfluous" next to this acreage in his returns). Meanwhile, the widow Routier lost four slaves, and, with little yield in March 1806, she or her son Augustin ordered that everything be planted in corn.[34] By contrast, Augustin's return on an even smaller parcel of land a few years later gives a better idea of a typical annual harvest that could be expected in a good year: 50 tons of coffee, 500 tons of corn, and 4,000 tons of vegetables of coffee, of corn and of vegetables.[35] That same year, 1812, in Sainte-Suzanne, Cyrille's newly planted clove trees began to produce a little, and his fields yielded 350 tons of wheat, 250 tons of rice, and a bumper crop of 1,000 tons of corn.[36] The land was very productive when the weather cooperated.

The Return of Furcy

PERHAPS THE CRISIS OF 1806 strained the widow Routier's health or confined her to the Sainte-Marie plantation, since she signed her census return there on 1 January 1807.[37] Living with her was the freedman and La Mare overseer Jeannot, the man who had journeyed home with Madeleine from France in 1773 and was freed with her in 1789.[38] With Eugénie and Joseph Lory having moved to town, the 69-year-old widow delegated the completion of her census forms for the townhouse to her son-in-law, who signed it on her behalf on 31 December 1806.[39]

The 1806 census form that Joseph Lory prepared for the widow may have been a strategy to re-enslave Furcy, nineteen, who until then had likely enjoyed a tacit paperless freedom. The French had a name for such informal manumissions: *libre de fait*, or "free in fact," as opposed to *libre de droit*, "free by law."[40] Without formal documentation, such people were vulnerable to re-enslavement. Furcy had not been declared on any of the widow Routier's census forms for the Saint-Denis or Sainte-Marie properties since his mother's manumission in 1789. Other enslaved children had been readily declared on her returns, so the omission of Furcy's name was not due to his age and was apparently deliberate.[41] The likeliest explanation is the widow meant for Furcy to be free as a toddler along with his mother. By inscribing Furcy's name on the widow's return in 1806, Lory restored Furcy as a slave of the Routier family.[42]

According to a much later account, based on Furcy's memories and composed by a legal advisor, "Furcy, having been at first a domestic, then became the head butler staff [*maître d'hôtel en chef*] at Madame Routier's house." By now the widow was likely incapacitated, and Furcy was working for Joseph and Eugénie Lory. When asked how he was treated, he told his interlocutor:

> He was so abused of his strength that when he had completed the service of the house, he was sent after dinner to the plantation house [in Sainte-Marie], a distance of three leagues [about seven and a half miles], to search for provisions and from which he was required to return the same night.[43]

What is more, Furcy was forced to help carry Eugénie Lory, who, along with her husband, had moved into the Saint-Denis townhouse, in a palanquin, as well as various female friends and relatives. "Furcy was so exhausted from this service that he began to spit blood."[44] He probably found these duties, reminiscent of those of a beast of burden, humiliating as well as physically taxing. Even if the point of recording the story was to elicit sympathy for his civil suit, the incident suggests that the transition from youth to adult service involved exercises designed to bring him under submission to Joseph and Eugénie Lory. Witnesses to this treatment, also living with the Lorys in the widow's Saint-Denis residence, were Madeleine (48), Constance (21), and Constance's son, Auguste (3), all listed in the census as free.[45]

The youngest of the widow's sons, Élie Routier, thirty years old, married Marie Anne Vincente Calixtine Jams Adam, divorcée of the notary Claude Louis Faciolle, on 13 February 1808.[46] Present before the notary for the prenuptial contract, standing in for their deceased father, was Élie's older brother, Augustin, and his brother-in-law, Joseph Lory.[47] Other members of the family (including the widow Routier, whose oversized, slightly wobbly signature reflects her deteriorating condition) witnessed the contract.[48] With the last of her adult children married off, the widow's work was nearly done.

Meanwhile, Joseph Lory's business transactions during the island's economic crisis suggest varied enterprises, from real estate speculation to an interest in importation, including—potentially—slaves. On 18 January 1808 Lory paid one Montalant, purveyor for the navy, 1,200 piasters (a little over $20,000) for the purchase of two capstans (heavy winches used, for example, to wind an anchor cable) and six boats: one *chaloupe* (rowboat or launch) of seven tons, another of fourteen tons, another small rowboat, a canoe, and two dugout canoes.[49] Likewise, on 31 May 1808, Lory advanced Montendre Adam Jams—the man whose mortgage he had purchased or swindled from the free woman of color Anne Luce two years earlier—1,000 piasters for the purchase of ten slaves; the slaves were to remain in the employ of Monsieur Adam Jams, who was responsible for their care and nourishment, until 31 July 1809. None of these names appear on Lory's 1810 census; most likely, Adam Jams was able to pay off his debt to Lory and keep the slaves as his own.[50] In September, Lory teamed up with a business partner, Pierre Gamin, and the two of them purchased a bakery in Saint-Denis from Victor Boyer and his wife for 8,000 piasters ($136,000). The plot, located across a narrow path from the state bakery and bordering the Saint-Denis ramparts, included a small watermill.[51] No doubt the recent damage to the wheat crop had made the Boyer bakery insolvent. By 1814, Lory had become sole proprietor.[52]

Constance, Married

THE 1808 CENSUS WOULD be the last signed by the widow Routier.[53] She had returned to her residence in Saint-Denis with Madeleine (now 50),

Constance (22), and Constance's two sons, Auguste (6) and Eugène (1½). The widow's census again enumerated her five domestic slaves, including Madeleine's two sons: Maurice, 29, and Furcy, 20.

On 30 May 1808 Constance appeared before the Routier family's notary with her fiancé, a freedman named Jean Baptiste Euphémie, to sign a marriage contract.[54] Little is known about Jean Baptiste's ancestry or early life. According to the contract, he was 24 1/2 years old, born in Saint-André, and was currently living in Sainte-Suzanne, "at the place of the River of Mât."[55] His former owner was supposedly a free woman of color named Madeleine, but there is no mention of when or where she had freed him. Formulaic prescriptions stated that their future marriage would merge their property but not their debts; each was to liquidate the latter prior to celebrating the marriage.

Jean Baptiste brought to the union two pieces of land in Sainte-Suzanne and three slaves, all shared jointly with Luce and Adélaide, also former slaves of the free woman Madeleine of Saint-Suzanne.[56] Constance brought with her three slaves, Euphrosine (*caffrine*, 27), Elisa (*malgache*, 18), and Georges (*créole*, 8), recently purchased from a Monsieur Duperier[57] and Matthieu Vetter and evaluated at a total of 500 piasters (about $9,000).[58] Owning slaves that could be rented out as day laborers or otherwise put to work in productive labor was a common strategy for single women in the colonies to support themselves; it is not surprising that Constance was investing in slaves as a form of capital.[59] Although slaves came with their own expenses—primarily the food they ate and a change of clothing once a year—their labor could produce a far greater return than a cache of coins buried in a special place.

The prenuptial contract reveals several startling facts. First, Jean Baptiste identified himself as the natural (i.e., unmarried) father of Constance's son Auguste; the future marriage was designed to legitimize the boy before the law.[60] There is no mention of Constance's infant, Eugène. Second, one of the witnesses to the contract was Matthieu Vetter, Constance's putative father.[61] While Constance signed her name with a clear hand, Jean Baptiste "declared that he did not know how" and so confirmed the contract by voice in front of the witnesses.

Although Constance contracted marriage with Jean Baptiste before the notary, she apparently did not celebrate the marriage in a church or before the colony's civil authorities immediately. In her 1808 Saint-Denis census report, filed and signed by her on December 31, Constance, *libre*, 22, still appears as an unmarried head of household with her two sons, Auguste and Eugène.[62] Before long, however, Constance would join Jean Baptiste on his property in Sainte-Suzanne, where they would begin their married life together.

Death of the Widow Routier

IN JUNE 1808, THE widow Routier began putting her affairs in order.[63] At the end of the month she arranged for the clerk of the Saint-Denis Tribunal of First Instance to record a copy of Madeleine's 1789 manumission. Unlike the original act, which made no mention of an amount for Madeleine's sustenance,[64] this new document specified that Madeleine was to receive "a pension of six hundred livres [about $ 2,770] and supplies [*vivres*] so that should will never become a cost of the Colony."[65] The cumulative sum owed Madeleine since her 1789 manumission should have been nineteen times that amount (11,400 livres, or $37,000). Clarifying Madeleine's pension retroactively might have been a way for the widow to work around the fact that, according to the 1723 Code Noir and the Code Decaen, people of color were "incapable of receiving from the white population any gift or inheritance."[66]

On 4 October 1808 Marie Anne Ursule Desblottières Routier died at the age of seventy, a ripe old age for a colonial widow.[67] Although later documents—once again dating from Furcy's later appeal—refer to, and even quote verbatim, the inventory of the widow's belongings and the act of their distribution in subsequent weeks, the original papers are missing from the archival repositories.[68] According to these later accounts, the inventory described Furcy as: "creole, age twenty, domestic and head butler, estimated at the value of 3,700 livres [about $11,000]."[69] Madeleine's cumulative savings should have been ample for her to purchase Furcy's freedom from the Lorys.

Although Augustin was the deceased widow's eldest son, either she had entrusted her affairs to her son-in-law before her death, or the heirs decided to make Lory executor of the estate, no doubt because of his business experience. In late 1808 and early 1809 Lory commenced the series of notarized transactions that would clear the way for the final distribution of the widow Routier's estate. She had left her eldest grandchildren—Charles, Adéline, and Marie Charles—500 piasters (less than $10,000) apiece. Joseph Lory paid each of them on 30 November 1808.

In January 1809, Joseph Lory arranged a meeting before the notary Michault d'Emery with Jeannot, the overseer of the widow's Sainte-Marie plantation since he was freed in 1789.[70] At the time of his manumission, the widow had promised to provide for Jeannot's sustenance with an annual food allowance of 600 livres ($2,770) plus supplies. However, Lory offered Jeannot only twenty piasters ($339) for the year 1808. Jeannot, illiterate ("[He] declares neither to be able to write nor sign"), agreed to these terms, although he may not have fully understood them.[71]

On 16 February 1809, all of the widow Routier's heirs (or their representatives) gathered before the notary Michault to conclude a sale of the portions of the estate to her oldest surviving son, Augustin.[72] To accomplish the
consolidation, the La Mare plantation was first divided amongst the widow's surviving children (Augustin, Cyrille, Eugénie) and the children of her
deceased husband's first marriage.[73] Then Augustin bought his siblings out of
their shares, paying them a total of 63,334 livres ($181,000), divided propor-
tionately. The heirs likewise renounced their ownership in the widow's slaves
(*noirs*) in exchange for 43,787 livres ($125,000), which was to be paid out of
a sum previously allocated by "Sir Panon Desbassayns" by an act of property
distribution (*partage des biens*) of 27 October 1808 and paid over four years
in separate installments.[74] This wealthy broker was likely the widow's first
cousin, Philippe Panon Desbassayns, the future commissioner general of the
colony. The net result of the redistribution of the widow's property was that
Augustin retained the main plantation, La Mare in Sainte-Marie, intact.[75]
Eugénie and Joseph Lory became proprietors of the Saint-Denis townhouse.
It was probably through this process that Maurice became the slave of Cyrille
Routier[76] and Furcy became the slave of Joseph and Eugénie Lory.[77]

Madeleine: Inheritance and Betrayal

THREE DIFFERENT EYEWITNESS ACCOUNTS shed light on Madeleine's
life following the death of the widow. Together, these documents portray
Joseph Lory as an unscrupulous cheat who deprived Madeleine of her just
compensation and Furcy of his freedom. The first is a notarized receipt
stating that Madeleine had received from Lory a sum of money owed her
by the widow's estate.[78] The second is Constance's petition, originating in
1817, almost a decade after the widow's death, in the midst of Furcy's legal
dispute with Joseph Lory.[79] The third is a lengthy document titled "Notes
written under the dictation of Furcy" that offers critical evidence about
Furcy's life as Joseph Lory's slave.[80] The events recounted in this third document (including private dialogue between himself and Joseph Lory) took
place between 1808 and 1829 and could only have been reported by Furcy
himself, but the account was written down sometime later, in the third
person, probably as Furcy appealed his slave status in Paris in the 1830s.[81]
All three documents contain demonstrable inaccuracies, those of the latter
two probably introduced by faulty memory or wishful thinking over the
intervening years. However, together they point to an inescapable conclusion: Lory tricked Madeleine into ratifying a receipt that cheated her out

of money owed her by the widow Routier, and he reneged on an oral promise to free Furcy.

At the time of Madame Routier's death, Madeleine was about fifty years
old. According to Constance, this was when Madeleine learned for the first
time that the widow had formally freed her nineteen years earlier, in 1789.[82]
The manumission papers had been kept secret from Madeleine for almost two
decades. Moreover, according to the second copy of the manumission, filed in
the months prior to the widow's death, Madeleine, like Jeannot, was supposed
to have been paid nineteen years of wages since the time of her manumission.[83] The cumulative debt of 11,400 livres ($37,000) was worth about at
least three skilled adult male slaves, a significant savings for a woman facing
retirement.[84]

Any joy that Madeleine felt at this windfall must certainly have been tem-
pered by Joseph Lory's claims over Furcy, for whom he had carefully laid a
paper trail to claim him as his slave. Madeleine immediately offered to trade the
entire debt of those back wages for Furcy's freedom. Lory, however, rejected
this offer.[85] While a mother purchasing the freedom of her enslaved son was
not strictly forbidden by the Code Decaen, her proposal certainly violated
the spirit of the law of 20 June 1805: "A master cannot free a slave through
self-purchase via the slave's savings; it is especially recommended to citizens
and to the public ministry to oppose any manumission that has a motive of
this nature."[86] As Constance's legal advisor later put it, Madeleine was

> spurned in her request, rebuffed with anger, intimidated by Sr. Lory's
> threatening words, and, fearing to see her unhappy son indirectly hurt
> by the effects of [Lory's] anger, Madeleine did not insist. She opposed
> the injustice with silence, holding hope in her heart that, sooner or
> later, her complaint would see justice.[87]

In other words, according to Constance, Madeleine withdrew, hoping that
Lory would eventually see his way to freeing Furcy. Furcy's memory is somewhat different. He recalled that Madeleine threatened to leave for Isle de France
to seek justice directly from General Decaen.[88] In fact, there is a hint that she
initiated a lawsuit but abandoned it because she lacked the funds to see it
through.[89] Whereas Constance remembered her mother's forbearance and suffering, Furcy recalled her assertive resistance to Lory. These memories strikingly
reflect their own gender expectations and perhaps also each child's personality.

Maybe Madeleine's threat to appeal to a higher authority worked. Lory
came back to Constance and suggested that if Madeleine would sign a receipt

for the nineteen years of back wages, he would free Furcy in two years, when Lory planned to return to France, and would give Furcy a sum of 4,000 livres ($11,300) to live on.[90] According to Furcy, Lory told him to go find Madeleine, "who no longer lived at [Lory's] house" and to "bring her to the home of M. Michault d'Emmery, the notary of his family."[91] The notary informed Madeleine that she was due nineteen years of back wages specified in her manumission and that, "if she would give a receipt for the nineteen years of wages, Monsieur Lory would undertake to free Furcy within six months or a year."[92]

However, when Madeleine arrived at the office of Michault d'Emery on 7 August 1809, Lory told her that she needed a witness. She stood up to go find one, but she was told, "Wait, here is Monsieur Hirne [a lawyer], who will do it for you."[93] Lory said that he would prepare an act whereby Furcy would be freed within six months or a year, and, according to Furcy, he extracted from Madeleine a fee of 4,000 livres ($13,300), which he said was required when a slave was manumitted.[94] As Furcy put it many years later, "Madeleine believed Monsieur Lory, believed the notary, believed that Monsieur Hirne would not betray her!"[95] Instead, Madeleine unknowingly acknowledged receipt from Lory of one year of back wages (paid in corn and ten livres cash [about $175]), "recently delivered outside of the presence of the undersigned notaries," thereby implicitly renouncing the remainder of the debt owed her.[96] As Joseph Lory's earlier transactions with free people of color (Anne Luce and Jeannot) showed, the verbiage about the amount being paid outside the presence of the notaries is formulaic, but it clearly misled Madeleine, who profoundly misunderstood the paper record that she verbally ratified. The notarial quittance did not mention the condition of freeing her son Furcy (whether in six months, a year, or, as stated elsewhere, two years).[97] By this omission, Furcy remained a slave in Joseph Lory's possession.[98] The notarial quittance concludes, "The said Madeleine declares not to know how to write or sign."[99] Illiterate, Madeleine was at the mercy of the unscrupulous and powerful men surrounding her.

In Furcy's narrative, as soon as Madeleine ratified the papers, she immediately came to him, insisting that he accompany her back to the notary to demand a copy of the act that had been signed. Upon their arrival in his office, Michault d'Emery told her that she didn't need a copy. Furcy later insisted that the notary's actions made him suspicious, but he told his mother he was going to wait, find another slave ["noir"] to replace him, and then seek to fulfill the conditions of the agreement.[100] This detail—that Furcy would try to find a replacement to serve as Lory's slave—is particularly interesting.

Perhaps he intended to use either his own or his mother's savings to purchase a young man to serve as the Lorys' head of domestic service. It suggests that, at least at this point, Furcy had no principled objection to slavery per se and that his single concern was to achieve his own personal freedom, unjustly denied him by Lory. This is consistent with Constance's investment in slaves. Brother and sister were operating within the slave system they had known since birth.

As Furcy later elaborated, Madeleine went back to Lory in 1811, saying, "You have promised to give freedom to my son within six months to a year, but after two years of delays, I am going to attempt the execution of our agreement again." Lory replied, "Everything that has been done has been done correctly; to undo it is impossible, and if you have the money, we will spend it."[101] Lory knew that Madeleine could not afford to purchase her son's freedom without the money owed her for back wages. Furcy remained Lory's slave.[102] Furcy's version of events, recorded with the assistance of a lawyer in Paris, was clearly self-serving, but it also clarifies his own understanding of why he was entitled to his freedom. Madeleine's loyal service had resulted in the widow's providing a sum for the purchase of Furcy's freedom. Lory cheated Madeleine out of her peculium and refused to free Furcy.

According to Constance, it was at this point that Madeleine finally decided to sue the heirs of the Routiers for her back wages.[103] But she couldn't afford to pursue the lawsuit against Madame Routier's heirs, so she "was reduced to live in inaction, deploring the state of servitude in which her son was held in violation of his rights . . . until death put an end to her misery."[104]

According to Lory's lawyer decades later, Furcy officially became Lory's slave in 1812, when Augustin Routier paid the final settlement (*échut en partage*) of his mother's estate to each of the co-heirs. As Lory's lawyer described it in 1838: "Furcy, who desired Monsieur Lory as a master, came to solicit him to purchase him. Monsieur Lory gave in to his pleas and assured him a condition as happy as was ever enjoyed by those of his condition."[105] It is conceivable that in the interim Lory had sent Furcy to the rural Sainte-Marie plantation and that Furcy, indeed, lobbied to be among those transferred to the Lory household in Saint-Denis. Furcy was now a young man in his early twenties, and the city promised people and encounters that were more stimulating than the daily routines of farming. But Lory's account of Furcy's pleas is plainly self-serving. Moreover, like the receipts produced by Joseph Lory for the first time in 1821 and 1837 to authenticate Madeleine's slavery in Chandernagor, the evidence of this transfer from Augustin to Lory only appears for the first time during Furcy's later appeal.[106] Moreover, Lory's own documentary evidence belies his version of his acquisition of Furcy. Two years earlier, in 1810, Lory's census return declared "Furcy, *créol*, 22," the first among his slaves.[107]

History and Memory

THE EVENTS THAT TOOK place after the widow Routier's death were crucial for Madeleine and her children. Despite jumbled, missing, and contradictory evidence, it is clear that Madeleine, who had served her mistress loyally for thirty-five years, from the delivery of Eugénie while crossing the ocean until the widow lay on her deathbed, expected a sum of money that would sustain her as she faced her own old age as a free woman. She was willing to trade this pension for her youngest son's freedom, which there is every reason to believe he had anticipated since his mother's paper manumission in 1789. During the island's worst recorded economic crisis, Joseph Lory, who came to be Furcy's owner by unclear means (through paperwork that is mysteriously missing from the archives), refused to honor Madeleine's expectation of back wages and instead made her acknowledge on a paper signed by others a paltry quantity of corn and cash as the reward for her years of service. Lory would continue to write Furcy's name at the top of the list of his slaves for the next 23 years, despite Furcy's best efforts to gain his freedom.

This tragic episode in Furcy's family's life is symptomatic of the broader challenges historians face in recovering the truth about unequal relationships. Isle Bourbon's creole elites bent the rules dictated by colonial officials by creating, modifying, and even falsifying the necessary paper trail. Even if the widow Routier acted with the best of intentions in revising the manumission papers to leave Madeleine the means to purchase her son's freedom, the fact remains that this powerful slaveholder held the power over her loyal but illiterate servant. Lory's wily and cynical manipulation of the notarial record would have remained unquestioned were it not for Constance's and Furcy's later, admittedly interested, charges. The historical archive is laced with these threads of power. Only by carefully comparing the disparate versions of the story can we begin to approach something like the truth.

6

A Perfect Storm

AS CONSTANCE LATER REMEMBERED, her older brother Maurice died "in July 1810, in the service of Monsieur Cyrille Routier, when the island was taken by the English."[1] Perhaps Maurice died in combat, trying to earn his freedom by one of the few means left open to black men under the Code Decaen, which offered freedom to slaves who fought on behalf of the French government.[2] However, since the French lost, there would be no commemoration of the fallen like Maurice. Indeed, this brief comment is the only passing mention in any surviving record of the fact that the Routiers' slave, Maurice, was Constance's and Furcy's brother. It underscores how much oral knowledge of family life has been lost outside the written records left by the church and the French state.

The British invaded Isle Bonaparte on 7–8 July 1810, and from there conquered Isle de France, restoring the names Isle Bourbon and the original Dutch name Mauritius (Isle Maurice) to Isle de France. They held the two islands until Napoleon's defeat. The 1814 Treaty of Paris restored Isle Bourbon to France, but the British retained Mauritius as the spoils of war. The imperial control of each island would have a direct impact on Furcy's future as his future passage between the two islands would determine his status as slave or free. With Napoleon removed, the Bourbon monarchy resumed its reign as a constitutional monarchy. In 1817, the French Ministry of the Navy and the Colonies commenced an effort to reform Isle Bourbon's judiciary, sending new magistrates and administrators to ferret out colonial corruption. The newly appointed justices came to clash with slaveholding creole elites precisely as Isle Bourbon's planters increasingly demanded more slave labor for sugar production on the island. This conflict quickly escalated into a colonial constitutional crisis, with the executive and the judicial branches of Isle Bourbon's government at complete loggerheads, each challenging the other's authority over personnel and extrajudicial arrests. The confluence of these events gave Constance and Furcy the perfect opportunity to challenge Furcy's enslavement, although both had family reasons to do so as well.

British Occupation and the Slave Trade Ban

WHEN THE BRITISH CONQUERED Isle Bourbon and Isle de France, the occupying forces were too small to effectively run the government by themselves. Instead of completely overhauling the political and judicial infrastructure of their newly acquired colonies, the British navy implemented a kind of "indirect rule," demanding an oath of loyalty and retaining the French colonial laws and personnel.[3] Thus, when the British Parliament extended the 1807 transatlantic slave trade ban to the Indian Ocean region in 1811, an inherent tension arose between the laws of the occupying power, which prohibited the transoceanic commerce in slaves, and local French law and the expanding sugar industry, which depended upon the ongoing importation of slaves.[4]

The British governor of the two islands, General Farquhar, tended to favor slavery and planters' interests, paying lip service to the slave trade ban while pleading to his London superiors that the islands be exempted. During this time, records show a steady increase in both islands' slave populations, apparently due to illegal imports from the Indian Ocean basin.[5] Among the planters who likely purchased black market African slaves during the period of British occupation were Joseph Lory and Cyrille Routier, who would soon begin to invest in Isle Bourbon's sugar revolution.[6]

Since the loss of Haiti to independence in 1804, French demand for colonial sugar had increased, making it a more profitable crop.[7] While Bourbon planters had grown small amounts of sugar for internal consumption on the island in the late eighteenth century, they rapidly accelerated cane production during and after the English occupation.[8] In 1812, the English lifted the ban on distilling liquor, and the local rum, arrack, began to flow. Charles Panon Desbassayns became the first colonist to install a sugar mill on an Isle Bourbon plantation, known as Le Chaudron ("The Cauldron"), which produced 110 tons of sugar in 1815. The following year he set up a steam engine on his property, replacing a windmill that had been destroyed in a windstorm.[9] With the new technology, processing the sugar harvest was both more efficient, since it was no longer dependent upon steady winds, and more brutal for the workers, who had to stoke the engine's flames with cane debris around the clock for weeks during the twice-annual harvest seasons.[10] Unlike the sugar revolution in France's Caribbean colonies, which took place in the late seventeenth and eighteenth centuries, Isle Bourbon's turn toward sugar occurred precisely as the government began to suppress the slave trade, drawing smugglers to flout the law in response to colonists' demand for more labor.[11]

Constance and her husband, the farmer Jean Baptiste Euphémie, must have sold the property he brought to the marriage, for by 1811 they had purchased a larger farm in the Saint-André district at Champ Borne, near the coast. There they lived with their four young children and four slaves, growing rice, corn, and vegetables.[12] At the beginning of their married life, they were relatively well-off for a family only a generation removed from slavery, with a horse and three pigs and a second, much smaller plot of land in the Saint-André district.[13] Constance began to teach her husband to read and write; Jean Baptiste's annual census returns reflect his growing literacy and attention to spelling.[14] By 1813 he no longer defined himself as farmer (*cultivateur*) but as a planter (*abitant* [*sic*]).[15]

There is no direct testimony as to how Constance and Jean Baptiste Euphémie treated their slaves, but several clues suggest that they—or at least he—rejected the planter model of labor exploitation for maximum productivity. The year they purchased their new land, they brought in a bountiful harvest of about 110 tons of vegetables, 220 tons of corn, and 165 tons of rice.[16] Then in December, Jean Baptiste freed his oldest slave, Dauphine, 39, and sold George, 9; perhaps he allowed Dauphine to purchase both her son's freedom and her own.[17] Jean Baptiste, and later Constance, would retain the other two female slave hands, Eliza (*malgache*, 18 in 1811) and Imogène (*caffrine*, 27), until 1826 and 1837, respectively. This is the very little that can be deduced about the adults in the household from the limited records.

However, after the first good year of Constance and Jean Baptiste's married life, something changed. They reported planting nothing in 1812 and gathered less than a fifth of the previous year's harvest: two tons of corn, the same of rice, and four tons of vegetables. The year 1813 was little better, as they planted extra corn, but the vegetable harvest was barely half a ton; these subsistence rations were hardly enough to support this household of four adults and four children. The weather was not the problem; there were no reported cyclones or droughts.[18] It is hard to know whether they lacked the seed to plant, whether Jean Baptiste—after working diligently for another master for so many years—had decided to live a simpler life, or whether there was something significantly wrong with his health. Did the quashed 1811 slave revolt in Saint-Leu, on the other side of the island, cause him to reconsider his position as a planter, leading him to reject the exploitive model of farming for the commercial market?[19] To make matters worse, over the next few years the couple had two more mouths to feed; one of their children died as a toddler.[20]

Meanwhile, Furcy, age 22 in 1810, continued to serve the small Lory family—Joseph, Eugénie, and their daughter Euphémie—in the Saint-Denis townhouse. [21] Despite his youth, Furcy was appointed head butler, supervising the rest of the domestic staff of six slaves, including a Malagasy man five years his elder who eventually became Lory's cook. [22] In marked contrast to the pattern established on the Routier estate in the 1780s, only one child was born to Lory's nine enslaved women of childbearing age. This was the mulatto Pauline, born to one of these women in 1812. [23]

The same year, Joseph Lory purchased a second building in Saint-Denis at the corner of rues du Conseil and de la Pompe, perhaps a storehouse or shed from which he did business. [24] His equipment hints at the diversified labor that his dozen or so non-domestic slaves probably performed: carts (*charettes*) and logging carts (*trinqueballes*) suggest land clearing and agricultural production. [25] The stills (*alambics*) were for the distillation of liquor. The rowboat (*chaloupes*) and canoes (*canots, pirogues*), purchased from Montalant, would be used for conveying merchandise from ship to shore. [26] As an urban dweller, Lory probably rented out both equipment and slaves at a profit. He also hired local artisans. For instance, in 1814, upon receipt of an elaborately refinished chair, he hired a colonial craftsman, Renoyal de Lescouble, to wallpaper his living room. [27]

Furcy, in his late twenties, was, according to one observer, "a young, intelligent, brave mulatto." [28] But his life had changed irrevocably following his mother's battle with Joseph Lory. After the widow Routier's death, Madeleine had moved into a house on the rue du Bazard, just a few blocks from the Lory household, where she could remain in touch with Furcy, rather than imposing upon Constance and her family in Saint-André. [29] At the age of "around sixty," and without the support or protection of her former mistress, she must have fallen on hard times. [30] On 18 January 1814, she died at two o'clock in the morning. It was Joseph Lory who reported the death to city officials. According to Furcy, she had died "of sadness [*chagrin*]" over having failed to secure his freedom from Joseph Lory. [31] Her actual cause of death cannot be known, but surely her limited finances must have played a role.

The grieving Furcy turned to a young free woman of color for consolation. Although the evidence is scant, it seems that he wooed Virginie Béga, the daughter of Célerine, a free woman of color, seamstress and hat maker, and granddaughter of an enslaved Indian woman named Bondi, living in Saint-Denis. [32] Virginie eventually gave birth to two daughters, who may have been Furcy's: Marie Anne Nelcine (b. 28 July 1815) and Olympe Joséphine Augustine (b. 27 July 1817). [33] That Furcy became a father before 1817 is certain, [34] but the link with Virginie and her children is inferred, never specified in any historical document. [35] If Virginie was indeed Furcy's companion, it is interesting that he successfully courted a free woman, who probably earned her own living, while he was still Lory's slave. In any event, bound in slavery and therefore unable to marry the mother of his children without his master's consent, Furcy could neither visit them freely nor provide for them; any savings he might muster technically belonged to Lory. Perhaps the birth of his second daughter contributed to Furcy's decision to claim his freedom, so that he could fully enjoy his status as father.

Under Joseph Lory, Furcy's treatment declined dramatically. As he later testified, though supervisor of Lory's domestic force, he was forced to do demeaning manual labor as a gardener and Eugénie's palanquin porter.[36] Moreover, Furcy

> was often beaten. If, in planting the garden, he didn't plant the flowers of the flowerbed symmetrically, in contrasting colors, Madame Lory had him beaten. If the younger slaves under his direction at the service of the table broke something, such as porcelain, glass, or crystal, the clumsy one was beaten, but so was Furcy, for his lack of careful supervision.
>
> One day, Monsieur Lory had dinner at the home of Antoine de Parny and had passed the evening gambling. The weather was bad—it rained terribly—Furcy was sleeping and at first didn't hear Monsieur Lory knock. Finally he woke up and opened the door for his supposed master. Immediately, the latter laid out a kick in the stomach and punched him in the face so forcefully that the next day the muddy boot print could still be seen and his shirt was covered with the blood that had flowed from Furcy's nose. Madame Lory, who knew of this fact, claimed that Furcy had [deliberately] cut his gums, so as to stain his shirt.[37]

Furcy's legal advisors in Paris, who recorded this testimony many years later, were looking for evidence of maltreatment, which—though perfectly legal, since masters had almost unlimited power to punish their slaves[38]—might garner some sympathy from the metropolitan judges, especially from those already beginning to question the legitimacy of colonial slavery. In addition to describing Lory's violence, the anecdote portrays Eugénie's capriciousness and willingness to lie to cover up her husband's behavior.

Furcy's testimony also sheds light on his financial relationship with his master. French law permitted slaves to amass savings, the peculium, though these funds ultimately belonged to the master.[39] In Furcy's case, the Lorys used the peculium as a means to punish him for perceived infractions: "He was made to pay for the little spoons that were lost by the domestics responsible for clearing the table and cleaning up." A final anecdote reveals Furcy's ongoing battle for dignity with his mistress and (and likely half-sister) Eugénie:

> Someone had asked 50 piasters [about $700] to reupholster a carrying chair, but Furcy proposed to do it [himself] and he apparently succeeded because Madame Lory gave him a piaster, but she expressed regret about it so often, as though it didn't merit anything, that he ended up returning the piaster. Then Madame Lory fell on him and overwhelmed him with blows herself.

We can imagine the youthful Furcy, hearing Eugénie's complaints about the artisan's rates, seeing an opportunity to earn some cash. Perhaps his amateur upholstering was not to her satisfaction, or—worse—he did an excellent job and she resented his success. In a moment of exasperation, Furcy returned the wages, probably regretting that he had ever offered to improve the palanquin in which he was forced to carry his mistress. She received his gesture as a thinly veiled challenge to her authority, resulting in her physical attack on him. The stories of punishment suggest that it was hard for Eugénie to exert control over Furcy.

Was Furcy aware of his kinship with Eugénie? The taboo against bastard children publicly naming their fathers was powerful, and Furcy never recorded the name of his father in any surviving record. Yet his declaration a few years later of being "the son of a Frenchman" suggests that he knew his father's identity, perhaps whispered to him by Madeleine or Constance.[40] The awareness that Eugénie was his half-sister probably intensified his sense of humiliation and complicated her need to dominate him. As a sister, Eugénie should have owed Furcy the respect due a male relative; as his mistress, she was due Furcy's "appropriate" deference. These battles reflected the ambiguity of their standing and her desire to break him to her will.

A Gust of Parisian Air

WHILE FURCY WAS BEING harassed by the Lorys in Saint-Denis, the restored monarchy in Paris pondered how it might reform conditions in the colonies. First, it bowed to British pressure by acquiescing to the slave trade ban, though the French government did little to enforce it.[41] Unfortunately, banning the slave trade intensified the terrible shipboard conditions for slaves smuggled into the island and may have increased the brutality of plantation working conditions as masters sought to extract the most labor from their slaves.[42] If the conditions of slavery worsened during the early years of the Restoration, policy slightly improved toward free people of color as the French ministry quietly lifted some of Napoleon's harshest racial policies. Under Napoleon no one with African ancestry had been lawfully permitted to enter the French kingdom (although, in practice, of course, there were many black soldiers in Napoleon's army). Likewise, blacks (though, curiously, not people of mixed ancestry) had been denied the right to marry whites of either sex in the metropole.[43] Although the new government continued to prohibit the entry of "blacks, mulattoes, and other people of color," the ban on mixed marriages was rescinded in 1818.[44]

More immediately important for Furcy than these measures, however, was the royal government's plan to reform the colonial legal system, increasingly seen as corrupted by local planter influence. The ministry's attempt to modernize the colonial courts, orchestrated from Paris, would set the stage for Furcy to challenge his enslavement to Lory. It would also initiate the encounter between Furcy and his lifelong ally, an idealistic magistrate who would champion his cause and ultimately produce and archive the records that preserved Furcy's story.

On 14 October 1816, Louis Gilbert Boucher, a magistrate whose career had advanced steadily under Napoleon and the Restoration with appointments in Italy and France, was invited by Baron Portal, the king's counselor of state charged with supervising the legal and judicial regulation of colonies, to join a committee to discuss plans for two new ordinances "on subjects of colonial interest."[45] The committee successfully executed its charge, and on 30 November 1816, the viscount Dubouchage, minister of the navy, sent instructions to the administrators of Isle Bourbon dictating the reorganization of the colonial court system. A lower court, the Tribunal of First Instance, would be retained, but with a different staff, and the Appeals Court would be replaced by the Royal Court of Bourbon. Each of the new courts would be presided over by the attorney general (*procureur général*)—a magistrate with prosecutorial powers—plus a president, and a second president.[46] Implicit in this reorganization was greater royal control over the appointment of the judges and other officers of the appeals court. On 13 December 1817, the ministry selected Boucher as the new attorney general to the Royal Court of Bourbon, the highest judicial officer in the colony.

Boucher must have been waiting excitedly for this opportunity, for within weeks, on the eve of his departure for Isle Bourbon, he contracted marriage to Marie Josephine Louise Sonthonax, the step-daughter of a counselor in France's highest appeals court, the Cour de Cassation in Paris.[47] Sonthonax is a rare and suggestive name in French colonial history; Léger Félicité Sonthonax was the commissioner who had decreed the emancipation of slaves in Saint-Domingue in 1793, catalyzing France's general emancipation decree of 1794.[48] Marie Sonthonax was undoubtedly a relative, perhaps even his niece.[49] That fact that a rising star like Boucher sought an alliance with the notorious Sonthonax family, held under surveillance during Napoleon's rule, hints at both his liberal, republican sentiments and his colonial aspirations; the fact that her stepfather, Joseph Julien Le Gonidec de Kerdaniel, was highly placed in the Paris legal profession likewise made her an attractive bride.[50] Boucher must have seen his impending mission to Isle Bourbon as one of reform: to bring the enlightened logical principles of French civil law to the corrupt, aristocratic pretensions of the planter elite.

As part of the clean sweep of the colonial order, the king also appointed completely new administrators for Isle Bourbon. These men boarded a royal fleet in Brest, which weighed anchor on 16 March 1817, arriving in Saint-Denis three and a half months later, on June 28—a much faster voyage than Madeleine's six-month journey in 1772–1773, probably due to improvements in naval construction.[51] The first ship, *L'Éléphant*, carried the two chief colonial officers: the commissioner general organizer Philippe Panon Desbassayns, Baron de Richemont, the chief civil officer of the crown, responsible for overseeing colonial tax revenues and expenditures, and Commander General Hilaire Urbain de Lafitte du Courteil, charged with the military governance of the colony. This dual-executive system, central to French administration since the seventeenth century, functioned as a kind of check and balance, ensuring that the king received regular dispatches from two rival officers, leaving his distant authority intact. However, in this case, Panon Desbassayns and Lafitte were not functional equals. Philippe Panon Desbassayns, brother of Charles Panon Desbassayns, the sugar entrepreneur, was a wealthy creole descendant of the original Panon dynasty.[52] Lafitte du Courteil had connections to the royal family, but he had no local knowledge, which allowed Panon Desbassayns to assert greater control over the daily life of the colony.[53]

After finishing their business in Paris and Rochefort, Boucher and his new wife boarded a second ship, *La Normande*, along with several new judicial officers destined for the lower and the appellate courts of Isle Bourbon. Immediately below Boucher in the Royal Court's hierarchy was its first president, Jean Romain Bussy de Saint-Romain, also a Frenchman with no colonial ties.[54] As the judge who served as chief administrator of the colony's appeals court, Bussy de Saint-Romain did not necessarily have bureaucratic functions that required him to attend hearings on a regular basis. Also on the ship was Boucher's junior colleague, fresh out of law school, the 23-year-old creole Jacques Sully Brunet. Son of a Saint-Denis watchmaker, Sully Brunet was descended from five generations of colonists; his great-great-grandmother may have been a Malagasy woman, which tainted his reputation among the colonial elite.[55] While his family owned a large plantation in Saint-Benoît with a hundred slaves, Sully Brunet was a rare liberal among creole planters.[56] The final member of the party aboard *La Normande* was Boucher's secretary, Jean Louis Testard, a cousin of Panon Desbassayns and probably his spy.[57]

The Tropical Low Pressure System

WHEN BOUCHER AND HIS party arrived in Saint-Denis in late June 1817, the middle of winter in the southern hemisphere, they would have been charmed, then disappointed, by the small colonial city laid out before them. As they entered from north of the city, behind the battery and artillery yard, the streets of Saint-Denis rose gradually from the shore, intersecting in intervals to form more or less regular city blocks. The commissioner's residence, the *intendance*, where Philippe Panon Desbassayns would reside, functioned as the center of civil government and was an elegant home, with formal gardens laid out in patterns reminiscent of Versailles. Walking east and uphill, past the warehouses and the treasury, the newcomer passed the Catholic church next to the graveyard and faced the barracks and the hospital. Turning left, to the north, one passed the bazaar, staffed by Malagasy, Indian, and Arab merchants, with its pungent spices, open-air booths of fresh ocean fish, and butcher shops selling skinned goats with their tongues hanging out. Only after passing this center of commercial life would the new justices have arrived at the judicial compound: the tribunals and jailhouse sat side by side, next to the post office. In the background to the southwest, past the commander general's elegant gardens and officers' quarters, rose the dramatic rocky heights and waterfalls of the Rivière des Pluies (the River of the Rains), where the original Routier concession resided.

Upon closer examination, Saint-Denis began to look shabby to Parisian eyes. The capital city, the second largest on the island, held only 7,846 people, in contrast to Paris' 700,000.[58] Since the English occupation in 1810, free people of color had streamed in from rural districts to Saint-Denis, causing overcrowding in the older housing stock.[59] As another contemporary described the island's residents:

> There are no colossal fortunes in Isle Bourbon.... Almost the entirety of the population lives in the manner of the slaves; amongst the whites there is a great quantity [of residents] who are equally contented with very little. ... Work is not valued there; diverse trades are only performed by slaves, of which it is more economical to be the owner than to have to pay their master for their labor, who does not release them without payment.[60]

Already, the free-flowing arrack led to public drunkenness among the slaves.[61] The free population of color, according to this visitor, included the island's "laziest: the fences [of stolen goods] and the prostitutes," though he also noted that there were some who "by their talents and their conduct have almost caused to be forgotten the prejudice that attaches to them despite themselves, due to the difference in color."[62]

The new colonial administrators arrived at an island in severe economic crisis. As the commander, Lafitte de Courteuil, lamented to the minister in Paris, "Since the 1816 hurricanes and subsequent ones, the soil of Bourbon has lost its fertility. The coffee and clove trees are almost irrecoverably lost; the grain fields produce less; the diseases and the boll weevil have almost completely destroyed cotton as a source of revenue."[63] Yet, as is so often the case, natural disaster proved an opportunity for elites to consolidate their wealth and power. Lafitte du Courteil urged the minister to consider major changes to colonial inheritance law to permit the joining of land for sugar plantations: "The production of sugar, newly introduced here, will not be able to support itself unless the government reforms the laws of succession. Establishments of this type require considerable expenses, [and] are incompatible with the subdivision of lands and especially of slaves."[64] In other words, the commandant proposed, no doubt at the behest of a few large-scale planters, including Panon Desbassayns and his coterie, that the customary inheritance law of Paris, which insisted on the equal distribution of property, be revised to allow would-be sugar barons to consolidate land and slaves, presumably in the hands of the eldest son. Coming from the aristocracy himself, Lafitte de Courteuil was receptive to the principle of primogeniture.

Soon after their arrival, the new officers of the Royal Court—Boucher, Bussy de Saint-Romain, and Sully Brunet—were introduced to their local colleagues, all of whom would eventually be drawn into Furcy's freedom suit.

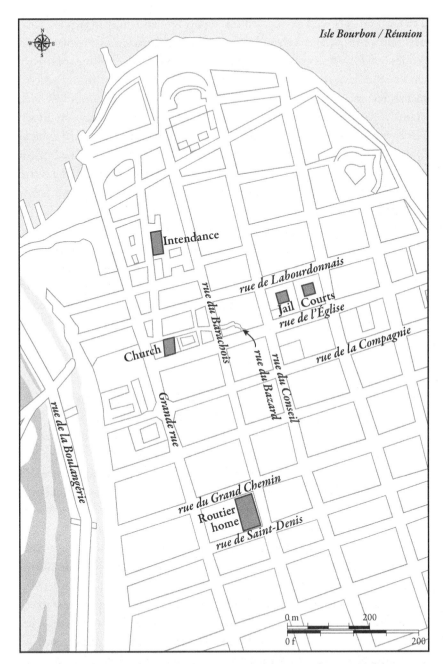

Fig. 6.1 Map of Saint-Denis, Isle Bourbon. The Routier home, on the main road downtown, was mere blocks from the courthouse and other government buildings. At the end of her life, Madeleine lived at *rue du Bazard* (Bazaar Street), a small walkway between the church and the courts. In 2015, *rue de la Compagnie* (Company Street) was officially renamed *Lavnu Furcy* ("Furcy Avenue" in Kreyol). Map based on D. Roussin, Louis Antoine. Souvenir de l'Ile de la Réunion n° 123. Plan de Saint-Denis. Lithographe. 1849.

The local officers were connected through extended family networks, business relationships, and a shared stake in the perpetuation of the plantation economy, which depended on using the courts and legal procedures to strictly enforce the slave regime. The man who had lost the most with the government's new court reforms was the assistant public prosecutor (*avocat général*), François Xavier Aimé Gillot de l'Étang, a neighbor of Augustin Routier.[65] Another wealthy descendent of the Panon clan, Gillot de l'Étang had worked his way up through the colonial legal system under Napoleon and the English occupation until he held the position of interim attorney general of the Royal Court. To his frustration, the king gave this position to Boucher, and Gillot de l'Étang was demoted to the outsider's assistant.[66] Another member of Royal Court of appeal, answering to Bussy de Saint-Romain, was the president, Jean Baptiste Pajot, brother-in-law to Philippe Panon Desbassayns.[67] Heading the lower court was the royal prosecutor (*procureur du roi*), Pierre Hippolyte Michault d'Emery, who, as notary in 1808, had witnessed (and thus legitimized) Lory's tricking Madeleine out of the money she intended to use to free Furcy.[68]

Hostilities

WITHIN DAYS OF THE new officers' arrival, Boucher delivered an "energetic" speech at their installation ceremony denouncing the unscrupulous professional activity and private lives of some members of the Isle Bourbon bar, warning obliquely of the reforms that he intended to undertake.[69] Henceforward, Boucher proclaimed, the court would operate independently from the colonial administrators and answer directly to the crown. Boucher's words rankled Commissioner Panon Desbassayns, who asked Boucher to revise the wording of his speech for the official published bulletin.[70]

Thus began a series of squabbles, moves, and counter moves, primarily between the chief judicial officer, Boucher, and the chief civil administrator, Panon Desbassayns, which eventually escalated into a full-blown colonial constitutional crisis.[71] First, Boucher removed three of the weakest lower magistrates from their posts for corruption, drunkenness, and moral turpitude (one was divorced), which provoked their partisans to protest.[72] At the beginning of September, he wrote to his superior in Paris of the positive response of the opposing faction of the colony to his reforms:

> It would be difficult for me to describe the enthusiasm, or, I should say, almost the furor, with which the magistrates coming from France have

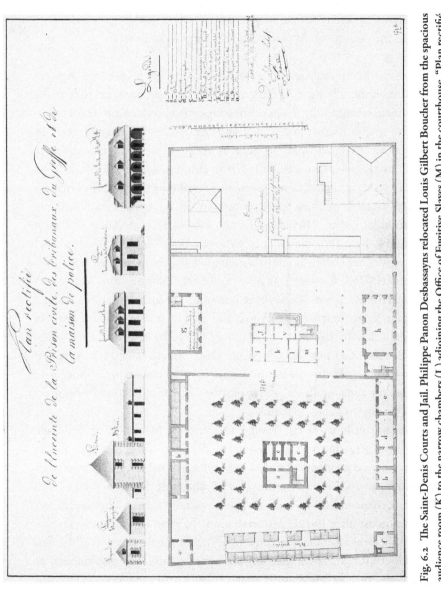

Fig. 6.2 The Saint-Denis Courts and Jail. Philippe Panon Desbassayns relocated Louis Gilbert Boucher from the spacious audience room (K) to the narrow chambers (L) adjoining the Office of Fugitive Slaves (M) in the courthouse. "Plan rectifié de l'enceinte de la prison civile, des tribunaux, du greffe et de la maison de police [de Saint-Denis]," 1821, copy by Prion. (ANOM France 23 DFC 171B).

been received in the colony. This people seem to have been deprived for a long time of the benefit of an impartial justice. Unchained passions disputed the victory amongst themselves with an equal indecency, nothing was spared to obtain it, and the unhappily too famous decisions [to depose some of the judges] attest to the ignorance of some, the illnesses of the others, and the fragility of them all.[73]

Proposals and counterproposals were debated for the magistrates' replacements, but eventually the two sides settled on one appointment, that of the young creole Jacques Sully Brunet as hearings officer (*conseilleur auditeur*).[74]

Overt tensions between Boucher and the creole elite erupted again in mid-October 1817. In order to hold meetings in a space commensurate with his status, Boucher ordered the lawyer Brulon and the Tribunal of First Instance to vacate their hearing room and installed himself, along with his secretary, Testard, in these spacious ceremonial quarters. Brulon and the tribunal's chief justice, Michault d'Emery, must have complained to Panon Desbassayns, for the commissioner wrote to Boucher that the municipal judge's room could barely hold the members of the council, much less a public audience. While Boucher was away from Saint-Denis, Panon Desbassayns instructed the municipal officers to relocate the city court back to its original spot and to move Boucher's "few books and cartons" to the Office of Fugitive Slaves opposite the jail. Michault d'Emery would be restored to the room where Boucher had put the city judge. Over Boucher's objections, Panon Desbassayns insisted that the attorney general could remain in the office next to the cell for runaway slaves or move to the post office to conduct his oversight of the colony's court system.[75]

Tensions continued to rise through October and November with the austral spring's increasing heat and humidity. Boucher skirmished with Panon Desbassayns and members of the colonial judiciary, debating legitimate lines of authority and jurisdiction in the colony.[76] The most volatile of their clashes was the 23-year-old Sully Brunet's court opinion against Philippe Panon Desbassayns' brother, Joseph.[77] In retaliation, the commissioner general commanded the hearings officer to come to his office, where Panon Desbassayns snarled in front of witnesses that Sully Brunet's decision was "yet another outrage . . . and that he could assure that . . . [such] things would never occur in the colony."[78] Sully Brunet would later cite this conflict with the commissioner general's brother as the true reason for his abrupt dismissal from his position as hearing officer (*conseiller auditeur*) to the Tribunal of First Instance a month later.[79]

Furcy Takes His Freedom

THE GROWING CONTROVERSY BETWEEN Boucher and Panon Desbassayns—not to mention rumors of Boucher's marriage to a member of the abolitionist Sonthonax family—must have prompted gossip among colonists, likely overheard by their slaves and transmitted to free people of color. Boucher's reputation as a champion of righteousness against local judicial corruption and his conflict with the former notary Michault d'Emery eventually reached the ears of Furcy and Constance, who realized that this was the moment to try and seize his freedom.[80]

However, other factors also fed into Furcy and Constance's decision. If Virginie, daughter of Célerine, was indeed Furcy's companion, their second daughter, Olympe Joséphine Augustine, had been born just three weeks after Boucher's arrival in the colony.[81] Furcy must have felt renewed urgency to declare his freedom so that he could live with and support his growing family. Then, sometime between the conception of Constance's daughter Joséphine early in 1817 and the child's birth on October 8, her husband, Jean Baptiste Euphémie, died.[82] Constance, now 31, was alone with her six children under the age of sixteen, without a male provider in an overwhelmingly patriarchal society. She needed her brother Furcy more than ever.[83]

At her farm in Saint-André parish, Constance retained copies of the documents that her mother had used to try to obtain Furcy's freedom from Lory in 1808–1810.[84] In October 1817, immediately after the birth of her daughter, Constance wrote to her friend Célerine (the mother of Furcy's likely partner, Virginie) in Saint-Denis and made arrangements to visit her for a few weeks.[85] Upon arrival in Saint-Denis, Constance approached Joseph Lory, requesting to purchase her brother's freedom. Lory "again made to her the same response that he had made to her mother, that 'everything that had been done was done well and that if they [Constance and Furcy] have the money, they will spend it.'"[86] Of course, Constance and Furcy did not have Madeleine's pension, as Lory knew full well.

So, taking advantage of Commissioner Panon Desbassayns's temporary absence from the capital,[87] while Furcy and Maurice were in Sainte-Marie for the christening of the new mill belonging to Boucher's secretary M. Testard,[88] Constance recruited a young, educated man of color, Adolphe Duperier, to assist her. The two used Célerine's home in Saint-Denis as the base from which to strategize Furcy's legal claim to freedom.[89]

Adolphe's alliance with Constance was crucial to her navigation of the island's judicial system, but his identity and the precise nature of his relationship to Constance is obscured by ambiguous language. Sully Brunet referred to Adolphe as Furcy's "relative [*parent*]."[90] Panon Desbassayns claimed that Adolphe was "the bastard son of Monsieur Dupérier, former merchant in this island," who had received his education in Germany.[91] Supposedly Constance had cared for him in his infancy, but since she was only 31 and Duperier must have been at least in his late teens, this seems unlikely; moreover Adolphe was never listed on Constance's census. Desbassayns may have wished to slur Constance and Adolphe by implying that she had been his wet nurse. The bailiff Huard described Adolphe as Constance's son-in-law, but this makes no sense, as her oldest daughter, Madeleine, was only nine years old in 1817.[92] The ambiguous language of familial ties probably obscures a relationship deemed illegitimate by the state, but one that was nevertheless important to Constance, perhaps a companion who stepped in before or after the death of her husband, Jean Baptiste.

On 9 November 1817, the attorney general Boucher's wife gave birth to their first child.[93] The same day, Constance took the paperwork that she held from Madeleine's earlier lawsuit against Joseph Lory to Boucher's home to request his assistance in winning Furcy's freedom.[94] This raises a very interesting but ultimately unanswerable question: Did Constance, who had just given birth to Josephine, offer her services as a wet nurse to Boucher's wife? If so, he declined, probably because they already had someone else under contract.[95] Nevertheless Boucher, persuaded that Furcy had a case, told Constance that if her brother could obtain a certificate of poverty (*indigence*) from local officials, he was eligible for legal representation at no cost.[96] The next day Boucher told Constance to visit his junior colleague, the hearing officer Sully Brunet, stating, "I have told him what he must do."[97]

When Constance and Adolphe arrived at Sully Brunet's office the next day, she asked the hearings officer "what he thought of Furcy's case, adding that, if there was any doubt on its success, she would rather abandon everything than expose her brother to any troubles."[98] Sully Brunet reassured her that he thought Furcy's freedom suit was on solid ground.[99] He then asked Adolphe if he knew how to write. (If he asked Constance about her literacy first, there is no record of this, but perhaps Adolphe, who had received an education in Europe, had a more fluid hand.) Finding that he could, Sully Brunet dictated the words of Furcy's petition to Adolphe, who set it down in his own handwriting; Sully Brunet made a few corrections and told Adolphe to make a fair copy to be submitted the next day, but he warned the pair to be discreet about his authorship, sensing that the case was volatile.[100] After meeting once more with Boucher, Constance returned to Célerine's home joyfully, saying that the attorney general "had been sent by God."[101]

Thus Constance initiated the freedom suit on behalf of her brother and continued to act as intermediary until a male guardian (*patron*) was later assigned to represent Furcy before the law. The fact that Constance brought Adolphe Duperier as her assistant is telling. As the "widow Jean Baptiste" (as she is called in the records), Constance did not trust that she could successfully negotiate this unfamiliar territory without a male representative.[102] Even with the backing of the two Paris-trained magistrates and her assistant Adolphe Duperier, Constance's actions constituted the height of courage. In helping to emancipate her brother from Joseph Lory's authority, Constance risked being charged with aiding and abetting a fugitive slave in direct violation of the Code Decaen.[103] Likewise, Furcy, in addition to whatever violence his master might mete out, risked imprisonment in chains for a year for a first offense as a fugitive slave. So it was that Constance and Furcy took advantage of the Paris reformer Louis Boucher to press their case against Joseph Lory. The many letters, briefs, and reports generated by the island's chief authorities in the ensuing crisis make it possible to reconstruct subsequent events on a day-to-day basis. The crisis was not entirely of Constance and Furcy's making. The underlying political tensions between Boucher and Panon Desbassayns would have erupted one way or another. Together, sister and brother inadvertently sparked the island's political powder keg.

7

Incendiary Arguments, Justice Suspended

ONCE LOUIS GILBERT BOUCHER and Jacques Sully Brunet agreed to help Furcy sue for his freedom in Isle Bourbon's courts, they entered a series of legal quagmires. The issues raised by Furcy's freedom suit would be invoked again and again in arguments and opinions for the next three decades as Furcy struggled to release himself legally from Joseph Lory. First and foremost, there was the question of Furcy's standing: Was he a slave suing for his freedom or a free man wrongfully held in slavery? The answer would determine whether he could represent himself in court or whether a legal guardian had to be appointed on his behalf. There was also Furcy's—and Constance's—understanding of the injustice of his enslavement. For them, it was a matter of overturning a personal wrong committed by Joseph Lory. Finally, there were the lawyers' arguments for Furcy's freedom, which depended on laws and procedures rather than Furcy's own understanding of injustice.

Under the 1723 Code Noir of the Mascarenes, slaves seeking relief from masters who neglected to feed or clothe them properly or who maltreated them excessively had the explicit right to appeal directly to the colony's attorney general (*procureur général*).[1] But the law also stated that slaves could not be parties in civil or criminal suits.[2] This created a conundrum, since to permit a freedom suit in the name of the aggrieved was tantamount to admitting that the person had legal standing and was therefore already recognized as free; conversely, to assign a guardian could imply that the plaintiff was incapable of representing himself, a bias toward a finding of slave status.[3] General Decaen's imperial slave laws offered one way out of this dilemma. The new, onerous bureaucratic procedures for manumitting slaves had instituted a proxy system whereby both slaves and freedmen had to be represented judicially by a free *patron*, or guardian, who would act legally on their behalf. This *patron* system relegated not only slaves but also free people of color to the status of a minor, much as Napoleon's civil code provided that wives be legally represented by their husbands.[4] By this reasoning, Boucher and Sully Brunet first drafted a petition for Furcy's freedom in Constance's name. As "the widow Jean Baptiste," she had legal authority to pursue a civil suit in her own name.

The Spark

CONSTANCE'S PETITION FOR HER brother's freedom, originally drafted on 9 November 1817 and entered into the court record on 3 December, is fascinating on several levels.[5] It offers the best summary of Furcy and Constance's understanding of the injustice that he and Madeleine had suffered at the hands of the Routier and Lory families. It also contains the first articulation of the legal grounds by which Furcy could claim his freedom; these would be foundational for all of his future legal actions. Finally, it contains the argument that Indians could not be enslaved, an assertion that would be deemed "incendiary," the potential cause of a slave revolt.[6] For all these reasons, it merits careful attention.

Constance's petition makes it clear that the primary basis of Furcy's complaint was the duplicity of the Routier and the Lory families. (Although Constance never says so, she might have stood to gain from her mother's accumulated wages as well.) In this document Constance described how the Routier family had originally contracted with Mademoiselle Despense to free Madeleine upon arrival in Isle Bourbon, assured her a lifetime pension, and even promised (or so said Constance) to find a husband for her. Constance's petition reveals how she understood that her mother was supposed to live as a free woman.[7] Yet, her petitioned continued, the Router family had waited until after Charles Routier died to free Madeleine in 1789, at which point no one told Madeleine that she was free. Madeleine served the widow until her death in 1808.[8] Constance's petition gives the first explicit description of how Joseph Lory tricked Madeleine into signing the receipt owed by the widow's estate, leaving Furcy in slavery, and of Madeleine's death soon after.[9]

Furcy's lawyers needed to craft arguments that would be upheld by judges, and Lory's trickery was both difficult to substantiate and, ultimately, irrelevant, since his carefully notarized paper trail "proved" that Madeleine had received her back wages and that Furcy had been censused as both the widow's and Lory's slave in the year before her death. Therefore, Furcy's freedom needed to be argued on other grounds.

Sully Brunet's petition for Constance offered four legal arguments for Madeleine's free status. The first was that because she was Indian, not African, Madeleine could not be a slave. The petition asserted that Indians were not subject to slavery, since all prior French legislation authorizing the slave trade specified regions in Africa and referred to "negroes" (*nègres*), never Indians.[10] This was a curious and particularly provocative assertion, since thousands of Indians and their descendants were in fact enslaved in Isle Bourbon.

The petition's second argument—the closest to Constance's position that her mother had been cheated—charged the Routier family with negligence, since they had delayed Madeleine's promised manumission for nineteen years. However, since Madeleine's manumission papers had been duly filed in 1789, and there was no proof that Madame Routier had withheld Madeleine's status from her, this argument could have little traction in court and would eventually be omitted from future justifications for Furcy's freedom.

The third argument, closely linked to Madeleine's Indian origins, was based in natural law: that the foundational condition of humanity is freedom.[11] Ancient Roman law held that freedom was the natural state of man, and this could only be altered by jus gentium, the law of nations.[12] Likewise, Islamic Sharī'a, the dominant legal system along the east African coast and in parts of India, presumed all persons freeborn unless they were non-Muslims, taken in war, or born to enslaved mothers; any adult who claimed to be held wrongfully in slavery was presumed free, and it was up to the master to prove ownership.[13] Medieval Spanish law was consistent with these two traditions, declaring, "By nature all the creatures of the world love and covet liberty. How much more do men who have understanding above all others, and especially those who have a noble heart."[14] France, however, had no positive law on the presumption of freedom.

To these justifications, Sully Brunet added a fourth argument: when Madeleine was manumitted in 1789, Madame Routier had intended Furcy to be free as well, since, according to Sully Brunet: "Children under the age of seven of the woman who has been manumitted follow the condition of the mother."[15] Here the young court officer was implicitly referencing Decaen's 1805 act, but also the 1723 Code Noir, which prohibited mothers and "prepubescent children" from being sold to different masters.[16] The problem was that the earlier legislation, which was in force when Madeleine was freed, did not explicitly state that manumitting the mother likewise freed the child. This argument was therefore shaky, since the 1805 law would not necessarily apply retroactively.

What Sully Brunet's petition for Constance did not proffer is the Free Soil argument: that because Furcy's mother Madeleine had set foot on metropolitan soil in 1772, she was free before Furcy was born. Apparently neither Sully Brunet nor Boucher was yet aware of the legal precedents.

Fuel to the Flame

AFTER BOUCHER AND SULLY Brunet drew up Constance's petition, they reconsidered their strategy and decided that Furcy must declare himself free, rather than having Constance act on his behalf. On November 21, Constance and Adolphe returned to Sully Brunet, who took a sheaf of papers from his desk and dictated a new writ (described as a *signification* or *exploit* in different documents), or legal notice, for Adolphe to copy in his own hand and to be served to Lory by a bailiff. The writ opens with the following words, designed to obscure the authorship, but also to allow Furcy to legally act on his own behalf as a free man through the court bailiff, Étienne Huard:

> At the request of *le nommé* Furcy, son of deceased Madeleine, Indian, free man of color, without position, living in Saint-Denis, residing at the home of Célerine, free woman of color, living at the rue des Prêtres, city of Saint-Denis, I, Étienne Toussaint Huard, bailiff to the tribunals of this island, hearings of the Royal Court, living in the district and city of Saint-Denis, undersigned, served and declared to Joseph Lory, merchant living in Saint-Denis, in his residence and speaking to his domestic servant named Alphonse, Furcy left his residence from this day on the grounds that he is free and wishes to enjoy the rights attached to this condition.[17]

This was the legal wording that Sully Brunet and Boucher had decided upon, but in his memoirs, Sully Brunet later paraphrased Furcy's petition as follows:

> I am Furcy. I was born free in the Routier house, to the free Indian woman Madeleine, then in the service of this family. I have been held as a slave by Monsieur Lory, son-in-law of Madame Routier. I claim my freedom. Here are my papers.[18]

Hearing the words by which Furcy would claim his freedom in his own name, Adolphe responded, "That's too strong!!" to which Sully Brunet responded, "I know what I'm doing. It must be like that."[19] Constance asked if it was really necessary to name Célerine's home as Furcy's place of residence, but Sully Brunet said that the writ needed an address for Furcy that could not be the same as Joseph Lory's house. Furcy would need a place to stay, and the home of Virginie's mother, Célerine—who was also hosting Constance while

she was in town—made the most sense. Sully Brunet instructed Constance
to tell her brother that he should leave the Lory household during the day
and that once this was done, Constance and Adolphe should return to Sully
Brunet's office at 2:30 p.m.

And so Furcy took his freedom on 21 November 1817. He put on his
best suit of clothes and waited for an opportunity to leave, as though on an
errand. He gathered the few things that belonged to him and would not be
missed (he did not want to be charged with theft) and moved one last time
through the rooms of the Lorys' splendid townhouse. As he walked through
the garden, heading for the gate, Furcy turned to Alphonse, another of Lory's
slaves, saying, and said (in words no doubt supplied to him by his lawyers), "[I
am] free and wish to enjoy the rights attached to this condition." Then Furcy
shut the Lorys' gate behind him, and stepped into the streets of Saint-Denis,
a self-declared free man.[20]

How did Furcy feel as he made his way to Célerine's house? These were
the same streets he'd walked all his life. He passed the same people. The same
strong sun beat down upon his head. And yet everything must have felt different: brighter, more exciting—and perhaps frightening as well. What would
Lory do when he learned of Furcy's defiance?

Once Furcy was safely housed at Célerine's home, Constance and Adolphe
delivered the writ to the bailiff, Huard, at dusk.[21] The bailiff was initially
reluctant to receive the document, but Adolphe assured him that it had been
dictated by Sully Brunet and thus had support from one of the officers of the
colonial high court. Huard told him to return the next day with two copies,
which he did the next morning.[22]

This second document justifying Furcy's freedom, the writ, recorded
by the bailiff Huard on November 22, is much shorter than Constance's
November 9 petition and includes only brief summaries of three essential
arguments for Furcy's freedom. The first—that Indians could not legally
be enslaved—reiterated the opening argument of Constance's petition, but
the other two grounds proffered were completely new. The writ added that
Madeleine's "appearance on the soil of liberty (France)" made her free and that
Mademoiselle Despense's sale or gift of Madeleine to the Routiers in France
had been illegal.[23] Between Constance's November 9 petition and Furcy's writ
filed November 22, Boucher and Sally Brunet must have consulted the Old
Regime legislation regulating the presence of colonial slaves in France.

Furcy's writ is the first articulation of the Free Soil argument that would
ultimately confirm his freedom under French law. From at least the middle of
the sixteenth century, the principle that every slave who set foot on French soil

thereby became free was a considered a fundamental maxim,[24] but as France's overseas colonies became increasingly dependent on plantation slavery, planters and their merchant allies lobbied the crown for exceptions to it. Two royal laws, issued in 1716 and 1738, allowed masters to bring their slaves to France for up to three years, provided that they had obtained the requisite permission from colonial administrators, that they paid a hefty deposit (1,000 livres, about $5,000), and that they registered the slaves with port authorities upon arrival in France.[25] By 1777 the law eschewed the word "slave" and instead prohibited the entry of all "blacks, mulattoes, and other people of color" into the metropole, regardless of status.[26] The Revolution reversed these policies and wrote France's Free Soil principle into statutory law for the first time in 1791: "Every individual is free as soon as he has entered France."[27] Then, weeks after Napoleon's Consulate reestablished Old Regime slavery, the government restored the racial quarantine with an act prohibiting the entry of "blacks, mulattoes, and other people of color, of either sex, without authorization into the continental territory of the Republic."[28] Coincidentally, on 17 October 1817, precisely as Furcy and Constance began to strategize in Isle Bourbon, Louis XVIII's minister in Paris issued new ministerial directives reforming the Consulate's treatment of blacks. Colonial masters were still required to obtain permission and leave a deposit for the blacks they wanted to bring from the colonies to France, but the people of color who arrived in the metropole were no longer required to notify authorities of their whereabouts, and the new policy omitted Old Regime provisions for their arrest, confiscation, and return to the colonies as royal property.[29] Although distance prohibited Isle Bourbon's administrators and magistrates from knowing about these new instructions for some months, it is possible that the minister had discussed his intentions with Boucher prior to his departure, sensitizing him to the ministry's evolving attitudes toward French Free Soil.

Furcy's writ concluded with an attack against Joseph Lory, stating that he had "profited by his situation, which allowed him to enslave a freeborn man, without education or fortune, to serve him," and demanded that Lory appear before the appropriate magistrates to prove his claims over Furcy or let him enjoy his freedom. The writ also reserved Furcy's right to claim "compensation, wages, damages, and interest resulting from the use he [Lory] made of his labor."[30] However, the writ was merely an assertion of Furcy's position; if challenged by Joseph Lory, Furcy's status would have to be decided by the courts.

The hodgepodge of arguments contained in the two documents drafted by Sully Brunet with input by Boucher—free Indians, separation of mother and child, negligence in delaying manumission, natural law, free soil, illegal sale or gift in France—were a far cry from Furcy's and Constance's perception of the injustice perpetrated against their mother almost a decade earlier. In framing Furcy's freedom suit for legal argumentation before the colonial courts, Sully Brunet and Boucher made no mention of Joseph Lory's fraud, which, in the absence of a paper trail, could not be legally proven.

Ignition

BECAUSE OF THE UNDERLYING tensions between the judicial reformers and creole elites, Commissioner General Philippe Panon Desbassayns seized upon Furcy's assertion of freedom as the means by which to drive out his rival and enemy Boucher. Over the weeks that followed, all parties began to issue letters and replies, sometimes multiple times a day. The resulting flurry of correspondence and the subsequent reports to the ministry in Paris, not to mention the confessions obtained through police detention, allow for an almost hourly reconstruction of events. They must also be read critically, since each party sought to justify its actions, especially to the royal ministry in Paris, once the crisis reached an impasse in the colony.

Furcy's writ, with its direct attack on Joseph Lory, prompted immediate retaliation. At eight o' clock on the morning of Saturday, November 22, within an hour of receiving Huard's document, Lory arrived home at the home of Boucher in a "highly agitated state and with the impatience of a man who becomes irritated at the least opposition."[31] Lory demanded that Furcy be put in chains and the bailiff fined for accepting and delivering the writ. Boucher responded that the writ did not give Lory permission to seize Furcy and that his own authority as the king's representative superseded "arbitrary measures."[32] Boucher told Lory to go see the president of the Tribunal of First Instance, Joseph Boulley Duparc, who would deliver Furcy to him.[33] Duparc instructed Lory that he should report Furcy missing as a fugitive slave, "since he couldn't enter into a lawsuit with his slave without colliding with all the accepted principles."[34] In other words, Duparc realized that if Lory entered into a civil suit with Furcy, it was tantamount to acknowledging that Furcy was a free man. Lory accordingly went to the Office of Fugitive Slaves and reported Furcy as a "rebel slave," demanding his arrest.[35]

The lawyer, Brulon (one of the men whose offices had been displaced by Boucher a month earlier), and several guards showed up at Célerine's house just after noon, demanding that Constance produce Furcy, who must have been hiding in another room.[36] They attempted to take him away immediately, but Constance pleaded for them to allow him to get properly dressed. They relented, and Furcy grabbed his hat and waistcoat before they led him off to jail.[37] Constance knew that her brother's appearance dressed as a proper free man of color would be essential in swaying public opinion. Furcy was then interrogated and locked in a jail cell.[38] Constance, alarmed, went to Boucher, who told her (if Panon Desbassayns's report can be trusted), "It is nothing, my girl. Let them put him in the cell for fugitive slaves. Tell Furcy not to worry."[39]

On the evening of Furcy's arrest, Panon Desbassayns's military counterpart, General Lafitte du Courteil, visited Boucher and indicated that he favored Lory's position. Boucher responded that he disapproved of Lory's anger, insisting that no one is above the law. Meanwhile, Constance tried to find a lawyer to represent Furcy, but when she approached a "Monsieur Delaunay," he stated that he had "obligations at the Lory house" and so was unavailable to take the case.[40] Boucher found Delaunay's rejection "incredible." Instead, on her own initiative, Constance went to Eugene Prévost de la Croix, saying (at least as quoted by Panon Desbassayns), "I am a poor girl; but [if you agree to take the case,] you would do business with one who is not ungrateful, and if there are damages and interest, we will share them together."[41] Prévost accepted the case graciously, supposedly saying "that nothing was owed him, that even if she offered him 20,000 piasters [$367,000], he would not defend her with more zeal."[42]

The following day, November 23, was Sunday. After mass, General Lafitte paid another visit to Boucher. This time he was "anxious and suspicious." Lafitte told Boucher that he would exile the authors of the writ to Madagascar if he could figure out who they were. Boucher commented, "In the insolent intensity of the general, I recognized the intrigue and the manipulations too common in the colonies."[43] Boucher laid out the legal arguments in favor of Furcy's freedom and reminded the general that the king's orders specifically forbade him from engaging in contentious legal disputes.[44]

Lafitte's intervention clarified to Boucher that the colonial power base was uniting against him and that the racial argument—that Indians could not be legally enslaved—was a lightning rod for the colonial elite. Boucher urged Lafitte to consider that it would be better for Lory to settle the case than to allow the public declaration that Indians could not legally be enslaved.[45] Then, a few days later, he wrote to Michault d'Emery, the former notary who had drafted the original document signed by Madeleine in 1809 and now the royal prosecutor (*procureur du roi*) of the Tribunal of First Instance: "It's a delicate affair," he wrote. "On the one hand, it is necessary to keep the slaves obedient; on the other it would also be as dangerous as it is impolitic to give some people of color a pretext for sedition in refusing them impartial justice."[46] Boucher was applying subtle pressure—and crafting alternative arguments, such as Free Soil—to try to secure Furcy's freedom, while brandishing the Indian Freedom argument to pressure Lory, through the other colonial officials, to settle out of court. Recognizing that the crisis was escalating and his own position in the colony was under direct attack, Boucher spent the day of November 25 summarizing events thus far for the minister of the colonies.[47]

A Meeting of the Justices

ON NOVEMBER 26, BOUCHER called for a meeting of the officers of both the Saint-Denis Tribunal of First Instance and the appellate Royal Court of Bourbon. The meeting took place at noon at his home, since his quarters near the Office of Fugitive Slaves lacked ceremony. Its purpose was to examine the essential issues presented in Furcy's case.[48] As the colony's highest judicial authority, Boucher enjoyed powers of investigation, prosecution, and judgment. Also present was his subordinate and rival, the assistant public prosecutor (*avocat général*), Gillot de l'Étang, who had been displaced from the higher office by Boucher's arrival. The third member of the appeals court, the Royal Court of Bourbon, was the hearings officer (*conseiller auditeur*), Sully Brunet. The chief officer of the lower court, Michault d'Emery, royal prosecutor to the Tribunal of First Instance, was seconded by the newly appointed 22-year-old substitute king's prosecutor, Gabriel Auguste Fédière. Based on Constance's petition, Furcy's writ, and several other texts, the panel of judges debated four legal questions.[49]

The first question addressed was the flashpoint: whether Indians could legally be enslaved in Isle Bourbon.[50] Gillot de L'Étang immediately attacked the assertion offered on Furcy's behalf that Indians were not subject to slavery: "The slave trade in Indians has been conducted under royal authority," he asserted. Moreover, "It pose[s] the gravest danger to raise even the slightest doubt on the condition of the Indians brought to the colony as slaves.... Close to 20,000 individuals would have to be declared free in Isle Bourbon" if Furcy were freed on these grounds.[51] Gillot de L'Étang's wild guess was surely an exaggeration. According to the 1818 census taken just two months later, the island held 54,249 slaves, of whom only about 1,700 had been designated as Indians in 1808.[52] Even if one took into account the descendants of the Indians brought as slaves since the earliest days of the colony, given the massive increase in Malagasy and African slaves imported since the middle of the eighteenth century, it was implausible that the mix of Afro-Indian slaves constituted over a third of the enslaved population. Nevertheless, Michault d'Emery agreed with his creole colleague on the appeals court; the enslavement of Indians was well known and tacitly approved by the royal government in France as evidenced by the censuses, which specifically called for an itemization of Indian slaves along with Malagasies and Africans. Given that colonial slave legislation specifically referenced Indian slaves, these men had a valid point.

On the question of Indian Freedom, Sully Brunet equivocated. He reminded his senior colleagues of the 1767 letter from the minister of the navy underscoring the freedom of "Indians" under French law and the fact that fundamental eighteenth-century legislation (the laws of 1716, 1738, and 1777) all referred to *nègres* or *noirs, mulâtres,* and *autres gens de couleur,* never explicitly mentioning Indian slaves.[53] Nevertheless, Sully Brunet agreed that while Isle Bourbon's administrators had permitted the Indian Ocean slave trade, thereby introducing a large number of Indian slaves to the colony, the security of the colonists necessitated that Indians not be permitted to "change their condition" (i.e., become free) against the wishes of their masters.[54] The youngest of the judges, Fédière, perhaps sensing the way that the wind was blowing, agreed that the slavery of Indians must be maintained. Boucher conceded the point: "Without examining the basis of the question, [I agree] that it is a sound policy not to change the status of the Indians reduced to slavery in the colony."[55]

The judges then turned to the second question raised by Furcy's case: whether slaves taken to France recovered their liberty simply by setting foot on French soil. Here Gillot de l'Étang stated that he was unaware "whether the provisions of the slave code that permitted [masters] to bring their slaves to France without risk of seeing them freed . . . was inscribed in a formal law." Nevertheless, he said, "There are a thousand examples in the colony of slaves brought to France as such and returned as such. . . . Many have even been arrested in France, by virtue of orders emanating from authority, and sent back to the ports to be returned to the colonies."[56] The lower court officers, Michault l'Emery and Fedière, simply stated that the slaves did not recover their freedom via sojourning in the metropole. Sully Brunet, however, insisted on the capacity of French soil to free slaves unless the master had fulfilled the necessary requirements and made arrangements immediately upon arrival to return the slaves to the place from which they came. Boucher, perhaps seeking to strike a compromise, offered an interesting spin. Arrival in France *did* free slaves, he insisted, "especially an Indian . . . , [but] if he returns to the colonies with his master, he cannot claim to be master of his person solely on the basis of his residence in France or his intermediate state of liberty."[57] Boucher's continued references to Madeleine's Indian origins is odd. He may have been trying to rile his adversaries. However, he was incorrect in asserting that French law had never addressed the question of whether slaves who voluntarily returned to the colonies were thereby re-enslaved; a (no doubt long forgotten) 1707 ministerial directive had specifically stated that by returning to the colonies, those who became free by the Free Soil principle in France waived their right to freedom.[58] Perhaps he was equivocating on this point to seek compromise on others.

The third question the judges addressed was whether "an Indian" (as Boucher continued to insist) sold "in India" as a slave could be the object of a contract of sale or gift (*un contrat à titre onéreux ou gratuit*) in metropolitan France. Here the justices were unanimous in agreeing that slaves could not be bought, sold, or gifted in France. Gillot de L'Étang qualified his agreement, suggesting that "some Indian slaves could be sent from France and sold in the colony at the expense of the owner," but Sully Brunet and Boucher objected. Neither the sale nor the gifting of slaves in the kingdom could be conditionally postponed for realization in the colonies, for, as Sully Brunet put it, in such cases "the lawful clause required for the validity of the obligations would not abide."[59] With virtually all judges in agreement that the original contract between Mademoiselle Despense and the Routiers was probably illegal, the original transaction could theoretically be nullified.[60] Even so, declaring the implied contract or deed illegal was not the same as finding Madeleine (and therefore Furcy) free. According to the Declaration of December 1738, once the illegal transaction had been nullified, Madeleine should have been confiscated as royal property and returned to India at Mademoiselle Despense's expense; there Madeleine should have been sold or put to labor for the state (e.g., as a laundress or nurse). It is completely unclear, then, what this would have meant for Furcy.

Having weighed in on the three primary questions of law, the lawyers discussed the necessary procedures for, as Boucher put it, "a person of the Indian race" (*de race indienne*) to claim his freedom. Gillot de L'Étang fairly bristled at Boucher's continued emphasis on Indians: "Not only an Indian but any individual who finds himself in slavery and who believes [himself] to have rights to liberty" should address the courts to seek a judgment on his claims.[61] The custom in the colony, he added, was to appoint a guardian (*patron*) to act on his behalf. Michault d'Emery was doubtful that standardized procedures existed—"Very few examples have arisen in the past thirty years that [I have] been on the island"—but he agreed that once the public ministry had reviewed the claim to determine whether it was founded, a *patron* could be named. Once again Fédière agreed with Gillot de L'Étang. Sully Brunet, by contrast, objected vehemently to the appointment of a *patron* for Furcy, whose liberty, he insisted again, derived from his Indian origins:

> Freedom is essential to the quality of being an Indian. In subjecting these sorts of men to slavery, the general principle has been infringed without positive law.... If an Indian claims to be free, the presumption must be for freedom, the opposite of which must be proved.... It would be otherwise for the negroes, whose trade used to be legally authorized.... Therefore from the instant that a man has proven his Indian origin and claimed his freedom, the public ministry must watch over his security.[62]

Sully Brunet could see that if Furcy was assigned a *patron*, his standing in the eyes of the law was diminished to that of a slave seeking freedom, perhaps subjecting him to continued detention, whereas full recognition by the court would allow Furcy to wait for the court's decision at liberty. With regard to the contentious Indian Freedom argument, while both of Furcy's legal allies conceded that the racial argument was dangerous and impractical, they continuously injected the idea that Indians were naturally free and threatened that the argument could be raised publicly. They were using the threat of a public hearing to pressure Lory's confederates to urge him to settle for damages and interest out of court.

In the meeting Boucher outlined another dilemma in determining the proper procedure. Admitting that he did not know the colonial laws on this point, he pointed out (no doubt recalling Roman law) that "a slave, being civilly dead, cannot have legal standing before the tribunals."[63] The problem was that "to assign [a free person] a *patron* is to prejudice the question against him; the stain ... imprinted on him can only be removed by a formal judgment."[64] Nevertheless, Boucher sided with the creole jurists and agreed that a *patron* should be assigned to Furcy to represent him before the courts. Indeed, he had already instructed Michault d'Emery to assign a *patron* for Furcy the previous day.[65] The lawyer selected by Constance, Eugène Prévost de la Croix, was formally recognized as Furcy's *patron*.[66]

An Assault upon the Public Order

BOUCHER'S WILLINGNESS TO COMPROMISE on the question of Furcy's representation by a *patron* marked the critical turning point for Furcy and ultimately the magistrate's career. Before the Tribunal of First Instance could render a decision, both Lory and Commissioner General Panon Desbassayns moved swiftly to punish those who had supported Furcy's petition. On November 28, Joseph Lory brought charges against the bailiff Huard, charging him with an "assault upon the public order" by formally receiving Furcy's petition.[67] In Lory's indictment, the two problematic clauses in Furcy's writ were the assertions that Indians could not be legally held as slaves and the attacks upon Lory's character, which he considered "a libel."[68] Huard would pay dearly for having accepted Furcy's petition against his better judgment when he was fired a week later.[69]

As tension mounted between the chief executive and judicial officers of the colonial government, Panon Desbassayns received word that "a crowd of free blacks show up regularly at the jail to visit Furcy" and that a Monsieur Boniat had "heard three slaves discussing Furcy and his freedom amongst themselves and that their own freedom could result from it, which had led him to punish them severely."[70] Whether or not these charges were true, it gave Panon Desbassayns the excuse he needed to isolate Furcy from his supporters. On November 29, he sent orders to the mayor of Saint-Denis that Furcy, held in the jail, be denied all outside contact until 4:00 p.m.[71] He then ordered that Constance and Adolphe Duperier be arrested and conducted individually to his office in order to question them separately so as to discover who had composed Furcy's anonymous writ for freedom.[72]

At 11:30 a.m., Mayor Pitois, accompanied by several police guards, arrested Constance at Célerine's home "in broad daylight, before the eyes of several thousand blacks"[73] (Boucher alleged) and took her to the Intendancy, the commissioner general's ornate official residence and office.[74] Panon Desbassayns let Constance know that she had placed her brother in danger "by giving him the idea to rise in rebellion against his master," but that if she revealed the names of those who had helped compose the writ, he "would not pursue judicial proceedings against her brother, herself, nor any of those who had enlisted her to conduct herself in such a manner."[75] Then Panon Desbassayns called a guard into his office to persuade Constance to confide to him, stepping out of his office to leave them alone for this conversation.[76] One can only imagine the ways that the guard attempted to intimidate Constance.

When Constance still refused to name the author of the petition, Panon Desbassayns returned to the room and, seating Constance before him, called the chief justice of the Tribunal of First Instance, Michault d'Emery who, according to Constance, spoke to her "like a pig."[77] Now the man who had notarized the document that deprived Madeleine of her pension sat in judgment of Constance's petition for her brother's freedom. She claimed that Michault "had the air of being so well satisfied that I was mute.... I was really angry to see what bad counsel I had been given."[78] Constance began to waver in her confidence in Boucher and Sully Brunet. But she did not yield until Panon Desbassayns revealed that he already knew from his interrogation of the bailiff Huard that it was Sully Brunet who had drafted the petition and dictated the writ. Then she finally confessed that she had seen Sully Brunet several times at the court. According to Panon Desbassayns, "Relieved by this declaration, this woman, dissolving in tears, threw herself at my feet, embracing my hands, saying to me that she depended upon my promise to harm neither her nor to her brother."[79] Boucher, who must have heard of the incident secondhand from Constance, described her reaction quite differently, stating that she was forced to her knees in terror.[80] Panon Desbassayns promised that if Constance wrote to Furcy, persuading him to beg Lory's forgiveness and to withdraw his freedom suit from the courts, he would intervene on his behalf with Monsieur Lory.[81] The commissioner then concluded Constance's interrogation by swearing her to silence. Here, her statement about the interrogation suddenly shifts into first person: "In the end, Monsieur [Boucher], I was tortured. It was a veritable inquisition."[82]

When Constance reported her arrest and interrogation to Boucher, he became livid. He wrote to Michault d'Emery, demanding, "By what right do you want to force a woman of color to declare to you, under the saber of the police guards, the name of those whom she has taken into her confidence?"[83] Boucher was not merely venting; his letter laid the groundwork for discrediting anything damaging that Constance might have said under coercion while insisting upon his sole authority to rule on colonial judicial officers' competency. Constance's questioning took place "in terms and expressions capable not only of intimidating her but also of disturbing her mind, as she is in fragile health."[84] Indeed, Constance had given birth to her sixth child less than two months earlier. If she had left her baby with others in all the tumult, especially while she was under arrest, she was now highly susceptible to systemic mastitis. Boucher chastised Michault d'Emery for his involvement in the interrogation, warning the lower court official that it was "at the prosecutor's office that you must receive the acts of your ministry and not at the Intendancy," and, further, that he should not be doing so in secret but should "draw up a formal statement [*procès verbal*] of what you are doing."[85]

Boucher's protests were to no avail. On December 1, Lafitte du Courteil and Panon Desbassayns issued orders to suspend Sully Brunet from his position as hearing officer to the Royal Court.[86] A squadron of police armed with pikes showed up at Sully Brunet's home and escorted him into exile at his plantation in Saint-Benoît, a little over twenty miles from the capital, where local authorities checked up on him regularly, ostensibly to make sure that he was not agitating his slaves to rebellion.[87] Indeed, in the days that followed, Eugénie Lory's oldest brother, Augustin Routier, among others, spread rumors that Sully Brunet was fomenting such a revolt, a serious crime carrying severe penalties.[88]

Anticipating the need for a permanent record, Boucher ordered the court clerk to transcribe Constance's original petition into the court register on December 3,[89] prompting court officers from the creole cabal to protest his actions.[90] But the ultimate blow was Panon Desbassayns's refusal to pay Boucher's salary. The attorney general, perhaps urged on by his wife, who was unwilling to raise her new baby in this hostile environment, finally gave up. On December 6, Boucher wrote a short letter to the Panon Desbassayns and Lafitte du Courteil, requesting permission and funding to return to France on the next available ship.[91]

As Boucher and his family packed up to leave, Constance, who had returned to her home in Saint-André, was arrested a second time on Panon Desbassayns's orders.[92] She described her ordeal later in a letter addressed to Boucher before his departure, the wording clearly indicating that it was drafted with Boucher's assistance, but in her own handwriting and spelling. Constance declared that guards had brought her (and possibly her baby) in a palanquin to Panon Desbassayns's home in Saint-Denis for questioning without allowing her to speak to anyone.[93] The commissioner general held her there in secret for two days, during which she was incessantly interrogated about her brother's case in the presence of the Saint-Denis mayor Pitois and Michault d'Emery. They wanted her to retract her previous statement about the first interrogation, saying that she had "misunderstood," but Constance continued to insist that she had well understood what she was saying, and it was all true. Although she refused to acquiesce to Panon Desbassayns's version of the events, a secretary was writing the whole time, preparing a new statement in concordance with her interrogators' interpretations, which she finally concluded she was obliged to sign "without knowing why, always fearing these gentleman, for they questioned me at night."[94]

When Boucher learned of Constance's second arrest, he composed a flurry of letters to various officials—Lafitte du Courteil, Michault d'Emery, Gillot de l'Étang, the mayor of Saint-André—chastising them for undermining his judicial authority and for participating in Constance's arbitrary arrest and detention for forty hours, as well as the grievances committed against Sully

Brunet.[95] Boucher's letter to Gillot de l'Étang was especially pointed, accusing him of participating in a security meeting (*conseil de haute police*) that was "illegal, arbitrary, and holding to nothing less than to intervene in the order of jurisdictions."[96] Finally, Boucher resorted to subterfuge. He wrote to Fédière, the young lower court's substitute royal prosecutor, entrusting him "with a very delicate mission that can only be executed by you." He instructed Fédière "to have *la nommée* Constance, sister of Furcy, arrested wherever she might be found, and to order her placed in the house of detention. You will then retire to the residence of the royal prosecutor [Michault d'Emery], your supervisor, who will communicate my orders to you."[97] Then Boucher immediately wrote to the mayor of Saint-André, ordering him to arrest Constance as well.[98] One can only imagine the confusing scenario when various parties converged on Panon Desbassayns's house to arrest Constance. But Boucher's campaign apparently worked. Lafitte du Courteil issued orders to "suspend all actions against *la nommée* Constance, widow of Jean Baptiste."[99] Boucher immediately communicated this suspension to the mayor of Saint-André, effecting her release.[100]

Boucher's pen continued to fly during his remaining weeks on the island.[101] He exchanged additional threatening messages with Gillot de l'Étang, Michault d'Emery, and the administrators, Panon Desbassayns and Lafitte du Courteil.[102] He also set about making copies of the key documents issuing from the crisis in anticipation of having to justify himself before the ministry in Paris.[103]

In the end, Boucher was forced to humiliate himself before his enemies. On December 16, he requested two favors from his opponents, Panon Desbassayns and Lafitte de Courteuil. The first was payment of his salary for the month of December: "The passage for myself and my family costs me 700 piasters [almost $13,000] beyond that which the government has allowed me, and I am without fortune."[104] The second was permission to bring along a black wet nurse (*négresse nourrice*) without payment of the legally mandated security deposit, promising to "return her to the colony as soon as she is no longer necessary for my child."[105] In other words, Boucher was begging the administrators to waive the fee spelled out in the very same laws that he had offered as the foundation of Furcy's freedom. Was he aware of the irony, setting a legal trap to demonstrate their willingness to bend the law, or simply desperate? The alternative for Boucher and his wife was to leave the wet nurse behind. Since his wife had never nursed the baby and no longer produced milk, this would be tantamount to a death sentence for his newborn child. There is no record of Panon Desbassayns's reply. Boucher apparently decided to take matters into his own hands, perhaps hoping to help the wet nurse, Marie Jeanne, obtain her freedom in France, though at the evident cost of separating her from any family and community in Isle Bourbon, including, perhaps, her own baby.[106]

Immediately before his scheduled departure, Boucher received orders from Panon Desbassayns and Gillot de l'Étang insisting that he leave all the paperwork from Furcy's case in the colony, a request that he apparently ignored.[107] On 23 December 1817, Boucher, his wife, and their baby, accompanied by a white servant (Julie Saint-Germe, "a lady's companion of Madame Gilbert Boucher"); Louis Testard, "Monsieur Gilbert Boucher's secretary"; and "Marie Jeanne, wet nurse of the child of Madame Gilbert Boucher," sailed for Bordeaux on *Le Télémaque,* with all expenses paid by the royal treasury.[108]

No Decision Is a Decision

LATER LEGAL PROCEEDINGS REFER to two court decisions emanating from Furcy's and Constance's actions in November 1817. Supposedly, the Tribunal of First Instance issued a decision on a later petition issued by Furcy's *patron,* a "Monsieur Petitpas, a lawyer who often worked for Monsieur Lory," who succeeded Prévost de la Croix as Furcy's legal guardian.[109] Several dates were given in subsequent records for the tribunal's supposed decision: 17 May, 17 October, and 17 December 1817.[110] Clearly, the first two dates are erroneous; Boucher and Panon Desbassayns did not arrive in the colony until June, and Constance and Furcy initiated their actions on 9 November 1817. The date of December 17 is plausible, since Boucher had clearly thrown in the towel by that point and Michault d'Emery's court could have rendered its decision while the fleeing magistrate awaited his departure. However, if the Tribunal of First Instance ruled on a petition submitted by Furcy's *patron* on 17 December 1817, the text of this petition was never recorded in any legal record at the time, including the hundreds of pages of correspondence emanating from the battle between Boucher and Panon Desbassayns.[111] Indeed, the text of the supposed decision by the Tribunal of First Instance was only "exhume[d]" (in the words of one lawyer) and quoted for the first time in 1843, after Furcy's lawyer went to considerable lengths to recover it.[112] It seems quite plausible that the Tribunal of First Instance in fact never formally ruled on Constance's petition and that the petition by Furcy's *patron,* in the employ of Joseph Lory, never materialized. Furcy was left to languish in jail while his case simply petered out.[113]

There is similar ambiguity about the alleged "decision" of the colonial appeals court, the Royal Court of Bourbon.[114] According to much later records, it was either on 12 or 18 February 1818, as Louis Boucher and family sailed toward France, that the Royal Court of Bourbon issued its ruling on Furcy's appeal of the (nonexistent?) lower court ruling.[115] If the quoted text of that decision (which first appears in 1836, after Furcy began his appeal in Paris) can be believed, the Royal Court accepted the paper trail proffered by Lory—the two bills of sale establishing Mademoiselle Despense's just title to Madeleine in India in 1768 and the 1789 manumission stating that Madeleine had been given to the Routier family "in Europe"[116]—as proof that Madeleine had been Madame Routier's slave when she gave birth to Furcy in 1786.

Just as with the decision of the Tribunal of First Instance, there is no contemporary record of a colonial appeals court's decision issued in February 1818 in the archival repositories.[117] Indeed, when Isle Bourbon's future colonial delegate Pierre Conil was instructed to look for the text of the second decision in the 1830s, he reported to the ministry that "it does not exist in the collection of decisions by the Royal Court of Bourbon for 1818; there is not even any decision of that date," and that "it cannot be known whether this decision was in fact rendered in the colony."[118] Therefore, there is substantial doubt as to whether the formal appeal of the (questionable) lower court decision to the Royal Court of Bourbon ever took place.[119]

According to Furcy, after he lost his case, Panon Desbassayns himself came to visit him in prison around midnight to tell him that "it was only by humanity that he was not condemned to the gallows, along with his sister."[120] Presumably the death penalty was warranted, in the commissioner's view, because of the political turmoil and public disquiet it had triggered. On the other hand, Panon Desbassayns must have been pleased with the outcome. The colonial oligarchy had removed its challengers by sending Sully Brunet into exile on his plantation and Boucher back to France. Their opponents deposed, the creole court officers and Joseph Lory effectively abandoned Furcy. For eleven months he remained in the cell block of Saint-Denis, with the exception of six weeks when, near death, he was chained to a hospital cot. There a doctor took pity on him and gradually nursed him back to health.[121]

In September 1818, a new governor, Pierre Bernard Milius, came to Isle Bourbon, replacing Panon Desbassayns. "Unable to leave a man in prison without judgment" (further evidence that the court never subjected Furcy to criminal charges or a hearing), he authorized Furcy's release.[122] Furcy was no longer useful to Joseph Lory as a butler, so the merchant decided to wreak even greater vengeance by removing Furcy from the island of his birth and forcing him to work on an active sugar plantation in Isle de France, now British Mauritius.

8

English Liberties

ON THE EVENING OF 26 October 1818, on Lory's orders, Furcy was collected from the Saint-Denis prison and sent to Mauritius under the supervision of the captain aboard *La Clélie*, a trusted vessel used by Lory in the past. Furcy arrived in Port Louis on 7, 10, or 12 November 1818, and—despite the British ban on importing slaves—no port official interfered with, or even recorded, his disembarkation.[1]

Thus began Furcy's new life in Mauritius. The recent transformation of Isle de France into a British colony placed the island's French creole elite under a thin veneer of British officialdom. The sugar revolution—decades more advanced in Mauritius than Isle Bourbon—and the island's easily accessible harbors, large and small, accelerated the colony's commercial culture, both licit and illicit. While sailing ships collected legitimate products from the capital city of Port Louis, slave smugglers unloaded human cargo into Mauritius's hidden harbors. At first, the English governor appointed French creole officers to administer the colony's traditional laws and institutions, but the colony increasingly came under the scrutiny of the antislavery lobby in London. Furcy's crossing to Mauritius separated him from his partner and children in Isle Bourbon, but the island also offered him the opportunity to create a new life at a distance from Joseph Lory. It was in Mauritius that Furcy described his experience for the first time in his own voice in letters he wrote to Louis Gilbert Boucher between 1821 and 1836 as he tried to elicit sympathy and legal assistance from his old ally.

The Lory Plantation

UPON LANDING IN PORT Louis, Mauritius, Joseph Lory's agents led Furcy directly to the Lory family plantation in Trois Ilôts, in the fertile region of Flacq, presently undergoing rapid conversion to sugar production.[2] As Furcy's legal team later described it:

> Arriving [at the plantation] the same evening, at 11:00 p.m., after having walked 10 leagues [about 25 miles] (despite having lost the

capacity to walk during his year in prison), his legs were excessively swollen and his fatigue was extreme. The next morning, the oldest son of Mrs. Lory came to purchase him from his uncle for 700 piasters [about $14,600].[3]

"Mrs. Lory" was Joseph Lory's sister-in-law, the widow of his eldest brother, André Lory. By this account, then, at age 32 Furcy became the property of Joseph Lory's nephew, Adolphe Lory, age 25.[4]

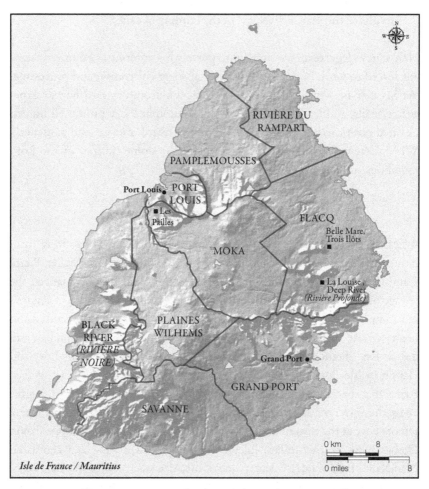

Fig. 8.1 Map of Mauritius. The Lory family owned two plantations: Belle Mare in Trois Ilôts and La Louise in Deep River, Flacq. Furcy would eventually live in Port Louis and Les Pailles.

Furcy was allowed to recover his health for about ten days, but was then put to work on the Lorys' sugar factory at their plantation, La Louise, in Rivière Profonde, Flacq.[5] Once again, Furcy's legal scribe evoked his recollections in the third person:

> The 21st of [November 1818, Adolphe Lory] made him walk to the sugar factory, two [miles?] from the plantation, and made him work at sugar (very hard work, as a kind of punishment, because it is necessary to empty, with the aid of an enormous spoon, five large cauldrons in which the sugar is boiling). He was subjected to this labor for five months. For three years, he was forced to the same sugar works for six months of the year, as [well as] in the farming of cane.[6]

Here Furcy's legal team was at pains to portray his suffering as a domestic servant forced to work in the grueling cycle of sugar cultivation and processing. Yet his new master eventually came to recognize and reward Furcy's experience, skills, and leadership. After a time, Adolphe Lory promoted him to elevated positions within the slave hierarchy: "third overseer and gardener."[7] Within a few years, Furcy was selected for the domestic staff of the Lory townhouse in Port Louis.

Joseph Lory: Slave Trade Financier

WHILE FURCY TOILED IN Mauritius, Joseph Lory was profiting from numerous ventures in Isle Bourbon with his primary business partner, Pierre Gamin, including slave smuggling.[8] In 1820, Lory and Gamin financed the voyage of a newly constructed ship, the *Succès*, out of Nantes, one of France's most important slave-trading ports. The *Succès* transported manufactured and luxury goods, including brandy, wine, hats, boots and shoes, umbrellas, and dresses from France to Isle Bourbon and, after being resupplied by Lory and Gamin in Isle Bourbon, set off for Zanzibar, an island off the coast of East Africa that specialized in the trade of cloves, ivory, and slaves.[9] On 31 August 1820, the *Succès* returned to Isle Bourbon, unloading 215 slaves at Cascades, a remote cove at the eastern end of the island, into the hands of Philippe Panon Desbassayns's brother-in-law, Jules Mourgue (the man who later translated Madeleine's bills of sale).[10] Thirty-one of the Africans had died of smallpox or starvation over the five-week passage, while another 26, "thin and sickly," were offered at discount prices to Mourgue.[11] Although Isle Bourbon's authorities caught the captain and crew, and the officers were charged with illegal slave trading, they were found not guilty, because, as the ship's supercargo noted, "All the judges are the same colonists who purchased the slaves from our cargo."[12]

Once the *Succès*'s captain was cleared of charges in Isle Bourbon, Lory and Gamin financed a second slaving voyage to Zanzibar in February 1821, purchasing a total of 309 slaves.[13] This time, however, the British antislavery crusader Captain Fairfax Moresby, commanding officer of the *Menai*, spotted the *Succès* near the Seychelles, gave chase, and eventually captured the French ship.[14] On board Moresby discovered 324 slaves (including fifteen undeclared in the inventory prepared for the ship's owner back in France) and seized the ship and its contents, with the many papers produced as evidence in the subsequent trial held in Mauritius.[15] On 8 May 1821, the British Admiralty Court condemned the brig *Succès* for transporting slaves in violation of the ban; the French ship and all its contents were forfeited to the British crown.[16]

The maiden voyages of the *Succès* had been anything but a success. Against the 102,929.38 francs (about $429,000) advanced by the owner in Nantes to build and outfit the ship in 1820, after the sale of French consumer goods and African slaves in Isle Bourbon, Captain Bertrand had come up short by 68,500 francs (about $286,000) from the first voyage. Now he had lost the ship itself and the value of all the slaves, purchased at 9,497 piasters (about $205,000) but worth about 64,800 piasters ($1.4 million) in resale value in Isle Bourbon. Whether this represented a net loss to the financiers Lory and Gamin is hard to know. When the *Succès* had left Isle Bourbon in December 1821, Captain Bertrand had signed papers saying that he and the ship's supercargo owed Lory and Gamin 9,467.34 piasters (about $197,000) on the trade goods that they had advanced for the voyage.[17] Consequently, the financial risk of the journey was carried by the Nantes ship owner and Captain Bertrand, not their colonial intermediaries. Since the *Succès* had failed at an illegal venture, it would difficult for the owner and the captain to recoup any of their losses from Lory and Gamin. In the end, Joseph Lory's role as financier of the trips went unprosecuted in either Mauritius or Bourbon, and consequently he was never punished. Was this his first attempt at smuggling slaves, or just the only one to have been caught and thus recorded in the British archives?

Antislavery: Britain and France

AS THE CASE OF the *Succès* makes clear, although the French government paid lip service to the slave trade ban, colonial officials in Isle Bourbon applied the laws selectively and to their own advantage. In Britain and Mauritius, however, things were different. Since the late eighteenth century, a committed group of antislavery activists in England had organized to educate the public about the cruelty of the slave trade and colonial slavery. Their first success was the case of Somerset in 1772, which effectively liberated slaves who arrived in Britain, much as France's Free Soil principle had.[18] English abolitionists had their second major success with the banning of the slave trade in 1807, extended to the Indian Ocean in 1811. However, the expected outcome of this ban—the gradual withering and natural death of colonial slavery—had not come to pass any more than it did in the southern United States, and in the 1820s Britain's antislavery movement began to bring even greater pressure on Parliament in the form of letters and petitions signed by millions of British citizens.[19]

Across the Channel, Restoration France, with its monarchy, Catholic culture, and limited democratic structures (in a nation of thirty million people, only about one hundred thousand men were eligible to vote), did not witness the deeply populist antislavery movement that evangelical Protestants and Quakers forged in the United States and Britain. A very small coterie of liberal French intellectuals denounced the slave trade but made little headway in the French government, where ties to the colonial elite dampened antislavery sentiment.[20] However, a celebrated case prosecuted in France's Caribbean colony of Martinique, known as the Bissette Affair, stirred Parisian hearts against racism, at least when applied to wealthy men of color.

Cyrille Bissette was a prominent slave owner, the son of free parents of mixed French and African ancestry in Martinique, who also happened to be an unacknowledged blood relative of Empress Josephine.[21] Charged with sedition for harboring a pamphlet advocating equal rights for free men of color, Bissette and dozens of other black and brown free men living in Martinique were convicted, their property was confiscated, and they were sentenced to branding and exile. As a result, many of Bissette's compatriots scattered throughout the Atlantic world, but he and three colleagues made their way to Paris, where they defended themselves in pamphlets and in the courts, stimulating public opinion for the justice of their cause. After years of debate in the French press, their original sentences were ultimately reduced by the Parisian Appeals Court (Cour de Cassation). As a result of the Bissette Affair, the French government undertook another reorganization of the colonial court system in 1828.[22] More generally, French liberals increasingly questioned the arbitrary racial regime of the slave colonies, at least regarding the colonies' wealthiest people of color, now several generations removed from slavery, some of whom were as rich as, or even richer than, many whites. Even so, in

1824 Louis XVIII's hardline successor, Charles X, instituted new restrictions on slave mobility, forbidding the departure of slaves from any of the French colonies.[23]

While metropolitan French opinion showed increasing sympathy toward established people of color, in the 1820s the English antislavery campaign began to bear down on slavery in Mauritius.[24] Once again, Furcy seized an opportunity afforded by the disjuncture between European and colonial authority to pursue his freedom from the Lory clan. A handful of letters from Furcy during this period illuminate exactly what freedom meant to him.

Furcy's Letters

REMARKABLY, TEN LETTERS AUTHORED by Furcy have survived. Letters written by slaves in any language are exceedingly rare, though this may have as much to do with the lack of institutional preservation in archives as with the limited original creation of such letters.[25] To my knowledge, Furcy's series of letters are unique in their efforts to seek assistance in establishing the legal grounds for freedom. Furcy took advantage of moments of crisis in the Lory family to seek help from legal officials in France and in Mauritius, especially the man who had come to his aid in 1817, Louis Gilbert Boucher.

Furcy's letters are also problematic. While teaching a slave to read and write was not against French law, most slaves never learned these skills.[26] In 1817, Sully Brunet had described Furcy as "without education,"[27] and until 1836 the signatures on Furcy's letters bear little resemblance to one another; one even bore an "X," indicating an inability to sign his name.[28] It is clear, then, that Furcy, like most people throughout the world in the early nineteenth century, could not write. Instead, Furcy made use of a common practice in such societies: he hired someone to write these letters for him—an amanuensis. At some point before 1821, Furcy relocated from the Lorys' plantation in Flacq to the townhouse in Port Louis.[29] There, running errands in the city, he must have found someone who could compose the letters on his behalf. Their wording must therefore be considered a product of both Furcy's will and his interlocutor's style. Nevertheless, Furcy's letters shed light on his living conditions, his family, and his aspirations in a way that no other surviving documents can.

On 13 June 1821, within weeks of the British capture of the *Succès*, Joseph Lory departed Saint-Denis for Mauritius, perhaps to follow up on business in the aftermath of the failed slaving voyage.[30] Lory's presence in Mauritius stirred Furcy to renew his struggle for freedom. Shortly after Lory's arrival, on 1 July 1821, Furcy wrote to his old ally, the metropolitan justice Louis Gilbert

Fig. 8.2 Port Louis, Mauritius. Port Louis's multiethnic heritage and thriving commercial culture was celebrated in this image from the late nineteenth century. The street signs show an undertaker, a tavern, and a poster for a coming theatrical, *La dame blanche* (The White Woman). "A Street Scene in Port Louis, Mauritius," *The Graphic*, 3 September 1881, 256. © Look and Learn.

Boucher, then serving as the attorney general in Bastia, Corsica, to request help in renewing his freedom suit.[31]

Furcy's plea to Boucher opens in a plaintive tone, requesting that the magistrate remember "the promises that you made to me at the time of your departure for France to interest yourself in my case." The letter continues in a romantic language of sympathy and pity, asking Boucher whether "the plaintive cries of a wretch [*un malheureux*] whose rights you know, can still move that sensibility with which your generous soul is endowed." Furcy's specific requests of Boucher are vague, asking only "that you give [me] the honor of one of your least regards, and continue the protection that you have afforded [me]," rather than asking for any tangible favor or intervention. This letter had no other immediate goal but to reestablish contact. If Boucher had any further knowledge that might be useful to Furcy, he was requested to "honor [him] with a response" via a Monsieur Rougevin. After an effusive, obsequious salutation, the scribe signed Furcy's name with a flourish.[32]

Details of Furcy's everyday life can be gleaned from the 1821 letter. Its very existence indicates that Furcy enjoyed some freedom of movement in Mauritius. That he was able to commission its composition away from his master's surveillance and post it to Boucher in Europe suggests that he had at least temporarily traveled from the Lorys' Flacq plantation to their townhouse on the rue de la Corderie, centrally located in Port Louis.[33] As a servant, Furcy would be sent on errands or left to wait while his master visited or conducted business, allowing a degree of privacy, sociability, and leisure in the bustle of urban life. The return of his former master, Joseph Lory, who no doubt visited his sister-in-law and nephews during his stay, must have been disconcerting, but Furcy would have picked up scraps of news about the trial of the *Succès* and maybe his family in Isle Bourbon. Furcy's reference to "Monsieur Rougevin" means that he found someone he trusted who was sympathetic to his plight.[34]

Boucher must have returned from Corsica to Paris, where Furcy's letter followed him, arriving on 1 February 1822.[35] If Boucher replied (and there is no evidence that he did), it is possible that his response was intercepted and never reached Furcy. After waiting a few months, Furcy grew impatient and dictated another appeal to the magistrate sometime in 1822.[36] He began by explaining that he was writing in triplicate, in the hope that one of the letters would reach his esteemed champion. In a respectful and subservient tone, he caught Boucher up on his whereabouts: "Since your departure, I was incarcerated, and I had only left prison to be embarked upon a vessel that carried me to Isle Maurice, where I am at the home of Madame Widow Laury [*sic*], always in slavery."[37]

The core content of Furcy's 1822 letter, however, is striking and specific. He asks the magistrate to help him locate particular documents in France to renew his freedom suit in Mauritius:

> You might perhaps, Monsieur, be of great help to me in this affair, if you had an opportunity to send [someone] to Lorient [to research] at the convent where Mademoiselle Despense was; to inquire [there] in which notarial cabinet she deposited her archives; doubtless you will find the contract and conditions that were passed between Madame Desblottières Routier with Mademoiselle Despense the nun for *la nommée* Marie Magdelaine, who was at this time thirteen years old. [As] the certified copy of this act, brought by the said woman [Routier], has been removed [*soustraite*], there is no doubt that the legitimacy of my rights would soon be recognized. My mother was then only thirteen years old and could not have yet had any children; she only had them upon arriving in Bourbon, which proves authentically that those that she had are free.[38]

Clearly Furcy—or someone close to him—understood the legal system and his case in particular, including the papers it would take to prove his freedom. Furcy needed written documentation of his mother's presence in France; the contract between Mademoiselle Despense and Madame Routier would provide this proof. Even the language of his letter includes several legal formulations: "*la nommée* Marie Magdalene" and "the said woman" (*laditte femme*), suggesting that Furcy's letter writer was a legal professional assisting him to build his case. The final argument, about Madeleine's age, was meant to show that her children could only have been born in Isle Bourbon after her residence in the metropole.

Furcy concluded his 1822 letter with a pleading tone, followed by a conventionally submissive, even florid, salutation:

> For these reasons, please reflect, sir, upon my unhappy situation, and deign, I pray you, not to withdraw your protective eye from an unfortunate who implores you, and of whose gratitude for such a noteworthy good deed he will maintain and will remain as great as the very profound respect with which he begs you to believe him to be, very humbly,
> Monsieur, your very humble and very obedient servant,
>
> Furcy[39]

Even through another's words, Furcy's 1822 letter reveals much about his character. He is persistent and determined; having failed to elicit a response with the first letter, he tries again. He (or his scribe) demonstrates a sophisticated understanding of the power of documentation in legal disputation, even if he has not quite harnessed the lawyers' arguments. His experience with Joseph Lory and the officers of the Isle Bourbon courts taught him that he needed paper evidence to support his legal status as a free man. Underpinning his request for documentation is the idea that the Free Soil principle and his mother's residence in France made her free. However, the paper he requests—the contract between Mademoiselle Despense and Madame Routier—is precisely the kind of documentation that Joseph Lory could use to demonstrate continuity in property; it could actually undermine Furcy's case, depending on the wording of the act.[40] Finally, the obsequious tone of the closure—while certainly formulaic—may also be evidence of the awkwardness of Furcy's request. After all, Boucher was driven to leave his post in Isle Bourbon precisely because of his support of Furcy's cause in 1817. Furcy ran the risk of alienating Boucher with his request, but he called upon their shared respect for liberty, "the greatest thing that a man can possess."[41]

The facts presented in Furcy's letters about his life in Mauritius can be cross-checked against the "dictated notes" recorded from Furcy in the 1830s.[42] While the notes contain some errors of date, and potentially of other facts, many of the details confirm and expand upon information recorded in other, disinterested historical records. For example, Furcy survived two severe cyclones in Mauritius in 1818 and 1824. The notes indicate that the second storm prompted his deployment as a mason on the plantation:

In 1824, a windstorm destroyed the sugar works and the refinery [at the Lorys' plantation], and he was obliged to work for eight months as a mason to reconstruct with others a new building 140 feet long. Notwithstanding his work as a mason, when necessary, he was obliged to work as a carpenter and from there was charged with squaring the joists destined for the building. Since then, he went back to sugar labor during the cane season and continued at this occupation, so difficult and painful, until 1828.[43]

A cyclone indeed struck Mauritius on 23 February 1824, though it was not as severe as that of 1818, which may have been the one that Furcy recalled. In the former, the Lory's plantation had suffered, according to a visitor, "much damage."[44]

Furcy's lawyers, in trying to build a case of unjust brutality, placed Furcy at the sugar plantation for the duration of his enslavement. However, he was never censused on the Lorys' rolls there,[45] and his two letters to Boucher indicate that he occasionally came into Port Louis. Furcy later mentioned a third letter, now lost, written to Boucher "near the end of 1824," which he sent by way of "a woman who lives in Paris" but to which he received no reply.[46]

Several years would pass before Furcy's next surviving letter in 1826. In the meantime, members of the Lory family continued to travel rather frequently between the two islands.[47] In April 1824, a measles outbreak, originating in Saint-Denis, began to ravage Isle Bourbon.[48] On August 1, Joseph Lory, his wife, and their daughter returned home from Mauritius at the height of the epidemic.[49] Less than a week later, Eugénie's brother, Cyrille Routier (Maurice's former master), died at his home in Sainte-Suzanne at the age of 57.[50] By the end of September, Joseph Lory's unmarried eighteen-year-old niece, Jenny, was also dead.[51] The suddenness of these deaths surprised and frightened those who knew them.[52]

By 1825, Joseph's widowed sister-in-law, Jeanne Marguerite Malvezy Lory, and several of his nephews had decided to leave Mauritius and establish new, permanent homes in Isle Bourbon, even as they retained ownership of the plantation and slaves in Flacq.[53] The widow Lory, as she was known, arrived in 1824 with her servant Justine Siahime.[54] In 1826, she ordered five of her favorite household slaves to follow her from Mauritius to Isle Bourbon, forcing the separation of many family members. Each of these people would eventually receive their freedom in Isle Bourbon—probably in tacit recognition of the 1835 abolition of slavery in Mauritius, where they continued to be declared as slaves, though "absent in Bourbon," into the early 1830s.[55]

Several of the widow Lory's sons relocated to Isle Bourbon in 1825 and 1826, including the eldest, Adolphe Lory, now a married merchant with a child, to whom Furcy believed himself to have been sold.[56] Yet Furcy is not listed among Adolphe Lory's slaves in Isle Bourbon, nor among the widow Lory's slaves in Mauritius; rather, Joseph Lory continued to itemize Furcy as the very first of his domestic slaves in every one of his Saint-Denis census returns from 1822 to 1833.[57] If Furcy believed he had been sold to Adolphe or the widow Lory in Mauritius, Joseph Lory still claimed to be Furcy's master in Isle Bourbon.

Now an absentee planter, the widow Lory left the business of running the family plantation to her son Edouard, 23.[58] When he next submitted the census on her behalf in 1826, the number of slaves had declined from 149 in

1817 to 120.[59] While some may have died in the 1818 cholera epidemic, a majority of those missing from the later roster were men with valuable skills, carpenters and blacksmiths. Perhaps the widow had sold them to raise cash. She retained a single carpenter, Paul Samson, 25, which is perhaps why the family ordered Furcy to take up carpentry following the 1824 cyclone. No doubt he envied one of missing blacksmiths, Hippolyte, 23, who was listed as "escaped" (*marron*).

Rocks of Mauritius

IF FURCY HAD RECEIVED any reply to his earlier letters to Boucher, it has not been found. Discouraged, he waited, working on the Lorys' plantation and in Port Louis. Several events conspired to prompt Furcy to reach out to his former champion again in May 1826. The first may have been the death of his likely companion, Virginie Béga, in Isle Bourbon around this time, leaving Furcy's two daughters in the hands of their maternal grandmother, Célerine.[60] But the more immediate cause was probably the Lorys' decampment to Isle Bourbon. Furcy's later account of this period in the "notes" muddles the dates but explains how this occurred:

> Around this time, the eldest Monsieur Lory [i.e., Adolphe], having to pass to Isle Bourbon, rented Furcy to his father-in-law, Monsieur Genève in Rivière Noire. As soon as Monsieur Lory left for Bourbon in 1829 [actually 1826], Furcy asked to be authorized to work in the city (Port Louis, where he would earn more and would also return more to Monsieur Lory).[61]

Furcy's account of this period can be partially corroborated in passenger lists and censuses. On 4 September 1826, Adolphe Lory traveled with his wife and child from Mauritius to Saint-Denis, accompanied by at least two domestics, Zephir Joyeux and Martial Egiste.[62] Were it not for his quick thinking, Furcy would have been rented to Adolphe's father-in-law, Auguste Génève, 63, who lived on a large cattle ranch in Rivière Noire, the rural southwestern district of Mauritius, a good distance from city life.[63] By negotiating an urban placement in Port Louis, Furcy entered the wage market, where he was hired out, giving a percentage of the cash he earned to his master. Through this arrangement he had access to the market economy, scribes, and British colonial authorities. With these resources, he was able to mount a successful challenge of his enslavement to the Lory clan.

Meanwhile in Europe, Boucher, ever the vigorous challenger of corruption, once more got in trouble for his actions on behalf of the French state. Having sued the ministry and won repayment of his Isle Bourbon salary, he was prosecuting criminals in Corsica.[64] According to Boucher's nineteenth-century biographical notice,

> Corsica was then under an extra-legal regime and, one might even say the course of justice was entirely suspended. More than 800 [criminals] condemned in absentia were located in the island, where they enjoyed complete impunity. [Boucher] ordered the arrest of a good number and had them judged. This manner of proceeding displeased [those in] power, resulting, by May 1826, in a magistrate being discharged for having done his duty. In vain, the opposition attacked the minister in the Chamber of Deputies because of this act; the injustice, rather than being repaired, was as usual, excused by reticence and by perfidious insinuations.[65]

Boucher relocated to Paris, where he opened a private practice. Furcy's ally was clearly occupied with other problems and likely had neither the time nor the spirit to ponder Furcy's plight.

The same month that the liberal opposition protested Boucher's treatment in the Chamber of Deputies in Paris, May 1826, Furcy wrote to him his most urgent letter yet, this time clearly addressed from Port Louis.[66] Once again, an unnamed woman had agreed to carry his letter to Paris, where Furcy hoped it would ultimately reach the hands of Boucher via his father-in-law, Joseph Julian Le Gonidec de Kerdaniel, a counselor at France's Appeals Court in Paris.[67]

Furcy's May 1826 letter to Boucher began by summarizing his life since he left Isle Bourbon, adding several new details that help to clarify not only his condition as a slave but, conversely, his understanding of freedom:

> I was sold to the sister[-in-law] of the man who claimed to be my master, and for the last seven years I have been in Mauritius, far from my children, and even deprived of the benefit that so many other slaves enjoy, that of being master of my own time and my actions, though I offered to my supposed masters up to ten piasters [about $250] per month.[68]

This is the first explicit reference in any document that Furcy was a father and that his children remained in Isle Bourbon; the relationship with Virginie Béga and her two daughters has been inferred from records, but never explicitly stated. Most importantly, the letter clarifies Furcy's understanding of what it means to be free. If slavery meant separation from his children, freedom would allow him to live in the bosom of family. Slavery meant being at the beck and call of his mistress; freedom would make him "master of [his] own time and actions." Freedom would allow him to keep, save, and spend all of the money that he earned.

Unlike previous letters, whose tone begged for Boucher's pity and aid, this one strikes a note of frustration and anger:

> You know better than anyone, sir, if I had and if I still have the right to claim my freedom; you encouraged my petitions; you protected me. I was going to breathe the air of liberty, you said, [but] I am [still] a slave.[69]

Here Furcy is no longer the supplicant; he appeals as a wronged man to Boucher's sense of justice. There is also an undercurrent of betrayal because, were it not for Boucher's initial encouragement in his freedom suit and his failure, Furcy might still be home in Isle Bourbon. Why had his champion abandoned him?

Furcy's May 1826 letter redefines him in yet another way: as a French citizen. Defying both the taboo of the bastard and that of mixed ancestry, Furcy declares that he is the son of a Frenchman and worthy of the rights of a French colonist:

> It is from the rocks of Mauritius that I make you hear my voice to ask you whether I, the son of an Indian woman who had lived in France, can be counted among the number of the slaves, without being in violation of all the laws, all the institutions that are the safeguards of a country that you inhabit, to which I also belong—for I am born a French colonist, and I am the son of a Frenchman by birth.[70]

This passage is truly striking. In referencing his mother, as "an Indian woman who had lived in France," Furcy is recalling two of the legal arguments by which Boucher had justified his freedom in Isle Bourbon: the claim that Indians could not legally be enslaved and the Free Soil principle, by which any slave who touched the soil of metropolitan France would become free.

Moreover, this is the only explicit evidence anywhere that Furcy's father was a Frenchman. Furcy's assertion is important and all the more believable because the claim technically had no bearing on his legal justification for freedom. Furcy's assertion that he was "a French colonist and the son of a Frenchman by birth" offers a clear insight into how Furcy saw himself, much as many free men of color made similar demands for recognition and equality elsewhere in the French empire.[71]

Furcy concluded his letter with an appeal to Boucher as a powerful patron with access to royal favor:

> The king, I am told, has honored you with the title of attorney general to Bestia [*sic*]. It is claimed that you have come back from [this position with] the esteem of the sovereign. Why has he not been informed of my fate? Why are you not my interpreter before the law? Then I would be sure to return to my rights.[72]

By claiming for himself a French identity, Furcy constructs France in particular ways: as the place where his mother had resided that gave her freedom; as a country based on "laws . . . , institutions . . . and safeguards"; as Boucher's home; and as the source of rights that Furcy was entitled to by birthplace and descent. France is the site of liberty and the rule of law.[73] At the same time, Furcy calls upon the protection of both the former attorney general and the king, resonant of older forms of political belonging, of obligation and patronage. Furcy's letter perfectly encapsulates the hybrid nature of Restoration France: a constitutional monarchy founded on rights but dependent upon patronage for access to power.

Furcy's closing salutation resonates with the self-respect and assuredness of the rest of this letter:

> In waiting for [your] response, which I request, not of your goodness, which I know is very large, but of your Justice. Permit a man in the irons of servitude, irons that you alone can make fall, to assure you of his respect and his eternal gratitude.
>
> Furcy[74]

Gone is the formulaic "humble and obedient servant." Furcy is now a man secure in the knowledge of his rights as a French citizen, but dependent upon the assistance of another to make his case. Despite Furcy's appeal to Frenchness, his freedom would not come immediately from Paris.

Commission on Eastern Inquiry

PROMPTED BY THE ANTISLAVERY lobby in London, in the 1820s the British government established the three-member Commission on Eastern

Inquiry, an investigatory panel designed to review all aspects of colonial rule, especially slavery and slave smuggling, in the British colonies of the Indian Ocean, from the Cape of Good Hope to Ceylon.[75] Two officers of the commission, Major William Macbean George Colebrooke and William Blair, arrived in Mauritius five months after Furcy sent his previous letter, on 1 October 1826. They were joined by their colleague John Thomas Bigge in 1827, and they remained there through 24 February 1829.[76] The Commission on Eastern Inquiry collected hundreds of pages of testimony from colonists, slaves, and former slaves about the conditions of slavery in Mauritius, striking fear into the hearts of slaveholders throughout the colony. The commissioners' investigation provided Furcy with just the opportunity he had been looking for.

In October 1826, the widow Lory's fourth son, Edouard Lory, having returned to Port Louis, completed the requisite slave census on behalf of his mother for the Belle Mare plantation in Flacq, making no mention of Furcy.[77] Probably at the behest of his uncle, Joseph, Edouard tracked Furcy down in Port Louis and told him that it was time to return to Isle Bourbon. Years later, as Furcy recalled through his lawyerly scribe:

> One of the Messrs. Lory (Edouard) then came to find him and proposed to him that he return to Bourbon, which he [Furcy] had wished to do when he was at the [Flacq] plantation of Trois Ilôts. "No," responded Furcy, who did not trust any proposition emanating from his persecutors. "Why?" asked Monsieur E. Lory. "Because the scalded cat fears cold water."[78] "Well then, I will make you leave!"[79]

In addition to demonstrating Furcy's command of idiom, the exchange reveals why he had changed his mind about wishing to return to Isle Bourbon. The Lorys knew that they could not demonstrate legal title to Furcy in Mauritius because they had never declared him on their slave registers, but Joseph Lory had been carefully recording Furcy on each of his census returns in Saint-Denis, Isle Bourbon.[80] Although Furcy could not have known this, he certainly realized that if the proposal to return to Isle Bourbon was intiated by the Lorys, it could not be good for him.

On 3 November 1826, Furcy, who had not yet received a reply from his May letter to Boucher, prepared a near duplicate letter, with only a few slight corrections.[81] The strangest aspect of this letter is Furcy's signature, penned with an elaborate flourish, "Furcy Lory."[82] Given the depth of his resentment toward the Lory family, it is highly unlikely that Furcy would have adopted this last name by choice. Moreover, the handwriting is not like any of the other signatures. The letter is clearly the product of a copyist trying to assist Furcy.

Thanks to the Commission on Eastern Inquiry, Furcy's address in Port Louis is recorded as the home of a "M. Micoin, rue de la Corderie"—a few paces from the ancestral townhouse of the Lory family.[83] In an undated petition to the governor of Mauritius, Sir Lowry Cole, forwarded to the Commission on 9 December 1826, Furcy lamented his suffering at the hands of the Lory family, adding many new details (including some erroneous assertions) to his story.[84] In his petition, Furcy claimed that when negotiating with Lory in 1809, Madeleine had offered the exchange of two slaves for the freedom of her son, "and this proposal was rejected." He also recalled the Free Soil argument while scrupulously avoiding any mention of the argument that Indians could not be enslaved under French law. Furcy's new petition explains why his name never appeared in the Mauritius slave registers: "I can assure His Excellence that I was never reported on the census," and concludes: "This reason alone, moreover, would suffice for you to determine to consider me a free man whose civil status one wants to destroy."[85] So Furcy's December 1826 petition to the British Governor of Mauritius offered yet another argument for his freedom, this time based in English law and stimulated by the presence of the Commission on Inquiry. His enslavement was unjust because he had never been duly registered by his owners in Mauritius. Without his letters to Boucher and his complaint, there would have been no formal record of his presence in Mauritius.

Shortly after Furcy filed his petition, Edouard Lory filed manumission papers in Port Louis on his mother's behalf for her eight-year-old slave, Floriancia.[86] This was the "reddish" (*rougeâtre*, often connoting Malagasy ancestry) daughter of the thirty-year-old servant and seamstress Rosa Sylvie.[87] Rosa and her "black" (*noir*) son Felix were already living with the widow Lory in Isle Bourbon.[88] In freeing Floriancia, the widow Lory not only lost her value, but she also had to pay 300 piasters (roughly $7,400) in order to assure that the child would not become a burden on the colony.[89] However, the family's beneficence to Floriancia would not extend to Furcy. Furcy lamented to the governor that he was now in the custody of Edouard Lory, "to whom I must belong, and with whom I will return to the island of Isle Bourbon." Edouard's plan to compel Furcy to return to Isle Bourbon against his will would result in Furcy's perpetual slavery there:

> Time presses: my persecutors seem to want to make me leave this island; but if Your Excellence will permit it, if it is necessary, to give

him greater detail, orally or in writing, and I will confound those with whom I deal. It is not useless that you notice that, even supposing that in Isle Bourbon I appear to be a slave, I can in no way be one in Mauritius; because here a state such as mine is inconceivable, because here there are regular laws on the registration of slaves; because here one lives under a government that holds nothing more dear than to achieve the noble enterprise that it has taken: that of rendering to men the liberty that others have ravished.[90]

Thus, Furcy stated his intention to remain in the British colony, "part of the most liberal nation in the world," flattering Governor Lowry that his excellence would "not breathe while a free man remains in slavery."[91] He signed his petition with an X.[92]

As a result of Furcy's letter to the governor, his case was assigned to the public defender (*attorney des indigènes*) Raymond Brusaud.[93] According to Furcy's later recollection in the "Notes":

[Edouard] then conducted [Furcy] to the police, to establish his rights of property over Furcy in consulting the registers of the city hall of the period of his arrival in the colony. But Furcy had not been listed on the passenger roster that had brought him from Bourbon. Found there were the names of all the passengers who had been with him on the *Clélie* but for his.[94] And the infraction of the law of which he had been the object became his salvation. Monsieur Lory, not being able to establish his claimed rights over Furcy—neither at the police nor at the customs house where he had the same research done—was forced to let him go, and it is only since this period (1829) that he has been able to enjoy a bit of freedom and work for his own account.[95]

So the legal arguments that finally secured Furcy's freedom were not any of those originally offered by his legal team in 1817—Indian freedom, free soil, natural law, negligence, separation of mother and child—nor the lack of census documentation in Mauritius but the fact that the Lorys had arranged for Furcy to be smuggled past the custom's house officials in Port Louis when he arrived emaciated in November 1818.[96]

Furcy's case never came before Mauritius's slave protector, the new officer established by the British government to handle hundreds of slave complaints beginning in March 1829.[97] As this account makes clear, there was no formal legal decision authorizing Furcy's freedom in Mauritius. Edouard Lory simply realized that he could not prove title and gave up, allowing Furcy to live the life of a free man (*libre de fait*), but without the papers to prove it (*libre de droit*), at an unknown date. Furcy recalled this happening in 1829; it was certainly sometime after December 1826.[98]

A Free Man Bound

AFTER FURCY FINALLY ACHIEVED his freedom from the Lory family in Mauritius, he joined the island's free majority—68 percent of the free population was then reported as nonwhite—in the thriving Indian Ocean hub of Port Louis.[99] One of the most visible distinctions between slaves and free people was their feet; by custom, only free people wore shoes.[100] No doubt one of Furcy's first acts as a free man was to visit the cobbler and get fitted for a pair. How did it feel to enclose his calloused, broad feet in leather? The creole expression "Shoes are pretty, but they eat your feet" is a reminder that shoes brought blisters as well as protection from the streets' stones, mud, and manure.[101] Freedom likewise brought its own challenges.

Although most free people of color adopted surnames, Furcy did not, at least not immediately.[102] He went into business as a candy maker (*confiseur*) and pastry chef (*patissier*), and in 1835 he lived alone, without wife or children, in Port Louis.[103] He had associates, such as the baker Joseph Dioré, who owned a large bakery on rue Beaucaire and probably helped to train Furcy in the art of sugary confections.[104] Through his new position, Furcy acquired the skills and the savings to work toward economic independence.

Finally, on 26 July 1833, after the slaves of several Caribbean colonies rose up in revolt and years of lobbying by antislavery activists, the British Parliament passed its Slavery Abolition Act, which applied to most of Britain's colonies in the Atlantic world and to Mauritius (but not India or Ceylon).[105] This was a peculiar experiment in liberal politics, an effort to free colonial slaves but also to compensate their masters for their loss of property and to transition slaves into compliant wage laborers through a period of "apprenticeship." All slaves above the age of six, though nominally "free," would nevertheless be required to work for their former masters without wages for another four to six years, both as a method of "training" them for freedom and also as part of the compensation to their masters. Though each British colony was required to enforce the act, local governments defined the terms. The Mauritius Council defined those terms on 17 September 1834, and the law took effect there on 1 February 1835.[106]

"Freedom" under general emancipation in Mauritius did not look anything like what Furcy described in his earlier letters to Boucher. "Apprentices" in Mauritius were bound to the land like medieval serfs, and although they could no longer be bought and sold as individuals, they were attached to any real estate property transactions. Masters were responsible for feeding and clothing their apprentices, but the workers were allowed to raise their own food on small garden plots belonging to their masters, working there between four and eight hours per week. Apprentices were to be punished for tardiness or absenteeism by owing extra days of labor to their masters; desertion or vagabondage would be punished by the state through hard labor or up to thirty lashes. Resisters could be charged with conspiracy or riot and punished with six months to a year of hard labor. Indeed, this new "freedom" looked a lot like the old slavery.[107]

It is not surprising to learn that when the government offered compensation to slave owners for "freeing" their slaves, the widow Lory and several of her sons requested cash payments. Only the widow and her eldest son, Adolphe, were successful, collecting a little over £3,000 (about $350,000 in today's money).[108] The other sons' applications were rejected on the basis of Clause 46 of the Emancipation Act, which prohibited compensation for "persons held illegally in slavery."[109]

What is perhaps more surprising is that Furcy likewise received £84.18s.2d (almost $11,000) in compensation for two slaves, Victor Théophile, "an inferior tradesman," and Chouchou Ladérouille, Furcy's butler.[110] Like his sister Constance, Furcy had invested his savings in a pair of enslaved workers to launch himself in freedom. Unlike the United States, but similar to most other slaveholding societies of this era, freed people and their descendants in Mauritius often owned slaves.[111] Furcy's slaves—about whom little is known—probably assisted him in his sweetshop business. There they served as labor and capital all in one. As laborers, Théophile and Ladérouille enhanced the value of the ingredients he purchased and, through their culinary skills, transformed the sugar, flour, and flavorings into treats for sale at a profit. Less expensive than land, slaves, with proper treatment, held and perhaps even increased in value during their adulthood as they learned skills and gained maturity. For a freedman like Furcy, they were like a living savings account that could appreciate over time to generate revenue upon resale, allowing him to save in small portions until he could purchase land. Although there is no evidence one way or the other, Furcy may also have shared the disdain most free people had toward the island's Afro-descended population. In an effort to distinguish themselves from slaves and former slaves, many free people of color imbibed the dominant racial prejudice that valued the tangible benefits of Eurasian ancestry and networks made visible in lighter skin.[112]

Thus, freedom for Furcy, at least at this stage of his life, meant the capacity to work for himself on his own terms and at his own hours; to acquire and build savings, even in purchasing other human beings; to spend his money; and to be with his family. It was in this last regard that Furcy remained unsatisfied. Furcy's children remained in Isle Bourbon, where most of the Lory clan resided in alliance with the judicial and notarial creole elite. He could not risk traveling there, lest he fall under their control once more. In 1827 the British Admiralty Court in London had ruled that any former slave who willingly returned to the jurisdiction where she or he was held as a slave thereby submitted to re-enslavement.[113] Mauritius might be free soil for Furcy, but Isle Bourbon remained a rock of slavery.

9

Freedom Papers Hidden in His Shoe

IN PORT LOUIS, FURCY busied himself alongside Chinese merchants in the confectionary business making "suckers, diverse candies, nougats, molded sugars [*sucres façonnées*], tiny layered sweet pastries [*petits fours*], fruit gums [*gommes et pâtes*], . . . and other sugared and flavored products,"[1] all byproducts of the sugar revolution taking place in both Mauritius and Isle Bourbon.[2] His work as a candy maker (*bonbonnier*) was lucrative, as the rising demand for sugar in France lined the pockets of wealthy planters, merchants, and bourgeois functionaries, who in turn treated their families to newly invented pastries, cookies, and candies, previously available only to the aristocracy or on Easter and at Christmas. Furcy's long hours and imaginative creations launched a thriving business during his first years of freedom in Port Louis and eventually established his reputation as "one of the notables of the island."[3]

And yet Furcy was not satisfied with his new life. In the mid-1830s, just as general emancipation was coming to Mauritius, he decided to pursue a legal appeal for freedom to France's highest courts in Paris, an effort that would eventually occupy him for more than a decade. Why would a "free" man like Furcy resume his legal process for liberty? While the appeal itself generated literally hundreds of pages of documentation, there exists little explicit evidence of Furcy's motivations for pursuing a judgment in the Parisian courts halfway around the world. Was he caught up in the rising spirit of antislavery, to become a principled activist for social change? Or were there more tangible personal benefits that he believed he could secure through France's courts? Did he act alone, or were others pressuring him to advance his struggle? If Furcy did not leave a record of his intentions regarding his reengagement with the courts, his actions offer a glimpse Furcy's understanding of the meaning of freedom in a world where abolitionism was rapidly transforming the meaning of citizenship in France and Britain, and their overseas colonies.

Furcy's freedom suit would not have advanced without another revolution in Paris. The reign of Charles X (1824–1830), the last of the Bourbon kings, saw a sharp turn toward absolutism. His prime minister, Jean Baptiste de Villèle—brother-in-law of Philippe Panon Desbassayns—orchestrated the re-establishment of many Old Regime aristocratic privileges and benefits for the Catholic Church in the metropole. In the face of growing and vocal opposition by more liberal-minded reformers, the king ordered the invasion of Algeria and, in July 1830, suspended the constitution, dissolved the recently elected assembly, called for new elections under revised guidelines, and censored all opposition in the press. Reaction was immediate: journalists called for revolt; police shut down the papers; Parisians poured into the streets and erected barricades. The insurrection lasted three days, culminating in the abdication of the king and the reception at the legislative chamber of Louis Philippe, of the Orleans branch of the royal family, as the new French king.[4]

One of the first acts of this July Monarchy was to revisit the political institutions linking colonial citizens with the national government in Paris. After some deliberation over whether it was better to allow direct election by colonial landowners or legislative appointment by the colonial councils, Louis Philippe's government determined that colonial representatives to Paris would be appointed by the elected General Councils in the colonies.[5] The first representative selected by Isle Bourbon in 1831 was Jean Baptiste Pajot (Philippe Desbassayns's other brother-in-law, who had colluded to drive Louis Gilbert Boucher from Isle Bourbon), who nevertheless declined the honor. The two positions were then offered to Jacques Sully Brunet, who, having recovered from the setback over Furcy's case in 1817, was an elected member of the colonial General Council, and François Paul Etienne Azéma.[6] Once in Paris, Sully Brunet sat on the commission working to suppress the illegal slave trade; there he would begin to interact with French antislavery leaders, including François André Isambert, confidant of Cyrille Bissette.[7]

In the first two years of operation, the July Monarchy rapidly passed a burst of legislation favoring equal civil rights for free people of color and voluntary manumission of slaves. Prior to his ascent to the throne, Louis Philippe, "the Citizen King" (as he was called), had supported reformist causes, including antislavery.[8] He readily accepted and promoted the chamber's new laws, first requiring that the births, marriages, and deaths of blacks and whites be recorded in the same registers (7 September 1830), and eventually removing all restrictions on the civil rights of colonial free people of color (24 February 1831), suppressing manumission taxes (1 March 1831), increasing surveillance and penalties against the slave trade (4 March 1831), and simplifying the process for masters who wished to free their slaves voluntarily (12 July 1832).[9] As a result of these measures, some twenty thousand former colonial slaves—most of whom had already informally achieved an informal freedom as *libres de fait*—were recorded as free in the civil status registers and colonial censuses, ostensibly equal in rights to white French men and women.[10] However, the new government stopped well short of the 1833 British decision to abolish slavery. Indeed, British emancipation frightened France's colonial planter lobby, who quickly organized to delay or quash any legislative initiatives that could lead to general emancipation. It would take yet another revolution to finish off slavery in France's colonies.

Isle Bourbon

WHILE FURCY BUILT HIS confectionery business in Mauritius, Constance continued to live in her home in Saint-André, surrounded by diverse neighbors, including many free people of color. Sadly, her eldest son, Auguste, had died in 1823 at the young age of twenty-one. The notice of his death gives no clue as to the cause, but it was duly reported to authorities by two young free men of color, no doubt his friends and neighbors.[11] The loss of her son left Constance, by 1832, forty-seven years old, with five remaining adult children who continued to live on the family farm with Constance's six slaves.[12]

In contrast to the lean years of the British occupation, when her husband, Jean Baptiste, had farmed the land with only two female slaves, barely coaxing enough for his family to live on, following Furcy's exile to Mauritius, Constance gradually invested in new field hands, who in time improved her land's productivity, yielding an excess tonnage of vegetables, corn, and rice that could be sold on the island or to provision ships. In time she even added coffee and cloves. With profits from her investment in export crops, Constance re-entered the class of "planters" (*habitants*).[13]

Meanwhile, the Lory fortunes flourished in Isle Bourbon. Joseph Lory's retail business, Nau & Lory, established by 1825, sold a variety of imported necessities, and the shop's slaves also manufactured machinery for the expanding sugar industry.[14] In 1831, after the suppression of the slave trade, his other business partner, Pierre Gamin, "the pillar of commerce," went bankrupt,[15] but in the years since Furcy's deportation in 1818, Joseph Lory had purchased two large plantations in the fertile eastern district of Saint-Benoît that allowed him to profit from the sugar boom.[16] Together, the two parcels of land stretched for a little under a mile in width, "up to the tops of the mountains," yielding about 1,650 acres of cultivatable land entirely devoted to sugar.[17]

Lory's multifaceted and complex investments had greatly increased his wealth since his marriage to Eugénie almost three decades earlier. His Saint-Benoît plantations required several layers of managerial hierarchy, run by his nephew, Jules, 31, the manager (*régisseur*); two young white overseers

(*économes*); and five enslaved overseers (*commandeurs*).[18] The workforce of
249 slaves, twice as large as the Routiers' holdings in the eighteenth century, included a dozen specialized artisans, and unlike his carefully gender-
balanced slave accumulation at his town house in Saint-Denis, the sugar
plantation was overwhelmingly male (195 males to 54 females). The brutal
regime of sugar production had deprived two men, Oscar and Corentin, of
their arms (*manchot*). With the illegal slave trade more effectively suppressed
under the July Monarchy, Lory's field workers were aging, and the work force
was rarely replenished with new slaves. These two factors increased pressure
on the minority of female slaves to reproduce.

In 1831, Joseph (60), Eugénie (58), and their unmarried daughter,
Euphémie (28) continued to live at the townhome in Saint-Denis they had
inherited from the widow Routier, surrounded by some 33 domestic and
laboring slaves.[19] Each year that Joseph filed his census return, he duly noted
"Furcy, creole, domestic," at the top of the list despite Furcy's absence and life
as a free man in Mauritius. Unusually, in 1831 Joseph decorated the form with
a lightly drawn illustration of an hourglass, the sands slowly dripping away
time (Fig. 9.1).

On 30 November 1832, Euphémie died at home at the age of 28, probably of an epidemic fever then sweeping the colony.[20] From then on, Joseph

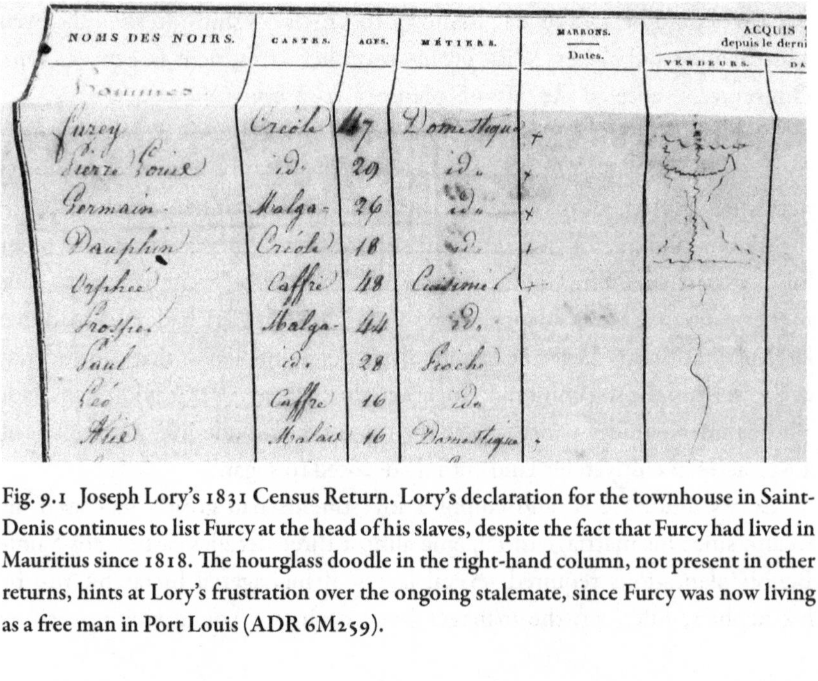

Fig. 9.1 Joseph Lory's 1831 Census Return. Lory's declaration for the townhouse in Saint-
Denis continues to list Furcy at the head of his slaves, despite the fact that Furcy had lived in
Mauritius since 1818. The hourglass doodle in the right-hand column, not present in other
returns, hints at Lory's frustration over the ongoing stalemate, since Furcy was now living
as a free man in Port Louis (ADR 6M259).

Lory had no living children that he could acknowledge and no heirs in his bloodline.

Tears of Joy

ALTHOUGH FURCY LIVED UNDER British rule in Mauritius, the liberal reforms of the July Monarchy offered him a ray of hope. After cooling his heels in private practice under Charles X, Louis Gilbert Boucher, following the 1830 revolution, received a new appointment as attorney general of Poitiers, an important city between Paris and the Atlantic coast.[21] Boucher's father-in-law, the judge to whom Furcy had confided his 1826 letter, Jean Julien Le Gonidec, remained on the bench of the Court of Cassation in Paris. Perhaps Boucher reminded Le Gonidec of Furcy's conundrum in light of the new political climate. Or perhaps it was Sully Brunet who brought Furcy to the attention of his co-councilor and antislavery reformer François André Isambert.[22] All three men—Boucher, Le Gonidec, and Isambert—were colleagues and even friends with André Dupin, who held dual offices of attorney general at the Court of Cassation and president of the Chamber of Deputies (1832–1840) and was confidant to the Citizen King.[23] It was Dupin who summarized Furcy's case before the Court of Cassation in 1835. Thanks to the 1830 Revolution, Furcy was now closely linked to France's elite antislavery establishment.

Early in 1835, Furcy boarded a ship in Port Louis, bound for France. His purpose, according to one reporter, was

> to present himself at the Court of Cassation, not with the decision from [Isle] Bourbon, which no one had deigned to make known to him, but with his complaint, which he had shielded from his masters' careful search by hiding it in the sole of his shoe.[24]

The reporter's polite expression about the Isle Bourbon court's missing decision ("which no one had deigned to make known to him") supports the theory the colonial courts never actually ruled on Furcy's original freedom suit or his appeal.

The "papers hidden in his shoe" is a colorful detail that may be apocryphal. As a slave, it is unlikely that Furcy wore shoes in Isle Bourbon or Mauritius, as they signified free status. Yet somehow Furcy had carefully secreted key documentation—perhaps copies of Constance's petition and his original 1817 writ—away from the Lorys' eyes in Mauritius. These papers would have been essential in helping Furcy's scribe compose the letters to Boucher while he was still enslaved to the Lorys. Or perhaps they were delivered to Furcy in Port Louis by one of his friends—M. Rougevin or the anonymous woman who carried his letters to Paris—after his arrival there. In 1835, Furcy, a free man clad in shoes, sailed to France.[25] But why would he need to hide the papers on board the ship? (And shoes would be a terrible place to protect such important documents on the high seas!)

Standing on deck, Furcy had ample time to contemplate his mother's own passage over these same waters sixty-five years earlier. Buoyed by his mission and traveling alone as an adult free man, Furcy's voyage in freedom was quite unlike his mother's crossing as a child slave. His ocean voyage connected him to powerful men in Paris and would eventually lead to securing his freedom under French law.

Furcy probably arrived in Bordeaux, Marseille, or one of the English ports, then continued on by a smaller boat or coach to Paris, or perhaps Boucher, Le Gonidec, or one of their servants met Furcy in Lorient and escorted him to the capital city. There Furcy make his way through the teeming streets, where almost a million people lived, worked, and begged. To reach the center, Furcy would have passed warrens of little alleys and narrow canyons lined by sagging homes, some centuries old. He eventually arrived at 13 rue de Savoie, the office and residence of Camille Godard de Saponay, the lawyer who would represent him in his appeal to the Court of Cassation on 12 August 1835.[26] From there, Furcy could walk just a block north to the Seine River, gazing across at the magnificent Palace of Justice, once a royal chateau, and the fabled Cathedral of Notre Dame.

Godard de Saponay had a problem: there was no documentation of the supposed decision by the Isle Bourbon court of appeal in February 1818.[27] How does a lawyer appeal a decision that was never recorded and probably never took place? Apparently, a date and the text of a decision was discovered (or invented), which Furcy's lawyer summarized as follows:

> The Royal Court of Bourbon, by decision of 12 February 1818, had judged that *la nommée* Madeleine, Indian by nation, and consequently free, had been able to be submitted to slavery, and that she had not ceased to be a slave, even though she had touched the welcoming soil of France and had resided there for more than five years [in fact it was only several months]; that the *sieur* Furcy, her son, born in the island of Bourbon after the return of his mother to this colony, was born a slave and remained as such, even after the manumission of his mother.[28]

Whereas Madeleine's status as a person of color was signaled by the expression *la nommée*," Furcy was awarded higher rank as "the *sieur* Furcy." This was the "decision" that Godard de Saponay needed to overturn.

In crafting his arguments, Furcy's lawyer began by establishing that Furcy was already a free man by English law: "The English government had no difficulty in recognizing [Furcy's freedom] and in proclaiming it." At the heart of his appeal, the lawyer lashed out at the corruption of the French colonial judiciary:

> Furcy, made free in an island submitted to English domination, remained no less under the blow of the decision of the French magistrates of Isle Bourbon. He profited by his liberty to come to France to demand the reform of a decision that he considered supremely unjust.[29]

Thus, from the beginning, the case crafted for Furcy's appeal was political, framed in the context of Britain's recent general emancipation and against the intrigues of the colonial courts of Isle Bourbon, the very name of which recalled to Parisian ears the arbitrary rule of both the executed Louis XVI and the abdicated Charles X.

More important than the lawyer's fashioning of Furcy's petition, however, were the conclusions of Attorney General Dupin, which offered the court a rationale for deciding that the case had sufficient merit to be heard by the Royal Court of Paris on appeal. Dupin framed Furcy's case in terms of three essential legal questions and supplied the answers that he felt were correct:

> Can a woman born INDIAN be legally reduced to the state of slavery? (No.)
>
> Supposing that her quality of being of free origin could be provisionally changed into one of slave in fact, has not the slavery ceased in law the instant that such a slave has touched the soil of France? (Yes.)
>
> The child, born of a mother of free origin, is he not free himself, despite the state of slavery of fact into which his mother may have been reduced; and in any case, can he not invoke, in support of his freedom, the manumission of his mother, which resulted from her having touched FRENCH soil? (Yes.)[30]

Thus, Dupin signaled that Furcy's case could be decided in his favor on the basis of three key arguments: Madeleine's Indian origins, her residence on France's free soil, and his condition following the maternal line.

Dupin's support of Furcy's case was invaluable, but he also introduced crucial, if unintentional, errors into the historical record. For example, in addition to establishing a date for the alleged colonial court decision, the attorney general speculated, based only upon Furcy's skin color, that he was born of a union between his mother and "a man of the negro race."[31] Furcy had already declared in his letter to Boucher that he was "born of a Frenchman."[32] Furcy's presence at the hearing was noted in the press, where he "awaited [the court's] decision with real anxiety, which was shared by the entire audience."[33]

Furcy needn't have worried. Dupin's forceful declarations, among them, "NO ONE IS A SLAVE IN FRANCE," carried the day.[34] The Court of Cassation's Petition Chamber found that Furcy's appeal had merit and summoned Joseph Lory, who had not come to France for the hearing, to appear before the Civil Chamber of the Court of Cassation to answer Furcy's charges.[35]

Furcy may have paid his own passage to France, but Dupin managed to finance his return voyage to Mauritius, giving a clue as to how and why the appeal was successful in 1835. Not one to hide his light under a bushel, Dupin spread word to the newspapers that

> upon the recommendation of the attorney general, the queen has arranged for the payment to the *sieur* Furcy, to aid him to return to his country, a sum of 150 francs; the Duke of Orleans for a similar amount, to which the attorney general himself added that of 100 francs; and that this magistrate actively presses the minister of the navy to obtain passage for Furcy, as a feeble compensation for the injuries that he has received in his status and in his freedom.[36]

So Dupin collected some 400 francs, worth a little more than $2,000 in today's money, to pay for Furcy's return. Having used public pressure "to aid the poor slave to return free to his country and to rejoin his family," Dupin was gratified to see, as his biographer duly noted,

> the leathered face of the Indian [as] his lawyer informed him of these charities and putting into his hands these unexpected gifts, his head lifted [*s'est renversée*], large tears fell on his cheeks: . . . "There is only heaven! . . ." [he said,] without being able to put his thoughts into words.[37]

Likewise, remembering this moment years later at Boucher's funeral, his eulogist wrote of Furcy, "It was a touching spectacle to see this poor Indian, yesterday a slave, and still a little uncertain, it seemed, of his liberty, to search for the gestures and the expressions to reconcile his respect with the enthusiasm of his appreciation."[38] On 23 October 1835, Furcy boarded *La Camille*, a commercial ship in Bordeaux, with his stated destination as Pondichéry, the capital of French India, though he would actually disembark at Mauritius.[39] Onboard he received the basic ration and sat with the sailors, apart from the wealthy passengers at the officers' table. The ship departed on 9 November 1835.

Dupin's support for Furcy's case was strategic in Paris's current political campaigns. Through it, he called attention to the Free Soil tradition, preparing the way for the Chamber of Deputies to pass new Free Soil legislation a few months later. The ordinance of 29 April 1836 clarified what had already become the default practice by the Ministry of the Navy and Colonies since the 1830 Revolution: it required colonial masters who wished to travel to France in the company of their slaves to manumit them formally before their departure from the colony. If a master failed to do so, the slave would be considered "free by right [*de plein droit*], from the time of his disembarkation in the metropole, and [would] consequently receive a title of liberty."[40]

A Free Man in Mauritius

FROM HIS HOME IN Port Louis, Mauritius, Furcy once again wrote to his old ally, Boucher—now embroiled in yet another controversy with rightist magistrates in Poitiers—on 1 October 1836.[41] Furcy began his letter warmly, celebrating the judge's commitment to justice:

> Monsieur, when one is unhappy, it is lovely to remember the charitable souls who have acted on one's behalf. It is lovely to tell of them again and what is felt above all when one is confident that he will be listened to, and that the person one addresses is just, and that he gives justice to those who merit it. My opening, sir, for anyone but you would appear a bit sycophantic, but you know me and will of course pardon me. Never, sir, do I utter your name without strong emotion. He who sees nothing but justice and has preferred perhaps to abandon his future, rather than to render an iniquitous judgment, he is someone who must be venerated. And so, as long as I have a breath of life, sir, I will never cease to think of all you have done for me. One day, sir, all this will be repaid to you, not by me but by God.[42]

Furcy's joyful expressions suggest that the two men had indeed reunited in Paris after seventeen years, through their mutual patron, Le Gonidec. If so,

Furcy would have heard of Boucher's woes in Corsica and the loss of his position there, as well as his new conflicts in Poitiers. The meeting would have been a tender reunion for both men.

The August 1835 hearing before the Court of Cassation in Paris had merely affirmed that Furcy's appeal could proceed. The rest of Furcy's letter describes his ongoing efforts to gather the necessary supporting evidence for his appeal to the Civil Chamber of the Court of Cassation. He writes:

> Since my arrival in Mauritius, I have done everything to procure for myself the documents necessary for my case from Isle Bourbon. I have been made many promises, but no one has kept them. I was obliged to send my nephew to search for them.[43]

Furcy's nephew was Eugène who at 29 was Constance's eldest surviving son. Her census returns, filed in February 1836 and February 1837, listed Eugène as "absent from the colony," perhaps in Mauritius, helping to deliver information he had gathered in Isle Bourbon to his uncle.[44]

According to Furcy, Eugène had "leafed through the registers, and those where my birth certificate should have been were missing several pages."[45] Although the absence of court decisions in December 1817 or February 1818 is not surprising, as these probably never took place, Furcy's claim that the pages recording his baptism are missing is odd, since these are clearly visible on microfilm today. However, in the 1780s, the slaves' parish registers were kept separately from those for whites and free people of color. Perhaps someone showed Eugène the wrong one.

Believing that he might have better luck himself, Furcy told Boucher that he "had decided to go myself to make a trip to [Isle] Bourbon, but before I left, I wrote a letter to the governor of Bourbon to ask for protection against those who could or would bother me, but quite the opposite [was the result]; my desires were frustrated."[46] Furcy included copies of his letter to Cuvillier and the governor's reply, which tersely warned Furcy that that he could not authorize his travel to Isle Bourbon and recommended that he contact the Court of Cassation's attorney general (i.e., Dupin) in Paris.[47] This was a subtle jab at Furcy, intimating that his success in Paris meant little in the colony and chastising him for the trouble he caused to the planter elite. Mail between Mauritius and Paris took months; in telling Furcy to stick to official channels, the governor indicated that he intended to support Joseph Lory's claims of ownership. A free man everywhere but Isle Bourbon, Furcy could not travel to his birthplace for risk of being re-enslaved.

Continuing his letter to Boucher, Furcy wrote that he had sent a copy of the governor's letter to his lawyer in Paris, Godard de Saponay, adding:

> You know, sir, that Monsieur Lorry [*sic*] has sent his power of attorney to Monsieur Richemond des Bassins [i.e., Philippe Desbassayns de Richemont]. You know, sir, that all my evils come from this latter [individual] and that all the judges except one (Monsieur [Bussy de] Saint-Romain) were relatives of Monsieur Lory. How can I, poor wretch, obtain justice from such judges?[48]

Nevertheless, Furcy now had strong backers in Paris who wanted to see his case succeed. And at 66 years old, Joseph Lory's stamina was beginning to fail. While he continued to tally up his property on the Saint-Benoît sugar plantation, he no longer filed census returns for the Saint-Denis home after 1833, the last year that he declared Furcy as his slave.[49]

Furcy signed his 1836 letter to Boucher with a unique signature. His handwriting—and this time there can be no doubt that it is Furcy's own, as it matches his signature on later documents—suggests basic literacy skills. Furcy must have studied and practiced the signatures made for him on earlier letters and documents by professional scribes, because he replicated the basic sense of the letters, but he had never learned to produce the elegant flourish above the capital "F" that began his name. Instead, Furcy wrote his full name, "Furcy," in one continuous cursive word, then returned the pen to the first letter and set it down again to approximate the fluid scrolling bar above his name. This signature would appear on all future documents that Furcy signed as a free man.

Furcy's sweet shop must have continued to thrive, even during his absence. Less than two weeks after putting his letter in the mail to Boucher, Furcy appeared at a notary office in Port Louis to purchase a piece of land in Mauritius from one Clément Galdemar.[50] The notary evidently demanded a surname, because although Furcy had not previously used one (in Paris he was and would continue to be called "the *sieur* Furcy," much as some people from India use a single public name today), on the notary record he offered the name "Furcy Madeleine," following the customary practice of former slaves in Isle Bourbon and Mauritius to take their mother's first name as a surname.[51] This convention subtly stigmatized the descendants of slaves by excluding them from the patriarchal order, even when they were the children of free white men. Furcy may have accepted the name as honoring the woman who gave him life, a sense of justice, and the foundation for his new quest for freedom under French law.[52] Nevertheless, when it came to his signature, he signed his name simply "Furcy," proud of his self-made freedom. The handwriting is identical to the signature in his recent letter to Boucher; thus we can be certain this is the same man.

The shop that Furcy purchased in the heart of Port Louis was at the corner of the rue de l'Église and the rue des Limites, not far from the opulent theatre, so playgoers might purchase sweets before or after performances.[53] Furcy paid 4,500 piasters cash toward the full purchase prices of 5,500 piasters, or about $127,000, for the two-story building, which included water rights to the recently constructed Bathurst Canal. Three years later, he moved out and resold the property at a profit to the confectionery merchant Jean Daniel Renaud Richard for 7,000 piasters, or about $157,000 in today's currency.[54] Then Furcy Madeleine, "bonbonnier," took the cash from the sale of his business property and, two weeks later, purchased a thirty-acre farm in Moka, Pamplemousses, south of Port Louis, along the main road to the sea, extending to Arsenal Bay. The property included twenty oxen (*bêtes à cornes*) and a bell mounted on the building.[55] In the wake of abolition, Furcy must have hired laborers to work the land, and perhaps rented out residences to the tenant farmer "apprentices." The move elevated Furcy from a bourgeois merchant to a wealthy landowner. His ascent from "slave" to planter had occurred in just a little over a decade.

The paperwork for these transactions gives additional clues into Furcy's life in Mauritius. The deed of sale of the sweet shop to Richard mentions that Furcy was never married and had no underage dependents.[56] His Isle Bourbon children with Virginie (or someone else), born out of wedlock, and now adults were not required to be listed in this document, and there is no indication if they were married or whether they continued to live in Isle Bourbon or—less likely—had followed their father to Mauritius.[57] Clearly Furcy had prospered in the candy business and his investment in property. He was able to purchase his new home outright in cash. Furcy thus enjoyed another valuable form of freedom: freedom from debt.

Constance

IN THE MONTHS FOLLOWING Furcy's purchase of the farm, he received terrible news. His sister, Constance, 54, had died at home on 13 July 1838.[58] Because of the new laws of the July Monarchy, Constance's property would be distributed like that of any other widow at her death, her birth as a slave and her mother's origin as an Indian notwithstanding. To date, neither

Constance's will nor the act distributing her property after her death have been found; perhaps she had not thought to prepare them. In February, prior to her demise, she was living with three of her adult children—Judith (26), Jean Baptiste (23; as the eldest male at home, listed as "planter" [*habitant*]), and Joséphine (20)—and three grandchildren: Judith's children, Arnold (5), and Constance (2), and Josephine's daughter, Amélina (5).[59] The faithful slave Irogine, probably in her fifties, had died on 7 September 1836, replaced by a Malagasy laborer named Sophie (41).[60] Olivette (81), "paralyzed," continued to remain in the household, evidently charitably supported as an invalid by Constance and her children.[61] Furcy had not seen his sister since he was removed from the Saint-Denis prison in 1818. Were it not for her actions in 1817, he would never have achieved the success he enjoyed as a free man in Mauritius. One can imagine his sense of loss over this irreplaceable tie to his youth.

Evidence and Arguments

THE PARIS COURT'S PERMISSION to Furcy to pursue his appeal had come as a blow to Joseph Lory, but the elderly planter was not ready to give up. On 21 February 1837, Lory deposited the small collection of extraordinary documents with the notary Maurice Desrieux, including what were supposedly the two original bills of sale for Madeleine, and their translation into French, helpfully provided by the slave smuggler Jules Mourgue, "sworn interpreter of the English and Spanish languages ... as there is no sworn interpreter of the Portuguese language in Isle Bourbon."[62] If these are forgeries—created by Lory and his circle to secure his original claim to Madeleine's enslavement in India—then they are fairly convincing. As Lory probably surmised, the invention of the appropriately named "Faustino" was indeed nearly impossible to discredit.

Lory's next step was to hire Émile Moreau, a lawyer and member of the royal commission on judicial affairs of the colonies in 1834, to represent him at the Court of Cassation in Paris.[63] Moreau prepared and published a pamphlet, known as a *mémoire*, or factum, summarizing the arguments on Lory's behalf.[64] His argument is interesting. Lory conceded from the outset that Furcy was a free man, but only as a result of English law (*l'autorité anglaise*).[65] Portraying Furcy as a pawn of "enemies of colonial interests," (i.e., the antislavery lobby in Paris), Moreau's *mémoire* for Lory claimed that a ruling on the basis of Indian Freedom would "deprive the residents of [Isle] Bourbon of the property of around six thousand slaves,"[66] an estimate considerably lower than

the figure of 20,000 given by the judge Gillot L'Étang in 1817.[67] While affirming Furcy's freedom in British Mauritius, Moreau's 1838 *mémoire* challenged
each of the arguments advanced on his behalf: that Indians were not subject to
slavery, that Madeleine achieved her freedom when she touched the Free Soil
of France, that the transfer or sale of a slave between Mademoiselle Despense
and the Routier family in Lorient was invalid, and that pre-adolescent children were necessarily freed by a mother's manumission.

While Furcy's appeal had backing within the king's own family, as evidenced by the queen's sponsorship of his voyage in 1835, correspondence
from the late 1830s and early 1840s shows that the minister of the navy,
charged with all colonial affairs, actively supported Lory in his effort to defeat
Furcy in appeal. In May 1838, Lory's lawyer Moreau sent a copy of the factum
to the minister, the admiral Claude Charles Marie du Campe de Rosamel,
who forwarded it to the minister of justice, Félix Barthe, with a letter stating his complete support of Lory's position.[68] The colonial ministry likewise
notified the current governor of Isle Bourbon of the impending appeal and its
support of Lory.[69]

Within nine months of the publication of Moreau's factum for Joseph
Lory, Furcy's lawyer, Godard de Saponay, responded with an opposing factum refuting the slave owner's claims.[70] Godard de Saponay argued that even
if local practices in India permitted the sale into slavery of children "of the
low castes, such as the caste of the Parias, that of the Pouliats, and that of
the Poulichis," French law had never recognized or authorized the transoceanic trade in Indian slaves.[71] Godard de Saponay's second argument, framed
as "No one is a slave in France," and "No sale, exchange or transfer of slaves in
France," was based on Madeleine's residence in France, where she supposedly
lived "for several years," and the royal legislation of 1716 and 1738 prohibiting sale, gifts, or transfer.[72]

Godard de Saponay made new allegations on Furcy's behalf: Madeleine
was never supposed to have been retained as the Routiers' slave; she was supposed to have been returned to India as a free woman:

> In reality, Madeleine, Furcy's mother, had been entrusted by
> Mademoiselle Dispense [*sic*] to Dame Routier, who, from Lorient,
> was leaving for Isle Bourbon to be sent to India, her natal country, and
> not to be retained in slavery. Dame Routier, abusing the confidence of
> Mademoiselle Dispense and the position of the young Indian, retained
> her as a slave in fact.

Are these facts contradicted? No, because the *sieur* Lorry [*sic*], who knew to produce a bill of sale, made in Chandernagor by Faustino Santiago to Mademoiselle Dispense, has in no way produced the deed of gift of Madeleine to Dame Routier; he has never produced it because there never was one.[73]

Furcy's lawyer stopped just short of accusing Lory of forging the original bills of sale, but the implication was clear. The absent contract between Mademoiselle Despense and the Routiers ruptured continuity of title and would have "proved" only the illegal sale or gift in France. The lawyer's larger point—that Mademoiselle Dispense intended for the Routiers to return Madeleine to India as a free person—is, however, overreach. In neither French nor Indian societies of the eighteenth century could a girl of thirteen or fourteen years old have been considered truly autonomous or free. Minors needed to belong to a household; the only way she could be returned to India in "freedom" would have been to restore her to her parents, an impossibility.

A New Freedom

BEFORE THE COURT OF Cassation could rule on Furcy's appeal, Joseph Lory died at his plantation house in Bras Panon on 20 April 1839 at the age of 69.[74] The extensive inventory of his property at the plantations and in Saint-Denis, catalogued over several days, reveals how his slaves' labor and the expansion of commercial culture throughout the French empire had improved Lory's standard of living, but also suggested the beginnings of wear. Officials noted that the spacious two-story home of the Saint-Benoît plantation, entered through "two Italian [doors]" facing east, was nevertheless "in poor condition." Perhaps he died in his office upstairs, containing "a little bed in local wood, furnished with a mattress, two pillows [*oreillers*], . . . and a mosquito netting," as well as two small tables and "a Huet barometer, in good condition." If so, he was within reach of his "library, in local wood, with six shelves" and glass doors, containing dozens of books with titles reflecting his reverence for Napoleon, a wish to imagine the salons of Europe beyond the seas, and letters and memoirs by the French aristocracy. An exterior locked storehouse held the Lorys' wine and liquor collection in bottles and barrels, carefully itemized, and other valuables, worth 1,331 francs (about $6,400).[75] The Lorys' displayed wealth showed how the family had advanced in material terms since the times of Eugénie's grandmother in 1767.

Furcy must have received the news of his adversary's death with unalloyed joy, relief, and triumph. Within months he proposed to a Mauritian woman, Mademoiselle Zulmé Maulgué, of Port Louis, and on 14 October 1839 they contracted marriage before the notary in the home of Zulmé's father.[76] Furcy brought to the marriage the land and house he owned in Moka, as well as the mortgage by which he continued to receive payments for the candy shop he had sold Jean Daniel Richard, worth 4,000 piasters (about $100,000). In addition, Furcy owned another 1,000 piasters ($25,000) in cash, as well as various unspecified belongings, in the notarial formula: "linens, personal effects [*hardes*] and jewelry."[77] Mademoiselle Maulgué likewise brought "linens, personal effects, and jewelry" into the marriage. Furcy joyfully signed his name in large but elegant letters, sprawling "Furcy Ma delaine" (as if pausing to consider whether to add the "g"), across the bottom of the page. His new wife likewise signed her name, evidence of expanding literacy within Mauritius's free community of color.

"The Free Soil of France"

EUGÉNIE LORY AND HER nephews were all named heirs of Joseph. Thus, when the Court of Cassation reached its decision in favor of Furcy in Paris on 6 May 1840, its conclusions affected all of them.[78] The decision contains a host of small errors, especially regarding dates, such as the assertion that Constance was still a slave when Madeleine was freed by her mistress in 1789, only to be subsequently freed by "her father, the *sieur* Weter," or the date of 17 May 1817 for the preliminary decision by Isle Bourbon's Tribunal of First Instance, months before the arrival of Boucher in the colony.[79] It quotes verbatim a supposed decision by the appeals court of Isle Bourbon dated 12 February 1818, thereby fixing it as "fact" into the judicial record, but noting that "it appears that the decision of the Royal Court of Bourbon had not been served to [Furcy]." Likewise, the court accepted Furcy's freedom in Mauritius, "by English laws and authority," as a fact that occurred in 1825 in contradiction to Furcy's letters, which indicate that he was not free until after sometime after December 1826.

More stunning, however, was the rationale for declaring Furcy a free man. The court found that

> although, since the beginning of the establishment of the colonies, several ordinances have prescribed certain formalities for the introduction of slaves in the metropole, it has not destroyed the principle of

freedom of French soil; they are limited to regulating the application thereof.[80]

In other words, the Court of Cassation determined—in full disregard of the eighteenth-century legislation in effect when Madeleine arrived in France— that the "ancient maxim of French public law" of Free Soil freed the slaves whose masters did not properly register them in France. By this rationale, the justices of the July Monarchy Court of Cassation ignored Article 4 of the king's Declaration of 15 December 1738, which said:

> Negro slaves of either sex who are brought to France by their master . . . will not be able to claim to have acquired their freedom, and will be required to return to our colonies, when their masters judge appropriate. But if the masters fail to observe the requisite formalities [i.e., obtaining permission from colonial administrators, paying a deposit, registering them upon arrival and at their ultimate place of residence] . . . the slaves will be confiscated at Our [the king's] profit, to be returned to Our colonies, and employed there in the labors that We command.[81]

In retrospect, it is clear that Mademoiselle Despense, despite ignoring the requirement to register Madeleine, was clearly trying to comply with at least one part of the royal law when she arrived with Madeleine in 1772 by arranging for her return to the colonies. The justices of the Court of Cassation held in 1840, however, that this clause of the king's law could not take precedence over France's "ancient" Free Soil tradition.[82]

The Court of Cassation reasoned that because Mademoiselle Despense had neglected to register Madeleine upon her arrival in Lorient in "1768" (another error), she thereby became free and that consequently "the children to whom she has since given birth [*donné le jour*] were born in a state of liberty and freedom [*ingénuité*]." [83] Thus the court set aside the other arguments advanced by Godard de Saponay—that Indians were not subject to slavery and that prepubescent children were automatically included in the manumission of their mothers—to conclude:

> For these reasons, and without needing to rule on the other justifications, the Court breaks and annuls the said decision rendered by the Royal Court of Bourbon on 12 February 1818 . . . and . . . returns the parties to the same status that they held before the said decision, [and]

returns the case and the parties before the Royal Court of Paris, there to be decided and legally ruled upon in this way.[84]

It fined Joseph Lory 180 francs and 5 centimes, a little less than $1,000 in today's money, plus costs.

The Court of Cassation's decision was a mixed bag. It established that Furcy was freeborn, which was certainly a triumph for him. It also elevated, in the name of "public law," the Free Soil principle over the royal statutory law of the Old Regime, thereby papering over the inconsistencies between positive law of the Old Regime and the more recent enactment of Free Soil legislation in 1836. On the other hand, the damages awarded against the Lory family were a mere slap on the wrist. The decision also required that the case be further reviewed by the Royal Court of Bourbon and France's highest court of appeal, the Royal Court of Paris, thus extending Furcy's engagement with the legal system and delaying an ultimate ruling on his condition.

Furcy's appeal did not really further an antislavery agenda in France. Even if his elite allies in Paris had supported his litigation to call attention to the need for formal Free Soil legislation, the resultant 1836 ordinance freed only the handful of individuals—no more than a hundred—who traveled with their masters to the metropole annually.[85] Like the statute, the court's 1840 decision reaffirmed France's two distinct legal regimes: the civil code for France and the slave code for the colonies. In this way, the state's support of the Free Soil principle actually helped to stabilize the colonial slave legal system. However, there is no question that Furcy's appeal to Paris had taken him quite literally into a new realm. Having met some of France's most powerful men in the great capital, he had become a man of the world.

Damages and Interest

FURCY HAD RETURNED TO Paris sometime in 1840, probably in anticipation of attending the hearings of the Court of Cassation, but arrived
only after the court reached its decision on May 6. However, he could not
remain in Europe long. As his lawyer, Godard de Saponay, explained in a
letter that Furcy received in Paris, the courts allowed him only one year to
collect the additional documentation necessary to support his appeal to the
Royal Court.[1]

While the Court of Cassation's decision had favored Furcy by declaring
him freeborn and overturning the 1818 Bourbon court of appeal's decision
that kept him in slavery, additional legal actions were necessary to render the
ultimate decision on his status and secure financial reparations. Godard de
Saponay instructed Furcy to pursue two parallel legal actions. First, the lawyer
would bring Furcy's appeal before the Royal Court of Paris to get a final judgment on his freedom suit. Meanwhile, Furcy had to return to Isle Bourbon to
seek reversal of the original Saint-Denis Tribunal judgment of 17 December
1817 in order to sue Joseph Lory's heirs for damages. To assist Furcy in pursuing both these claims, Godard prepared a list of the documents that Furcy
needed to procure in Isle Bourbon:

1. An official copy of the judgment of first instance of the tribunal of Saint-
   Denis of 17 December 1817.
2. You must request Monsieur Auguste Brunet to search to discover the
   succession of Monsieur Petitpas and to search to recover in the papers of
   his practice the dossier that concerned your complaint against the *sieur*
   Lory. In this dossier must be found, firstly, the original of the complaint
   of 22 November 1817; secondly, the writ given at your request to the *sieur*
   Lory.
3. The conclusions rendered at first instance and on appeal.[2]

These documents are precisely those that are missing in the original archival collections of Isle Bourbon's judicial records to this day. Yet, as Godard
de Saponay explained, "We need these documents to present to the Royal

Court of Paris the conclusions relative to the damages and interest that are due to you. Otherwise, we could only resume the case from the point of view of the question of your status." In other words, Furcy would likely be found free, but without compensation. While preparing the groundwork for these two legal appeals, Furcy was also to approach the widow Lory and the other heirs, explaining that he preferred to settle for damages out of court, in order to avoid "the annoying red tape [*tracasseries*] and the embarrassments of a lawsuit."[3]

In addition to the money that Furcy might be able to extract from the Lory clan, Godard de Saponay's letter gives another hint as to why the legally "freeborn" Furcy would want to pursue his appeal further under French law:

I learned with the greatest astonishment that the authorities of Mauritius had refused to process your civil marriage under the pretext that you did not supply your birth certificate.[4]

Here is yet another insight into Furcy's understanding of freedom: the right to marry the woman he chose. Godard de Saponay assured Furcy that the government's objections were groundless:

The [Napoleonic] Civil Code was promulgated in Isle de France and the principles must still be active there. Articles 70 and 71 indicate that lack of a birth certificate can be rectified by the production of an act of public knowledge [*notoriété*]. However, this act of public knowledge could not be forbidden to you even if the *sieur* Joseph Lory claimed you as his slave. It was impossible not to recognize that, finding yourself in Mauritius since 1818 or 1819, you were subject to the influence of the Bill of Emancipation emanating from the English government. As a consequence, in the eyes of current English law in Mauritius, you are free, and the civil authority cannot refuse to support your civil marriage. You would have the right to start proceedings before the tribunals for being constrained.[5]

Was Furcy heartened by his lawyer's words or exhausted? But what else could be done? He decided to follow the lawyer's advice "to proceed with this celebration [of marriage] so as not to leave any doubt regarding the status of your children."[6]

Who were the children that Furcy's lawyer referenced? They were not Virginie's two daughters in Isle Bourbon. Records show that Furcy had sired two additional daughters with Zulmée Maulgué before the couple married, Marie Euridice Madeleine and Louise Furcy Madeleine.[7] Godard de Saponay's letter makes it clear that these two were born before 1840, and subsequent documentation clarifies that they were born out of wedlock and later legitimated.[8] The fates of his earlier children born on Isle Bourbon have not yet come to light.

Furcy had become a rather wealthy man by the age of 55. Upon his return to Mauritius he purchased more property in 1841, this time from a Mademoiselle Barry, who sold him a large farm of about 33 acres (39–40 *arpents*) of her plantation in Moka, known as Les Pailles ("The Straws") for 6,500 piasters in cash (about $150,000 in today's money).[9] It is not clear whether the farm was in active production or primarily an investment property. Because slavery was abolished, we have no record of who worked the land, but it is likely that Furcy hired local laborers—probably those descendants of slaves already resident on the property—to maintain it. He seems to have continued to run his candy business in Port Louis as well.[10]

One month after the purchase of his new farm, Furcy returned to the same notary and completed a power of attorney authorizing the Isle Bourbon lawyer Pierre Gabriel Toussaint de Quièvrecourt to pursue "the recovery, by all means and avenues of law, for a debt or an indemnity due him by the Lory family of Bourbon."[11] The amount requested by Furcy was "at least ten thousand piasters, free and clear of any fees of procedure or otherwise." Furcy was asking for what is in today's money a quarter of a million dollars.

As Furcy pursued his legal struggle, he lost his longtime ally. Louis Gilbert Boucher died after "a long and painful illness" in Poitiers on 5 March 1841.[12] At his funeral, a colleague eulogized Boucher's life and career, noting that his fervent commitment to standing up to injustices had made for a challenging life and career. The stress from this lifetime ultimately "ruined his health." "But," added the eulogist, "what we could appreciate were the qualities of his heart. Misunderstood on this point, this man, who was said to have a hardness almost to the point of cruelty, was instead sensitive to the point of feebleness."[13] The person who retained the largest dossier of documents relevant to Furcy's pursuit of freedom did not live to see his case presented to the Royal Court of Paris.

Sugar Barons of Isle Bourbon

FOLLOWING GODARD DE SAPONAY's instructions, Furcy pursued his freedom suit in Paris against the heirs of Joseph Lory, now wealthy planters and entrepreneurs in the sugar industry.[14] Eugénie Lory, Joseph's widow, 67 in 1840, continued to live in her elegant Saint-Denis townhouse on the profits produced by her 260 slaves on her deceased husband's two sugar plantations in Bras Panon and Saint-Benoît.[15] Slaves had been directed to build one of the rare slave chapels on the island there, a sign, perhaps, of her devotion.[16]

The 1840 Isle Bourbon census began to require masters to supply specific descriptions of the skin color and hair texture of their slaves as well as their familial relations as "a means by which all the changes that will occur in this population may be followed and controlled."[17] The terms of physical description in the subsequent censuses are similar to those utilized in Mauritius after the colony came under British rule. Those descended primarily from mainland Africans were designated black (*noir*), while those descended from Malagasy ancestors were labeled "reddish" (*rougeâtre*). People born of mixed European and African heritage were "mulattoes" (*mulâtres*), a term rarely found in previous Isle Bourbon censuses.

The widow Eugénie Lory's 1840s return, completed on her behalf by her brother Augustin Routier, suggests that Joseph Lory may have been survived by children and grandchildren after all, but that these were enslaved, never recognized or legitimated by their father, and thus ineligible to inherit property. Pauline, a mulatto woman with long, curly hair, was born into the Lory household of an unnamed mother and father around 1812. By the age of 28, she had created a family with Alexis, a mulatto man from "Malaya" (*malais*—which might mean anywhere in the southeastern Asian archipelago or peninsular mainland), with straight black hair, the domestic slave of the youngest of the Lory nephews, Charles.[18] Pauline and Alexis's children—Frédérick (11), Eugène (10), Fanny (1), Victor Alexis (6 months)—following the condition of their mother, belonged to Eugénie Lory.[19] Likewise, the Malagasy woman Olympe's daughter, Nancy, born around 1820, had an unnamed white father. By 1840 Nancy (19), had two children with Baptiste, a mulatto man: Cécile (4), and Modeste (1 ½).[20] The census's unusual attention to the ages of these children, given in months as well as years, hints that Eugénie paid careful attention to their births, perhaps because they were the surviving grandchildren of her late husband.

Eugénie's sister-in-law, Jeanne Malvezy, the widow of André Lory, 65, a woman of independent means (*rentière*), lived close to Eugénie in one of the two houses that she owned on the rue du Barachois in Saint-Denis.[21] She was surrounded by many of the former slaves who had accompanied her or her sons from Mauritius, now all listed as free people, as well as five enslaved laborers.[22] Long accustomed to managing her own affairs, she completed and signed her own census return.

The sugar revolution, which concentrated larger and larger pieces of land in the hands of a few families, had made sugar barons of Joseph Lory's nephews, Adolphe, Thomy, Arthur, Edouard, Henry, and Charles, each of whom now owned plantations or worked in affiliate businesses.[23] Within months of Joseph Lory's death, his nephews had joined other associates to form the Society of Agriculture, with a mission to "propagate the principles of rural economy applicable to the soil and to the climate of the colony," a collection of the island's wealthiest and most powerful men.[24] All but the youngest nephew, Charles Lory, owned homes in the capital, Saint-Denis. It was from these well-connected Isle Bourbon colonists that Furcy sought a definitive ruling on his freedom from the Royal Court of Paris, as well as damages for the years that he had suffered as their slave.

Royal Court of Paris, 1843

ON 8 SEPTEMBER 1841, Furcy's lawyers subpoenaed the heirs of Joseph Lory to appear before the Royal Court of Paris. Two years would pass before the high court heard the case.[25] In the meantime, the antislavery movement in Paris, never as robust or widespread as that of the English-speaking world, had all but disbanded. Although a French delegation had attended the first World Anti-Slavery Convention in London in 1840, efforts to reciprocate by hosting the meeting in Paris in 1842 met with governmental interference.[26] The French legislative commission on slavery and the colonies—composed of half a dozen abolitionists, ranging from gradualists to "immediatists," equally balanced by pro-slavery interests, including representatives from colonies, port cities, and the royal administration—increasingly distanced itself from general emancipation at any speed. The net effect of this committee was, in the words of the historian Lawrence Jennings, "stalemate and regression," followed by "crisis and further setbacks."[27] Frustrated with this lack of progress, Cyrille Bissette continued to work outside government channels, often depending on funding through British abolitionists and going into personal debt for the cause. As Bissette's star was falling, a new abolitionist, Victor Schœlcher, began to champion French antislavery.[28] However, despite their shared cause, the two men became bitter political rivals.

On 8 December 1843, the new naval minister, Albin Roussin, contacted the minister of justice to lobby for a particular decision on Furcy's appeal. Noting that the Royal Court of Paris would soon rule on Furcy's freedom, but also the award of damages and interest for the period that he was held in slavery, he insisted that the grounds of the decision must be framed carefully lest they lead to disastrous consequences. Of the three legal questions that would be addressed by the court (the first two being whether Madeleine had been freed by Free Soil and whether Furcy had achieved freedom as the underage child with his mother's manumission), the third, he argued, was the most volatile:

> [Furcy's] right to liberty by birth as the son of an Indian mother ... if it would be affirmed [by the court], would cause incalculable disturbances in the status of the population of Isle Bourbon. Not only do a fairly large number of slaves from India still remain in the colony, but one would see lawsuits for liberty proliferate on behalf of all the individual slaves who could justify that they belong by descent to the same race.[29]

Just as royal policy was beginning to inscribe slaves in phenotypical and familial terms in the Isle Bourbon census, making it potentially possible to trace descent in racial categories, the minister in charge of colonies found it essential to block freedom on the basis of Indian descent. Although the naval minister framed the problem of declaring all Indians free in practical terms that the minister of justice could appreciate, he was no doubt mindful of the nightmare awaiting his colonial staff in certifying slaves' ancestry in the incomplete colonial records, not to mention the cost in reparations (for masters, but also potentially, the government) that would inevitably follow from a decision on the basis of Indian Freedom.

The Royal Court of Paris began hearings the next day in France's Palace of Justice.[30] Neither Furcy nor the heirs of Joseph Lory were present. Furcy was represented by a new lawyer, Nicolas Marie Edouard Thureau, of bourgeois origins and lifelong friend of the Duke of Chartres, son of the king of France. At 35, Thureau was "no longer an unknown"[31] and would be celebrated at his funeral as an "open and cultivated spirit" and an "erudite legal expert."[32]

Thureau's factum for Furcy is florid at times, punctuated by more than the usual number of exclamation points, as in this passage, summarizing his opening remarks:

> What I have just invoked in [Furcy's] name are the most sacred principles of natural law, the most ancient and glorious maxims of our national law, the regulations inscribed in our colonial legislation and

by religion and humanity! Should I add, Messieurs, that the man whose rights I defend is well worthy of your sympathies? This unfortunate, who should have been free, has passed more than half of his life in slavery: he was a slave for forty years! and the day when he dared to claim his liberty, he was thrown in prison to groan for an entire year![33]

The duration of Furcy's enslavement was the central question for any ruling on the amount of damages and interest owed. Thureau's rhetorical estimate—forty years a slave—was no exaggeration if Furcy's *de jure* freedom was to be dated from his birth in 1786 to his *de facto* freedom following successful negotiations with the Lory's under British authority in 1826.

Yet, mindful of the current political climate, the lawyer Thureau distanced both himself and his client from any whiff of abolitionism: "I have not come here to protest against slavery; it exists as a fact, even as a legal fact."[34] Instead, he carefully detailed the events of Madeleine's and Furcy's lives and five grounds (*moyens*) for Furcy's freedom: his birth to an Indian mother, Madeleine's arrival on France's free soil, Mademoiselle Despense's failure to complete the necessary formalities by registering Madeleine as her slave, the illegal bequest (*donation*) to Madame Routier, and—if none of these arguments were sufficient—the principle, supposedly implied in the Code Noir, that "the family must not be separated."[35]

Thureau's 1843 factum quoted for the first time the theoretical 17 October 1817 decision of the Saint-Denis Tribunal of First Instance.[36] That "decision" held that since Madame Routier had listed Madeleine on census returns for sixteen years, Madeleine only became free at the time of her manumission, in 1789. Moreover, Decaen's provision that children under seven would be freed along with their mothers clearly overturned prior colonial "common law," by which children and mothers were often freed independently of one another. On this basis, the Saint-Denis court had supposedly found Furcy's original lawsuit, actioned on his behalf by the patron Petitpas, "inadmissible" (*non-recevable*)."[37]

Where did the text of this decision come from? Furcy's lawyers needed such a ruling because it was the procedural foundation for his claim to damages and interest, which explains why Thureau included it in his appeal, but its source and author remain unknown. The probably fabricated document concluded with this important, if formulaic, passage:

Having considered everything, the Tribunal of First Instance, judging in the first instance, without deciding on the petition of Petitpas,

patron named on behalf of Furcy, holding that Lory be required to go
before the [colonial] administrators to obtain at his own cost a manumission for Furcy, and other demands, ends, and conclusions, declares
the demands, ends, and conclusions [of Petitpas] . . . inadmissible.[38]

These unspecified "demands, ends, and conclusions" would be the foundation for Furcy's civil suit for cash compensation—reparation—for his years
as a slave.

Thureau addressed finally why a free man like Furcy pursued his appeal to
the furthest ends in 1843:

> There is for [Furcy] and his children an immense interest to erase the
> stain imprinted on his birth. His emancipation [by English authori-
> ties] conferred upon him only a *freedom in fact*, but not the privileges
> that are the prerogative of a liberty in law [*liberté de droit*]. He has been
> refused until now any participation in the rights of free men [*hommes
> libres*], of the same ceremonies of marriage and the same burial. He
> therefore has a moral and a social interest to make fall all of these barri-
> ers and to make known and proclaim his natural freedom [*ingénuité*].[39]

While Furcy might enjoy many of the implicit rights of freedom—the ability to earn money and keep the wages he earned, the capacity to travel freely
between English and French territories without fear of arrest—he was denied
the right to establish legally recognized family ties, the foundation for the
passage of property to the next generation, something that the law explicitly
denied to slaves. Furcy was suing to become free in the ways that French patriarchy constructed freedom: to be a father, the head of a household, and the
founder of a dynasty.

On 16 December 1843, the lawyer for the widow Lory and his heirs,
Alphonse Gabriel Victor Paillet, presented his arguments to the court.[40]
Drawing heavily from the text that the lawyer Moreau had prepared for the
Court of Cassation hearings in 1840, Paillet argued against the proposition
that Madeleine's arrival in France in 1772 was sufficient to warrant Furcy's
freedom. Paillet pointed out that the medieval legislation cited as a foundation for the Free Soil principle concerned serfs, not colonial slaves.[41] The
Lorys, he insisted, should not be required to furnish proof of the registration
of Madeleine upon her 1772 arrival in Lorient, since these events occurred
more than fifty years earlier.[42] Moreover, according to Paillet, by the 1738
law then in effect, even if Despense had neglected to register Madeleine, the

explicit penalty was confiscation by the king and return to the colonies for labor or resale, not freedom by France's Free Soil.[43]

Paillet provided a devastating critique of the Free Indian argument, beginning with the fact that the Court of Cassation had not incorporated this justification into its ruling. Paillet insisted that the 1739 royal order prohibiting the enslavement of Indians and Caribs applied solely to the indigenous peoples of the West Indies; slavery in the East Indies, by contrast, was "an ancient and incontestable fact."[44] Drawing upon the detailed reports furnished by British Orientalist scholars in their expanding eastern empire, Paillet noted that Indian slavery was fed by children born out of wedlock, prisoners of war, debt bondage, and those who sold themselves or their children into slavery.[45] Paillet likewise dismissed the argument that Furcy was implicitly freed along with his mother in 1789, since that argument had been "abandoned by Furcy before the Court of Cassation," probably because there was no positive law providing explicitly for this provision prior to 1805.[46]

Paillet then introduced a lengthy new debate on the question of financial compensation for Furcy in the form of damages.[47] Furcy was demanding 80,000 francs (over $400,000 in today's money) on the grounds that he was held in slavery for 44 years (from his birth in 1786 to 1830). Paillet argued that the Lory heirs could not be held liable for this tort because it went against article 464 of the French Civil Code prohibiting compensation for the period prior to the initial 1817 decision.[48] Since the decisions of the Tribunal of First Instance and the Bourbon Royal Court did not award damages, Furcy could not be entitled to them. Even if, Paillet argued, Furcy were entitled to damages, these should be charged to *all* of Joseph Lory's heirs, not just his widow and nephews. Finally, to receive damages, Furcy would have to prove that Joseph Lory "had knowledge of his legal status as a free man and had, with this knowledge, unduly retained him in slavery."[49]

Paillet completely reframed the story of Furcy's enslavement to Joseph Lory as emanating from Furcy's own desires and actions:

> How can Monsieur Lory's good faith be doubted when he is seen to have acquired Furcy from Monsieur [Augustin] Routier, to whom he was awarded as the result of the division of the inheritance of Madame Routier, and for which he [Lory] paid the price? When Furcy, already close to 25 years old, had only so arrived in his possession, after having belonged to two preceding masters [Marie Charles and Augustin Routier] and after having himself solicited Monsieur Lory to acquire him?[50]

Archival evidence revealing how Lory came to be Furcy's master has never come to light, so it is impossible to know if Paillet was using the occasion to invent Lory's legal claim to property, much as Thureau apparently invented the wording of the 1817 Tribunal of Saint-Denis. Moreover, Paillet claimed, Furcy did not begin to demand his freedom until 1817, after he had willingly and without objection served Lory as a slave for five years. Finally, after Furcy was sent to Mauritius "immediately" (glossing over Furcy's year of imprisonment) after the colonial court decisions, he "obtained his manumission without obstacle on the part of his former master, who did not even include him in the annual census of his slaves."[51] Of course, this last claim was a lie. Unbeknownst to Furcy or any of the Parisian lawyers, Joseph Lory had continued to list Furcy among his slaves in Isle Bourbon until 1833.

A Freeborn Man

"AN UNUSUALLY ABUNDANT" AUDIENCE arrived early on 23 December 1843, pressing at the doors of the Royal Court of Paris to hear the attorney general's concluding remarks and the justices' decision.[52] When the "crowd" (*foule*) had entered and were finally quieted down, Attorney General Michel Hébert opened his remarks.[53]

Michel Hébert, known for his lively oration, began by noting that although Furcy was in fact free (*libre de fait*), he undertook this challenge to be recognized as legally free (*libre de droit*).[54] It was important to establish the exact moment that Furcy became legally free, because

> if, for example, a gift [*donation*] had been made to him, if some successions had been allotted to him or his mother, during the time when they were called slaves but they claimed to be free; if some alliances had been contracted, if he had had children—all things unknown to us . . . obviously [these] would be regulated and modified by the legal status of Furcy or of Madeleine.[55]

The importance of the case, averred Hébert, was its potential impact on others in a similar situation.

According to the attorney general, the question of whether Furcy's mother, Madeleine, was free by virtue of being Indian was "the first and the most important of the case."[56] Accepting Paillet's arguments, Hébert rejected the Indian Freedom argument: slavery had existed in "Hindustan" since ancient times, and Madeleine was incontestably a slave from the time that she was sold to Portuguese traders there.[57] However, he accepted the Free Soil reasoning articulated by André Dupin in the Court of Cassation's 1840 decision.[58] Hébert asked rhetorically, "Is it true to say that this maxim had been unrecognized here? It must be so, gentlemen, because truth demands it and demands especially not to say the opposite: no one challenged this incontestable maxim of our public law."[59] Thus the king's representative to the high court intentionally sided with pre-revolutionary Parisian legal minds who freed scores of slaves up until the Revolution on the basis of Free Soil principle, regardless of the contrary dictates of the 1738 Declaration.

According to Hébert, the sole relevant legal question was whether Madeleine's owner had fulfilled the requirements of the 1716 and 1738 laws in order to retain her legal title to the slave. Hébert pronounced the Court of Cassation's presumption that Despense had neglected the formalities, unless proven otherwise, "dangerous."[60] "It would suffice for a slave to claim [without evidence] that his progenitors, or at least one of them, made a voyage to France a century ago for him to be free."[61] However, in the case of Madeleine, both the registers in Isle Bourbon and Lorient had survived, making it clear that Madeleine was never registered according to the law. Some hapless clerk had been tasked with searching for her name fruitlessly.[62]

With regard to the final question—whether Madame Routier was obliged to manumit Madeleine immediately upon her arrival in Isle Bourbon—Hébert answered decisively, no. Since Despense had not specified a date for the Madeleine's manumission, Madame Routier was free to do as she pleased.[63]

After listening to Hébert's arguments "with a religious attention," the justices of the Royal Court retired to their chamber.[64] After only an hour of deliberation, President Séguier announced their decision: Furcy had been born free (*né libre*).[65]

According to the reporter of the *Gazette des Tribunaux*, the court refused to consider any of the legal questions except the Free Soil argument.[66] In truth, the case for Indian freedom was weak, at least as presented by Furcy's lawyer. The only legal directives he cited that specifically excluded Indians from slavery arose in the American colonies and were directed toward Native Americans.[67] He was apparently unaware of the 1727 East India Company directive barring the exportation of slaves from Chandernagor for Isle Bourbon and Isle de France.[68] Meanwhile, Free Soil was consistent with the July Monarchy's policy and legislation. It was also pragmatic: passenger records carefully recorded the arrivals of all colonial subjects, leaving an unambiguous paper trail of who was eligible for freedom (in contrast to the Indian Freedom argument, which required extensive genealogical documentation that was would not be readily forthcoming in Isle Bourbon's census or parish records). Finally, Free Soil conferred freedom to only a few hundred individuals; it would not undermine colonial slavery on a large scale. Consistent with the July Monarchy's tepid efforts at abolition, this decision freed Furcy, but few others.

The Royal Court of Paris's decision recognized Furcy's freedom on the basis of the enduring condition of French Free Soil:

> Considering that it was a maxim of public law in France that every slave who touched French soil became free; that, if some edicts in force at that time, relative to slavery in the colonies, permitted masters who brought their slaves to France to keep them as property, it was only under the conditions that they fulfill some formalities prescribed by the ordinances;
>
> Considering that there are in the case sufficient presumptions to establish that the girl [*fille*] Dispense [*sic*] did not fulfill these formalities; that, in effect, the girl Dispense had brought Madeleine to France with the intention of raising her in the Catholic religion; that one can nevertheless admit the wish of the girl Dispense to maintain Madeleine in slavery and to fulfill the costly formalities imposed by the regulations such that, a short time after her arrival in France, she made a gift to the dame Routier, charging her to procure her manumission in the colony which she herself could not give in France;
>
> [The Court] denies [Furcy's] appeal [of the Court of Cassation's 1840 decision; i.e., letting its conclusions stand]. Emending, discharges the appellant [Furcy] of the condemnations pronounced against him; and determining on the principle, says that Furcy was born in a state of liberty and of natural freedom [*ingénuité*]; gives act to the respondents [i.e., the Lorys] of the withdrawal [*désistement*] of the appellant in his demand of damages and interest; condemns the respondents to pay the costs of the principal case of appeal and petitions, etc.[69]

Furcy was now incontestably a "freeborn" man. But the Royal Court had not supported Furcy's claim to damages and interest. It would not award him any compensation or reparations for the decades he lived as a slave. For this he would have to return to the colonial courts of Isle Bourbon.

Furcy and the Abolitionists

THE PARISIAN COURT'S DECISION was publicized in the French legal press and traveled swiftly to London. On the same day, the London *Law*

Times ran a summary of the court's ruling in Furcy's case.[70] This account was then picked up and reproduced in the *British and Foreign Anti-Slavery Reporter.*[71] Within weeks, Cyrille Bissette, whose calls for immediate abolition in his journal *Revue des Colonies* had been virtually ignored, inaugurated a new journal, *L'Abolitionniste français*, in January 1844.[72] The very first issue reported on Furcy's victory in the Royal Court of Paris, calling Furcy "one of the celebrities of the island" of Mauritius.[73] Yet word apparently did not reach the United States; there is no mention of it in William Lloyd Garrison's abolitionist newspaper, the *Liberator*, though he regularly borrowed content from the London *Anti-Slavery Reporter*.[74] Only three years later, Dred and Harriet Scott would initiate their freedom suits in the former French settlement of Saint Louis, Missouri, on the grounds of Free Soil.[75] But no evidence has come to light that they or their lawyers had direct knowledge of Furcy's case.[76]

If Furcy's freedom was celebrated within the antislavery circles of London and Paris, can he be considered part of a French abolitionist movement? There is a slight suggestion that Furcy's success stimulated new populist antislavery actions in France. In the immediate aftermath of Furcy's victory, French labor activists began to imitate the English petition drives that had proven so effective in England. [77] In January, immediately following the high court's decision and the inauguration of Bissette's new journal, Parisian and provincial printers circulated France's first antislavery petition calling for immediate emancipation. However, none of these actions achieved serious widespread appeal. The printers' limited petition drive gathered only 8,832 signatures. A second petition drive in 1846–1847 garnered only 12,395 signatures.[78] French antislavery would never match the wide populist movements of England or the United States, which were propelled by both evangelical revivalism and the English trade unions.[79]

Yet even these small efforts prompted a legislative reaction—if not abolitionist momentum—in France. Immediately following the submission of the workers' first petition to the legislature, the minister Mackau introduced a series of bills into the Chamber of Peers that passed in the 1845 session. The Mackau laws, as they became known, clarified the legislative relationship between the metropole and the colonies, introduced ameliorative measures for the maintenance and living conditions of slaves, and encouraged gradual emancipation through self-purchase (*rachat*) and independent savings by slaves (*pécule*). All of these provisions sought to prepare certain slaves for seeking their freedom as individuals but did nothing to advance general emancipation. French and British abolitionists viewed the Mackau laws as a delaying tactic, designed to slow down movement toward general emancipation.[80] In the end, Furcy's role in French abolitionism was modest at best.

Colonial Justice

THE DECISION OF THE Royal Court of Paris was not the last word on Furcy's condition. Despite the high court having denied him damages, Furcy Madeleine (as he appears now in court records) continued to pursue his parallel appeal of the 1817 decision to the Royal Court of Bourbon, asking for damages and interest for the years he was unjustly held in slavery.[81] In this suit, Furcy sued not only Eugénie Lory, represented by the celebrated jurist of Isle Bourbon law Auguste Delabarre de Nanteuil,[82] and her six nephews but all of Joseph Lory's collateral or named heirs, collectively represented through power of attorney by the merchant Pierre Laurent Washington Terrasson.[83] When Furcy's lawyer, Toussaint de Quièvrecourt, approached the heirs directly in January 1845, they offered to pay Furcy one-tenth of what his lawyer was demanding: 5,000 francs (about $24,600) in damages. Furcy declined and pressed ahead with his lawsuit.[84]

The Isle Bourbon Royal Court's lengthy decision, rendered on 30 August 1845, portrays Joseph Lory as the unfortunate victim of Furcy's unreasonable demands.[85] The decision excused Lory's actions as the product of his historical context: "The most irreproachable acts in perfect harmony with the ideas of their time must necessarily lose their features [*physionomie*] and present themselves unfavorably to the critique of another era of which the opinions are completely different." In truth, Lory's actions—his cheating Madeleine out of her pension and his removal of Furcy from his family in Isle Bourbon to Mauritius—were hardly "irreproachable," nor were they uncontested within his own era, not only by visitors from Paris but also by creoles of Isle Bourbon. The judge portrayed Lory as a generous man, who, when the funds specified by Madame Routier in Madeleine's 1789 manumission came due in 1808, "of his own funds, paid Madeleine's alimentary pension . . . as proven by the two notarized quittances."[86] Drawing upon the narrative offered by the Lorys' Paris lawyer, Paillet, the creole justice claimed Furcy begged to be transferred from the rural Saint-Marie plantation to Joseph Lory in Saint-Denis with the final distribution of the widow's estate in 1812:

> Furcy . . . preferred to serve Sieur Joseph Lory and to live in town than to stay in the country with Sieur [Augustin] Routier, to whom he had been distributed in the division of the estate, had pleaded with Sieur

Lory to buy him from . . . Sieur Routier; all of which was executed according to his wishes and with his participation.[87]

A good lie has the ring of truth to it. And based on knowledge of Furcy, it seems plausible that, had Furcy been consigned to remain on Augustin's plantation, he might have approached Lory in 1812, so as to be closer to his mother and the city life of Saint-Denis. If that is so, however, why did Lory declare Furcy the widow Routier's slave in Saint-Denis in 1806 and his own slave on his 1810 census return, two years before the legal distribution of the Routier estate?[88] Furcy was never reported by Augustin as his property in any census return.

According to the 1845 Isle Bourbon Royal Court decision, "Until 1817, Furcy made no claim [to freedom] and considered himself Lory's slave." Joseph Lory's "good faith could only have been fortified by Furcy's claims in 1817, since the claimant for freedom had been declared non-receivable in all its demands." So the argument was that Lory had justifiably believed Furcy to be his slave before and after 1817. And yet here is another curious clue to the judicial chicanery of Furcy's original lawsuit. According to the justices in 1845, the undated decision of the Tribunal of First Instance of Saint-Denis had been "confirmed" by the Royal Court's previous decision of "12 February 1818," even though the latter was not entered into the judicial registers until 29 November 1834, after Furcy was already living as a free man in Mauritius; the late registration of the 1818 decision had been accepted, as the court noted, "without contradictory discussion."[89] The best possible explanation for the belated registration of the supposed 1818 decision in 1834 is that within weeks of the Mauritius Council defining the terms of general emancipation on that island (17 September 1834), Furcy realized that he was finally, uncontestably, legally free. He must have made it clear that he was going to appeal the decision to Paris, and someone in the Isle Bourbon justice system must have realized that they needed a record of the decision supposedly made in 1818.

The 1845 colonial decision contains further inaccuracies. According to the judge, after Furcy traveled to Mauritius in October 1818 thanks to "the generosity of Monsieur Lory," Lory

> preferred no longer to register Furcy in the census as his slave, to let him thereby enjoy a liberty in fact [*de fait*], which was cause for Furcy, once he had made a claim to the English government to obtain his manumission legally and without the least opposition on the part of his masters, which, by the fact of his voluntary release [*dépossession*] and

the state of manumission in which he had placed Furcy in Mauritius since 1818, had beforehand acquiesced and even rendered the said Furcy capable [*apte*] of the emancipation that he had demanded and obtained definitively in 1827 from the English authorities.

Joseph Lory—or, to be fair, his nephews, who had had direct authority over Furcy in Mauritius—now claimed that they did not force him to work at the sugar plantation or in Port Louis, nor did they admit that Edouard had searched the records of the Port Louis Customs House to prove that Furcy was their slave. Moreover, the justices blamed Furcy for not having "sooner petitioned the English government to regularize his condition as a free man by fact, which he enjoyed by the wishes of *sieur* Joseph Lory since his arrival in Isle Maurice in 1818." The court could not hold Joseph Lory responsible for Furcy's "careless or calculated inaction." Furcy was "the sole author [and] must alone suffer the consequences." Toward the end of this colonial apologia, Judge Bédier of the Royal Court of Isle Bourbon went so far as to say that Furcy "in some manner forced *sieur* Lory to buy him [in 1812] and to possess him as a slave."

Despite their exculpatory account of the relationship between Furcy and Lory, the colonial justices were forced to accept both superior courts' determination that Furcy was a freeborn man and entitled to damages. Therefore, Judge Bédier made every effort to minimize the number of years that Furcy was held in slavery. He limited the Lorys' liability from the day that Lory had supposedly purchased him from his brother-in-law Augustin in 1812 until the moment that he was recognized as free by the English government in 1827, at the rate of 300 francs ($1,250) per year for fifteen years of unjust enslavement. In conclusion, the court condemned Eugénie Lory and the other heirs to pay Furcy 5,000 francs (less than $25,000) in damages and interest, plus court costs.

Day of Reckoning

FURCY WAS NOT TOO proud to refuse the money. His lawyer, Toussaint de Quièvecourt, attended a meeting on Furcy's behalf with Maurice Desrieux, the Lorys' preferred notary, to receive payment from Eugénie Lory and the rest of the heirs.[90] Furcy was now a "shopkeeper" (*commerçant*) living in Port Louis, Mauritius; Eugénie was living on her sugar plantation in Saint-Benoît, Isle Bourbon, and was represented that day by her eldest brother, "Charles Routier de Grandval," that is, Augustin. Quièvecourt acknowledged receipt on

Furcy's behalf of the payment in "metal specie [*espèces métalliques*] . . . counted and delivered out of the presence of the undersigned notaries." But there is a surprise tucked away in this receipt. The amount paid by Eugénie, "from her own funds," was 15,000 francs (almost $75,000)—three times the amount awarded by the court. After listening to years of her husband cursing Furcy's resistance, did the widow Eugénie have a crisis of conscience and re-evaluate the debt that she owed Madeleine's son? Furcy's lawyer accepted the cash but reserved Furcy's right to appeal the decision.

The quittance cleared the way for Eugénie Lory to complete the succession of her husband's will. The Lorys' 143-acre plantations were efficiently planted in two crops of sugar, half of which would ripen that year and the rest in "young canes for the following year." Seventeen acres were set aside for manioc and two acres for potatoes to feed the 236 slaves and ten free people living there. The plantation house held a few valuable items—dishes "in gilded porcelain," silverware worth almost $3,800, twelve champagne flutes, four chandeliers gilded with silver, two large wooden sideboards with marble bases to inhibit ants, centipedes, and lizards—but all the furniture was made locally (*en bois du pays*), and several items in the various rooms were noted as "old" or in "very bad condition," as was the house itself. The Lorys' workforce was aging, with many men and women in their forties and fifties, since the slave trade had been effectively suppressed for more than a decade, but some were now married.[91] Altogether, the 236 slaves were evaluated at 322,875 francs (more than $1.5 million), representing more than 60 percent of the rural properties' total value of 535,575 francs ($2.57 million).[92]

Eugénie no longer lived at the plantation but in the two-story Saint-Denis townhouse she had inherited from her mother and grandmother, the place where Furcy had very likely been born. It was fronted by a large stucco porch embedded with stone decorations, at one end of a large urban plot surrounded by a stone wall, the gate through which Furcy had first walked as a free man almost four decades earlier. Eugénie had improved the house's furnishings during her tenure as the home's mistress. Open to light and fresh air by many windows, the house held lavish furniture, including chairs upholstered in red silk, two silver gilded candelabras decorated with flowers, another silver candelabra ornamented with crystals, and many knickknacks. The substantial library of hundreds of books reflected slightly more cosmopolitan taste than the smaller library at the plantation—*Letters to Emily on Mythology*, Madame de Staël's *Corinne*, a French-English dictionary, a French translation of Milton's *Paradise Lost*. In the granary was the "old palanquin" in which Furcy had carried Eugénie to and from her visits with neighbors in Isle Bourbon, and the cause of one of his beatings. Together with the outbuildings, including a kitchen and a laundry, the entire property was evaluated 60,000 francs ($288,000).[93] Strangely, the inventory of the Saint-Denis townhouse did not count the widow's slaves. Of the 29 she and her husband had owned for many years, she now retained a single enslaved family of four creoles: Adèle ("brown" or "black," long hair, 54), her daughter Lucile (mulatto, long hair, 32), and Lucile's two children, Clémence (mulatto, long hair, 13) and Auguste (mulatto, long hair, 5).[94] Lucile, "insane" (folle), would die of unknown causes the following year, after which Eugénie Lory freed her children.[95] What burdens had the mixed-race Lucile borne while waiting for her freedom?

Is it remarkable to consider that Eugénie Lory, after listening to her husband scheming and complaining about Madeleine, Constance, and Furcy for the last three decades of his life, only to be drawn into the lawyers' battle with Furcy, had a last-minute change of heart and tripled the amount awarded to Furcy for damages? Since Joseph Lory's total estate was worth almost $3 million, perhaps Eugénie decided that she could afford to pay Furcy $75,000 for the troubles her husband had caused. Indeed, as she faced her own mortality, did Eugénie begin to regret the life-long treatment of Furcy, the man who was likely her half-brother? When the distribution of Joseph Lory's fortune took place on 21 February 1848, it itemized not only the 15,000 francs Eugénie paid to Furcy plus 1,076.25 francs in interest on the above amount but also 9,048 francs in lawyer's fees, for a total of 25,125.15 francs, about $113,000 today.[96] When the damages paid to Furcy for the years he battled his enslavement are compared to the lawyers' billable hours, the relative compensation hardly seems just.

General Emancipation, 1848

THE DAY AFTER JOSEPH Lory's estate passed to his heirs, Paris rose again in a third revolution, one of a series of contemporaneous European uprisings challenging the remnants of aristocratic rule. In Paris, opponents of the increasingly censorious policies of Louis Philippe and his prime minister, François Pierre Guillaume Guizot, poured into the streets demanding the latter's ouster and fundamental political reforms. Guizot resigned the next day, but when a dozen protesters were fired upon by royal guards, Parisians rebuilt the barricades, set fires, and converged on the royal palace, prompting Louis Philippe to abdicate and flee to London. The revolutionaries abolished the monarchy once again and proclaimed the Second Republic on 26 February 1848.

In the years leading up to the 1848 revolution, Victor Schœlcher had eclipsed Bissette as the most prominent antislavery voice in Paris. Schœlcher was appointed to the provisional revolutionary government in February, and in less than two months the legislature passed Schœlcher's Act for General Emancipation (27 April 1848), mandating the abolition of slavery in each colony within two months of its promulgation. The government then passed a constellation of laws regulating the aftermath of emancipation. Key among these provisions was the accordance of full political and civil rights to former slaves.[97] The law of 30 April 1849 provided for the repayment of slaveholders for their loss of property at rates that varied by colony, including cash and credit, but these payments did not approach market value for the slaves.[98] On 14 April 1851, Joseph Lory's nephews and great-nephews received altogether 150,289.14 francs (about $692,000) for their 215 remaining slaves.[99]

Isle Bourbon became once again, and definitively, Réunion. The former slaves exercised their new rights to become mobile; many left plantations for unsettled small holdings in the volcanic hillsides, despite government regulations trying to fix them in wage labor contracts with their former masters. Plantation owners, desperate for workers, stepped up their efforts to recruit peasants from India, Madagascar, China, and other points within the Indian Ocean basin under contracts of indenture. These men were technically "free" laborers, but they were subject to physical punishment, and few could earn sufficient savings to return home, making their condition very much like that of slaves. They and their descendants remained in Réunion, and also Mauritius, as workers without land.[100] In contrast to the more vigorous political mobilization of former slaves in France's Caribbean colonies, where both Bissette and Schœlcher were elected to represent the colonies in the French legislature, Réunion whites used violence to intimidate former slaves, effectively preventing their registration and voting in significant numbers.[101] These rights were in any case short-lived. With the 1852 coup of Napoleon III, the liberating reforms of 1848 were summarily reversed, even to the point of restoring compulsory labor, if not slave ownership, in the colonies.[102] Many French republicans in the metropole were arrested or, like Schœlcher, fled into exile. Réunion enjoyed another surge in sugar production during the 1850s until the market collapsed in 1860, the result of free trade policies.[103]

By overturning the laws and regulations that upheld slavery, France's 1848 government abolished slavery in Réunion, much as England had in Mauritius fifteen years earlier. If Schœlcher's reforms tried to strike a balance between freedom for workers and compensation for their masters, he, like his peers, believed that former slaves remained separate from French society by their values and culture, attitudes that upheld the denial of equal rights to France's colonial subjects for almost another century.

Schœlcher continued to advocate for education and bourgeois norms, including Christian marriages and patriarchal families, as the hallmarks of freedom for former slaves. By this measure, Constance and Furcy had already become "free" in Réunion and Mauritius well before Furcy received token compensation for his years as a slave. This notion of freedom, however, comes with its own limitations and hierarchies. Furcy became a free man by becoming the father of a middle class family. Through his education and travel he probably came to believe himself superior to the laborers who worked in the sugar fields, at the docks, and on the seas. If he treated his wife and daughters with tenderness, they were not his equals before the law. France would not recognize full political rights for colonial subjects or women until after World War II.

Afterword

REMEMBERING FURCY

WHAT HAPPENED TO FURCY? How did he die? Where are his descendants today?

The answers to these questions have been much more difficult to find than this seasoned historian, with decades of experience hunting and sleuthing, ever would have imagined.

The investigative challenges were numerous: Furcy's contemporaries stole, destroyed, or invented documents to cover their tracks. I was looking in the wrong places. Laws prevented genealogists and historians from accessing key records. Popular culture mythologized Furcy's life and added misunderstandings. And, for more than a century, historians were simply not interested in the lives of slaves.

I hadn't found the ending yet, but I knew that I needed to discover what happened to Furcy. The lingering inequalities generated by European colonialism and slavery, together with the formal and informal racism they engendered, demanded that the complete story of Madeleine and her descendants be told.

IN JANUARY 2015, I traveled to Réunion and Mauritius for a final rummage in the archives, trying to figure out where Furcy had lived out his days after winning his freedom in Paris. In Réunion I met the anthropologist Gilles Gérard, an expert in the history of the island's enslaved families.[1] Gérard had painstakingly traced the births, marriages, and deaths of Constance's children there, including some branches reaching down to the present. He discovered that each of Constance's children had married into white families.[2]

A few days later, we traveled to Champ Borne, a seaside community in the district of Saint-André where Constance had lived out her days, to meet one of her descendants. This man—whom I'll refer to as Monsieur J. to protect his privacy—had heard a little of Furcy's story and agreed to talk with us. Arriving in the neighborhood a little early, we stopped at the seaside ruins of a church and the cemetery that holds some of the oldest graves in Champ

Borne. A massive tsunami had struck in 1962, flooding the graveyard and washing away many of the original tombstones and human remains. Only the largest mausoleums of the most prominent families remained intact. The cemetery struck me as an apt symbol of the permanence of a historical record created by those in power and the vulnerability of the memory of those who history has all too often been allowed to be swept away.

At his home, Monsieur J. showed us a genealogical chart created by a relative who had traced the family roots all the way back to his first French ancestor, a man who had arrived in Isle Bourbon early in the eighteenth century. Though deep, the family tree was incomplete, excluding most maternal branches. The power of patriarchal structures persisted in family lore, recalling the names of French fathers and grandfathers and forgetting the names of selected ancestral mothers, including Constance and Madeleine.

Today, the majority of Monsieur J's neighbors in Champ Borne are the descendants of later immigrants from India, brought to work the fields in the decades since the abolition of slavery in 1848. Some practice Christianity, but many are Muslim or Hindu. Monsieur J. commented that his own family was now the only white one in the area. "Not to be racist," he told us, "but we have never had any troubles with them," his Indian neighbors. The news that at least one of his own ancestors came from India—Madeleine—didn't seem to faze him.

Monsieur J. remembered the original boundaries of his paternal ancestor's land concession, long since reduced through inheritance and sale to a large sugar plantation. He knew of some families with the surname Jean-Baptiste, likely the descendants of one of Constance's sons, but was unaware that they shared ancestry. There are probably dozens of Madeleine's descendants living in Réunion today.

THE SEARCH FOR FURCY'S descendants has been a bit more, as the French say, *compliqué*. It appears that some of Furcy's contemporaries deliberately tried to erase the memory of his struggle from the historical record. Key documents are missing from various archives, suggesting a systematic effort to obliterate this troublesome and persistent man, Furcy, from history. The political crisis brought on by Furcy's initial lawsuit in 1817–1818 may well have prompted some of the less scrupulous participants to try to erase their tracks.[3] Other documents—such as the folder holding Furcy's appeal to the Cour Royale de Paris in 1843—were apparently removed from the Archives Nationales at a later date.[4] Other frustrating lacunae are probably accidental.[5]

I am not the first historian to tell Furcy's story (though scant prior attention has been paid to Madeleine or Constance). After a century and a half of oblivion, Furcy's legal battle first came to light in 1990 when the historian Hubert Gerbeau reported on the 1817 battle between Boucher and Desbassayns in a collection commemorating the bicentennial of the French Revolution.[6] Gerbeau relied upon the original commentary by Desbassayns, thereby unwittingly introducing some misleading details into his account (such as Furcy brandishing the Rights of Man and Citizen), but Gerbeau's discovery had an immediate and powerful impact on popular culture in Réunion. Furcy's courageous resistance inspired artists and scholars to produce a series of plays re-enacting Furcy's courtroom drama for the celebration of the 150th anniversary of the abolition of slavery in 1998–1999.[7] Yet this rendition ended with the initial lawsuit and its preliminary appeal in 1818.

In 2005, a cache of papers held quietly for decades in private hands—the vast majority of which almost certainly belonged to Furcy's champion, Louis Gilbert Boucher—were auctioned off in Paris and became the property of the Departmental Archives of Réunion. This event generated a Wikipedia entry in 2006, which stated, erroneously, that Furcy "died a slave." When I read that statement, I knew that my quest was on. Thanks to the legal memoir published by Furcy's Parisian lawyer that I had discovered in the Bibliothèque Nationale in 1990, I knew that Furcy had not died in slavery. He had ultimately won his freedom in 1843, but I didn't know whether he had lived out his life in Paris, returned to Réunion in time to witness the abolition of slavery there in the Revolution of 1848, or resumed his life in Mauritius, surrounded by his new wife and children.

How to begin searching for such a fine needle in widely strewn haystacks? While many advances in digitizing vital records have occurred over the past decade, most of these collections contain simple photographs of the originals and cannot be searched by keyword. Moreover, the Parisian birth, marriage, and death records from this era were destroyed in the terrible fires of the Paris Commune of 1871.

In 2008 I wrote to the director of the Departmental Archives of Réunion, requesting permission to read the dossiers purchased in 2005—some three hundred handwritten pages on yellowing eighteenth- and nineteenth-century paper. The Archives gave me access as the first historian to read these papers, but the papers did not reveal what had happened to Furcy after his appeal in Paris. Soon thereafter the Parisian journalist Mohammed Aïssaoui was invited to read the archives' dossiers as well. Aïssaoui's novel, *L'Affaire de l'esclave Furcy*, won two literary prizes in 2010 and has profoundly shaped the public's awareness of Furcy in Réunion and more widely in France.[8] The novel prompted the staging of new plays and inspired a popular song by the Réunionnais musician Kaf Malbar in 2014.[9]

The precise date, location, and circumstances of Furcy's death has been perhaps the most difficult truth to recover in this book, at least in part because of Mauritius' unique law that restricts access to historical civil status records. During my 2015 visit, I tried to discover the date and location of Furcy's death and the fates of his children with Zulmé, but the 1981 Civil Status Act restricts the release of vital records (birth, marriage, death certificates) to those who can prove themselves the spouse, direct lineal ascendant, or descendant of the individual in question. People outside the family may request typed extracts of the records from the Mauritius Civil Status Division, but these requests are subject to bureaucratic approval and omit any "extraneous" information that may in fact prove vital to historians, including handwriting. As a result, anyone seeking the history of his or her ancestors in Mauritius must be able to demonstrate a continuous paper trail from the present to the past or accept authorities' decisions regarding the appropriateness of any such request. Needless to say, the law severely restricts the kinds of inquiries performed in this book and limits the recovery of vibrant family histories in the island.[10]

It was only through the kind intercession of others—who have asked not to be named—that I was able at least to fix the place and date of the death of Furcy Madeleine, husband of Zulmée Maulgué, at his home in Pailles, Mauritius, on 12 March 1856. The terse formulaic typescript of the death certificate gives no clues to the circumstances of his passing. I imagine the seventy-year-old man lying in bed, surrounded by Zulmée and his children, feeling proud of his accomplishments and sorry to leave the ones he loved behind. I entrust to future researchers the task of uncovering the fates of his earlier children, born in Isle Bourbon, as well as his descendants in Mauritius.

TODAY ACTIVISTS HAVE CLAIMED Furcy as an important symbol for resistance to the legacies of slavery in Réunion. In October 2014, a local television station reported that an activist collective had designated Furcy as their icon and was spray-painting the Kreyol graffiti "Liber Nout Furcy" (We Free Furcy) on highway overpasses and rocks throughout the island. Among their demands were that a street in the capital city be named for Furcy and that his struggle for freedom be taught in schools. Their efforts have begun to achieve success: in 2015 the Rue de la Compagnie, in the heart of Saint-Denis, was quietly renamed in Kreyol "Lavnu Furcy": Furcy Avenue.

My reconstruction of Furcy's life will probably not satisfy either Réunion's activists or their opponents. Furcy's long struggle for freedom and his eventual success are undeniable, but his efforts to free himself—as near as can be detected in the historical record—were personal, not political. Freedom for Furcy ultimately meant exerting the patriarchal rights of a bourgeois head of household and landowner. Among Furcy's first actions as a free man was the purchase of two slaves. Likewise, Madeleine and Constance's efforts—clearly essential in instilling Furcy's belief in himself as a man entitled to freedom and in fighting the planter judicial bloc—were hardly aimed at improving the status of others beyond their immediate family. Furcy was no abolitionist.

There are others, no doubt, who feel that history's evils, like the nefarious actions of Lory and his allies, are better left forgotten. Why dredge up the master's perfidy and the abuses of government officials like Desbassayns? Why stoke fires of resentment today for events long past?

To these concerns, I recall the words of South Africa's Truth and Reconciliation Commission, which deemed it "necessary to establish the truth in relation to past events as well as the motives for and circumstances in which gross violations of human rights have occurred, and to make the findings known in order to prevent a repetition of such acts in future. . . . There is a need for understanding but not for vengeance, a need for reparation but not for retaliation, a need for *ubuntu* [kindness in shared humanity] but not for victimization."[11] History must seek the truth, however inconvenient or elusive.

In the words of Kaf Malbar's song "Furcy's Gold":

> Let's keep Furcy in our mind
> We all ought to know his story
> We shouldn't let it disappear
> It shouldn't fall into oblivion
> Let's free our Furcy, with gratitude. . . .
> Our children must know our history.[12]

Abbreviations

AD   Archives départementales
ADR   Archives départementales de La Réunion
ANOM   Archives nationales d'outre-mer
ASHDL   Les Amis du Service Historique de la Défense à Lorient
IREL   Instruments de recherches en ligne
NAM   National Archives of Mauritius
NAUK   National Archives of the United Kingdom
SHDL   Service historique de la Défense à Lorient

Notes

NOTE ON CURRENCY, MEASUREMENTS, AND PLACE NAMES

1. Richard B. Allen, "Licentious and Unbridled Proceedings: The Illegal Slave Trade to Mauritius and the Seychelles during the Early Nineteenth Century," *Journal of African History* 42, no. 1 (2001): 103, n. 49, citing *British Parliament Sessional Papers*, 1835 49 (53), 105; Victor Bulmer-Thomas, *The Economic History of the Caribbean since the Napoleonic Wars* (Cambridge, U.K.: Cambridge University Press, 2012), 495; Francis J. Grund, *The Merchant's Assistant, or Mercantile Instructor* (Boston: Hilliard, Gray, 1834), 157.

2. Samuel H. Williamson and Louis P. Cain, "Measuring Slavery in 2011 Dollars," *Measuring Worth*, https://www.measuringworth.com/slavery.php.

3. In hopes of rendering French place names easier to digest for Anglophone readers, I've rendered "Île" or "Ile" as "Isle," which was one of the variant spellings used in both French and English documents of the eighteenth and nineteenth centuries. Isle Bourbon was often rendered "Isle de Bourbon" in the seventeenth and eighteenth centuries, with the article "de" ("of") usually dropped after the Revolution. Many thanks to Nathan Marvin for this suggestion.

INTRODUCTION

1. Jacques Sully Brunet, "A mon Fils" (ANOM, 515Mi1, 190). Sully Brunet was one of the legal minds who helped Furcy craft his original freedom suit, discussed in detail in chapter 7. These words paraphrase the essential arguments he drafted into Furcy's original petition.

2. Historians, playwrights, a novelist, and even a popular songwriter, have recounted the story of Furcy's efforts to free himself from his master. Hubert Gerbeau, "Les libertés de Bourbon: D'une révolution à une autre," in *Révolution française et Océan Indien: prémices, paroxysmes, héritages et déviances: Actes du colloque de Saint-Pierre de la Réunion, octobre 1990*, ed. Claude Wanquet and Benoît Julien (Saint-Denis: Université de la Réunion, 1996), 347–360; Hubert Gerbeau, "L'Esclavage et son ombre: L'île Bourbon aux XIXe et XXe siècles" (doctoral thesis, Université de Provence Aix-Marseille I, 2005), 211–226, 942–948; Jérémy Boutier, "L'ordre public: Sully Brunet et les contradictions de la justice et de la politique dans l'Affaire Furcy (Ile Bourbon, 1817–1818)," *French Colonial History* 15 (2014): 135–163; Gilles Gérard, "L'esclave Furcy, une autre vie, un autre

procès," *L'Harmattan*, 2016 http://www.editions-harmattan.fr/auteurs/article_pop. asp?no=31010&no_artiste=22426.

It was Gerbeau's article that brought Furcy to the attention of a collective of Réunionnais artists, led by the legal scholar Johary Ravaloson and the sculptress Sophie Bazin (under the noms de plume Arius and Mary Batiskaf), who prepared and performed an extraordinary celebration of Furcy's memory in 1998–1999, timed to coincide with the celebration of the 150th anniversary of the 1848 abolition of slavery. Their performance piece, *Liberté plastiK*, included an art installation, a video, and, most importantly, a dozen staged performances of Furcy's lawsuit, scripted in Kreyol and French, brought to life by multiple troupes of "acteurs de circonstance"—local citizens, young and old, from a variety of backgrounds—in several dozen performances around the island of Réunion. The event is beautifully archived in a book and a website, both of which manage to capture in text and photographs the teamwork and the spirit of the event, as well as its historical, philosophical, and legal facets. Arius and Mary Batiskaf, eds., *Liberté plastiK* (Saint-Denis, Réunion: Grand Océan-Dodo vole, 2000). See also the website: http://batiskaf.blogspot. com/2007/09/libert-plastik.html.

In 2008, the Parisian journalist Mohammed Aïssaoui rendered Furcy's life history in a lively novel, based on original research in a large collection of nineteenth-century manuscripts recently purchased by the Archives Départementales de la Réunion, as *L'Affaire de l'esclave Furcy* (Paris: Gallimard, 2009), which won the Prix Renaudot and the Prix RFO in 2010. Patrick Le Mauff and Hassane Kassi Kouyaté adapted a play from Aïssaoui's novel, which was performed by Kouyaté in Paris in 2012 and Réunion in 2013; see the website for the performance, http://www.letarmac.fr/la-saison/archives/p_s-l-affaire-de-l-esclave-furcy/spectacle-31/ http://www.temoignages.re/culture/culture-et-identite/ l-affaire-de-l-esclave-furcy,65446. In October 2014, at the suggestion of Gilles Dégras, the Réunionnais musician Kaf Malbar released a song, "L'Or de Furcy," which has become an anthem of a Kreyol movement for dignity for the descendants of enslaved people. An animated film is in the works; see the articles "Tiktak Production (Réunion): L'affaire Furcy adaptée au grand écran," *Le Mauricien*, 2 June 2014, and "L'esclave Furcy en route pour devenir un film d'animation," *Le Figaro*, 3 March 2015.

3. Edouard Thureau, *Plaidoyer pour le sieur Furcy indien, demeurant à l'île de France, appelant, contre les veuve et héritiers Lory, demeurant à l'île Bourbon, intimés* (Paris: Imprimérie de J. Delalaine, 1844), 4, hereafter Thureau, *Plaidoyer pour le sieur Furcy*.

4. Here and throughout this book I use the term "creole" as it was employed in the eighteenth and nineteenth centuries to mean "born in the colony," rather than as a hybrid language developed at the convergence of two or more migration streams. For a critique of creolization in this latter sense, see Pier M. Larson, *Ocean of Letters: Language and Creolization in an Indian Ocean Diaspora* (Cambridge, U.K.: Cambridge University Press, 2009), 23–24.

5. Robert Bousquet's earlier genealogical study is an important precedent for Réunion, but it does not truly approach biography. Bousquet, *Trois Générations d'Esclaves à Bourbon: La Famille Jacques Lamboutique, 1670–1720* (Saint-Denis, Réunion: Service Educatif des Archives Départementales de la Réunion, 1993).

6. The French abolished slavery twice, first in 1794 as a result of the Saint-Domingue slave revolt during the French and Haitian Revolutions and again, after Napoleon restored slavery in 1802, during the Revolution of 1848. Marcel Dorigny, ed., *Les*

abolitions de l'esclavage: De L. F. Sonthonax à V. Schœlcher, 1793, 1794, 1848; Actes du colloque international tenu à l'Université de Paris VIII les 3, 4, et 5 février 1994 (Saint-Denis, Réunion: Presses universitaires de Vincennes, 1995); Lawrence C. Jennings, *French Reaction to British Slave Emancipation* (Baton Rouge: Louisiana State University Press, 1988); Lawrence C. Jennings, *French Anti-Slavery: The Movement for the Abolition of Slavery in France, 1802–1848* (Cambridge, U.K.: Cambridge University Press, 2000); Nelly Schmidt, *Abolitionnistes de l'esclavage et réformateurs des colonies, 1820–1851: Analyse et documents* (Paris: Karthala, 2000); Seymour Drescher, *Abolition: A History of Slavery and Antislavery* (Cambridge, U.K.: Cambridge University Press, 2009); Sue Peabody, "France's Two Emancipations in Comparative Context," in *Abolitions as a Global Experiment*, ed. Hideaki Suzuki (Singapore: National University Press of Singapore), 25–49.

7. Stories of Frenchmen captured by Barbary pirates and sold into slavery in North Africa were popular in the seventeenth and eighteenth centuries; Gillian Weiss, *Captives and Corsairs: France and Slavery in the Early Modern Mediterranean* (Stanford, CA: Stanford University Press, 2011); see, for example, Pierre-Raymond de Brisson, *Histoire du naufrage et de la captivité de monsieur de Brisson . . . en 1785*, ed. Attilio Gaudio (Paris: Nouv. éd. latines, 1984).

8. The scholarship is vast. An entry point is John Ernest, ed., *The Oxford Handbook of the African American Slave Narrative* (New York: Oxford University Press, 2014).

9. Some recent essays begin to look at individuals enslaved in the Muslim and Indian Ocean worlds. Indrani Chatterjee considers a rare autobiographical account of a Muslim slave held in Afghanistan in the eighteenth century in comparison with American slave narratives in her extraordinary essay "A Slave's Quest for Selfhood in Eighteenth-Century Hindustan," *Indian Economic Social History Review* 37 (2000): 53–86. Richard B. Allen explores the life of Marie Rozette in "Marie Rozette and Her World: Class, Ethnicity, Gender, and Race in Late Eighteenth- and Early Nineteenth-Century Mauritius," *Journal of Social History* 45, no. 2 (2011): 345–365. Edward Alpers notes that the earliest published captivity/freedom narrative for an East African slave dates from 1865; see "The Other Middle Passage: The African Slave Trade in the Indian Ocean," in *Many Middle Passages: Forced Migration and the Making of the Modern World*, ed. Emma Christopher, Cassandra Pybus, and Marcus Rediker (Berkeley: University of California, 2007), 21–22. On silences in the historical documentation of the experiences of enslaved people, see Sudel Fuma, ed., *Mémoire orale et esclavage dans les îles du Sud-Ouest de l'océan Indien: Silences, oublis, reconnaissance* (Saint-Denis, Réunion: Université de la Réunion, 2005).

10. On French Protestant salvation narratives, see Carolyn Lougee Chappell, "'The Pains I Took to Save My/His Family': Escape Accounts by a Huguenot Mother and Daughter after the Revocation of the Edict of Nantes," *French Historical Studies* 22, no, 1 (1999): 1–65.

11. Jean Fouchard, *Les marrons du syllabaire: Quelques aspects du problème de l'instruction et de l'éducation des esclaves et affranchis de Saint-Domingue* (Port-au-Prince, Haiti: H. Deschamps, 1953); Frédéric Régent, Gilda Gonfier, and Bruno Maillard, *Libres et sans fers, les esclaves racontés par eux-mêmes* (Paris: Fayard: 2015), Dominique Rogers, *Voix d'esclaves, Antilles, Guyane et Louisiane françaises, XVIIIe–XIXe siècles* (Paris: Karthala, 2015).

12. Christopher L. Miller, *The French Atlantic Triangle: Literature and Culture of the Slave Trade* (Durham, NC: Duke University Press, 2008).

13. [Claire de Durfort, duchesse de Duras], *Ourika* (Paris: De l'Imprimerie royal, 1823), became an immediate bestseller in Europe; Joan DeJean and Margaret Waller, "Introduction," in *Ourika: An English Translation*, trans. John Fowles, Texts and Translations 3 (New York: Modern Language Association of America, 1994), vii–ix.

14. Sue Peabody, "Window, Prism, Mirror: *Ourika* in the History Classroom," in *Approaches to Teaching Duras's Ourika*, ed. Mary Ellen Birkett and Christopher Rivers, Approaches to Teaching World Literature 107 (New York: Modern Language Association of America, 2009), 123.

15. Through these fictional works, they performed a kind of "ventriloquism." Wendy Dasler Johnson, *Antebellum American Women's Poetry: A Rhetoric of Sentiment* (Carbondale: Southern Illinois University Press, 2016), 51–75.

16. Work discussing the specificity of Indian Ocean slavery include James Warren, *The Sulu Zone, 1768–1898: The Dynamics of External Trade, Slavery, Ethnicity in the Transformation of a Southeast Asian Maritime State* (Singapore: Singapore University Press, 1981); Anthony Reid, ed., *Slavery, Bondage and Dependency in Southeast Asia* (New York: St. Martin's, 1983); Gwyn Campbell, ed., *The Structure of Slavery in Indian Ocean Africa and Asia* (London: Frank Cass, 2004), 1–15; Gwyn Campbell, ed., *Abolition and Its Aftermath in Indian Ocean Africa and Asia* (London: Routledge, 2005); Edward Alpers, Gwyn Campbell, and Michael Salmon, eds., *Slavery and Resistance in Africa and Asia* (London: Routledge, 2005); Shihan de Silva Jayasuriya, *African Identity in Asia: Cultural Effects of Forced Migration* (Princeton, NJ: Markus Wiener, 2009); Clare Anderson, *Subaltern Lives: Biographies of Colonialism in the Indian Ocean World, 1790–1920* (Cambridge, U.K.: Cambridge University Press, 2012); Richard Allen, "Slaves, Convicts, Abolitionism and the Global Origins of the Post-Emancipation Indentured Labor System," *Slavery and Abolition* 35, no. 2 (2014): 328–348; and Matthew S. Hopper, *Slaves of One Master: Globalization and Slavery in Arabia in the Age of Empire* (New Haven, CT: Yale University Press, 2015).

17. Ann Laura Stoler's highly influential work *Carnal Knowledge and Imperial Power* (Berkeley: University of California Press, 2002) is based in Dutch culture of the nineteenth and twentieth centuries. The Dutch case is interesting because it embodies, from the seventeenth century, the modern structure of colonialism organized around private joint stock companies and a flourishing middle class in Europe. France's colonial social fabric at the outset in the seventeenth century, by contrast, mirrored the feudal divide between aristocrats and peasants at home. French middle-class consumer culture only really began to flourish from the early nineteenth century; bourgeois gender relations and the widening gulf between public and private spheres likewise began to emerge somewhat later in France's slave colonies. These transitions, while not a dominant theme in this book, can be seen in the lives of Furcy's owners and, indeed, in his own life as an adult. For a nuanced analysis of family, gender, and the production of race in France's eighteenth-century Atlantic world, see Jennifer Palmer, *Intimate Bonds: Family and Slavery in the French Atlantic* (Philadelphia: University of Pennsylvania Press, 2016).

18. Orlando Patterson, *Slavery and Social Death: A Comparative Study* (Cambridge, MA: Harvard University Press, 1982), 2–3.

19. Orlando Patterson, "The Unholy Trinity: Freedom, Slavery and the American Constitution," *Social Research* 54, no. 3 (Autumn 1987): 556–557.

20. Igor Kopytoff and Suzanne Miers, "African 'Slavery' as an Institution of Marginality," in *Slavery in Africa: Historical and Anthropological Perspectives*, ed. Igor Kopytoff and Suzanne Miers (Madison: University of Wisconsin Press, 1977), 17.

21. Furcy, Port Louis, Isle Maurice, letter to Boucher, place unknown, 15 May 1826 (ADR 1Jp2007-1, no. 71).

22. The complexity of race in the Indian Ocean world as compared to the tripartite system (white, mixed, black) that developed in the French Caribbean and other parts of the Atlantic world is explored in these works: Edward A. Alpers, "Becoming 'Mozambique': Diaspora and Identity in Mauritius," in *History, Memory and Identity*, ed. Vijayalakshmi Teelock and Edward A. Alpers (Port-Louis, Mauritius: Nelson Mandela Centre for African Culture and University of Mauritius, 2001), 117–155, and "Mozambique and 'Mozambiques': Slave Trade and Diaspora on a Global Scale," in *Slave Routes and Oral Tradition in Southeastern Africa*, ed. Benigna Zimba, Edward A. Alpers, and Allen Isaacman (Maputo, Mozambique: Filsom Entertainment, 2005), 39–61; Pier M. Larson, *History & Memory in the Age of Enslavement: Becoming Merina in Highland Madagascar, 1770–1822* (Portsmouth, NH: Heinemann, 2000), and, more recently, Shihan de Silva Jayasuriya, *African Identity in Asia: Cultural Effects of Forced Migration* (Princeton, NJ: Markus Wiener, 2009); Megan Vaughan, *Creating the Creole Island: Slavery in Eighteenth-Century Mauritius* (Durham, NC: Duke University Press, 2005); Adrian Carton, *Mixed Race and Modernity in Colonial India: Changing Concepts of Hybridity across Empires*, Intersections 5 (New York: Routledge, 2012); Myriam Paris, "La page blanche. Genre, esclavage et métissage dans la construction de la trame coloniale (La Réunion, XVIIIe–XIXe siècle)," in "(Ré)articulation des rapports sociaux de sexe, classe et 'race,'" ed. Jules Falquet, Emmanuelle Lada, and Aude Rabaud, special issue, *Cahiers du CEDREF* 14 (2006): 31–51, available online at https://cedref.revues.org/459; Amitava Chowdhury, "Narratives of Home: Diaspora Formations Among the Indian Indentured Labourers," in *Between Dispersion and Belonging: Global Approaches to Diaspora in Practice*, ed. Amitava Chowdhury and Donald H. Akenson (McGill-Queen's University Press, 2016), 240–253.

23. Brett Rushforth shows how French policy in North America and the Caribbean colonies came to formally exempt indigenous people there from slavery, which contributed to the intensification of the association between African blackness and slavery in the French Atlantic, in *Bonds of Alliance: Indigenous and Atlantic Slaveries in New France* (Chapel Hill: University of North Carolina Press for the Omohundro Institute of Early American History and Culture, 2012), 73–75.

24. Categories of racial intermixture, such as mulatto (*mûlatre*) and quadroon (*quarteron*), persisted in French and American thinking and law into the nineteenth century, especially in Louisiana, with French, Spanish, and American legal traditions. Paul Schor, "Mobilising for Pure Prestige? Challenging Federal Census Ethnic Categories in the USA (1850–1940)," *International Social Science Journal* 57, no. 183 (March 2005): 89–101.

25. Article 59, *Le Code noir ou Recueil de Reglemens rendus jusqu'à présent: Concernant [. . .] les Negres dans les Colonies Françoises*, Paris, Chez Prault, 1788 (Reproduction, Basse-Terre & Fort-de-France, Sociétés d'histoire de la Guadeloupe et de la Martinique, 1980), 57.

26. Two junior scholars researching these dynamics are: Melanie Lamotte, "Before Race Mattered: Ethnic Prejudice in the French Empire, c. 1635–1767," (Ph.D. diss, Cambridge

University, 2016), and Nathan Marvin, "Mixed Bloodlines: Family, Race, and Revolution in the French Indian Ocean" (Ph.D. diss., Johns Hopkins University [forthcoming]).

27. Thureau, *Plaidoyer pour le sieur Furcy*.

28. My first book ended with the French Revolution; to do justice to Furcy's story required research into the history of French slave law through the emancipation of 1848. Sue Peabody, *"There Are No Slaves in France": The Political Culture of Race and Slavery in the Ancien Régime* (New York: Oxford University Press, 1996); Pierre H. Boulle and Sue Peabody, *Le droit des Noirs en France au temps de l'esclavage: Textes choisis et commentés*, Autrement Mêmes (Paris: L'Harmattan, 2014).

Some of the fine new slave biographies already under research in 2007 include: Annette Gordon-Reed, *The Hemings of Monticello: An American Family* (New York: W. W. Norton, 2008); Clifton Crais and Pamela Scully, *Sara Baartman and the Hottentot Venus: A Ghost Story and a Biography* (Princeton, NJ: Princeton University Press, 2009); Lea VanderVelde, *Mrs. Dred Scott: A Life on Slavery's Frontier* (New York: Oxford University Press, 2009); James H. Sweet. *Domingos Alvares, African Healing, and the Intellectual History of the Atlantic World* (Chapel Hill: University of North Carolina Press, 2011); Rebecca J. Scott and Jean M. Hébrard, *Freedom Papers: An Atlantic Odyssey in the Age of Emancipation* (Cambridge, MA: Harvard University Press, 2012); Sydney Nathans, *To Free a Family: The Journey of Mary Walker* (Cambridge, MA: Harvard University Press, 2013); Martha S. Jones, "The Case of *Jean Baptiste, un Créole de Saint-Domingue*: Narrating Slavery, Freedom, and the Haitian Revolution in Baltimore City," in *The American South and the Atlantic World*, ed. B. Ward, M. Bone, and W. A. Link (Gainesville: University Press of Florida, 2013), 104–128.

29. Claude Wanquet's studies of French Revolution in Réunion and Mauritius are foundational for recent works on the history of race and slavery in nineteenth-century France and its colonies: *Histoire d'une Révolution: La Réunion 1789–1803*, 3 vols. (Marseille, France: Jeanne Lafitte, 1981), and *La France et la première abolition de l'esclavage, 1794–1802: Le cas des colonies orientales, Ile de France (Maurice) et la Réunion* (Paris: Karthala, 1998). See also Sudel Fuma, *L'abolition de l'esclavage à la Réunion* (Saint-André, Réunion: G.R.A.H.T.E.R., 1998); Rebecca Hartkopf Schloss, *Sweet Liberty: The Final Days of Slavery in Martinique* (Philadelphia: University of Pennsylvania Press, 2009); Jennifer N. Heuer, "The One-Drop Rule in Reverse? Interracial Marriages in Napoleonic and Restoration France," *Law and History Review* 27, no. 3 (2009): 515–548; Gilles Gérard, *Famiy Maron, ou la famille esclave à Bourbon (Île de la Réunion)* (Paris: L'Harmattan, 2012); Prosper Ève, *Le corps des esclaves de l'île Bourbon: Histoire d'une reconquête* (Paris: Presses de l'université Paris-Sorbonne, 2013); Boulle and Peabody, *Le droit des Noirs en France*, chs. 7–9; Robin Mitchell, *Vénus Noire: Black Women, Colonial Fantasies, and the Production of Gender and Race in France, 1804–1848* (University of Georgia Press, forthcoming).

30. Several writers have tackled the life of Toussaint Louverture, the former slave who led the French colony of Saint-Domingue during the Haitian Revolution, but none of these were published during his lifetime. Among the most recent are Pierre Pluchon, *Toussaint Louverture* (Paris: Fayard, 1989); Madison Smartt Bell, *Toussaint Louverture: A Biography* (New York: Pantheon, 2007); Philippe R. Girard, *The Slaves Who Defeated Napoléon: Toussaint Louverture and the Haitian War of Independence* (Huntsville: University of Alabama Press, 2011); Philippe R. Girard, *The Memoir of*

General Toussaint Louverture (New York: Oxford University Press, 2014); and Philippe R. Girard, ed. and trans., *Toussaint Louverture: A Revolutionary Life* (New York: Basic Books, 2016).

31. Furcy's letters are discussed in detail in chapter 8.

32. The 1840 decision of the Cour de Cassation references "Two items of private agreement [*Deux pièces sous seing privé*], written in the presence of witnesses, and of which deposit was made in 1837 to a notary in Isle Bourbon." "Arrêt de la cour de cassation, relative à l'affranchissement de Furcy, né à Bourbon d'une mère indienne," in *Annales maritimes et coloniales, 26 année, 1841*, 2ᶜ série, 1ʳᵉ *partie: partie officielle* (Paris: Imprimerie Royale, 1841), 324.

CHAPTER I

1. Extrait des minutes du greffe de première instance de l'Isle Bourbon, arrondissement du vent, 16 February 1837, in Joseph Lory, Deposit of Items (Dépôt des Pièces), Notariat Desrieux (ADR 3 E 678, no. 41). Jules Mourgue had purchased slaves smuggled into Isle Bourbon aboard the *Succès* in 1820, "Tableau de 220 Nègres & Negresses de la Cargaison du Brick le Succès de Nantes. . .," and two with the same title: "Compte de vente et net produit de la cargaison du brick Le Succès . . ." (NAUK CO 167/92). Mourgue would later be incarcerated in Mauritius for his traffic in slaves in Madagascar. Great Britain, Foreign Office, *British and Foreign State Papers*, vol. 12, *1824–1825* (London: HMSO, 1846), 324–326.

2. *Bicha* is a French transliteration of the Bengali word *bachaa*, meaning infant, child, or small or young girl. Today, it is a derogative word in Portuguese slang for a gay man.

3. A rupee was worth about 28–42 French sous in 1759 (about $11–$17 today); Joly de Fleury, de la Roue, et Collet, *Mémoire signifié pour le nommé Francisque, Indien de Nation, Néophyte dans l'Église Romaine, Intimé; contre le sieur Allain-François-Xavier-Ignace Brignon, se disant Ecuyer, Appelant* (Paris: P. G. Simon, Imprimeur du Parlement, 1759), 3.

4. This receipt would place Madeleine's birth in 1755, a few years earlier than any of the subsequent accounts, which state that her birth occurred in 1759. See note 7.

5. A rupee minted in Arcot, the capital of the Carnatic region of India, near the British fort at Madras, and worth a little bit less than the rupee sicca. Alfred Martineau, *Dupleix et l'Inde française, 1722–1741* (Paris: Champion, 1920), 407.

6. The original Portuguese is difficult to decipher; this is Mourgue's translation. He offers the gloss "young Indian girl" on the term *bicha*. Extrait des minutes du greffe de première instance de l'Isle Bourbon, arrondissement du vent, 16 February 1837, in the pieces deposited by Joseph Lory, Notariat Desrieux (ADR 3 E 678, no. 41). Nineteenth-century documentation spells her name "Dispense," but all evidence from the eighteenth century uses "Despense" or, rarely, "Despence"; I use "Despense" for consistency throughout.

7. All accounts of Madeleine's life state that she was born in or near Chandernagor in the 1750s, and the most consistent suggest that this occurred in 1759. Several census records in the 1780s suggest that Madeleine was born around 1754, but such estimates were probably made without seeking any confirmation; Census, Isle Bourbon, Sainte-Marie, Messieurs Routiers, père et fils, 1780 and Les sieurs Routiers, 1784 (ADR 71 C). Her manumission papers in 1789 give her age as thirty (ADR 1Jp2007-1, 39), hence born in 1759.

Both sides in Furcy's legal case accepted 1759 as the year of Madeleine's birth: Godart Desaponay [sic], *Mémoire pour le sieur Furcy, homme de couleur libre, demeurant à Saint-Denis, Isle Bourbon, et maintenant à Maurice, contre, Le sieur Lorry, propriétaire et habitant de l'Isle Bourbon* (Paris: Casimir, Imprimeur de la Cour Royale, n.d.) (ADR 1Jp2007-2, no. 275), 5; *Annales maritimes et coloniales, 29ᵉ Année, 1844, 3ᵉ série, partie non officielle, tome III: Revue Coloniale* (Paris: Imprimerie Royale, 1844), 53, and *Gazette des tribunaux*, 21 December 1843, 1; Thureau, *Plaidoyer pour le sieur Furcy*, 3.

8. The name recalls Saint Mary Magdalene (*Sainte Marie-Madeleine*), venerated since the seventeenth century as an icon of repentance. In the eighteenth century, she came to be represented as a "fallen woman," a prostitute who nevertheless was redeemed through her relationship with Jesus and lauded as the first to witness his resurrection. Simone de Reyff, *Sainte-Amante de Dieu: Anthologie des poèmes héroïques du XVIIe siècle français consacrés à la Madeleine* (Fribourg, Switzerland: Éditions Universitaires, 1989), 5–22. This tradition has been repudiated more recently by the Catholic Church and by scholars. Katherine Rondou, "Echos de la Madeleine, figure évangelique, dans la litérature contemporaine," *Rivista di Storia e Letteratura Religiosa* 41, no. 2 (August 2005): 413–432.

   "Madeleine," alone or in composite form (Marie-Madeleine, Françoise-Madeleine), was among the most common first names in eighteenth-century France and its colonies. It was not a sign of stigma or sin but a symbol of the capacity for Christian redemption. Along with Marie, Anne, Louise, and Marguerite, Madeleine was the among the most common first name names for girls of all classes in eighteenth-century Quebec. Geneviève Ribordy, *Les prénoms de nos ancêtres: Étude d'histoire sociale* (Quebec: Éditions de Septentrion, 1995), 159–160. The common expression "pleurer comme une Madeleine" ("to cry like a Madeleine") recalled her mourning at the foot of the cross at Calvary.

9. G. Ugo Nwokeji and David Eltis have organized a database project whereby the names of Africans transported across the Atlantic can be searched, but the records are far from complete. African Origins, http://www.african-origins.org/.

10. Philippe Panon Desbassayns, "Organisation Judiciaire (1817). Plaintes contre Bussy de Saint-Romain, premier président et Gilbert Boucher," no. 1 (ANOM 3201 COL 22). Panon Desbassayns's report did not include the prior 1762 Sabino de Gomes receipt.

11. Other documents mentioning the sales, all related to the struggle for freedom of Madeleine's son Furcy, are France, *Annales maritimes et coloniales 26ᵉ année, 1841, 2ᶜ série, 1ʳᵉ partie: partie officielle* (Paris: Imprimerie Royale, 1841), 324 and *Annales maritimes et coloniales, 29ᵉ année, 1844, 3ᵉ série, partie non officielle, tome III : Revue Coloniale* (Paris: Imprimerie Royale, 1844), (1844): 4:53, the *Gazette des tribunaux*, 21 December 1843, 1, and Thureau, *Plaidoyer pour le sieur Furcy*, 3. The exact date in 1768 of the Santiago/Despense translation differs slightly in each instance. There is no record of the sale listed in Edmond Gaudart, *Catalogue des manuscrits des anciennes archives françaises*, vol. 3, *Chandernagor et les loges du Bengale, 1730–1815* (Pondichéry: Société de l'histoire de l'Inde française, 1933), which, however, is by no means a complete documentation of all slave transactions in French India.

12. A substantial body of recent literature addresses debt bondage in both the Indian Ocean and Atlantic worlds. Robert W. Harms, Bernard K. Freamon, and David W. Blight, eds., *Indian Ocean Slavery in the Age of Abolition* (New Haven, CT: Yale University Press, 2013); Gwyn Campbell and Alessandro Stanziani, eds., *Bonded*

Labour and Debt in the Indian Ocean World (London: Pickering & Chatto, 2013); Alessandro Stanziani, *Labour, Coercion, and Economic growth in Eurasia, 17th–20th centuries* (London: Brill, 2013); Gwyn Campbell and Elizabeth Elbourne, eds., *Sex, Power, and Slavery* (Athens, OH: Ohio University Press, 2014); Alessandro Stanziani and Gwyn Campbell, eds., *Debt and Slavery in the Mediterranean and Atlantic Worlds* (London: Routledge, 2016).

13. The most comprehensive study of European slave trading in the Indian Ocean to date is Richard B. Allen, *European Slave Trading in the Indian Ocean, 1500–1850*, Indian Ocean Studies (Athens, OH: Ohio University Press, 2014), but it is stronger for areas where the British influence was strongest (especially India and Mauritius); references to child slavery are scattered throughout. Elsewhere Allen focuses specifically on the trade in Indian children, noting that half of the Indian slaves in Mauritius in 1817 were imported there between the ages of six and fifteen. "Children and European Slave Trading in the Indian Ocean During the Eighteenth and Early Nineteenth Centuries," in *Children in Slavery through the Ages*, ed. Gwyn Campbell, Suzanne Miers, and Joseph C. Miller (Athens, OH: Ohio University Press, 2009), 36. On the prevalence of child trafficking in early modern India, see also Dady Rustomji Banaji, *Slavery in British India* (Bombay: D. B. Taraporevala Sons, 1933), 45, 53–63; Amal Kumar Chattopadhyay, *Slavery in the Bengal Presidency, 1772–1843* (London: Golden Eagle, 1977), 36, 46, 80–83; Lionel Caplan, "Power and Status in South Asian Slavery," in *Asian and African Systems of Slavery*, ed. James L. Watson (Berkeley: University of California Press, 1980), 182; Indrani Chatterjee, *Gender, Slavery and the Law in Colonial India* (Delhi: Oxford University Press, 1999), 11–12, 22, 179; Basanta Kumer Basu, "Notes on the Slave Trade in India during the Early Days of John Company," *Muslim Review* 4, no. 4 (1930): 22, 23, 26, 27; Marina Carter, "Indian Slaves in Mauritius (1729–1834)," *Indian Historical Review* 15 (1987/1988): 235–237; Pierre H. Boulle, "Les non-blancs de l'océan Indien en France," reprinted in *Race et esclavage dans la France de l'Ancien Régime* (Paris: Perrin, 2007), 144; Richard B. Allen, "The Constant Demand of the French: The Mascarene Slave Trade and the Worlds of the Indian Ocean and Atlantic during the Eighteenth and Nineteenth Centuries," *Journal of African History* 49 (2008): 44, 47, 54, 55. The transoceanic trade in Indian children was already underway in the late seventeenth century. J. M. Filliot, *La Traite des esclaves vers les Mascareignes au XVIIIe siècle* (Paris: ORSTOM, 1974), 177.

14. William Adam, *The Law and Custom of Slavery in British India in a Series of Letters to Thomas Fowell Buxton, Esq.* (Boston: Weeks, Jordan, 1840); Basu, "Notes on the Slave Trade," 21–34; Banaji, *Slavery in British India*; Chattopadhyay, *Slavery in the Bengal Presidency*; Caplan, "Power and Status," 169–194. Most of the history of slavery in Bengal has focused on the period of British rule, beginning in 1772, using sources generated by the colonial administration, especially from the early nineteenth century as the antislavery movement in the metropole pressured colonial officials to suppress first the slave trade and then slavery itself.

15. Thomas Law, Robert Palk, and E. Lane to Warrant Hastings, 4 August 1774, quoted in Narendranath Ganguly, "A Peep into the Social Life of Bengal in the Eighteenth Century," *Bengal, Past and Present* 69 (1950): 46–50.

16. Chatterjee, *Gender, Slavery and the Law*; Dharma Kumar, "Colonialism, Bondage and Caste in British India," in *Breaking the Chains: Slavery, Bondage, and Emancipation in*

Modern Africa and Asia, ed. Martin A. Klein (Madison: University of Wisconsin Press, 1993), 112–130.

17. For example, from the Brahminical tradition: "*Griha-jata* (the child of a female slave), *Krita* (purchased), *Labdha* (gifted), *Daya-dupagat* (inherited), *Anakal-brita* (taken in time of famine), *Rina-das* (a voluntary slave in payment of a debt), *Judh-prapta* (captured in war), *Ponejita* (won in a wager)" and so on. Basu, "Notes on the Slave Trade," 21, and Banaji, *Slavery in British India*, 209–213, 226–228. On the complexity of terminology for bonded people in India, see especially Gyan Prakash, "Terms of Servitude: The Colonial Discourse on Slavery and Bondage in India," in Klein, *Breaking the Chains*, 131–149.

18. Indrani Chatterjee emphasizes the relatively high-status skilled positions held by slaves in "A Slave's Quest," 64–66.

19. Marina Carter, "Slavery and Unfree Labour in the Indian Ocean," *History Compass* 4, no. 5 (2006): 805; Caplan, "Power and Status," 169–194, esp. 185–186. Although the Portuguese and Dutch empires participated in the Indian Ocean slave trade and utilized slaves in their eastern colonies and factories, plantation slavery for commercial export was not a major factor of these regimes; their use of slaves typically emulated local slavery paradigms.

20. John Thornton, *Africa and Africans in the Making of the Atlantic World, 1400–1800*, 2nd ed. (Cambridge, U.K.: Cambridge University Press, 1998), 118; David Eltis, *The Rise of African Slavery in the Americas* (Cambridge, U.K.: Cambridge University Press, 2000), 116.

21. Carter, "Slavery and Unfree Labour," 804–808.

22. Chatterjee, *Gender, Slavery and the Law*, 179–181; C. R. Boxer, *Race Relations in the Portuguese Colonial Empire, 1415–1825* (Oxford: Clarendon, 1963), 59–62. "An infamous traffic has, it seems, long been carried on in this country by the low Portuguese, and even by several foreign European sea-faring people and traders, in purchasing and collecting native children in a clandestine manner, and exporting them for sale to the French islands, and other parts of India." Lord Cornwallis, Governor-General of Bengal, letter to the Directors of the British East India Company, 2 August 1787, quoted in Chattopadhyay, *Slavery in the Bengal Presidency*, 82.

23. "Two persons in the Mahomedan courts, the Cauzee and Mooftee, share between them, on each occasion, the functions of the judge. The Mooftee attends in order to expound the sacred text; the *Cauzee* is the person who investigates the question of fact, and carries into execution what he receives as the meaning of the law." James Mill, *The History of British India*, vol. 2 (London: Baldwin, Craddock & Joy, 1826), 452.

24. British Board of Revenue Consultations, 17 May 1774, no. 214, Regulation 9, quoted in Chatterjee, *Gender, Slavery and the Law*, 179, and, with additional supporting documents, Ganouly, "A Peep into the Social Life," 46–50.

25. Thomas Law, Robert Palk, E. Lane to Warrant Hastings, 4 August 1774, quoted in Ganouly, "A Peep into the Social Life," 46–50. The Hindustani term *kabāla* means "a deed, writing; a bond, written agreement, contract, a bill of sale." Duncan Forbes, *A Smaller Hindustani and English Dictionary* (London: W. H. Allen, 1892), 214.

26. Chatterjee mentions another example where maternal authority of the sale of slaves is recognized (*Gender, Slavery and the Law*, 108). Jeyaseela Stephen notes that "even in Tamil society mothers or grandmothers enjoyed the sole authority to assign children to slave status"

(private correspondence, 1 May 2014). See also Jeyaseela Stephen, "Sale Deed of a Slave Girl in Pondichéry Drawn on 5 November 1781," *Revue Historique de Pondichery* 19 (1996): 141. Ramya Sreenivasan, "Drudges, Dancing Girls, Concubines: Female Slaves in Rajput Polity, 1500–1800," in *Slavery and South Asian History*, ed. Indrani Chatterjee and Richard M. Eaton (Bloomington: Indiana University Press, 2006), 146; Sumit Guha, "Slavery, Society and the State in Western India, 1700–1800," in Chatterjee and Eaton, *Slavery and South Asian History*, 167–171; Sylvia Vatuk, "Bharattee's Death: Domestic Slave-Women in Nineteenth-Century Madras," in Chatterjee and Eaton, *Slavery and South Asian History*, 215–216; Banaji, *Slavery in British India*, 235–238. Muslim contract law permits both verbal contracts and written contracts, without requiring consent of the mother or grandmother. Wael B. Hallaq, *Sharīʿa: Theory and Practice* (Cambridge, U.K.: Cambridge University Press, 2009), 239–243, 307.

27. Thomas Law, Robert Palk, E. Lane to Warrant Hastings, 4 August 1774, quoted in Ganouly, "A Peep into the Social Life," 47.

28. Thomas Law, Robert Palk, E. Lane to Warrant Hastings, 4 August 1774, quoted in Ganouly, "A Peep into the Social Life," 48.

29. Aniruddha Ray, *The Merchant and the State: The French in India, 1666–1739*, 2 vols. (New Delhi: Munshiram Manoharial, 2004), 1–13. See also Martineau, *Dupleix et l'Inde française*; Pierre Pluchon, *Histoire de la colonisation française*, vol. 1, *Des origines à la Restauration* (Paris: Fayard, 1991); Jean Meyer, Jean Tarrade, Annie Rey-Goldzeiguer, and Jacques Thobie, *Histoire de la France Coloniale: Des origines à 1914*, Histoires (Paris: Armand Colin, 1991).

30. For example, "Poivre, espicerie, est grain chaud & sec, prés du quatriesme degré, & parce il attire & deterge," in Guy de Chauliac and Laurent Joubert, *La grande chirurgie de M. Guy de Chauliac*, traict. 7, doct. 1 ch. 8 (Rouen: David du Petit Val, 1649), 698.

31. A series of former French trading companies attempted to establish regular trade with the Indian Ocean, with a hub in Madagascar, before 1664. Ray, *Merchant and the State*, 7–25. On the founding of the French colony in Madagascar, see especially Pier Martin Larson, "Colonies Lost: God, Hunger, and Conflict in Anosy (Madagascar) to 1674," *Comparative Studies of South Asia, Africa and the Middle East*, 27, no. 2 (2007): 345–366.

32. The original name was Compagnie française pour le commerce des Indes Orientales. Ray, *Merchant and the State*, 26–33. Ray's account of the company's foundation is based largely on Paul Kaepplin, *La Compagnie des Indes Orientales, 1664–1719, et François Martin* (Paris: A. Challamel, 1908). These concessions were modeled on the land-tenure system of metropolitan France, whereby the king ceded parts of his domain to his subjects, though they remained fundamentally property of the crown. Rafe Blaufarb, *The Great Demarcation: The French Revolution and the Invention of Modern Property* (New York: Oxford University Press, 2016), 148–152.

33. Louis XIV, *Déclarations du Roy, L'une portant établissement d'une Compagnie pour le Commerce des Indes Orientales, l'autre, en faveur des officiers de son conseil, & Cours Souveraines interessées en ladite Compagnie, & en celle des Indes Occidentales, … 1 Septembre 1664* (Paris: Imprimeurs ordinaires du Roy, 1664).

34. Carton, *Mixed Race and Modernity*, 64.

35. These were, in chronological order: Surat (1666), Tellichéry (Thalassery, 1669), Masulipatam (1669, renewed 1686), Saint-Thomé (briefly, 1673–1674), Pondichéry

(1674), Kaveripattanam (near Tranquebar, 1688), and Chandernagor (1690). Dating of the establishment of the Company's Indian factories is surprisingly difficult because Company employees sometimes traded for several years before they received official permission from local rulers (the *farman* from the Mughal emperor, which formalized the terms of trade and taxation, or a *parwana*, permission from the local authority). For consistency, I have selected the date of the *farman* or other permission authorizing each factory. Ray, *Merchant and the State*, 1:43, 48, 52, 98, 104–107, 216, 270, 296.

36. Ray, *Merchant and the State*, 1:282–309. The original town of Borokishenpur, capital of Boropargana, is also spelled Borokishanpur, or "Boroquichempour" in French. There is some disagreement as to the root of the name Chandernagor, which might take as its root *chandra* (moon) or *chandan* (sandalwood). Subhayu Cattopadhyay, "French Factory in Chandernagore: Facets of Overseas Trade, Urbanisation and Globalisation," in *Trade and Globalisation: Europeans, Americans, and Indians in the Bay of Bengal, 1511–1819*, ed. S. Jeyaseela Stephen (Jaipur, India: Rawat, 2003), 274. For a comparative history of two towns, see Rila Mukherjee, "Competing Spatial Networks: Kasimbazar and Chandernagore in Overland and Indian Ocean Worlds," in *Trade, Circulation, and Flow in the Indian Ocean World*, ed. Michael Pearson, Palgrave Series in Indian Ocean World Studies (London: Palgrave Macmillan, 2015), 129–51.

37. Om Prakash, *European Commercial Enterprise in Pre-colonial India*, New Cambridge History of India 2.5 (New York: Cambridge University Press, 1998), 211, 337.

38. George Bryan Souza, "The French Connection: Indian Cottons and Their Early Modern Technology," in *How India Clothed the World: The World of South Asian Textiles, 1500–1850*, ed. Giorgio Riello, Tirthankar Roy, Om Prakash, and Kaoru Sugihara, Global Economic History 4 (Leiden: Brill, 2009), 347–364; Céline Cousquer, *Nantes, une capitale française des indiennes au XVIIIe siècle* (Paris: Coiffard, 2003), 31–32, 44–45.

39. Cattopadhyay, "French Factory in Chandernagore," 273–291, esp. 277, 285. There is some debate about whether Chandernagor was essentially involved in silk manufacture and trade; see Mukherjee, "Comparative Study of the Many Networks."

40. The most comprehensive early studies are: Henry Weber, *La Compagnie française des Indes, 1604–1875* (Paris: A. Rousseau, 1904), and Martineau, *Dupleix et l'Inde française*, neither of which make any mention of the Indian Ocean slave trade. Philippe Haudrère, *La Compagnie française des Indes au XVIIIe siècle, 1719–1795*, 4 vols. (Paris: Librairie d'Inde Éditeur, 1989), pays more attention to the role of slavery in the Company trade (1:125; 2:556–557, 3:909–916). The renewed Company founded Mahé (1721), Yanaon/Yanon (on the Orissa coast, 1731), and Karikal (1739). Ray, *Merchant and the State*, 2:655, 782–791.

41. This was under the governorship of Dupleix (1731–1741). Jacques Weber, "L'Inde française de la compagnie de Colbert à la cession des comptoirs," *Mondes et cultures* 56 (1996): 236. The cowries were to be used in the West African slave trade. See Aniruddha Ray, "Structure and Problems of the French Trade in Bengal, 1719–1727," in Stephen, *Trade and Globalisation*, 248–272, esp. 250–253.

42. P. K. Chatterji, "The French in Bengal in the Generation after the Treaty of Paris (1763)," in *Les relations historiques et culturelles entre la France et l'Inde, XVIIe–XXe siècles / Historical and Cultural Relations Between France and India, XVIIth–XXth Centuries: Actes de la Conférence Internationale France-Inde de L'Association Historique de l'Océan Indien,*

Saint-Denis de la Réunion, 21–28 juillet 1986 (Sainte-Clotilde, Réunion: AHIOI, 1987), 1:371–373.

43. The fort was built between 1691 and 1697. S. C. Hill, *Three Frenchmen in Bengal: The Commercial Ruin of the French Settlements in 1757* (London: Longmans, Green, 1903), 13–14.

44. Wilbert Harold Dalgliesh, *The Companie of the Indies in the Days of Dupleix* (Easton, PA: Chemical Publishing, 1933), 155–160; Hill, *Three Frenchmen in Bengal*, 12.

45. Census, Chandernagor, 1756 (ANOM DPPC G1/481, fol. 100). Sushil Chaudhury, "The Imperatives of the Empire: Private Trade, Sub-Imperialism and the British Attack on Chandernagore, March 1757," *Studies in History* 8, no. 1 (1992): 1–12.

46. The most famous is Dupleix's wife, Johanna Begum, who is the subject of an extensive biography: Yvonne Robert Gaebele, *Créole et grande dame: Johanna Bégum, Marquise Dupleix, 1706–1756* (Pondichéry: Imprimérie Moderne, 1934). For the British case, see William Dalrymple, *White Mughals: Love and Betrayal in Eighteenth-Century India* (London: Harper Collins, 2002), and his essay "Assimilation and Transculturation in Eighteenth-Century India: A Response to Pankaj Mishra," *Common Knowledge*, 11, no. 3 (Fall 2005): 445–485.

47. Carton, *Mixed Race and Modernity*, 74.

48. The Chandernagor census gives the place of origin of "Anne Despense de la Loge" as Ligny-le-Châtel in the "Diocese of Langres." I presume that her parents were François Dispense de la Loge and his wife, Reine Matthieu. The Despense de la Loge lineage is discussed in *Bulletin de la Société archéologique de Sens* 9 (1846): 121, 150–153, 189–190. The digitized baptismal registers for Ligny-le- Châtel (Yonne, Conseil Général, État Civil, BMS 1724–1742 [5 Mi 521/3]) contain over six hundred pages, with about three or four entries per page, so I have not yet found her original baptism record. They are available online at the website of the Yonne archives, http://www.yonne-archives.fr/Archives-en-ligne/Fonds-numerises. By 1755, she appeared in notarial records as a *fille majeure*, an unmarried woman over the age of twenty-five legally capable of transacting business on her own. "Delivrée une expedition a Ma^{de}. Du Bocage," Notariat, Chandernagor, 7 January 1756 (ANOM O25). On the age of majority, see Sarah Hanley, "Engendering the State: Family Formation and State-Building in Early Modern France," *French Historical Studies* 16, no. 1 (Spring 1989): 9.

49. "Delivrée une expedition a Ma^{de}. Du Bocage," Notariat, Chandernagor, 7 January 1756 (ANOM O25).

50. Armament No. 46, *Le Silhouette*, Archives de la Compagnie des Indes, Lorient, 2P 38-II.1; photos provided in private correspondence by Jean-Michel André, Les Amis du Service Historique de la Défense à Lorient, 15 December 2015.

51. Dupleix to Hardincourt, 7 January 1739 (BNAFF 8981, fol. 60), or Dupleix to his brother, 10 January 1739 (NAF 9337, fol. 86), quoted in Dalgliesh, *Companie of the Indies*, 162.

52. "Delivrée une expedition a Ma^{de}. Du Bocage," Notariat, Chandernagor, 7 January 1756 (ANOM O25).

53. The chapel of Saint-Louis within the fort was staffed by priests and almoners who traveled to India at company expense, but Sunday services were reputedly poorly attended. A second, more popular church, run by the Jesuits, served the Catholics of the "black" town of Chandernagor; these included "native Christians"—local converts to Catholicism

through missions since the beginning of Portuguese colonization. Carton, *Mixed Race and Modernity*, 67.

54. *Annales maritimes et coloniales, 26ᵉ année, 1841,* 2ᶜ série, *1ʳᵉ partie: partie officielle* (Paris: Imprimerie Royale, 1841), 324.

55. "In his evidence before the Law Commission, Monsieur Cheap, the Magistrate of Mymensingh stated that children of both sexes were frequently brought from [Sylhet, Dacca, or Mymensingh] by Roman Catholics and Protestants, especially by the Portuguese and Greeks. They bought young children and brought them up, not as slaves, but as menials in their own creed," *Report of Law Commissioners and Evidence on Slavery in the East Indies*, 1:50–55, quoted in Chattopadhyay, *Slavery in the Bengal Presidency*, 50–51. For an extensive history of Christian conversion in the southeastern Tamil region, see S. Jeyaseela Stephen, *Caste, Catholic Christianity, and the Language of Conversion: Social Change and Cultural Translation in Tamil Country, 1519–1774* (Delhi: Kalpaz, 2008), and Chattopadhyay, *Slavery in the Bengal Presidency*, 34–46. However, this was not always the case. In 1791, a generation after Madeleine joined the household of Mademoiselle Despense, twenty-four slaves, ages four to seventeen, were "rescued" by a British magistrate from a ship owned by an Indian but sailing under French colors from Bengal to Pondichéry. Though most had originated in Bengal under masters with European names, only a few of these slaves had Christian names like "Mary," "Anthony," or "Hannah." Most bore names like Jannu, Jayah, Mirhan, Aunchi, or Jaggoo, suggesting that they had not been baptized. In general, Protestant slaveholders were less likely to seek the baptism of their slaves before the Methodist and Baptist movements of the late eighteenth and early nineteenth centuries; see Chattopadhyay, *Slavery in the Bengal Presidency*, 88–96.

56. Kumar, "Colonialism, Bondage and Caste," 113–115; Chattopadhyay, *Slavery in the Bengal Presidency*, 35–36. André Béteille, *Caste, Class and Power: Changing Patterns of Stratification in a Tanjour Village* (Berkeley: University of California Press, 1965), 46, on the basis of a community study of Sripuram in southern India, argues that castes, while they existed before the British period, were less important until then than subcastes (*jati* or *kulam*), which were somewhat flexible and varied from locality to locality, according to changing economic and social conditions.

57. "The Hindu slaves had thus to be divided into two classes, the pure and the impure. The Kāyasthas, Goālās, Chāsās, Vaidyas, Rājputs and Kshastriyas were the slaves of pure caste, while the Sûdras, Tānti, Hāri, Dome, Bāgdi, Kaibarta, Kewat, Barai, Nāpit, Rangri, Pān, Maity, Jele, Kāhār, Lat, Chandāl, Kumors, and Muchis were the slaves of impure castes." Chattopadhyay, *Slavery in the Bengal Presidency*, 35.

58. "Inde. Chandernagor. État Civil. Tables décennales de la Paroisse. St. Louis, 1690–1830," microfilm (ANOM 1 DPPC 5292), and "Actes d'état civil, 1690–1776," microfilm (ANOM 1 DPPC 4379).

59. Chaudhury, "Imperatives of the Empire," 9–10.

60. J. S. Stavorinus, *Voyages to the East Indies*, 3 vols. (London: G G. and J. Robinson, 1789), 1:531.

61. Carton, *Mixed Race and Modernity*, 50–51.

62. Amartya Sen, *Poverty and Famines: An Essay on Entitlement and Deprivation* (Oxford: Oxford University Press, 1982); David Arnold, *Famine: Social Crisis and Historical Change* (New York: Basil Blackwell, 1988); Jean Drèze and Amartya Kumar

Sen, *Hunger and Public Action* (Oxford: Clarendon, 1989); Urmita Roy, "Famine and Dearth in Late Eighteenth-Century Bengal," *Bengal: Past and Present* 112, nos. 1/ 2 (1993): 55–67; R. Datta, "Crises and Survival: Ecology, Subsistence and Coping in Eighteenth-Century Bengal," *Calcutta Historical Journal* 18, no. 1 (1996): 1–34.

63. Steven L. Kaplan, *The Famine Plot Persuasion in Eighteenth-Century France,* Transactions of the American Philosophical Society 72.3 (Philadelphia: American Philosophical Society, 1982), esp. 53–57. Kaplan emphasizes the social interpretation of the periodic dearths of 1725–1726, 1738–1741, 1747, 1751–1752, 1765–1770, and 1771–1775.

64. Datta, "Crises and Survival," 1–34.

65. Subhajyoti Ray, *Transformations on the Bengal Frontier: Jalpaiguri, 1765–1948* (Abingdon, U.K.: Routledge, 2002), 113–114.

66. Datta, "Crises and Survival," 13–14. Scarcity around Pondichéry in 1728 and 1729 drove unskilled laborers and artisans alike to French recruiters, who transported them as early settlers to the Mascarene colonies, Isle de France and Isle Bourbon. Marie-Claude Buxtorf, "Colonie, comptoirs et compagnie: Bourbon et l'Inde française, 1720–1767," in *Les relations historiques et culturelles*, 2:167.

67. Roy, "Famine and Dearth," 56–57.

68. Datta, "Crises and Survival," 5. I've simplified Datta's more complex analysis somewhat. According to Romesh Chunder Dutt, in 1760 "a fearful famine swept away a third of the population of Bengal and about a third of the cultivated area of land relapsed into jungle." *The Peasantry of Bengal* (Calcutta: Thacker, Spink, 1874), 196. This is the only reference I've found to an especially severe famine in 1760 (I suspect he confuses it with that of 1770), but Ralph W. Nicholas notes, "There was a severe financial crisis between 1757 and 1760; many zamindārs refused or were unable to pay their revenues to the treasury in Murshidabad. . . . In the period between 1760 and 1770, the zamindārs of Bengal were progressively impoverished. . . . It is probable that the zamindārs increased their revenue demands on the villagers in every way possible during this period." *Fruits of Worship: Practical Religion in Bengal* (New Delhi: Chronicle, 2003), 122. See also Martineau, *Dupleix et l'Inde française*, 418–419.

69. S. Jeyaseela Stephen, "The Slaves of the Tamil Coast," paper presented at Asia Research Center/MCRI/Indian Ocean World Center Conference on the Dimensions of the Indian Ocean World Past: Sources and Opportunities for Interdisciplinary Work in Indian Ocean World History, 9th–19th Centuries, Jointly convened by the Asia Research Centre, Australia Research Council Linkage Grant, Murdoch University, and the Indian Ocean World Centre, Major Collaborative Research Initiative, McGill University, the Western Australian Maritime Museum, Victoria Quay, Fremantle, 12–14 November 2012. Prof. Stephen's paper focuses primarily on the Tamil region of South India, but also references slaves taken from Bengal.

70. Unlike the very extensive 1753 Mahé census. Census, Chandernagor, 1751, 1753, 1756 (ANOM DPPC G1/481 F° 1, 3, 6, 9, and 100), and 1768 (ANOM DPPC G1/481 F° 103).

71. Census, Chandernagor, 1751–1768, ANOM DPPC G1/481.

72. Caste, a category once thought to designate fixed status, occupation, and kinship, is now understood to be changeable over time and in different communities. "Pariah," today "Dalit," was generally considered the lowest caste. Béteille, *Caste, Class and Power*;

André Béteille *Castes: Old and New. Essays in Social Structure and Social Stratification* (Bombay: Asia Pub. House, 1969); Susan Bayly, *Caste, Society and Politics in India from the Eighteenth Century to the Modern Age* (New York: Cambridge University Press, 1999); Norbert Peabody, "Cents, Sense, Census: Human Inventories in Late Precolonial and Early Colonial India," *Comparative Studies in Society and History* 43, no. 4 (October 2001): 819–850.

73. I have compiled these figures from itemized catalog references in Gaudart, *Catalogue des manuscrits*, vols. 4–5. I have not consulted the original deeds themselves, which may include more details. Unfortunately, none survive from Chandernagor.

74. There is one anomaly in this collection: the vast majority of the surviving bills of sale (thirty-seven of fifty-two) date from September–November 1774. While a profound famine raged in Bengal in 1773–1774, there is no evidence of a similar crisis in the south of India, where these sales occurred; Datta, "Crisis and Survival," 5. Instead, these deeds were probably stimulated by the British law requiring deeds of sale, issued in May of that same year. Long-distance traders and buyers would have wanted evidence that their transactions were legitimate under British law.

75. In some cases, the deeds of sale list the children's names and/or castes. For example, some of the slaves are identified as: "Chaveraye," "a slave . . . of Bengali caste," "Marie," "Camalahi," "Nianamerekan," "Marguerite, of Pariah caste," "Aly," "Vira," "a young girl of Pariah caste," "Poungavanom," "Antoine," and "a slave of Nair caste."

76. Of course, it is possible that she was approximately five years older at each transaction, if we accept the ages of the Isle Bourbon census records in the 1780s.

77. The average price for a slave in 1761 in Isle Bourbon was about 750 livres (today worth about $3,780). Ève, *Le corps des esclaves*, 135.

78. Lory was one of two merchants who helped finance two shipments of slaves from Zanzibar to Réunion and Mauritius in 1821 and 1822 (National Archives [Kew], CO 167/92). Allen, "Licentious and Unbridled Proceedings," 102–103.

   Further evidence of prices in India from slightly later in the eighteenth century reveals some higher prices. In Mahé almost two decades later, prices varied from twenty to thirty rupees (about $10,000–$15,000). Gaudert, *Catalogue des Manuscrits*, vol. 5. Evidence from nineteenth-century rural British Bengal suggests that prices for children ranged from ten to forty rupees around 1840 but were somewhat higher in the cities, especially Calcutta. See Chattopadhyay, *Slavery in the Bengal Presidency*, 46, 72, and "Translation of a Report Made by a Well-Known Native Gentleman to F. Jenkins," in Banaji, *Slavery in British India*, 135. Interestingly, African slaves were considerably more expensive than Indian slaves in India, due to their relative scarcity; see Chattopadhyay, *Slavery in the Bengal Presidency*, 49–50. Evidence from another Indian Ocean port, Zanzibar, off the coast of eastern Africa, shows declining prices for slaves from a peak in 1777 to the lowest point in 1840; see Abdul Sheriff, *Slaves, Spices and Ivory in Zanzibar* (London: James Currey, 1987), 64.

79. Gaudart, *Catalogue des manuscrits*, 134.

80. Āṇantaraṅkam Piḷḷai, *The Diary of Ananda Ranga Pillai*, trans. Henry Dodwell, 12 vols. (Madras: Printed by the Superintendent, Government Press, 1904–1928), 1:227.

81. Niklas Frykman, "Seamen on Late Eighteenth-Century European Warships," *International Review of Social History* 54 (2009): 69–73.

82. Gaudart, *Catalogue des manuscrits*, 4:144. The conversion rate is based on *The Penny Cyclopædia of the Society for the Diffusion of Useful Knowledge* (London: Charles Knight, 1839), 15:325 and *Measuring Worth*, http://measuringworth.com.

83. The remainder had Indian names. Ange Marie Nicolazo, notary clerk at Karikal (four deeds); Alexandre de Rosaire (three deeds); Poly d'Aurbigny, master surveyer at Karikal (three deeds). The rest are missing or ambiguous, as, for example: "Pavy, gunner" or "the widow of Étienne Canni."

84. Adrian Carton, "Shades of Fraternity: Creolization and the Making of Citizenship in French India, 1790–1792," *French Historical Studies*, 31, no. 4 (Fall 2008): 581.

85. Including one Pierre Gomez, a soldier, married to Isabelle du Rosaire.

86. Gaudart, *Catalogue des manuscrits*, vols. 3, 4, 5, and 6. Nor do they appear in a Google Books search, except for the reference to the nineteenth-century Lory litigation.

87. For example, the census tables of 20 December 1753 list 256 Topas (men, women, and children) resident in "Chocnossirabat" and 423 Topas in "Boroquichempour." Census, Chandernagor, 1751–1768" (ANOM DPPC G1/481).

88. Copy, "Mémoire de Constance en faveur de Furcy," 9 November 1817 (ADR 1Jp2007-1, no. 3). The language "in the care of," offered by Furcy's legal team decades later, tells us nothing about Madeleine's actual status. The lawyers' goal was to show that Furcy was not descended from an enslaved mother, so the papers they produced avoid characterizing her as Mademoiselle Despense's slave.

89. The sixty-eight white women constituted 23 percent of the 293 European inhabitants censused in Chandernagor in 1768. Carton, *Mixed Race and Modernity*, 72–73.

90. "One of the drawbacks to life in India was the small number of European women in the colonies. Some were sent out from France, but these were mostly absorbed by Pondichéry. 'No European women come here to us, except those not wanted at Pondichéry' wrote Dupleix from Chandernagore in 1739." Dalgliesh, *Companie of the Indies*, 161–162.

91. The short-lived presence of French Ursulines in Pondichéry (1738–1739) is well documented; see Dalgliesh, *Companie of the Indies*, 67, 73, 160; Adrien Launay, *Histoire des missions de l'Inde*, 5 vols. (Paris: Ancienne Maison Charles Douniol, 1898), 1:xxxvii and 457, 458, and, more recently Heidi M. Keller-Lapp, "Who Is the Real Sovereign of the Ursulines of Pondichéry?" *French Colonial History* 13 (2012): 111–140. The Ursulines' arrival was the catalyst for a sustained attack on the Jesuits on the eve of their suppression, discussed in in C. P. Platel, *Mémoires historiques sur les affaires des jésuites avec le Saint-siége* (F. L. Ameno, 1766), Book 1.

92. Alternatively, Rila Mukherjee notes that Chandernagor was "a great centre for the sex trade from its inception." One must consider the possibility that Mademoiselle Despense de la Loge was the madame of a brothel. However, given her name's proximity in the census to the niece of the colonial elite, M. Sinfray, this seems unlikely. Mukherjee, "A Comparative Study of the Many Networks."

93. Census, Chandernagor, 1768 (ANOM DPPC G1/481 F° 103). The 329 servants tallied (but not listed named) in the census include 22 male slaves, 39 female slaves, 100 free males, and 168 free females.

94. *Kitāb-i-Qiṣṣa-i Tahmās Miskin*, fol. 1, translated in Chatterjee, "A Slave's Quest," 72.

95. Yet another possibility, I suppose, is that Madeleine was the out-of-wedlock child of a French-Indian couple in French India, placed in the service of Mademoiselle Despense

(conceivably even Despense's own child). However, there is absolutely no documentary evidence for such a supposition, and the frequent references to Madeleine as a *négresse* may suggest that her skin tone was darker than one might expect to find in such a child. The most likely scenario is that she was of Indian parentage and pawned to Mademoiselle Despense.

96. *Kitāb-i-Qiṣṣa-i Tahmās Miskin*, fols. 8–9, translated in Chatterjee, "A Slave's Quest," 66. I have substituted "learned people" for her term "intellectuals."

97. For example, Jeremy Hayhoe found that only 11.6 percent of daughters ages 12–20 living with their parents in rural Burgundy could sign their names; for servants the same age, the literacy rate dropped to 3.9 percent. "Rural Domestic Servants in Eighteenth-Century Burgundy: Demography, Economy, and Mobility," *Journal of Social History* 46, no. 2 (Winter 2012): 554.

98. Colin Haynes, *The Complete Collector's Guide to Fakes and Forgeries* (Greensboro, NC: Wallace-Homestead, 1988), 118.

99. This is essentially what the archives' director told me in private correspondence of 7 May 2015. He added, "And even if one arrives at proving that the document was fabricated after the fact, this does not prove that its contents are false; one could have wished to reconstitute a lost document that had truly existed."

CHAPTER 2

1. For example, Passengers, Lorient, Arrivals, 22 May 1772, *Hector* (ANOM COL F/5B/21); Passengers, Lorient, Departures, 12 September 1773, *La Brune*, (ANOM COL F/5B/50). Pierre H. Boulle makes it clear that slaves of African origin and descent were also present in Bengal. "Les déclarations parisiennes de non-blancs entre 1738 et 1790: Permanence des catégories et interchangeabilité des statuts," *Nuevo Mundo* (2010), paras. 24–26, available online at http://nuevomundo.revues.org/58021. However, there is no indication that Madeleine was one of them, since all records, discussed in subsequent chapters, described her as "Indienne," despite the occasional reference to her as a *négresse*.

   Nineteenth-century anthropological obsessions with defining race tended to classify the very diverse populations of India into two categories: the northern Aryan, with lighter skin and Mediterranean features, and the darker southern Dravidian race. See, for example, Herbert Hope Risley, *The Tribes and Castes of Bengal: Ethnographic Glossary* (Calcutta: Bengal Secretariat, 1892), 1:xxxi–xxxiv. However, they admitted that people of varying shades lived throughout India. A third racial type for Risley in India was the "Mongoloid."

2. These included: Antoine Julie (cook), Jean Poupe, Soubisse Marie (wet nurse), Lucy, Simon, Hirame, Mercure, Caron, Marianne, Crach, Louison, Carnaval, Narcisse, Hector, Samedy, Lucie, Jean, Lubin and two Césars. Passengers, Lorient, Arrivals, 22 May 1772, *Hector* (ANOM COL F/5B/21), and Muster Roll, *Hector*, Disarmament, 22 May 1772 (SHDL 2P 44–II.6). Two additional servants sported last names and no racial designation: Jean Pitard and Pierre Lekimas. Passengers, Lorient, Arrivals, 22 May 1772, *Hector* (ANOM COL F/5B/21).

3. Pierre H. Boulle, "La construction du concept de race dans la France d'Ancien Régime," *Outre-mers* 89, no. 336 (2002): 155–175, and "Francois Bernier (1620–88) and the Origins

of the Modern Concept of Race," in *The Color of Liberty: Histories of Race in France*, ed. Sue Peabody and Tyler Stovall (Durham, NC: Duke University Press, 2003), 1–28.

4. "Nouvelle division de la Terre, par différentes Espèces ou Races d'hommes qui l'habitent, envoyée par un fameux Voyageur à Monsieur **** à peu près en ces terms," *Journal des sça-vans* 13, no. 12 (24 April 1684): 148–155.

5. Benjamin Braude, "The Sons of Noah and the Construction of Ethnic and Geographical Identities in the Medieval and Early Modern Periods," *William and Mary Quarterly* 54 (January 1997): 103–142.

6. Andrew S. Curran, *The Anatomy of Blackness: Science and Slavery in an Age of Enlightenment* (Johns Hopkins University Press, Baltimore, 2011), 118–129.

7. India Office Records, Home Miscellaneous, vol. 102, p. 94, quoted in Datta, "Crises and Survival," 6.

8. Most historians believe Warren Hastings's estimation of ten million deaths (one-third of the population) an exaggeration but agree that the event was calamitous. Roy, "Famine and Dearth," 57; Datta, "Crises and Survival," 6–11. Although the drought primarily affected crops in the western and northeastern districts, its impact on refugees and trade would have been visible in Chandernagor.

9. Chatterji, "French in Bengal," 385–386.

10. Philippe Haudrère, "Les Routes maritimes entre la France et les Indes orientales au XVIIIe siècle au temps de la Compagnie des Indes," in *Les relations historiques et culturelles*, 155.

11. His name is spelled "Janot" here; I've retained this spelling throughout for consistency (so as not to be confused with the Routiers' slave Jeannot). The disarmament of the ship *Hector* (Port-Louis, 1772), gives the date of departure from Chandernagor as 11 January 1771, *désarmé* in Lorient, 22 May 1772 (Désarmement, Le V^eau Particulier l'*Hector*, 22 mai 1772, Archives de la Compagnie des Indes, Lorient, 2P 44–II.6; photos provided in private correspondence by Chantal Plévert, Les Amis du Service Historique de la Défense à Lorient, 25 January 2013); Passengers, Lorient, Arrivals, 22 May 1772, *Hector* (ANOM COL F/5B/21).

12. Muster Roll, *Hector*, Disarmament, 22 May 1772 (SHDL 2P 44–II.6).

13. Michael H. Fisher, "Bound for Britain: Changing Conditions of Servitude, 1600–1857," in Chatterjee and Eaton, *Slavery and South Asian History*, 203, quoting William Hickey, *Memoirs of William Hickey*, ed. Alfred Spencer, 3rd ed., 4 vols. (London: Hurst & Blackett, 1919–1925), 4:405–406. This occurred a few decades later. Munnoo would go on to embrace Christianity, marry an Englishwoman, and raise a family in England; he was buried there in the 1830s.

14. Jacques Henri Bernardin de Saint-Pierre, *Voyage à l'Ile de France*, 2 vols. (Paris: Hiard, 1835), 1:27–28. Bernardin de Saint-Pierre just missed Charles Routier, who would move to Isle Bourbon before the writer arrived in Isle de France, and to France before the author arrived in Isle Bourbon on 20 November 1770 (2:5).

15. There is a growing body of research on South Asian sailors, known as lascars. A good place to begin is the special issue "Asian Sailors in the Age of Empire," ed. Jesse Ransley, *Journal for Maritime Research*, 16, no. 2 (November 2014).

16. Passengers, Lorient, Arrivals, 22 May 1772, *Le Hector* (ANOM COL F/5B/21); Muster Roll, *Hector*, Disarmament, 22 May 1772 (SHDL 2P 44–II.6). Travel was dangerous between April and September; Bernardin de Saint-Pierre, *Voyage à l'Ile de France*, 2:9.

17. Anthony S. Cheke and Julian P. Hume, *Lost Land of the Dodo: The Ecological History of Mauritius, Réunion and Rodrigues* (London: A & C Black, 2009), 14, 76–83.

18. By 1771 the original hub of the colony, Grand Port, in the southeast, had been more or less abandoned by the French government. Vaughan, *Creating the Creole Island*, 35–55 and Stephen, "Slaves of the Tamil Coast."

19. Vaughan, *Creating the Creole Island*, 71; and Auguste Toussaint, *Port-Louis, deux siécles d'histoire, 1735–1935* (Port-Louis, Mauritius: Imprimé par La Typographie moderne, 1936), 107.

20. Under their dominion, the island's most famous indigenous creature, the dodo, had become extinct, along with many other animals unique to the island, including birds and tortoises, which fell prey to—or competed unsuccessfully with—humans and the rats, cats, and pigs that accompanied them. Cheke and Hume, *Lost Land of the Dodo*, 14, 76–83. Vaughan, *Creating the Creole Island*, 7–10.

21. Muster Roll, *Hector*, Disarmament, 22 May 1772 (SHDL 2P 44–II.6); Passengers, Lorient, Arrivals, 22 May 1772, *Hector* (ANOM COL F/5B/21).

22. Toussaint, *La Route des Isles*, 118. With the right winds, ships from Isle Bourbon could reach Isle de France overnight, but because of prevailing currents the reverse course might take ten days.

23. Passengers, Lorient, Arrivals, 22 May 1772, *Hector* (ANOM COL F/5B/21).

24. The vulnerability of poor women, especially slaves and women of color, to harassment and violation is an all too common feature in maritime and colonial cities, not to mention plantations, in the eighteenth century. There is considerably more literature on this topic for the British Empire and early United States than for France's colonies, but more will certainly emerge. Trevor Burnard, *Mastery, Tyranny, and Desire: Thomas Thistlewood and His Slaves in the Anglo-Jamaican World* (Chapel Hill: University of North Carolina Press, 2004), 156–162, 209–239; Sharon Block, *Rape and Sexual Power in Early America* (Chapel Hill: University of North Carolina University Press for the Omohundro Institute of Early American History and Culture, 2006), esp. 63–74; Wendy Anne Warren, "'The Cause of Her Grief': The Rape of a Slave in Early New England," *Journal of American History* 93, no. 4 (March 2007): 1031–1049; David Brion Davis, "Slavery, Sex and Dehumanization," in *Sex, Power, and Slavery*, ed. Gwyn Campbell and Elizabeth Elbourne (Athens, OH: Ohio University Press, 2014), 43–60; Richard Goldberg, "William Byrd's Flourish: The Sexual Cosmos of a Virginian Planter," in *Sex and Sexuality in Early America*, ed. Merril D. Smith (New York: New York University Press, 1998), 135–163; Edward E. Baptist, "'Cuffy,' 'Fancy Maids,' and 'One-Eyed Men': Rape, Commodification, and the Domestic Slave Trade in the United States," *American Historical Review* 106, no. 5 (December 2001): 1619–1650. See Sophie White, "Les Esclaves et le droit en Louisiane sous le régime français, carrefour entre la Nouvelle-France, les Antilles, et l'océan indien," in *Thémis Outre-Mer: Adapter le droit et rendre la justice aux colonies (16e–19e siècles)*, ed. by Eric Wenzel and Eric de Mari (Editions universitaires de Dijon, 2015), 57-67.

25. Muster Roll, *Hector*, Disarmament, 22 May 1772 (SHDL 2P 44–II.6); Passengers, Lorient, Arrivals, 22 May 1772, *Hector* (ANOM COL F/5B/21).

26. Bernardin de Saint-Pierre, *Voyage à l'Ile de France,* 1:13–15.

27. The origins of this maxim are complex, but it seems to have emerged from disputes over fugitive slaves escaping from Spanish territories on France's southern border. Sue Peabody, "An Alternative Genealogy of the Origins of French Free Soil: Medieval Toulouse," in *Free Soil in the Atlantic World*, ed. Sue Peabody and Keila Grinberg (New York: Routledge, 2014), 341–362. In the late sixteenth century, the French political theorist Jean Bodin articulated the principle thus: "Servitude . . . has no place in this kingdom, even such that the slave of a foreigner is free and liberated as soon as he has set foot in France." Jean Bodin, *Les six livres de la République* (Lyon: Jean de Tournes, 1579), 43. Antoine Loisel was the first to call the principle a maxim, and he included the condition of baptism in his seventeenth-century formulation of the Free Soil principle: "All people are free in this kingdom, and as soon as a slave has set foot here, having been baptized, he is free." Antoine Loisel, *Institutes coutumières* (Paris: Abel l'Angelier, 1608), 1.

28. Peabody, "*There Are No Slaves*," 88–94; Boulle and Peabody, *Le droit des Noirs en France*, 81–83.

29. Antoine Boucher, "Mon discours," or "Mémoire d'observations sur l'isle Bourbon, adressé à M. de Foucherolle, directeur général de la Royale Compagnie des Indes, par son très humble serviteur Boucher" (1714), quoted in Isidore Guët, *Les origines de l'île Bourbon et de la colonisation française à Madagascar: d'après des documents inédits tirés des Archives coloniales du Ministère de la Marine et des colonies* (Paris: C. Bayle, 1888), 229, 232.

30. Filliot, *La Traite des esclaves vers les Mascareignes*, 53; Jean Barassin, "Aperçu sur l'évolution des groupes ethniques à l'Isle Bourbon depuis les origines jusqu'en 1848," in *Mouvements de populations dans l'Océan Indien* (Paris: Honoré Champion, 1979), 245; Prosper Ève, *Naître et mourir à l'Île Bourbon à l'époque de l'esclavage*, (Saint-Denis: Université de la Réunion and Paris: l'Harmattan, 1999), 16.

31. Antoine Boucher, "Mon discours," quoted in Guët, *Les origines de l'Île Bourbon*, 229, 232.

32. The Martinique Superior Council upheld the Free Soil principle in a slave's freedom suit in 1704; Rushforth, *Bonds of Alliance*, 73–75.

33. M. L. E. Moreau de Saint-Méry, *Loix et constitutions des colonies françaises de l'Amérique sous le vent*, 6 vol. (Paris: Chez l'auteur, chez Quillan et chez Mequignon jeune, 1784–1790), 2:99.

34. Such evidence would have been important to both sides of Furcy's case. The fact that it was not produced strongly indicates that Madeleine was never registered as an entering black there. Furthermore, Pierre H. Boulle, who has worked extensively with the Admiralty registrations of nonwhites in French ports found no record of the slave Madeleine in the Lorient registers, though he has not examined the Lorient registers for 1772 (private correspondence, March 16, 2007), nor did subsequent lawyers when the case came to court.

35. Pierre H. Boulle, *Race et esclavage dans la France de l'Ancien Régime* (Paris: Perrin, 2006), 148–149.

36. Yvan Debbasch, *Couleur et liberté: Le jeu du critère ethnique dans un ordre juridique esclavagiste*. vol. 1, *L'affranchi dans les possessions françaises de la Caraïbe, 1635–1833* (Paris: Dalloz, 1967), 53–71; John Garrigus, *Before Haiti: Race and Citizenship in French Saint-Domingue*, Americas in the Early Modern Atlantic World (New York: Palgrave, 2006), 162–169; Robert Taber, "The Issue of their Union : Family, Law, and Politics in Western Saint-Domingue, 1777-1789" (Ph.D. diss., University of Florida, 2015), 89–91. Such racialist policies were contested in Guiana, where some administrators actively sought to recruit free people of color from Gorée and even maroons to settle and maintain

the colony for the French; Barbara Traver, "After Kourou: Settlement Schemes in French Guiana in the Age of Enlightenment" (PhD diss., University of Washington, 2011), 205–208, 254–265, 325–331.

37. Investigators of the natural world, especially the Swedish naturalist and inventor of our modern system of biological taxonomy, Carl Linnaeus, were beginning to sort humanity into essential subcategories with fixed attributes within a hierarchy, but the French scientist George Louis LeClerc, Count of Buffon, argued for a more empiricist anti-classificatory description of the world modeled on the great chain of being. Curran, *Anatomy of Blackness*, 75; Sue Peabody, "Furcy, la question raciale et le 'sol libre de France': Une micro-histoire," *Annales* 64, no. 6 (2009): 1305–1334.

38. No slaves may be sent from Pondichéry or Chandernagor to the islands of Bourbon and of France. Penalties against offenders. Order to the councils to modify the said prohibitions, and to those of Pondichéry and of Chandernagor to require captains to submit in writing to not conduct any commerce directly or indirectly in the said slaves or foodstuffs or merchandise from Europe or the Indies. It is to be very expressly forbidden for the councils of Pondichéry and Chandernagor to permit the embarkation of any Indian slaves on the Company's vessels, for any pretext or reason there might be. Under penalty against the offenders of the confiscation of the said slaves. And also against the captains of the said vessels making their return to Europe of the loss of their port permit and salaries of their campaigns. And against the captains of the commercial establishments in India likewise of the loss of their salaries. (Isle Bourbon Correspondance générale 1727, ANOM C3/5 fol. 206.) Many thanks to Mélanie Lamotte for sharing this document with me.

39. Peabody, "*There Are No Slaves*," ch. 4; Boulle and Peabody, *Le droit des noirs en France*, 61, 75–78; *Mémoire signifié pour le nommé Francisque*. Nor was the 1727 Company regulation ever mentioned in Furcy's nineteenth-century freedom suits. This may be because it prohibited only trade on Company vessels, not private trade in slaves. Moreover, the penalty for trading in Indian slaves was their confiscation by the crown, not their freedom, so the ban would have been of little use to Furcy's lawyers and of ambiguous utility to his opponents. If the 1727 law, issued by Company officials in the metropole, was ever enforced in the Indian Ocean colonies, it apparently fell into disuse and was forgotten.

40. Ordinance of 9 March 1739 (ANOM COL B 68, fol. 15–15v). Rushforth notes that these instructions merely reinforced royal policy dating from the first decade of the eighteenth century; *Bonds of Alliance*, 120–121, 135–136, 356–337.

41. Thureau, *Plaidoyer pour le sieur Furcy*, 13; and Moreau de Saint-Méry, *Loix et constitutions*, 5:80. Rushforth argues that, following France's defeat and the transfer of governance in North America to the British in 1763, the French government no longer had a stake in preserving ethnic distinctions among Indian nations as its allies or foes. This facilitated the simplification of racial policies whereby "Indians" were not subject to slavery, while "Negroes" were naturally destined to be slaves, thus "ellid[ing] a century of experience in New France, where thousands of enslaved Indians [had] labored under French colonial control"; *Bonds of Alliance*, 381.

42. Passengers, Lorient, Arrivals, 1771–1772, *La Paix* (ANOM COL F/5B/21). Captain Augustin Louis Desblottières is probably Madame Routier's elder brother, François Augustin Desblottières (1732–?), although Ricquebourg lists his profession as "assistant merchant." L.J. Camille Ricquebourg, *Dictionnaire généalogique des familles de*

l'Ile Bourbon (la Réunion), 1665-1810, 3 vols. (Mayenne: Imprimerie de la Manutention [chez l'auteur], 1983), 1:691. Marie Anne Ursule had two more brothers: Pierre Marie Desblottières de Vermont, ship captain and François Gilles Desblottières, ship captain and commander of the French *comptoir* in Bengal (*idem.*, 1:692). According to a much later document, Despense roomed with Madame Routier in Lorient. Emile Moreau, *Mémoire pour le Sieur Lory, Propriétaire, demeurant à Saint-Denis (Isle Bourbon), défendeur, contre le Sieur Furcy, Homme de Couleur, Demeurant à l'Isle de France, demandeur* (Saint-Denis, Réunion: Imp. de Pollet, Soupe et Guillois, 1838) (ANOM FM GEN/158/1307), 2.

43. Article 11 of the Edit du Roi, Concernant les esclaves Nègres des colonies, donné à Paris au mois d'octobre 1716, prohibited the sale and exchange of slaves in France; *Le Code noir, ou Recueil des réglemens rendu jusqu'à présent. Concernant le gouvernement, l'administration de la justice, la police, la discipline & le commerce des Nègres dans les colonies françoises* [...] (Paris: Chez L. F. Prault, 1788), 169–180. The updated regulation, Déclaration du Roi du 15 décembre 1738 (*Le Code noir*, 382–395), still in force in 1772, did not alter this provision.

44. Affranchissements, no. 727, 6 July 1789 (ANOM 6 DPPC/3742).

45. Since 1579, the French state had required priests to submit sworn copies of parish registers to civil authorities; Hanley, "Engendering the State," 14.

46. Jean Nicolas Routier, was born in Elbeuf, Seine-Maritime, to Claude Routier and Marie Flavigny on 10 June 1706. Registres Paroissaux et d'État Civil, Elbeuf (Paroisse Saint-Jean) (Archives Départementales de Seine-Maritimes, 3^E 00999), http://recherche.archivesdepartementales76.net/. The entry is very difficult to read, but there is no profession or trade listed for the parents. Ricquebourg mistakenly says that Jean Routier was born in Saint-Vigor, Eure, Normandy (a village midway between Paris and Le Havre). Ricquebourg, *Dictionnaire généalogique*, 3:2589, n. 1; "Jean Routier dit Routier (#189), soldat passager, solde 30, embarqué à Lorient [le 15 mars. 1729], via Cadix et l'Inde, débarqué à l'Isle de France, le 25 août 1729, pour Pondichery," Muster Roll, *Duc de Chartres*, Disarmament (transcription) (SHDL 2P 24–I.4), in *Mémoire des Hommes*, French Presence in the World, India Company, Crew and Passengers, http://www.memoiredeshommes.sga.defense.gouv.fr; Ricquebourg, *Dictionnaire généalogique*, 3:2589.

47. Huguette Ly-Tio-Fane Pineo, *Isle de France, 1715–1746*, vol. 1, *L'Emergence de Port Louis* (Moka, Mauritius: Mahatma Gandhi Institute, 1993), 101–104, 110.

48. Françoise Busson was born, probably before 1709, in Lorient, parish of Saint-Louis; she was the widow of Antoine LeDoux. She married Jean Nicholas Routier on 3 May 1730 in Port Bourbon (today Vieux Grand Port), Isle de France. Ricquebourg, *Dictionnaire généalogique*, 3:2589, n. 1; Vaughan, *Creating the Creole Island*, 46–47.

49. Jennifer Palmer, "Women and Contracts in the Age of Transatlantic Commerce," in *Women and Work in Eighteenth-Century France*, ed. Daryl Hafter and Nina Kushner (Baton Rouge: Louisiana State University Press, 2015), 133–134.

50. Charles Gabriel Routier was born 25 March 1731 in Port Bourbon (today Grand Port, Mauritius); Ricquebourg, *Dictionnaire généalogique*, 3:2589. In fact, the environmental degradation and unsanitary conditions left by the earlier Dutch settlers had caused them to abandon the island colony early in the eighteenth century.

51. Vijaya Teelock, *Bitter Sugar: Sugar and Slavery in 19th Century Mauritius* (Moka, Mauritius: Mahatma Gandhi Institute, 1998), 34–38; Blaufarb, *Great Demarcation*, 148–152.

52. Between 1731 and 1736, Jean Routier received five concessions on the island but ultimately ended up reselling or abandoning all but his primary estate in the Plaines de Wilhelm. Concessions, Isle de France, to 1749 (ANOM DPPC G/1/511). Jean Nicholas Routier bought the first piece of land several months after his marriage in 1730, consisting of "450 paces [*pas géometriques*] in length along the river up to the boundary stone [*borne*] of the concession of Giblon, the duke Sir Dueray, in depth from the side of the mountain, conceded 20 October 1730." He would hold this until he resold it to the island's governor, Mahé de la Bourdonnais in 1739. The Trois Ilôts concession was purchased from the original concessionaire, Dupleix, in 1731. Marcelle Lagasse, *L'Isle de France avant La Bourdonnais, 1721–1735*, Mauritius Archives Publication 12 (Port Louis, Mauritius: M. Coquet, 1972), 11, n. 3, 62. As the East India Company shifted its center of operations from Grand Port to Port Louis, Jean Routier petitioned the Company council, asking for the forgiveness of his debts and permission to abandon his concession in Trois Ilôts for land in Pamplemousses to the north, because "the distance [of the former is] an insurmountable obstacle for the delivery of food and supplies suitable for the refreshment of the vessels" in the new port. Jean Routier de Grandval, petition to the Provincial Council, 2 December 1732, quoted in Lagasse, *L'Isle de France*, 97. In 1732, he bought, then abandoned (in 1733), property in Port Bourbon, i.e., Grand Port. The other three properties were bought and resold; it is not clear whether at a profit or loss. These were: L'Enfoncement des Hollandais (1732, sold, n.d.); Pamplemousses (1733), which he sold in 1735 after being denied permission to farm there; a property in Montagne Longue (1735), which he sold to a neighboring landowner in 1736. Concessions, Isle de France, to 1749 (ANOM DPPC G/1/511).

53. Census, Isle de France, 1738 (ANOM DPPC G/1/505).

54. "Routier de Grandvalle, Sr. (#149), troop commander, passenger, embarqued at fitting out, [7 February 1738], disembarqued at Isle de France, 15 July 1738, passenger for Isle de France with his wife and son, at the [officers'] table," Muster Roll, *Apollon*, Disarmament (transcription), 1738–1739 (SHDL 2P 28–I.14), *Mémoire des Hommes*, French Presence in the World, India Company, Crew and Passengers, http://www.memoiredeshommes.sga.defense.gouv.fr.

55. A 1745 proclamation issued by the governor of Isle Bourbon, quoted in Buxtorf, "Colonie, comptoirs et compagnie," 2:171.

56. "Charles Routier (#208), son of Jean Nicholas, age 15, size m[edium], hair ch[estnut], origin Isle Bourbon [*sic*: Isle de France], volunteer, pay 25, passenger, embarqued at armament [10 January 1746 at Lorient], disembarked at Isle de France, 25 June 1746," Muster Roll, *Brilliant*, Disarmament (transcription), 1746–1750 (SHDL 2P 33–II.12), in *Mémoire des Hommes*, French Presence in the World, India Company, Crew and Passengers, http://www.memoiredeshommes.sga.defense.gouv.fr. His father, "Sr Routier de Grandval, officier des troupes à la charge à la Compagnie," and mother traveled on board the same ship, along with George, their servant; Passengers, Lorient, Departures, 14 November 1764, *La Paix* (ANOM COL F/5B/49).

57. Personnel colonial ancien: Routier, Charles, major des milices à Bourbon 1746/1779, ANOM COL E 358 bis. The Moka concession dates to 1755 (NARM LC 3/63). A second

concession (also named Consistance) went to "Jean Claude Routier" in Flacq (LC 3/95); I haven't been able to determine whether these are the same individual, or whether they were brothers or otherwise related.

58. The marriage took place on 20 October 1752 in Grand Port, Isle de France (Ricquebourg, *Dictionnaire généalogique*, 3:2589). Françoise Panon was one of 36 grandchildren of Augustin Panon, originally of Toulon, who arrived to settle Isle Bourbon in 1689.

59. Routier *fils* received a concession of "500 pas geometriques sur 1000, ou 312 arpents," about 264 acres, also part of the land known as the "habitation de la Consistence," in Moka in 1754. The following year, he bought another 312 *arpents* between the rivers of Terre Rouge and la Cascade, next to a concession belonging to his wife's uncle, Augustin Panon, *fils*. (ANOM DPPC G1/511). Once Jean Routier had established his son, he returned briefly to France in 1754 during a lull in warfare with the British. Muster Roll, *Achille*, Disarmament (transcription), 1752–1754 (SHDL 2P 36–13), in *Mémoire des Hommes*, French Presence in the World, India Company, Crew and Passengers, http://www.memoiredeshommes.sga.defense.gouv.fr. He returned to Isle de France; Passengers, Lorient, Departures, 14 November 1764, *La Paix* (ANOM COL F/5B/49).

60. Vaughan, *Creating the Creole Island*, 64.

61. Vaughan, *Creating the Creole Island*, 53–55.

62. *Edit du Roi, portant confirmation de l'établissement de Compagnie des Indes, sous le tire de Compagnie commerçante*, August 1764.

63. The couple's three daughters were Françoise Marguerite (b. 1753 in Port Bourbon, Isle de France), Marie Elie (Louise; b. 1761 in Saint-Denis, ADR GG13), and Marie Euphrasie (b. 1763). Francois Marguerite Routier would marry Michel Front Duclaud in Isle de France in 1781 (NARM LC 13, pp. 301–303). She obtained a new concession in Petite Riviere Noire, Isle de France, on 7 Jan. 1784 (NARM Land Concessions, LC 13/293) and then divorced Duclaud in 1794 (NARM KJ2, Reg. 9, fols. 74–44), remarrying Alexandre George Vergoz in 1809 (NARM KA 178, Reg. 45, fols. 117v–119r); she lived until 76, dying in Port Louis 2 February 1830. At age fifteen, Charles Routier's second daughter married a much older man, Guy Maurice de Fayard (age 35) in 1776 and remained in Saint-Denis (Ricquebourg, *Dictionnaire généalogique*, 3:2589 and NARM KA 178, KJ 2). Unmentioned in Ricquebourg's study is Euphrasie Routier, wife of Monsieur D'Orge, b. 1763, probably married in Isle de France, who died in 1805 (28 Germinal, An 13) in Port Nord-Ouest, Isle de France (NARM KA 160). Neither I nor Ricquebourg have been able to find a death record for Françoise Busson Routier, as the Port Louis parish registers for the years 1762–1765 have not survived.

64. Just a decade earlier, Marie Anne's father, Jean Louis Gilles François Desblottières, owned the third-largest number of slaves on Isle Bourbon, with 148 on his plantation in Saint-Denis. Michèle Dion, *Quand La Réunion s'appelait Bourbon* (Paris: L'Harmattan, 2006), 114–115.

65. Marriage of Charles Routier and Mary Anne Ursule Desblottières, 8 February 1764 (AD Morbihan, État civil, Port Louis, BMS 1748–1779, photo 483/891, http://recherche.archives.morbihan.fr); Ricquebourg, *Dictionnaire généalogique*, 3:2589. Charles Gabriel Routier's two wives were cousins, one the daughter of Joseph Panon-Lamare, and the second of Marie Panon, wife of Jean Louis Gilles François Desblottières, Écuyer, of Marseille, who arrived in Isle Bourbon in 1722, a Company officer. Charles's second wife was the

daughter of (Jean Louis Gilles) François Desblottières (born around 1697 in Marseille, d. 27 September 1755), a Company officer, and Marie Panon (1706–1769), the youngest child of the early settler, Augustin Panon. Desblottières's testament, drawn up as he lay on his deathbed, 16 September 1755, evinces his fervent Marian faith and, after paying off his debts, leaves 100 piasters for the construction of the parish church of Saint-Denis; likewise he requests an annual mass be said on the anniversary of his death, to which is added (at the urging of the parish curate Philippe?), another 100 piasters to the church. Likewise, he donates 200 piasters to the poor ("aux pauvres"), and the remainder to his heirs (ANOM DPPC REU 76, Notariat Amat-Laplane, Saint-Denis, 1755–1758).

66. Ricquebourg, *Dictionnaire généalogique*, 3:2097; Guët, *Les origines de l'Île Bourbon*, 105–106, 112–120, 163.

67. Augustin Panon's original land concession, known as La Mare ("the pool"), between the Ravine des Figuiers and the Chemin de la Rivière des Pluies, to the base of the mountain, would be passed down to through the generations, a portion of which eventually came to Charles Routier and his second wife, Marie Anne Ursules Desblottières. A second concession, known as Du Hazier ("of the beech tree") passed to other descendants. "Contrat de concession d'Augustin Panon . . . La Mare à Sainte-Marie," 4 April 1697, f. 23, 22 November 1698, f. 24, and 26 July 1724 (ADR CO 1921).

68. These were Marie Joseph Louise Emilie, Augustin Marie François, Marie Charles Eugénie, Marie Charles Euphémie, and Charlies Marie Élie.

69. Charles François Augustin, Charles Thomas Cyrille, Marie Charles Eugénie, Marie Charles Euphémie, and Charlies Marie Élie.

70. They were accompanied by her brother-in-law, Monsieur Launay, Marie Anne Ursule's sister-in-law, Madame Vermont Desblottières, and a black female servant, Jeanneton. The ship was bound for Moka, but their ultimate destination was Isle de France. Passengers, Lorient, Departures, 14 November 1764, *La Paix* (ANOM COL F/5B/49).

71. Marie Joseph Élie Louise, a daughter, was baptized shortly after their arrival in Port Louis, Isle de France, on 6 June 1765. Two sons, Augustin and Cyrille, were born there subsequently in 1766 and 1767. Augustin's full name was Charles François Augustin Routier (b. 19 June 1766, Port Louis, Isle de France); Cyrille's full name was Charles Thomas Cyrille Routier (b. 20 June 1767, Port Louis, Isle de France). Their fourth child, François, was baptized in Isle Bourbon's capital city, Saint-Denis, on 15 August 1768. Ricquebourg, *Dictionnaire généalogique*, 3:2590. Strangely, this record does not appear in the Saint-Denis 1768 register digitized by ANOM IREL, which seems to mainly include slaves and free people of color, though the register is labeled "whites and blacks."

72. Historians debate the degree to which white families utilized enslaved wet nurses in the American colonies and the antebellum South. Janet Golden, *A Social History of Wet Nursing in America: From Breast to Bottle* (Columbus: Ohio State University Press, 2001), 25–27, 73–74.

73. In early modern Europe, the infant was typically sent out for the first three years to be raised by another woman in the countryside until it could be weaned, but as urbanization advanced, it became more common to invite the nurse to live with the employer; as print culture accelerated, newspaper advertisements helped to connect nursing women with employers. Christiana Klapisch-Zuber, "Blood Parents and Milk Parents: Wet-Nursing in Florence, 1300–1530," in *Women, Family, and Ritual in Renaissance Italy*, trans. Lydia G.

Cochrane (Chicago: University of Chicago Press, 1985), 137–164; Marissa C. Rhodes, "Domestic Vulnerabilities: Reading Families and Bodies into Eighteenth-Century Anglo-Atlantic Wet Nurse Advertisements," *Journal of Family History* 40, no. 1 (2015): 39–63; Clodagh Tait, "Safely Delivered: Childbirth, Wet-Nursing, Gossip-Feasts and Churching in Ireland, c. 1530–1690s," *Irish Economic and Social History* 30 (December 2003): 1–23; Ping-Chen Hsiung, "To Nurse the Young: Breastfeeding and Infant Feeding in Late imperial China," *Journal of Family History* 20, no. 3 (June 1995): 217–239.

74. Londa Schiebinger, "Why Mammals Are Called Mammals: Gender Politics in Eighteenth-Century Natural History," *American Historical Review* 98, no. 2 (April 1993): 382–411; Sünje Prühlen, "What Was the Best for an Infant from the Middle Ages to Early Modern Times in Europe? The Discussion Concerning Wet Nurses," *Hygiea Internationalis* 6, no. 2 (July 2007): 195–213. French policy focused on licensing wet nurses to help curb infant mortality. George D. Sussman, *Selling Mother's Milk: The Wet-Nursing Business in France, 1715–1914* (Urbana: University of Illinois Press, 1982), 19–20; Antoinette Fauve-Chamoux, "Innovation et comportement parental en milieu urbain (XVe–XIXe siècles)," *Annales: Économies, Sociétés, Civilisations* 40, no. 5 (1985): 1023–1039; Joan Sherwood, *Infection of the Innocents: Wet Nurses, Infants, and Syphilis in France, 1780–1900* (Montreal: McGill-Queens Press, 2010); Marie-France Morel, "Images de nourrices dans la France des XVIIIe et XIXe siècles," *Paedagogica Historica* 46, no. 6 (December 2010): 803–817.

75. Klapisch-Zuber, "Blood Parents," 137–138; Sussman, *Selling Mothers' Milk*, 56; Bianca Premo, "'Misunderstood Love': Children and Wet Nurses, Creoles and Kings in Lima's Enlightenment," *Colonial Latin American Review* 14, no. 2 (December 2005): 240.

76. Jacques Henri Bernardin de Saint-Pierre, *Paul et Virginie* (Paris: L'Imprimérie de Monsieur, 1789), 18.

77. Jennifer M. Spear, *Race, Sex and Social Order in Early New Orleans*, Early America (Baltimore: Johns Hopkins University Press, 2009), 75–76. In Lima, Peru, "the idea was that the milk passed from non-white subordinates to creole [colonial] infants debased American-born Spaniards, making them, in essence, the same as the women who suckled them"; Premo, "'Misunderstood Love,'" 243.

78. An anecdote recounted in British India a few decades later suggests that the "little black infant[s]" of the Indian wet nurses were neglected by their mothers once the *daye* (wet nurse) was hired to nurse a British child, a trope deconstructed by Denise K. Comer, "'White Child is Good, Black Child His [or Her] Slave': Women, Children and Empire in Early Nineteenth-Century India," *European Romantic Review* 16, no. 1 (January 2005): 39.

79. Lyndal Roper discusses the ambivalence of mothers to their surrogates in "Witchcraft and Fantasy in Early Modern Europe," in *Oedipus and the Devil: Witchcraft, Sexuality, and Religion in Early Modern Europe* (New York: Routledge, 1994), 200–227.

80. Ricquebourg, *Dictionnaire généalogique*, 3:2098; ANOM IREL, Réunion État civil, Saint-Denis, recorded 8 November 1769.

81. The heirs and their representatives included Charles Routier (listed first, "captain of the city militia" the husband of her eldest local daughter, Marie Anne Desblottières), Pierre Desblottières de Vermont (ship captain, resident in Saint-Denis), Pierre Augustin de Launay (former captain in the regiment of Touraine and major of the militia of Sainte-Suzanne, "residing in this quarter [Saint-Denis] because of his wife Marie Marc Benoîte Desblottières"), Jean Pierre Parny (major in the militia of Saint-Denis, standing in for his

wife, Marie Adelaide Desblottières, and also on behalf of "François Gilles Desblottières, ship captain and commander of the *comptoir* of Karikal in Bengal [*sic*] and [Marie Françoise Catherine] Desblottières, the eldest daughter and wife of Jean Jacques Venerosy Pesciolini, commander of the Isle of Croix in Brittany"). The Company's National Troops were reorganized as militia by Governor Bellecombe in 1768.

82. "Scellés chez Desblottières," 7 November 1769 (ADR 41B).

83. In 1745, the Rivière des Pluies had become the border of a new district (Sainte-Marie) within the old capital district of Saint-Denis.

84. "Scellés chez Desblottières," 7 November 1769 (ADR 41B).

85. Robert Bousquet, *Les Esclaves et leurs maîtres à Bourbon au temps de la Compagnie des Indes, 1665-1767. Livre 2 : La mise en valeur de l'île. Les esclaves dans la guerre en Inde. Commandeurs et économes* (Self-published online: http://www.reunion-esclavage-traite-noirs-neg-marron.com/), ch.1, p. 149, Table 1.46. The widow's husband had owned 148 slaves just before his death in 1755. Dion, *Quand La Réunion s'appelait Bourbon*, 114–115. Since then, she had lost or sold more than a quarter of her human property.

86. The average price in 1761 comes from Ève, *Le corps des esclaves*, 135.

87. The original concession went to Lacour en Saulais on 22 November 1698. Élie Pajot, *Simples renseignements sur l'Isle Bourbon* (Paris: Challalmel Aîné, 1887), 30–31.

88. Palmer, *Intimate Bonds*, 70–79, 89–95.

89. I have not found documentation about these transactions, but the net result was that Charles and Marie Anne Routier came to own both properties in Isle Bourbon.

90. "Auguste" Routier departed Isle Bourbon aboard *Le Choiseul* for France, accompanied by his servant, Rhemy Avril; this must be Charles and Marie Anne's oldest son, Augustin; Passengers, Saint-Denis, Departures, 22 January 1770, *Le Choiseul*, (ADR 58C). Charles, his wife, and Élie Louise (age 6) and "Cyrile" (3), accompanied by the enslaved domestic servants, Jeanneton and Jannot, set out from Isle Bourbon on 11 March 1770; they arrived in Lorient on the *Paix* 18 August 1770; Passengers, Lorient, Arrivals, 18 August 1770, *La Paix* (ANOM COL F/5B/21). Jeannot would return to Isle Bourbon with Madeleine and the Routier family.

91. Bernardin de Saint-Pierre, *Voyage à l'Ile de France*, 1:248.

92. Bernardin de Saint-Pierre, *Voyage à l'Ile de France*, 1:248–249.

93. Dion, *Quand La Réunion s'appelait Bourbon*, 194.

94. Ève, *Naître et mourir à l'Île Bourbon*, 37. The census, which was based on property, under-counted the number of free people of color in the island, especially those who could not be taxed or who passed for white.

95. Ève, *Naître et mourir à l'Île Bourbon*, 37.

96. ". . . died at sea, 26 April 1770, . . . ~~Marie~~ Élie Louise, age seven." Passengers, Lorient, Arrivals, 18 August 1770, *La Paix* (ANOM COL F/5B/21).

97. The baptismal record for Jean Nicholas François Routier (25 November 1770, Port Louis, Morbihan) lists the father as "Capitaine des troupes nationals de l'isle de France." The grandfather, Jean Nicolas Routier, "lieutenant du roi des ville et château de l'Arche," stood as godfather, while his aunt, Marie Française Catherine Desblottières, wife of Jean Jacques Venerozy Pesciolini, "commandant pour le roy de l'isle de Groais," served as god-mother (Archives départementales de Morbihan, État civil, Port Louis, 1748–1779, recherche.archives.morbihan.fr/). This son does not appear in Ricquebourg, *Dictionnaire généalogique*.

98. "Extrait d'une Mémoire déposé au greffe de la Cour Royale de l'Ile de Bourbon le trois Décembre 1817 par M. le Procureur général pour servir s'il y a lieu, à intenter toute procédure criminelle ou correctionnelle" (ADR 1Jp2007-1, no. 36).

99. Furcy to Governor Lowry Cole, Mauritius, n.d. [1826] (NAUK CO 415/4).

100. This was Furcy's lawyer, before the Cour de Cassation in 1838; Desaponay [sic], *Mémoire pour le sieur Furcy*, 56.

101. A Indian man named Jean Baptiste ("Janique") duly reported to admiralty officers in Eu-et-Tréport on the English Channel that Despense had given him an education for a few years, until 1775, after which he entered the service of the vicomte de Saint-Estevan, captain in the regiment of the cuirassiers; when Janique made his declaration, his putative new master was hundreds of miles away, living in his chateau, not far from the Spanish frontier in southwestern France. Extr. Reg. Adm. Eu & Tréport, 3 Oct. 1777 (ANOM COL F/1B/4, fol. 124), Pierre H. Boulle, private correspondence, 18 September 2008 The fact that Janot was living so far from his purported master when he declared himself makes his account of being in the service of the vicomte somewhat suspect. If the story of his new master was fabricated to satisfy French authorities, Janot clearly knew enough about French geography to give a story that would take days or weeks to verify, perhaps allowing him sufficient time to make his escape from official surveillance.

102. Boulle, *Race et esclavage*, 171–173. These figures are based on those for whom the age and sex were declared in the registers.

103. This was the baptism of one Anne Françoise Gondre, the daughter of Pierre and Marie François Foulni. Many thanks to Chantal Plévert of Les Amis du Service Historique de la Défense à Lorient (SHDL) for this reference (private communication, 1 February 2013). Of course, this could have been Anne's female relative, but if so, both had ventured far from their family's estate in Ligny-le-Châtel, Burgundy.

104. To locate Anne Despense de la Loge in convent records would be truly daunting without further advances in digitization, especially the transcription of convent records. Even if we limit the search to Brittany, the Archives Departementales de Vannes (60H–78H) hold papers for two abbeys, four priories, and seven Ursuline establishments in Hennebont, Josellin, Malestroit, Muzillac, Ploërmel, Pontivy, and Vannes, any of which could have received her. Many of these collections contain registers of dowries and pensions, and sometimes burials of the nuns housed there, but the period when Despense is most likely to have entered the convent (ca. 1771–1779) is often missing from these collections.

105. Passengers, Lorient, Departures, 12 September 1773, *La Brune* (ANOM COL F/5B/50).

106. See chapter 1, n. 7.

107. Vaughan, *Creating the Creole Island*, 171; Cissie Fairchilds, *Domestic Enemies: Servants and their Masters in Old Regime France* (Baltimore: Johns Hopkins University Press, 1984), 164–192; Sara C. Maza, *Servants and Masters in Eighteenth-Century France: The Uses of Loyalty* (Princeton, NJ: Princeton University Press, 1983), 176–188. This access was explicit under Islamic law. Kecia Ali, *Marriage and Slavery in Early Islam* (Cambridge, MA: Harvard University Press, 2010), 164.

108. An unusual study of American masters and female slaves suggests one model: "Rather than directly order his dependent to have sexual relations with him, each master

took advantage of the woman's status to create a situation in which her ability to consent or refuse was whittled away. . . . Servants and slaves could not only be forced *to* consent, but this force was also reconfigured *as* consent." Block, *Rape and Sexual Power*, 68.

109. Registre paroissiaux de Ste-Marie, Isle Bourbon, baptême de Marie Charles Euphrosie [*sic*] Routier (ADR 1Mi19 B49–50), (ANOM IREL, Réunion État civil, Sainte-Marie, 23 July 1774).

110. Patterson, *Slavery and Social Death*, 2–3.

CHAPTER 3

1. Their disembarkation is confirmed by Jean-Paul Even, ASHDL, in a personal message from Chantal Plévert, dated 6 January 2014. The armament records (SHDL 2P 13–III.10 and 2P46–I.9) summarized on the *Mémoire des Hommes* site (http://www.memoiredeshommes.sga.defense.gouv.fr/), French Presence in the World, India Company, Ship Outfitters, list a "Routier" as proprietor of the ship. A black male servant, Jeannot (Charles Routier's enslaved male servant who had accompanied him to France in 1770, not the same person as Mademoiselle Despence's Janot), is listed among their entourage upon arrival, though strangely not in the outbound passenger record from Lorient.

2. These images are drawn from Auguste Billiard, *Le Voyage aux colonies orientales*, ed. Jean Alby and Mario Serviable (Sainte-Clotilde, Réunion: Ars Terres Créoles, 1990), 112.

3. Gérard, *Famiy Maron*, 35–36.

4. Vincent Dubut, François Cartault, Christine Payet, Marie-Dominique Thionville, and Pascal Murail, "Complete Mitochondrial Sequences for Haplogroups M23 and M46: Insights into the Asian Ancestry of the Malagasy Population," *Human Biology* 81, no. 4 (August 2009): 495–500. The Malagasy individuals selected for genetic sequencing were residents of Réunion, rather than modern day Madagascar. The term *rougeâtre* does not appear frequently in Isle census records until the 1840s, but it clearly applies to slaves and their descendants from Madagascar.

5. At the time, the French called the island "Mascareigne." Larson, "Colonies Lost," 361. Larson emphasizes the trigger for the revolt as the violation of "a neat politics of race," when the French Protestant leader, Jacques Pronis, married the daughter and niece of Malagasy rulers, but then notes that the it was the rebels who were sent into exile with their Malagasy wives. This would seem to be a conflict over clan alliances rather than a problem of violating racial norms. Étienne Flacourt's seventeenth-century account stresses that the rebels' chief complaints were that their leader was careless with their rice, that he made them "work like the slaves," and that when the elites (*grands*) of the country (i.e., local rulers) asked who the French were, he responded that they were his "slaves." "This contempt much enraged them and they began to murmur against him." Flacourt makes no mention of the convicts' wives in their exile to Mascareigne (Bourbon). Étienne Flacourt, *Histoire de la grande isle Madagascar, composée par le sieur de Flacourt, . . . avec une relation de ce qui s'est passé ès années 1655, 1656 et 1657 . . .* (Troyes, France: N. Oudot and Paris: G. Clouzier, 1661), 208, 219, 267–269.

See also, Guët, *Les origines de l'Île Bourbon*, 47–63, 69, 77–78, 94. Guët was the archivist and librarian of the Central Administration of the Colonies in 1885. I draw upon his history of the early years of settlement for its colorful anecdotes. However, it must be noted that one of Guët's chief occupations was to identify the earliest white women to colonize the island and to elevate their descendants over those of mixed or non-European ancestry—in other words, to create a genealogy of whiteness for the island's elite. As such, one needs to read his account critically.

6. Guët, *Les origines de l'Île Bourbon*, 121–157.

7. Philippe Haudrère, *L'empire des rois, 1500–1789* (Paris: Denoël, 1997), 135–140; Guët, *Les origines de l'Île Bourbon*, 49, 53.

8. Cheke and Hume, *Lost Land of the Dodo*, 75–95.

9. Examples abound. Such was the case in the marriage of the French governor of Madagascar, Jacques Pronis, to Dian Ravellom Manor, daughter and niece of two powerful Malagasy lords. Larson, "Colonies Lost," 361. Likewise, two merchants and leaders of the French establishment of Chandernagor, Jacques Vincent and Joseph-François Dupleix, successively married the Indo-Portuguese Johanna Bégum in 1719 and 1741. Gaebele, *Créole et grande dame*, 7, 80; Martineau, *Dupleix et l'Inde français*, vol. 1, ch. 12.

   In 1666, Colbert began to promote intermarriage between Indian women and French men in North America, even to the point of allocating several thousand livres as dowries for native brides. Saliha Belmessous, "Assimilation and Racialism in Seventeenth and Eighteenth-Century French Colonial Policy," *American Historical Review* 110, no. 2 (April 2005): 328. In the Antilles, where the indigenous Caribs mostly rejected Christian conversion, priests performed a small number of interracial marriages with the Africans who arrived as slaves before 1700. Guillaume Aubert, "'The Blood of France': Race and Purity of Blood in the French Atlantic World," *William and Mary Quarterly*, 3rd ser., 61, no. 3 (July 2004): 452–453. For Louisiana, see, Spear, *Race, Sex and Social Order in Early New Orleans*, chs. 1 and 3. In Senegal and Asia, French traders followed the pattern of intermarriage *à la façon du pays* ("in the local manner") established by the Portuguese and Dutch; see Hilary Jones, *The Métis of Senegal: Urban Life and Politics in French West Africa* (Bloomington: Indiana University Press, 2013); Carton, *Mixed Race and Modernity*; and Jean Gelman Taylor, *The Social World of Batavia: Europeans and Eurasians in Colonial Indonesia*, 2nd ed. (Madison: University of Wisconsin Press, 2009).

10. Colbert transported almost eight hundred French *filles du roi* to New France (Quebec) between 1663 and 1673. Aubert, "Blood of France," 454.

11. Guët, *Les origines de l'Île Bourbon*, 105–106, 112–120. Nathan Marvin argues that Guët deliberately obscured the Asian and Malagasy origins of the founding settlers in "'Le Débris de Madagascar': Whiteness and Myth on Isle Bourbon in the Eighteenth Century," paper presented at A Journée d'étude on the Francophone Indian Ocean, Florida State University, 8 April 2016.

12. J. Barassin, *Naissance d'une chrétienté: Bourbon des origines jusqu'en 1714* (Saint-Denis, Réunion: Cazal, 1953), 137.

13. Many of the hybrid Topas community of South Asia used Portuguese last names, so their ancestry is more likely hybrid, but Catholic.

14. Guët, *Les origines de l'Île Bourbon*, 141.

15. The Lamboutique and Le Herachy clans date from this early period; Gilles Gérard, *Famiy Maron*, 65–68; Bousquet, *Trois générations d'esclaves à Bourbon*, 1993.

16. Guët, *Les origines de l'Île Bourbon*, 141.

17. Mélanie Lamotte, "Economic Developments and the Growth of Colour Prejudice in the French Empire, c. 1635–1767" (Ph.D. diss., Cambridge University, 2015), 152.

18. August 1664 Edict of the King (establishing the Compagnie des Indes), Article 38, cited in Marvin, "Débris de Madagascar." The terminologies deployed to describe the offspring of mixed relations varied across the French empire. In New France (Canada), Illinois country, and Louisiana, where Native Americans intermarried with French, the category of *métis* (mixed Indian and European) came to be an important descriptor; Aubert, "Blood of France," 452–453; Spear, *Race, Sex and Social Order in Early New Orleans*, 14–15; Sophie White, *Wild Frenchmen and Frenchified Indians: Material Culture and Race in Colonial Louisiana*, Early American Studies (Philadelphia: University of Pennsylvania Press, 2013), 24–27. In Saint-Domingue, especially in the southwestern districts, a few families "of color" owned significant portions of land and slaves, but they increasingly faced racial discrimination in the middle and later eighteenth centuries. Garrigus, *Before Haiti*, 7–16, 158–162; Yvonne Fabella, "Redeeming the 'Character of the Creoles': Whiteness, Gender and Creolization in Pre-Revolutionary Saint-Domingue," *Journal of Historical Sociology* 23, no. 1 (March 2010): 40–72. Likewise, racial intermixture produced free families of color in Guadeloupe, though some of the terminology differed from that used in Saint-Domingue. Frédéric Régent, *Esclavage, métissage, liberté: La Révolution française en Guadeloupe, 1789–1802* (Paris: Grassat, 2004), 22. Racial divisions were less uniformly enforced in French Guiana, where the government was desperate to attract permanent settlers; Traver, "After Kourou"; Barbara Traver, "'The Benefits of Their Liberty': Race and the Euro-Africans of Gorée in Eighteenth-Century French Guiana," *French Colonial History* 16 (2016): 1–25.

    This pervasive policy within France's seventeenth-century empire stands in marked contrast to Ann Stoler's observation about Dutch policies promoting concubinage over marriage: "Interracial unions (as opposed to marriage) between European men and colonized women aided the long-term settlement of European men in the colonies while ensuring that colonial patrimony stayed in limited and selective hands" (*Carnal Knowledge*, 76). Two factors explain the difference in French policy: first, the stronger influence of the Catholic Church in French promotion of marriage over concubinage, and second, the wide gulf between French promotion of marriage and the lived experience on the ground, where sexual access to enslaved women was the norm in slave colonies. While Dutch culture seems to have presumed monogamous unions even outside formal marriages, French toleration for elite men's extramarital sexual partners was more permissive.

19. Larson, "Colonies Lost"; Carton, *Mixed Race and Modernity*.

20. Buxtorf, "Colonie, comptoirs et compagnie," 2:167–168. See also Urbain Lartin, "Les Indiens dans la société Bourbonnaise," in *Les relations historiques et culturelles*, 2:190. However, sometimes even these artisans were held on the island against their will; they came under contracts that they understood to be voluntary, but then found that local authorities would not let them return home; now they were slaves.

21. Helen M. Hintjens, "From French Slaves to Citizens: The African Diaspora in the Réunion Island," in *The African Diaspora in the Indian Ocean*, ed. Shihan de Silva Jayasuri and Richard Pankhurst (Trenton, NJ: Africa World Press, 2003), 102.

22. Nevertheless, this ratio was low compared to France's Caribbean island colonies. Sue Peabody, "'A Dangerous Zeal': Catholic Missions to Slaves in the French Antilles, 1635–1789," *French Historical Studies* 25, no. 1 (2002): 53–90.

23. Europeans brought a variety of religious traditions—Roman Catholic, Huguenot, Reformed, Armenian, Jewish—to their colonies throughout the globe. While Roman Catholicism offered a means for fusing immigrants from many locales in Isle Bourbon, colonial law there (unlike the 1685 Caribbean Code Noir) did not impose religious uniformity.

24. Lamotte, "Economic Developments and the Growth of Colour Prejudice," 153–154.

25. Unlike contemporary Mauritius, where the term *créole*, in Megan Vaughan's definition, connotes the descendants of African slaves, "those who are *not* . . . Hindus nor Muslims nor Tamils nor Chinese nor 'whites' of either the Franco or Anglo variety" (*Creating the Creole Island*, 3), in most eighteenth-century French colonies, including Isle Bourbon, the term *créole* was applied to anyone born in the colony. If there was a negative connotation, it applied to French creoles, who were often looked down upon by their continental counterparts.

26. Royal declaration of September 1698, Article 28 (ANOM F2a/12, f. 208–208v). Moreau de Saint-Méry, *Loix et constitutions*, 1:615, cites an identical article for the Saint-Domingue Company in "Édit en forme de Lettres-Patentes pour l'Établissement de la Compagnie Royale de Saint-Domingue, dite de la Nouvelle-Bourgogne," September 1698. Mélanie Lamotte (private correspondance) notes that a similar provision (Article 38) was promulgated earlier in 1664 by the Compagnie des Indes for Madagascar and "adjacent islands"; it is cited in Barassin, *Naissance d'une chrétienté*, 57. The 1698 declaration was not, as suggested by Frédéric Régent, specifically ordained for Isle Bourbon, in "Le métissage des premières générations de colons en Guadeloupe et à l'Isle Bourbon (Réunion)," in *Mariage et métissage dans les sociétés coloniales: Amériques, Afrique et Isles de l'Océan Indien (XVIe–XXe siècles)*, ed. Guy Brunet (Bern: Peter Lang, 2013), 125. Rather, it applied to French residents anywhere where the Company established settlements, including India, China, and so on. According to the compilation where it was recorded, it was renewed in "Lettres Patentes du mois d'aout 1717," art. 23; "Edit du mois de May 1719," art. 13; and "Edit du mois de Juillet 1720," art. 13. Many thanks to Nathan Marvin and Mélanie Lamotte for sharing their research on this document.

27. Ève, *Naître et mourir à l'Île Bourbon*, 17.

28. Wanquet, *Histoire d'une révolution*, 1:215–218, citing Jean Baptiste Geneviève Marcellin Bory de Saint-Vincent, *Voyage dans les quatre principales îles des mers d'Afrique*, 3 vols. (Paris: Year XIII [1804]), 2:311.

29. This was part of the worldwide intensification of French slave trading in both the Atlantic and Indian Oceans, rather than a shift of preference from earlier sites to the other. Edward A. Alpers, "The French Slave Trade in East Africa (1721–1810)," *Cahiers d'études africaines* 37 (1970): 80–124; Filliot, *La traite des esclaves vers les Mascareignes*; Edward A. Alpers, *Ivory and Slaves: Changing Patterns of International Trade in East Central Africa to the Later Nineteenth Century* (Berkeley: University of California Press, 1975); Jean Barassin,

"Aperçu général de l'évolution des groupes ethniques à l'Isle Bourbon depuis les origines jusqu'en 1848," in *Mouvements de populations dans l'Océan Indien: actes*; Thomas Vernet, "Le commerce des esclaves sur la côte Swahili, 1500–1750," *Azania* 38 (2003): 69–97; Vernet, "Slave Trade and Slavery on the Swahili Coast, 1500–1750," in *Slavery, Islam, and Diaspora*, ed. Behnaz Mirzai, Ismael Musah Montana, and Paul E. Lovejoy (Trenton, NJ: Africa World Press, 2009, 37–76; Vernet, "La première traite française à Zanzibar: Le journal de bord du vaisseau l'Espérance, 1774–1775," in *Civilisations des mondes insulaires (Madagascar, canal de Mozambique, Mascareignes, Polynésie, Guyanes): Mélanges en l'honneur du Professeur Claude Allibert*, ed. Chantal Radimilahy and et Narivelo Rajaonarimanana (Paris, Karthala, 2011), 477–521; Henri Médard, Marie-Laure Derat, Thomas Vernet, and Marie P. Ballarin, *Traites et esclavages en Afrique orientale et dans l'océan Indien* (Paris: Karthala et CIRESC, 2013). See also Allen, *European Slave Trading in the Indian Ocean*), esp. 65–69, 100–103. Note that the term "Mozambique," assigned by slave traders, comprised people from a wide range of ethnic and linguistic groups. Alpers, "Becoming 'Mozambique,'" and Alpers, "Mozambique and 'Mozambiques.'"

30. Megan Vaughan offers an exceptionally nuanced view of the multiplicity of ethnic and religious "roots" of people, enslaved and free, migrating into French colonies in the Indian Ocean in *Creating the Creole Island*, esp. 99–122. A variant eighteenth- and nineteenth-century spelling of *caffre* is *cafre*.

31. The "Letters patent in the form of edict" of December 1723 were registered in Isle Bourbon on 18 September 1724. Articles 1 (expelling all Jews), 5 (requiring Huguenots to send their slaves for Catholic instruction and worship), 7 (prohibiting markets on Sundays and holidays), and 8 (nullifying non-Catholic marriages) were omitted in the 1723 Indian Ocean code. J. B. E. Delaleu, *Code des îles de France et de Bourbon*, 2nd ed. (Port-Louis, Mauritius: chez Tristan Mallac et Cie, Imprimeurs du gouvernement, 1826), Isle de France (hereafter IF), 247–252. Delaleu's compendium contains separate sections for Isle de France and Isle Bourbon, each paginated separately. When the laws are identical, the Bourbon section (henceforth IB) often refers the reader back to the Isle de France pages, where the law is printed in full.

32. "Ce que la Compagnie Ordonne au Sujet des Noirs de L'Isle (ANOM F3 205, p. 108)," quoted in Lamotte, "Economic Developments and the Growth of Colour Prejudice," 324. The law was later incorporated into Ordinance 159 (7 September 1767), article 6, in Delaleu, *Code des îles de France et de Bourbon*, IB, 61.

33. Ordinance 159, article 20, in Delaleu, *Code des îles de France et de Bourbon*, IB, 62.

34. "Instructions du Ministère de la marine, concernant la tolérance envers l'islam et l'hindouisme dans les colonies françaises de l'Océan indien sous l'Ancien Régime," transcribed by Nathan Marvin, *Outre-mers, revue d'histoire*, 388–389 (2015): 285–290.

35. As Jean-François Niort, Jérémy Richard, and Brett Rushforth and have pointed out, the term "Code Noir" was not the official title of the 1685 legislation. Jean-François Niort and Jérémy Richard, "L'édit royal de mars 1685 touchant la police des îles de l'Amérique française dit 'Code Noir': Versions choisies, comparés et commentées," in "L'esclavage: la question de l'homme. Histoire, religion, philosophie, droit," special issue, *Droits* 50 (2009): 143–162; Rushforth, *Bonds of Alliance*, 355. It is noteworthy that the original title of the 1685 edict references "negroes and slaves," probably to include the presence of enslaved Indians in the Caribbean colonies. The term "Code Noir" did not begin to be

used until the early eighteenth century; its earliest use that I am aware of is in administrative correspondence originating in Martinique: Governor Phélypeaux du Verger, Letter to the Secretary of State for the Navy, 6 April, 1713 (ANOM COL, C8A 19, fol. 84). By 1718, it was the title of a published version of the Caribbean law: *Le Code noir, ou édit . . . servant de règlement pour le gouvernement et l'administration de justice et la police des isles françoises de l'Amérique . . .* (Paris: Veuve Saugrain, 1718).

36. See, for example, Louis Sala-Molins, *Le code noir ou le Calvaire de Canaan*, Pratiques théoriques (Paris: Presses Universitaires de France, 1987), 15, 85; Spear, *Race, Sex and Social Order in Early New Orleans*, 53; Jean-François Niort, *Le Code noir. Idées reçues sur un texte symbolique* (Paris: Éditions du Cavalier Bleu, 2015), 23.

37. "Lettres patentes en forme d'édit, concernant les esclaves nègres des Isles de France et de Bourbon," in Delaleu, *Code des îles de France et de Bourbon*, IF, 258.

38. Aubert, "The Blood of the French," 474. In 1667, the same year that Colbert formally encouraged marriages between Frenchmen and Indians in New France, the Sovereign Council of Guadeloupe prohibited marriages between blacks and whites, but this measure was never ratified by the crown. Debbasch, *Couleur et liberté*, 48. In 1758, colonial administrators in Guadeloupe requested again that such a ban be issued, but for reasons unexplained, the crown decided not to implement the ban there. Régent, "Le métissage des premières générations," 130. Vincent Cousseau, "Le métissage dans la Martinique de l'époque esclavagiste: un phénomène ordinaire entre déni et acceptation," in Brunet, *Mariage et métissage dans les sociétés coloniales*, 133–158. For Saint-Domingue, see Dominique Rogers, "Les libres de couleur dans les capitales de Saint-Domingue: Fortune, mentalités et intégration à la fin de l'Ancien Régime (1776–1789)" (thesis, Université Michel de Montaigne, Bordeaux III, 1999), 545; Garrigus, *Before Haiti*, 42; Taber, "Issue of their Union," 110. Although methodologically somewhat dated (because it takes the racial ascriptions of the censuses at face value), see also Jacques Houdaille, "Le métissage dans les anciennes colonies françaises," *Population* 36, no. 2 (1981): 267–286.

39. Marie Polderman, "Populations pionnières et métissage en Guyane (1680–1737)," in Brunet, *Mariage et métissage dans les sociétés coloniales*, 159–184.

40. In 1724, the Louisiana slave population (about one thousand) was just beginning to surpass number of free people. Gwendolyn Midlo Hall, *Africans in Colonial Louisiana: The Development of Afro-Creole Culture in the Eighteenth Century* (Baton Rouge: Louisiana State University Press, 1992), 10. By contrast, Isle Bourbon now held about eight thousand residents, three-quarters of whom were enslaved. Dion, *Quand La Réunion s'appelait Bourbon*, 23.

41. "Frenchmen are prohibited from marrying negresses; this would give black men distaste [*dégoûterait les noirs*] for service"; the marriage of white women to black men was "a confusion to avoid." Guët, *Les origines de l'Île Bourbon*, 125. Interestingly, the prohibition did not apply to the Portuguese or Dutch men living in Isle Bourbon.

42. Article 9 (1685) levied a heavy fine against informal unions between free men and female slaves and the confiscation of the resulting offspring, but made an exception for "Free men who will have had one or more children by their concubinage with slaves, as well as the masters who have permitted it." "Édit du Roi, touchant l'Etat & la Discipline des Esclaves Nègres de l'Amérique Française, donné à Versailles, au mois de Mars 1685," in France, *Recueils de reglemens, edits, declarations et arrets: concernant le commerce, l'administration*

de la justice et la police des colonies françaises de l'Amérique, & les engagés avec le code noir et l'addition audit code (Paris: Hachette, 1744–1745), 1:85. No doubt this provision of the 1685 Caribbean law resulted from the "most Christian king" Louis XIV's desire to encourage legitimate Catholic marriages (even as he himself famously maintained a series of mistresses and naturalized his illegitimate sons).

43. Ève, *Naître et mourir à l'Île Bourbon,* 49; Ordinance 159, article 7, in Delaleu, *Code des îles de France et de Bourbon,* IB, 61.

44. Lamotte finds that these interethnic marriages were frequent in Isle Bourbon in the late seventeenth century. "Economic Developments and the Growth of Colour Prejudice," 195–197, 229–230. Nathan Marvin has identified at least sixteen biracial marriages between 1767 and 1789 and twenty more for the decade of the Revolution, 1790–1802 (private correspondence, 23 May 2016).

45. "Lettres patentes en forme d'édit, concernant les esclaves nègres des Isles de France et de Bourbon," article 43, in Delaleu, *Code des îles de France et de Bourbon,* IF, 250–251.

46. Articles 55–59 of the 1685 Caribbean code and articles 49–53 of the 1723 Indian Ocean code.

47. "Lettres patentes en forme d'édit, concernant les esclaves nègres des Isles de France et de Bourbon," article 51 (1723), in Delaleu, *Code des îles de France et de Bourbon,* IF, 251, formerly article 57 (1685). Similar regulations were subsequently reissued for the Windward Islands as "Déclaration du roi interprétant l'édit de mars 1685 sur les esclaves nègres des Isles du Vent, et particulièrement l'article 39 sur les châtiments à infliger à ceux qui donneraient retraite aux nègres fugitifs, ainsi que l'article 52 de l'édit de mars 1724, qui interdit les donations entre vifs par des blancs à des affranchis (no. 34)," 5 February 1726 (ANOM COL A 25 F° 59).

48. Dominique Rogers finds that colonial judges "systematically favored [illegitimate free colored children] over legitimate, but less closely related, heirs residing in France." "On the Road to Citizenship: The Complex Route to Integration of the Free People of Color in the Two Capitals of Saint-Domingue," in *The World of the Haitian Revolution,* ed. David Patrick Geggus and Norman Fiering, Blacks in the Diaspora (Bloomington: Indiana University Press, 2009), 71.

49. The arrival date is not known. Eugénie was born at sea on 27 February 1773, so it must have been sometime thereafter.

50. Census, Isle Bourbon, 1776 (ANOM DPPC G1/479).

51. Bernardin de Saint-Pierre, *Voyage à l'Île de France,* 1:238.

52. The property is described in the 1780 census: "A parcel of land from the sea, situated in the Sainte-Marie parish 650 × 42.5 *gaulettes* [about 162 acres]; another at 9,000 *pieds* [9,600 feet] from the border of the sea, situated in the Sainte-Marie parish . . . 110 × 150 *gaulettes* [about 97 acres]; another from the [illegible] to the summit of the mountains, situated in the Sainte-Marie parish300 × 28 *gaulettes* [about 32 acres]; another parcel at 700 *gaulettes* [8,960 feet] from the shoreline, situated in the parish of Saint-André, 33 × 55 *gaulettes* [almost 7 acres]." Census, Isle Bourbon, Sainte-Marie, "Sieurs Routier Père," 1780 (ADR 71C).

53. Census, Isle Bourbon, Sainte-Marie, "Sieurs Routier Père," 1780 (ADR 71C).

54. Census, Isle Bourbon, Sainte-Marie, 1776 (ANOM DPPC G1/479). That eighteen of the children were boys and only seven were girls suggests that the family was purchasing boys directly from the transoceanic slave trade.

55. Census, Isle Bourbon, Sainte-Marie, "Sieurs Routier Père," 1780 (ADR 71C).

56. Ève, *Le corps des esclaves*, 246–253.

57. ANOM IREL, Réunion, État civil, Sainte-Marie, Baptism, 23 July 1774. Although the baptismal record for the younger daughter clearly says "Euphrosie," she is listed in the subsequent censuses as Euphémie, which I will use for consistency.

58. Ricquebourg, *Dictionnaire généalogique*, 3:2590. Their full names are Marie Charles Euphémy and Charles Marie Élie. Since most of the Routier children had a version of Charles Marie in their names, I have abbreviated them here, as they will appear in later censuses, to the shorter, more distinguishable versions of their names.

59. Passengers, Isle Bourbon, Departures, 27 December 1774, *La Brune* (ADR 58C). The grandfather will remain in France until his death in 1786.

60. Charles Routier is found on two passenger lists, returning from Isle de France in 1780 and 1783. Passengers, Isle Bourbon, Arrivals, 19 November 1780, *L'Europe* (ANOM, COL, F/5B/6) and Passengers, Isle Bourbon, Saint-Denis, Arrivals, 22 November 1783, *L'Osterley* (ANOM, COL, F/5B/6 and ADR 58C).

61. There is always the possibility that she lost other children as infants, leaving no memory to her future children. Since slaves are not grouped in families in these records, there is nothing to indicate their relationship to Madeleine. Census, Isle Bourbon, Sainte-Marie, sieurs Routier, père et fils 1780 (ADR 71C); Census, Isle Bourbon, Sainte-Marie, Veuve Routier, 1787 (ADR74C).

62. Gerbeau, *Family Maron*, 70, 128. I searched for evidence of Maurice's baptism in the microfilms of the ADR Saint-Denis parish records for 1775–1777 (2Mi-EC11 [J22–J25]) and the digitized Sainte-Marie parish records, 1774–1779, on ANOM IREL, without success. A note added to the 1775 register states that it contains only "whites and free blacks."

63. Maurice Coëffard is listed as *économe, rentier*, at the Saint-Denis residence of ~~Etienne~~ "Augustin Rotier" in 1776; Census, Isle Bourbon, Sainte-Marie, 1776 (ANOM DPPC G1/479). Coëffard was listed in the 1787 census as 56 years old; Census, Isle Bourbon, Sainte-Marie, Veuve Routier, 1787 (ADR74C).

64. Matthew Gerber, *Bastards: Politics, Family, and Law in Early Modern France* (New York: Oxford University Press, 2012), esp. 90–91.

65. A series of local acts issued in Guadeloupe (1763), Martinique (1773), and Saint-Domingue (1773) prohibited free people of color from using white surnames; Debbasch, *Couleur et liberté*, 69–71. This was never formally decreed in Isle Bourbon, and the recognized mixed children of the Indian Ocean colony inherited their father's last name. However, mixed children born out of wedlock typically took their mother's first name as a surname.

66. Because Maurice was born in the colony, he is merely listed as "creole," without any descriptor that would indicate his father's color or race.

67. It is only because of a single mention by his sister Constance many years later that we know of Maurice's relationship to Madeleine and his siblings. She mentioned that Maurice died "in July 1810, in the service of Monsieur Cyrille Routier, when the island was taken by the English." "Extrait d'une Mémoire déposé au greffe de la Cour Royale de l'Ile de Bourbon le trois Décembre 1817 par M. le Procureur général pour servir s'il y a lieu, à intenter toute procédure criminelle ou correctionnelle" (ADR 1Jp2007-1, no. 36).

68. Madeleine, age 26, appears as one of 27 adult female slaves in the 1780 census, as well as her son, "Morice, *créol*, 5." Census, Isle Bourbon, Sainte-Marie, sieurs Routier père et fils, 1780

(ADR). The return is signed "Routier," but he could have delegated the drafting of the census to someone else. Gilles Gérard, who has worked intensively with the Bourbon census rolls, notes that the ascriptions of origin are not always consistent or accurate from census to census (*Famiy Maron*, 62). However, we can be sure that this is indeed "our" Madeleine, because in the subsequent census, in 1784, she appears again, this time as "[Mad]elaine, indiene, 27." Census, Isle Bourbon, Sainte-Marie, Sieurs Routier Père, 1784 (ADR 71C). There is some damage at the extreme margins of this document, but I am certain that this is Madeleine. Maurice's name has been obscured by damage to the paper.

69. Inconsistency regarding ages is not uncommon for slaves or free people, especially in the eighteenth century. However, the lack of attention to his year of birth implies that he was not especially important to the Routier family.

70. Michèle Dion lists 57 storms retroactively designated level five, the highest possible force, for Isle Bourbon between 1657 and 1799 (*Quand La Réunion s'appelait Bourbon*, 180–81). Emmanuel Garnier and Jeremy Desarthe, tracing the impact of 89 cyclones in La Réunion and Mauritius between 1656 and 2007, conclude that the period from 1750 to 1849 was the most destructive, but, by their own admission, these records are incomplete and tend to be more systematic and reliable after 1789; E. Garnier and J. Desarthe, "Cyclones and Societies in the Mascarene Islands 17th-20th Centuries," *American Journal of Climate Change*, 2 (2013): 3-4, available online at http://www.scirp.org/journal/PaperInformation.aspx?PaperID=29074.

71. Garnier and Desarthe, "Cyclones and Societies," 8.

72. S. K. Devi, "History of Cyclones on the Coromandel Coast with Special Reference to Tamil Nadu, 1800–1900" (Ph.D. diss., Bharathidasan University, 2011), 12–18, 34–48, 76–77.

73. Ève, *Le corps des esclaves*, 65–75.

74. Ricquebourg, *Dictionnaire généalogique*, 3:2590.

75. Dion, *Quand La Réunion s'appelait Bourbon*, 181.

76. Ève, *Le corps des esclaves*, p. 70.

77. Census, Isle Bourbon, Sainte-Marie [torn], Sieurs Routier père et fils, 1784 (ADR 71C).

78. Census, Isle Bourbon, Sainte-Marie, Sieurs Routier père et fils, 1780 (ADR 71C).

79. Men: 32.9; women: 29.6.

80. Unlike the 1776 census table, which categorized slaves only by age and sex, the Routiers' individual 1780 census recorded place of birth. In general, the Routiers' slaves were predominantly Malagasy (47 percent) and creole (30 percent), with only a quarter—all adults—originating in the African mainland (*cafre*, 22 percent).

81. Charles Routier made a trip to and from Isle de France in October and November 1783; Passengers, Isle Bourbon, Saint-Denis, Departure, 11 October 1783 and Arrival, 22 November 1783 (ANOM COL F/5B/6). He then left for France on *La Beauté* on 16 April 1784. An unnamed son (probably Élie) arrived in Isle Bourbon from Isle de France on 5 November 1784 (ANOM COL F/5B/6).

82. "B[aptized]: a little female slave belonging to M. Routier. Constance, illegitimate daughter of Magdelene, negress and slave of Monsieur Rotier [*sic*]. The godfather was Monsieur Charles Routier and the godmother Euphémie Routier. [Signed] Father Bourdet. Euphémie Routier, Charles Routier." Baptèmes, Mariages, Sépultres des Esclaves, 1784 (ADR, 2 MIEC11 [J35–36]). Unusually, no date is listed for this entry, but it appears in the register between 10 and 13 April 1784.

83. Prosper Ève, *Variations sur le thème de l'amour à Bourbon à l'époque de l'esclavage* (Saint-André, Réunion: Conseil Générale de la Réunion/Océan Editions, 1998), 128.

84. During the 1780s, 21.5 percent of the 566 recorded baptisms for whites in the Saint-Denis parish were for illegitimate children. Ève, *Variations sur le thème*, 42. What is perhaps more surprising is the dramatic increase in illegitimate births in Réunion over the twentieth century, surpassing 50 percent in 1987 (Ève, *Variations sur le thème*, 8).

85. Ève's study is a little incomplete on this point; his statistics on named godparents for slaves in Saint-Denis go only through 1757, when the proportion of slaves reaches 51.7 percent, but the trend toward appointing slaves rather than whites as godparents for slaves is clear. Ève, *Naître et mourir à l'Île Bourbon*, 114. Palmer shows how slave owners' selection of godparents for their slaves was strategic (*Intimate Bonds*, 63–68).

86. ADR 2MIEC11 (J38). "Registre Paroissale de St. Denis, 1786." "Marie Louise, bastard daughter of *la nommée* Marie Joseph, slave belonging to M. Rotier [*sic*]," had Calixte and Marie Louise, both slaves, named as godparents; another Routier slave, Etienette, daughter of Marie Françoise, had Antoine Brocard and Dorothé Rattier named as godparents.

87. Charles Routier departed on April 16, 1784 aboard *La Beauté*, returning to Isle Bourbon a little over six months later. Passengers, Isle Bourbon, [Saint-Denis], 5 November 1784, *L'Asie* (ANOM COL F/5B/6).

88. Sometimes spelled "Wetter." The 1814 census says that Vetter arrived in 1782 aboard *Les Trois Amis*; Census, Isle Bourbon, Saint-Denis, 1814 (ADR L166.2). The 6 May 1840 decision of the Cour de Cassation identified "Weter" as her father and stated that he purchased her from the Routier family (ANOM FM GEN 158/1307). No extant contemporaneous documents indicate how or when this "sale" occurred.

89. Of 1,029 free people of color censused in 1788, more than 75 percent were of children; Ève, *Naître et mourir à l'Île Bourbon*, 37. On the higher proportion of women and children among the freed in the French Caribbean, see Arlette Gautier, *Les soeurs de Solitude: Femmes et l'esclavage aux Antilles du XVIIe au XIXe siècle* (Rennes, France: Presses Universitaires de Rennes, 2010), 153; Garrigus, *Before Haiti*, 60; and Palmer, *Intimate Bonds*, 101.

90. Wanquet, *Histoire d'une Révolution*, 219; Ève, *Naître et mourir à l'Île Bourbon*, 24.

91. "under the offer to give her the gift of the one named Suzanne, an Indian woman of thirty years, and to have care of her forever at all times in such a way that she will not be a burden to the colony." Actes d'affranchissement, 1767–1786 (ADR 1B9J25, no. 439); the manumission petition was submitted on 9 September 1785 and approved on 13 January 1786. Constance's later *mémoire* (factum) refers to him as "Monsieur Weter" ("Extrait d'une Mémoire déposé au greffe de la Cour Royale de l'Ile de Bourbon le trois Décembre 1817 par M. le Procureur général pour servir s'il y a lieu, à intenter toute procédure criminelle ou correctionnelle" (ADR 1Jp2007-1, no. 36]). The Routier family owned a slave named Suzanne in 1781, but she was much older (38) and continues to be listed as their slave in the 1787 census and so is probably not the same person (ADR 71C and 74C).

92. *Annales maritimes et coloniales Annales maritimes et coloniales, 26ᵉ année, 1841, 2ᵉ série, 1ʳᵉ partie: partie officielle* (Paris: Imprimerie Royale, 1841), 324.

93. Testimony by enslaved women narrating their sexual experiences with free men are rare, particularly before the nineteenth century, since the law did not recognize their capacity to be raped. A few legal records suggest that free men might use flattery and insinuation as preambles to their pressure, but the word "seduction" is inappropriate, since their positions of power always carried the imminent threat of violence should women refuse; Block, *Rape and Sexual Power*, 72–74. See also Christine Hünefeldt, *Paying the Price of Freedom: Family and Labor among Lima's Slaves, 1800–1854* (Berkeley: University of California Press, 1995), 130, and Melton A. McLaurin, *Celia, a Slave* (Athens, GA: University of Georgia Press, 1999), 20–24.

94. NARM, OA 69, Procureur Général: Régistre pour la consignation de divers plaints et declarations, December 1772–May 1794, quoted in translation by Vaughan, *Creating the Creole Island*, 168–169. The 'Ky' in Kymorseven is a mistranscription of the usual handwritten abbreviation of the Breton "Ker."

95. Félicité Constance Douyere (1767–ca. 1846), Ricquebourg, *Dictionnaire généalogique*, 3:2815.

96. In 1787, the 31-year-old Vetter and his young wife were living in a 25' x 16' house with their newborn daughter, Catherine Margueritte Joséphine, age one month, with land in Saint-Denis. He owned seven slaves, two goats, three pigs, and three horses. His signature suggests basic literacy, but without a flourish. Census, Isle Bourbon, Saint-Denis, Mattias Wetter, 1786 (ADR 73C, no. 271). Ricquebourg gives his year of birth as "near 1757 in Molsheim, Lower Rhine, Saint-George parish." Ricquebourg, *Dictionnaire généalogique*, 3:2815–2816.

97. Census, Isle Bourbon, Saint-Denis, Mattias Wetter, 1788 (ADR 75C, no. 271).

98. Census, Isle Bourbon, Sainte-Marie, *Veuve* Routier, 1787 (ADR 74C). There is a 31-year-old slave named Suzanne itemized on the Routier slave inventory in 1787, but this is a common name; the Routiers own a second Suzanne, age 22.

99. See Constance's census returns discussed in chapter 6 as well as her letter to Louis Gilbert Boucher, 15 December 1817 ANOM 3201 (SG REU) COL 97/684.

100. Ève, *Le corps des esclaves*, 70.

101. Ève, *Le corps des esclaves*, 66.

102. A "Sieur" Routier (certainly Charles), major in the militia of Saint-Denis, boarded the *Chameau*, bound for France on 25 February 1786, but a marginal note mentions that he got off again [*redébarqué*] before it set sail, while "Routier *particulier* [private individual]" arrived from Isle de France on 14 June 1786; Routier, Major of the Saint-Denis militia (Charles again), returned from Isle de France on 16 October 1786 aboard the *Prudent*; Passengers, Isle Bourbon, Arrivals and Departures, 1785–1786 (ADR 58C). "Routier fils, v[olontai]re de marine," probably Augustin, departed to Isle de France aboard *Le Prudent* on 14 August 1787 and again on 13 November 1788, this time as "captain of the Merchant Navy"; Passengers, Isle Bourbon, Arrivals and Departures, 1786 (ANOM COL F/5B/7 and ADR 58C). "François Routier, v[olontai]re de Bourbon" (probably Augustin), seated at the officers' table, traveled aboard *La Genevieve*, on 8 April 1788 (ADR 58C), while his younger brother, Jean Nicholas François "Fauchin" traveled to Isle de France on the *Duc de Chartres* on 16 April 1788; Passengers, Isle Bourbon, Saint-Denis, Departures, 1788 (ANOM COL F/5B/7).

103. Jean Nicholas Routier was buried in Port-Louis, France (not Isle de France), on 24 October 1786; of course, the news would not have reached Charles Routier until months later (AD Morbihan, État civil, Port-Louis, photo 228/462, http://www.archives.mor-bihan.fr/rechercher/. Many thanks to Jean-Michel André and Annie Blayo for this reference.

104. ADR, Registre Paroissial de Saint-Denis, 1786 (2 MIEC11 [J38]). The entry was recorded by Father Bourdet, a member of the Recollet order. A later record states that this was also the date of his birth, but this is not certain. "Extrait d'une Mémoire déposé au greffe de la Cour Royale de l'Ile de Bourbon le trois Décembre 1817 par M. le Procureur général pour servir s'il y a lieu, à intenter toute procédure criminelle ou cor-rectionnelle" (ADR 1Jp2007-1, no. 36). The *Gazette des tribunaux* erroneously gives the year of his birth as 1788 (24 December 1843).

105. Roman law had reserved the term "natural" for the children of concubines and per-mitted them to inherit from their fathers, but since the sixteenth century French law had excluded all children born out of wedlock from recognition and inheritance, even forbidding the mother to name the father. Such attitudes, however, were beginning to change in the eighteenth century. Matthew Gerber, "Illegitimacy, Natural Law and Legal Culture on the Eve of the French Revolution," *Proceedings of the Western Society for French History* 33 (2005): 240–257.

106. ADR, Registre Paroissial de Saint-Denis, 1786 (2 MIEC11 [J38]). Strangely, neither name appears in Ricquebourg's voluminous *Dictionnaire généalogique* of Isle Bourbon, suggesting that they may have been free people of color. For the godmother, the closest possible match is Anne Louise Thérèse Charlotte Sophie Fabus de Vernan, future wife of a prominent colonist, but in October 1786 Anne Louise was only six months old and probably had not yet arrived from her natal Bordeaux. Several "Silves" appear in Bousquet, *Les esclaves et leurs maîtres*, 45, 112. Antoine Silve "Indien," served as a witness to a slave wedding in 1709.

107. On 2 August 1793, a proud Parisian father named his newborn son Fédéré Furcy Clair. Several months later, on 4 Brumaire II (9 November 1793), as the Terror was in full swing, the father received permission from the Société populaire to change Fédéré's first names to Réunion La Fraternité, clearly signifying his enthusiasm for the new regime. However, by 1812, this name no longer had the same cachet, and the father was permitted to rename his son Furcy Clair, which he presumably carried through the rest of his life. Pierre-Henri Billy, "Des prénoms révolutionnaires en France," *Annales historiques de la révolution française* 322 (2000), http://ahrf.revues.org/document125.html.

108. A Saint-Furcy church was built during the Renaissance in the town of Lagny-sur-Marne, east of Paris, but the building was mostly destroyed by republicans during the Revolution. Ministère français de la Culture, Mérimée database, "Eglise Saint-Furcy (ancienne): par-tie subsistante," http://www.culture.gouv.fr/.

109. *Le Gazette de Maurice*, 8 November 1817, 29 November 1817, 10 January 1818, 7 March 1818, 28 March 1818, 18 April 1818, 6 June 1818, 13 June 1818, available online at http://la-gazette-de-maurice.blogspot.com/. A keyword search for slaves in Mauritius by the name of Furcy in the genealogical database Ancestry turned up 24 listings (approximately eighteen individuals) with the last name Furcy and 81 listings

(approximately sixty individuals) with the first name Furcy, born between 1752 and 1830; http://www.Ancestry.co.uk. The originals of these records can be found in "Office of Registry of Colonial Slaves and Slave Compensation Commission Records" (NAUK T71 566–573). Additionally, there were free men with "Furcy" as a first or a last name in Isle Bourbon and Isle de France. For example, just a couple of years before Furcy was born, Monsieur and Madame Maillot christened their son Adrien Ferreol Furcy in the parish of Saint-André, Isle Bourbon; ANOM IREL, Réunion, État Civil, Saint-André, Baptism, 14 August 1783. A Furcy Dennemont testified regarding the discovery of a dead slave in 1804 (Ève, *Le corps des Esclaves*, 359). Likewise, four slaves escaped from a "Sieur Furcy Galenne" when he threatened them with extreme punishment in 1835, and a slave named Henry fled his new master to return to his former master "Sieur Furcy Ribenaire" in 1844; ADR 168 U, cited in Prosper Ève, *Les esclaves de Bourbon: La mer et la montagne* (Paris: Karthala, 2003), 103, 287.

110. Eugénie, Constance, and Furcy shared their names with three of Joseph Lory's nieces and nephews: Etienne Helene Constant Hulot (b. 1783) and André Furcy Hulot (b. 1789). Albert Révérend, *Titres, anoblissements et pairies de la restauration 1814–1830* (Paris: Honoré Champion, 1904), 4:26.

111. *Gazette des tribunaux*, 14 August 1835, 1.

112. Furcy to Boucher, 15 May 1826 (ADR 1Jp2007-1, no. 71).

113. Thureau, *Plaidoyer pour le sieur Furcy*, 4. The *Gazette des tribunaux* also gives Furcy's occupational title (22 December 1843, 1).

CHAPTER 4

1. "Furci, créol, 1," and "Magdelene, indienne, 29." Census, Isle Bourbon, Sainte-Marie, Routier, 1787 (ADR 74C).

2. Census, Isle Bourbon, Saint-Denis, "Dame Vve Routier et héritiers de feu Sieur Routier" (hereafter "Routier"), 1787 (ADR 74C).

3. Billiard, *Voyage aux colonies orientales*, 125.

4. He was buried 21 December 1787 in Saint-Denis (ADR 4E2–55, via microfilm: 1Mi28 [B23–27]).

5. Routier fils, "v[olontai]re de Bourbon," departed 14 August 1787, and again 16 April 1788. Colonies, Passengers, Departures and Arrivals, Isle Bourbon, 1787 and 1788 (ANOM COL, F/5B/6).

6. Census, Isle Bourbon, Sainte-Marie, Routier, 1787 (ADR 74C).

7. Census, Isle Bourbon, Sainte-Marie, Routier, 1787 (ADR 74C). Janot, *créol*, 35, is also listed. A Suzanne, *malgache*, 31 is part of the Routier holdings as well.

8. Ève, *Le corps des esclaves*, 65.

9. Ève, *Le corps des esclaves*, 84–95.

10. Prior to the Revolution, only three slave revolts were prosecuted in Isle Bourbon, each of them fairly small. On the other hand, in 1,270 judicial prosecutions of slaves in Isle Bourbon between 1750 and 1848, violence was implicated in 36 percent of these; their frequency climbed dramatically after the introduction of sugar and the abolition of the slave trade in around 1817. Audrey Carotenuto, "Un autre regard sur les complots serviles

à l'île Bourbon (XVIIIe–XIXe siècles)," in *Villes portuaires du commerce triangulaire à l'abolition de l'esclavage*, ed. Eric Saunier, Cahiers de l'histoire et des mémoires de la traite négrière, de l'esclavage et de leurs abolitions en Normandie, no. 1, (Le Havre: Université du Havre, 2009), 147, 159, 163.

11. Prosper Ève, "Les formes de résistance à Bourbon de 1750 à 1789," in Dorigny, *Les abolitions de l'esclavage*, 49–71.

12. Teelock, *Bitter Sugar*, 34.

13. Richard S. Dunn, *Sugar and Slaves: The Rise and Fall of the Planter Class in the British West Indies* (Chapel Hill: University of North Carolina Press, 1972), 188–223, and Teelock, *Bitter Sugar*, 93–96, 152–154, but see a revisionist approach, stressing how little time was actually spent by slaves in the sugar harvest compared to other tasks. Justin Roberts, "Working between the Lines: Labor and Agriculture on Two Barbadian Sugar Plantations, 1796–97," *William and Mary Quarterly*, 3rd ser., 63, no. 3 (July 2006): 551–586.

14. I base this on a reading of Ève's *Le corps des esclaves*, esp. the chapter "Les corps Violentés," 343–399, analyzing dozens of postmortem investigations. Gilles Gérard and Martine Grimaud narrate a story of such abuse dating to late in Isle Bourbon's period of slavery, as both economic pressures intensified on slaveholders and humanitarian interest increased in the general public. *Des esclaves sous le fouet: Le procès Morette à l'Île Bourbon* (Paris: L'Harmattan, 2016). By contrast, whippings and other forms of brutality were more common (or more visible) in the United States and Saint-Domingue. Thavolia Glymph, *Out of the House of Bondage: The Transformation of the Plantation Household* (Cambridge, U.K.: Cambridge University Press, 2008), 30–38, 40–48, 55–57, 68–70; Malick Ghachem, *The Old Regime and the Haitian Revolution* (Cambridge, U.K.: Cambridge University Press, 2012), 12–14, 62–63, 127–140, 167–199.

15. Ève, *Le corps des esclaves*, 116–118.

16. Ève found that the number of recorded suicides increased during the period of royal rule, 1767–1789, moderated slightly during the Revolution, and then increased dramatically during the Restoration, as sugar came to dominate the island's agriculture, though they also tended to cluster in particular years; *Le corps des esclaves*, 344–345.

17. Thureau, *Plaidoyer pour le sieur Furcy*, 4.

18. All three petitions were submitted on July 3 and granted on 6 July 1789. Affranchissements, Nos. 725, 726 and 727 (ANOM 6DPPC 3742). Jeannot had accompanied the Routiers to France in 1770; Passengers, Lorient, Arrivals, 18 August 1770, *La Paix* (ANOM COL F/5B/21, SHDL 2P 13–III.10 and 2P46–I.9). He appears as "Jannott" and "Janot" at the head of the list of the Routiers' slaves in the censuses of 1780 and 1784 (Sainte-Marie, ADR 71C), and, age 35, in 1787 (Sainte-Marie, ADR 74C). Jeannot was freed in 1789 "in recognition of the good services he had rendered to the deceased Monsieur Routier."

The other slave freed by the widow Routier was a boy, Maximilian, *créole*, 10, the son of an unnamed wet nurse, "who has rendered great services to the Desblottières family and who Madame Desblottières Vermont [Mary Anne Ursule's niece] has given the gift of a slave, and gives the sum of three thousand livres in silver so that he will not become a burden to the colony." Presumably Maximilien was freed as compensation to his mother for her services, yet the widow's role in this transaction is odd. "Maximilien" has never appeared on her slave census, so it is not clear why she was performing the manumission of what was presumably one of her niece's slaves. The niece, aged twenty, already the mother of three children (one deceased), would die within the year after giving birth to her fourth child. Was the liberation of Madeleine and the two others somehow an act of conscience, a ritual in recognition or anticipation of important deaths in the family?

19. There are numerous copies of this document. The earliest (the contemporaneous copy sent to the ministry in France in 1789) does not mention of the name Despense or any stipulation that Madeleine would receive a pension, though Jeannot's and Maximilien's pensions are specified: Affranchissements, no. 727 (ANOM 6DPPC 3742). Other copies of the manumission include: Copy, "Acte d'affranchissement de la nommée Madelaine indienne," 6 July 1789, registered by the clerk of the Tribunal du 1er Instance de l'Isle Bonaparte, 30 June 1808 (ADR 1Jp2007-1, nos. 37 and 39); a version "verified against the original, inscribed in the register of acts of liberty no. 2, f° 65 [signed] le Contrôleur colonial L Gérard" (ANOM FM SG REU 97/684, no. 2); Thureau, *Plaidoyer pour le sieur Furcy*, 3–4; and *Gazette des tribunaux*, 21 December 1843. Gérard retired from the position of *controleur colonial* on 7 November 1821, so this copy probably dates from the period around Furcy's initial freedom suit.

20. Wanquet places the proportion of freedmen and women at 2.6 percent of the 1788 slave population (*Révolution*, 3:135–136). Prosper Ève, by contrast, enumerates Isle Bourbon's 1788 population as 42,588 slaves (78.4 percent), 8,182 whites (17.3 percent), and 1,029 free people of color (2.2 percent) (*Naître et mourir à l'Île Bourbon*, 16–17), but Ève's figures do not correlate with the figures given by Barassin, cited as Ève's source. Barassin, "Aperçu général de l'évolution des groupes ethniques à l'Isle Bourbon," 246–247.

21. Ève, *Variations sur le thème*, 72. Ève gives the same total figure in *Naître et mourir à l'Île Bourbon*, 17. The *libres* census total for 1787 was only 919 (ANOM COL G1/479).

22. "Extrait d'une Mémoire déposé au greffe de la Cour Royale de l'Ile de Bourbon le trois Décembre 1817 par M. le Procureur général pour servir s'il y a lieu, à intenter toute procédure criminelle ou correctionnelle" (ADR 1Jp2007-1, no. 36).

23. "Janot" will be listed as the widow's free overseer (*commandeur*) on her Sainte-Marie plantation in 1807; Census, Isle Bonaparte, Saint-Marie, "Dame Ursule Desblottières, Vve Routier," 1807 (ADR L171). It is unclear whether he, like Madeleine, knew of his status as a free man.

24. An example of such an informal understanding can be found in the declaration made by Marie Anne Touchard, the widow Dian, regarding her fifty-year-old slave and domestic servant Anne, in Marseille, "that [she] is very satisfied with the services, the fidelity, and the good conduct of the said negress, and that she regards her in her house as her own child, to the point that, for a long time, she would have manumitted her if the formalities for this act had been practicable in France, but that this liberty, in addition, would only be pure ceremony, considering the fact that the negress is free by the agreements that she enjoys with her mistress and by the complete confidence that she has merited" (ÀNOM, F/1B/4, fol. 268-v). Many thanks to Pierre H. Boulle for providing this example.

25. Droits de l'Homme et du Citoyen, 1789, in *Archives parlementaires de 1787 à 1860: Première série (1789–1799)*, ed. Jérôme Mavidal, Émile Laurent, et al., 102 vols. (Paris: E. Dupont [etc.], 1862–2012), 67:143–144.

26. Much has been written about the Haitian Revolution and its impact on world history. See especially Carolyn E. Fick, *The Making of Haiti: The Saint-Domingue Revolution*

from Below (Knoxville: University of Tennessee Press, 2000); Laurent Dubois, *Avengers of the New World* (Cambridge, MA: Harvard University Press, 2004); Jeremy D. Popkin, *You Are All Free: The Haitian Revolution and the Abolition of Slavery* (Cambridge, U.K.: Cambridge University Press, 2010), Alyssa Sepinwall, *Haitian History: New Perspectives* (New York: Routledge, 2012); David Patrick Geggus, *The Haitian Revolution: A Documentary History* (Cambridge, MA: Hackett, 2014); and the classic C. L. R. James, *The Black Jacobins* (New York: Dial, 1938).

27. This is Dubois's emphasis in *Avengers of the New World*, 42. David Geggus does not quibble with the figures, but he believes that since most of the leaders of the revolt were creoles and the revolt broke out in regions where creole slaves were in the greatest proportion, the African-born slaves were less implicated in the revolt than has been argued elsewhere. "The French Slave Trade: An Overview," in "New Perspectives on the Transatlantic Slave Trade," special issue, *William and Mary Quarterly* 58, no. 1 (January 2001): 131. The impact of the transatlantic slave trade in stimulating West and Central African warfare, as advanced by Walter Rodney and Paul Lovejoy, has been challenged by J. D. Fage, David Eltis, and, most recently, John Thornton. The debate is summarized by John Thornton, *Africa and Africans in the Making of the Atlantic World*, 2nd ed. (New York: Cambridge University Press, 1998), 72–74. However, if the sheer volume of the slave trade in the eighteenth century had led to "demographic exhaustion" (as Thornton states on p. 117), it is hard to resist the conclusion that the Atlantic trade stimulated such raiding parties to an unprecedented degree.

28. Yves Bénot, *La Révolution française et la fin des colonies, 1789–1794: Postface inédite* (Paris: La Découverte, 2004).

29. The revolutionary calendar, designed to remove all traces of Catholic "superstition" (in the eyes of its secular authors), passed by the National Convention legislature on 24 October 1793 and took as its start 22 September 1792, the date of the establishment of the French Republic. The neologisms offered for the months (e.g., Vendémiaire for the grape harvest of late September to October) defy easy translation, but one British satirist rattled them off as: "Wheezy, Sneezy and Freezy; Slippy, Drippy and Nippy; Showery, Flowery and Bowery; Hoppy, Croppy and Poppy." Anon., "Feast of Wit, or, Sportsman's Hall," *The Sporting Magazine* 15 (January 1800), 210. The Gregorian calendar was finally resumed on 1 January 1806 under Napoleon.

30. Miranda Frances Spieler, "The Legal Structure of Colonial Rule during the French Revolution," *William and Mary Quarterly*, 3rd ser., 66, no. 2 (April 2009): 369–370.

31. The law of 20 September 1792 permitted either spouse to initiate divorce on a wide range of grounds, including the no-fault "incompatibility of temperament," for which no supporting evidence was required. In the metropole, the majority of divorce petitions emanated from women. Divorce would be significantly restricted by the 1804 Napoleonic Civil Code, which limited the acceptable grounds and made the procedures more rigorous and expensive; it was finally suppressed altogether in favor of legal separation, without the possibility for remarriage, in 1816, only to be restored in the 1880s. Divorce appears frequently in Isle Bourbon colonial records but has not yet been analyzed by historians as carefully as in the metropole. Suzanne Desan, *The Family on Trial in the French Revolution* (Berkeley: University of California Press, 2006), 96. On the transition of family law during the Revolution, see also Roderick Phillips, *Family Breakdown*

in Late Eighteenth-Century France: Divorces in Rouen, 1792–1803 (Oxford: Clarendon, 1981); Elaine Marie Kruse, "Divorce in Paris, 1792–1804: Window on a Society in Crisis" (Ph.D. diss., University of Iowa, 1983); Jennifer Ngaire Heuer, *The Family and the Nation: Gender and Citizenship in Revolutionary France, 1789–1830* (Ithaca, NY: Cornell University Press, 2005).

32. Claude Wanquet, *Histoire d'une révolution: La Réunion 1789–1803,* 3 vols. (Marseille: J. Laffitte, 1980–1984; hereafter *Révolution*); Claude Wanquet, *La France et la premiére abolition de l'esclavage, 1794–1802: Le cas des colonies orientales, île de France (Maurice) et La Réunion* (Paris: Karthala, 1998; hereafter *Abolition*). See also Uttama Bissondoyal, ed., *L'Île de France et la Révolution française: Actes de colloque Mahatma Gandhi Institute, 4–8 August 1989* ([Moka], Mauritius: Mahatma Gandhi Institute Press, 1990); Wanquet and Julien, *Révolution française et Océan Indien.* Although there were rumors of a slave plot in Isle Bourbon in 1769 and the prosecution of a plot in 1779, as well as a mass episode of marronage from one plantation in 1788, there was no outbreak of organized violence prior to the Revolution. Wanquet, *Révolution,* esp. 1:196–214, 1:736–751.

33. Wanquet, *Révolution,* 1:200–205, 2:333–334; 3:117–121, 377–388, 487–488.

34. Gabriel Debien, "Marronage in the French Caribbean," in *Maroon Societies: Rebel Slave Communities in the Americas,* ed. Richard Price, 3rd ed. (Baltimore: Johns Hopkins University Press, 1996), 107–134.

35. Richard B. Allen, "A Traffic Repugnant to Humanity: Children, the Mascarene Slave Trade and British Abolitionism," *Slavery and Abolition* 27, no. 2, Special Issue: "Children in European Systems of Bondage" (2009): 219–236.

36. Sugar enhanced the masters' efficiency of their labor force in the Southern Hemisphere. Beginning in the nineteenth century, the sugar harvest took place during the dry season, from July through November, when slaves' harvest of grain was already complete. Ève, *Le corps des esclaves,* 246–253. Historians of Atlantic slavery have long noted the cruel effect of sugar cultivation on slave demographics, treatment, and resistance. Michael Craton, "Proto-Peasant Revolts? The Late Slave Rebellions in the British West Indies, 1816–1832," *Past and Present* 85 (1979): 99–125; Richard B. Sheridan, "The Crisis of Slave Subsistence in the British West Indies during and after the American Revolution," *William and Mary Quarterly* 33, no. 4 (1976): 615–641; Barbara Bush-Slimani, "Hard Labor: Women, Childbirth And Resistance In British Caribbean Slave Societies," *History Workshop* 36 (1993): 82–99; Alphons M. G. Rutten and Peter C. Emmer, "Harmful Silica Fibres and Slave Demography," *Itinerario* 23, nos. 3/4 (1999): 69–72.

37. Giesey, "Rules of Inheritance and Strategies of Mobility," 272–275. Since the *acquêts* belonged equally to both spouses, they could only be distributed upon the second death.

38. Ricquebourg, *Dictionnaire généalogique,* 3:2361–2362. Both of Duvergé's daughters had been born in Pondichéry, the capital of French India, during his stationing there. Cyrille married the older sister, Anne Adélaïde Rathier-Duvergé (age 16), on 27 April 1790, followed several months later by Augustin's marriage to Thérèse-Agnès Rathier-Duvergé (age 15) on 21 June 1790; Ricquebourg, *Dictionnaire généalogique,* 3:2364–65 and 3:2590. Cyrille and Adélaïde apparently waited until Augustin's divorce before beginning to produce their nine children, starting in 1794.

39. Those received from his mother include the African manservant L'Éveillé and five Malagasy field hands. Augustin would divest himself of nearly all of these in the next decade, retaining only L'Éveillé and Bephirame, whom he would appoint driver (*commandeur*) of his other slaves in 1810. Census, Isle Bourbon, Sainte-Marie, Augustin Routier, Year XIII (1804), 1806, 1807, and 1812 (ADR L168, L170, L171, L172.1).

40. The divorce was registered on 8 Prairial Year III (27 May 1795) in the Sainte-Marie parish (f° 9v°); Ricquebourg, *Dictionnaire généalogique*, 3:2363–64 and 3:2590–91 and ANOM IREL, État Civil, Réunion, Sainte-Marie. Several months after the May divorce, Augustin turned all of his business over to his brother-in-law, Joseph Lory, and prepared to travel to France on the *Minerve*; Procuration, Routier ainé à Lory, Notariat Michault D'Emery (ANOM DPPC NOT REU 1790).

41. Augustin's second wife was Marie Charlotte Pauline Malcy Latouche. Census, Isle Bourbon, Sainte-Marie, Charles Routier, Year XIII (1804) (ADR L168), Year XIV (1805) (ADR L170), 1806 (ADR L171). Latouche's mother was Françoise Modeste Panon, another descendant of Augustin Panon.

42. He received only one of his mother's slaves at the time of his marriage: the creole woman Blandine, 24, probably intended as a gift for his wife. Census, Isle Bourbon, Sainte-Suzanne, Cyrille Routier, 1805 (ADR L183.2). She would remain with him through 1819, when she is listed as "60" (ADR 6M422).

43. Ricquebourg, *Dictionnaire généalogique*, 3:2590–2592.

44. Maurice appears as a slave on the widow Routier's Sainte-Marie plantation census in 1787, catalogued as "créole, 10" (ADR 74C), and again in 1808 at her Saint-Denis residence as "créole, domestique, 29" (ADR L 141). Constance later recalled that he died "in July 1810, in the service of Monsieur Cyrille Routier, when the island was taken by the English"; Copy "Mémoire de Constance en faveur de Furcy," 9 November 1817 (ADR 1Jp2007-1, no. 3).

45. Ricquebourg, *Dictionnaire généalogique*, 2:1753. Joseph Marie "Lorry" was baptized 20 December 1770; État Civil, Pamplemousses, Isle de France, 1767–1770 (ANOM 1DDPC 2927; 85MIOM/1176). The parish register for Pamplemousses 1770 is missing from the Mauritius National Archives' digitized *état civil*.

46. Ricquebourg's *Dictionnaire généalogique* names Lory's parents as André Lory, *avocat* from Nantes, and Jacquette Perrine Bertin (2:1753). André Lory was born 8 October 1716 in Nantes and baptized two days later; Parish Register, Nantes, Sainte-Croix (AD Loire-Atlantique, CG44), http://archives.loire-atlantique.fr/jcms, image 24/30. He married Jacquette Perrine Bertin (some sources say in Rennes, but I was unable to confirm in the parish registers) on 30 September 1749.

47. André Lory arrived aboard the royal flute *La Nourrice* ["the wet nurse"], departed from Rochefort in 1769, sailing past the Cape of Good Hope, and arriving in Isle de France on 22 March 1770. Desroches to the minister of the navy, 23 March 1770 (AN Col C/4/26, f. 75). See also "Rôle de l'équipage de la flute du Roi, *La Nourrice*," 1 January 1769–26 November 1771 (NARM 392 [OC 61]). Perrine Jeanne Lory (b. 1758) would marry Gurit Hulot in Pamplemousse, Isle de France, on 16 August 1774 and would bear five children. Albert Révérend, *Titres, anoblissements et pairies de la restauration 1814–1830* (Paris: H. Champion, 1904), 4:26. Soon after Sieur André Lory married off his daughter, he obtained

a concession of land for a shop or a stall (10′ x 12′) in the "Bazard" of Petite Montagne (near Port Louis), Isle de France, on 22 September 1774 (NARM LC 14, p. 100).

48. On October 8, 1791, he boarded the ship *La Faune* in Lorient, arriving at Port Louis, Isle de France, on February 13, 1792; Passengers, Departures, Lorient (ANOM COL F/FB/ 51), Captain Latouche.

49. The name of the ship is listed in Census, Isle Bonaparte, Saint-Denis, Joseph Lory, 1810 (ADR L 165).

50. In 1776, at the age of 59, the planter (*habitant*) André Lory lived with his wife, son, and three daughters in Montagne Longue. He had also invested in cattle (32 adults and 14 calves) and pigs (44). His land measured 1,092 *arpents* (about 923 acres) yet was worth only 500 livres ($14,000 in today's prices) and was planted in corn and manioc, grains deemed only fit for slaves. With 69 slaves (44 men, 19 women, four boys, and two girls), André Lory *père* was neither the wealthiest nor the poorest planter in the district. Census, Isle de France, 1776 (ANOM DPPC G/1/473). By 1780, André Lory was 65 and still owned pretty much the same land (1000 *arpents*, worth 400 livres) in Montagne Longue, but his wife and children no longer appear to be living there. He owned 68 slaves (41 men, 19 women, six boys, and two girls) and had liquidated some of his pigs to purchase one horse and more cattle. Census, Isle de France, 1780 (ANOM DPPC G/1/474).

51. Marriage of Joseph Marie Lory and Marie Charles Eugénie Routier, 7 April 1794 (ADR GG72/4^E2G2, via microfilm: 2MiEC774 (J11) and ANOM IREL État Civil, Réunion, Saint-Denis). The witnesses included Vice Admiral Armand Philipe Germain de Saint-Félix; the former commissioner general of the colonies Augustin François Motais de Narbonne (maternal uncle of the bride); Guy Desrieux, secretary of the colonial government's correspondence (paternal cousin of the guardian and nephew of the bride); Pierre Augustin de Launay, former major of the infantry (maternal uncle of the bride), and Eugénie's brothers and aunt Grayell.

52. She was born in her grandmother's house, 8 Nivôse Year III (28 December 1794) at 11:00 a.m. État Civil, Saint-Denis, 10 Nivôse Year III, f. 6 (ADR 4E2–61, via micro-film: 2MiEC774 (J13–15)).

53. Ricquebourg, *Dictionnaire généalogique*, 2:1753.

54. Wanquet, *Révolution*, 3:333–338.

55. Marie Charlotte Eugénie Lory's death was reported as 9:00 a.m., 27 Nivôse Year VII (16 January 1799) (ADR 4E2–74 via microfilm: 2MiEC12 (J20)).

56. Buried 19 Pluviôse Year VII (7 February 1799) (ADR 4E2–74 via microfilm: 2MiEC12 (J20)).

57. She was baptized Marie Charlette Augustine Euphémie Lory; Ricquebourg, *Dictionnaire généalogique*, 2:1753.

58. Death of Marie Charlette Augustine Euphémie Lory, 1 December 1832 (ANOM IREL État Civil, Réunion, Saint-Denis).

59. None of the Lory's slaves eventually censused as "mulatto" in the 1840s were born before 1812.

60. "M^c Vve Lory, pour l'habitation dite Belle Mare, Flacq," *Slave Registers of Former British Colonial Dependencies, 1812–1834*, Mauritius (NAUK T 71/573, 1248–1254), via Ancestry database, http://www.Ancestry.co.uk.

61. The name Eraste also raises the possibility that Lory, having fulfilled his husbandly duty of providing an heir, turned his attention to men. If so, there might have been further implications for Furcy's life that were never recorded.

62. Garnier and Desarthe list no cyclones for either Mauritius or Réunion between the late 1780s and 1806 ("Cyclones and Societies," 5).

63. Wanquet, *Révolution,* 1:699.

64. Wanquet, *Révolution,* 1:699.

65. The Colonial Assembly passed a law on 14 June 1792 chastising slaveholders for neglecting to adequately feed their slaves and categorically prohibited them from "unburdening themselves of this obligation by permitting slaves to work for themselves several days per week for their own sustenance" in garden plots or provision grounds. ADR L 12, quoted in Ève, *Le corps des esclaves,* 68.

66. Wanquet, *Révolution,* 1:699, and the regulation of 14 June 1793 (Wanquet, *Révolution,* 2:327–328).

67. Wanquet, *Révolution,* 1:699; Ève, *Le corps des esclaves,* 66–69.

68. C. G. de Vaux, *The History of Mauritius, or The Isle of France, and the Neighbouring Islands, from Their First Discovery to the Present Time* (London: W. Bulmer, 1801), 568.

69. "Décret qui supprime la prime pour la traite des noirs," 11 August 1792, in J. B. Duvergier, ed., *Collection complète des lois,* 2nd ed. (Paris: Guyot, 1834), 4:297.

70. A transcription of the Pondichéry ban, "Interdiction de la présence d'esclaves à Pondichéry," registered 15 March 1793, was published in *Lettres du C.I.D.I.F* 36 (4 January 2009): 131-134, and can be found on the website of the Centre d'information et de documentation de l'Inde francophone (http://cidif2.go1.cc/index.php/lettres-du-c-i-d-i-f), but it must be used with caution. It references a royal act of "19 Janvier 1792," but this act does not appear in Duvergier, *Collection complète des lois.*

71. The dates of these acts are February 16 (Isle de France) and August 7 (Réunion). Claude Wanquet, "La Suspension de la Traite négrière par les Mascareiagnes durant la révolution française, anticipation ou leurre?" in *Droit et anthropologie de la complexité: Mélanges dédiés à Jean Mas* (Paris: Economica, 1996), 397–406.

72. Wanquet, "La Suspension," 394.

73. Ève, *Naître et mourir à l'Île Bourbon,* 25, 37.

74. Wanquet, *Révolution,* 1:749.

75. Wanquet, *Révolution,* 2:333–336.

76. Wanquet, *Révolution,* 3:134–137.

77. Wanquet, *Révolution,* 3:386, 484–485.

78. Ève, *Le corps des esclaves,* 70–71.

79. Notariat Michault D'Emery, 1789–1811, 7 Pluviôse Year III (9 February 1795) (ANOM DPPC NOT * REU 1788).

80. Notariat Michault D'Emery, 1789–1811, 21 Pluviôse Year III (9 February 1795) (ANOM DPPC NOT * REU 1788). The final payment was due 11 Nivôse Year IV (1 January 1796).

81. Notariat Michault D'Emery, 1789–1811, 25 Pluviôse Year III (13 February 1795) (ANOM DPPC NOT * REU 1788).

82. Jeremy D. Popkin, *A Concise History of the Haitian Revolution* (Chichester, U.K.: Wiley-Blackwell, 2012), 54–60.

83. Popkin, *You Are All Free*, 212–213, and ch. 8.
84. Robert Stein, "The Abolition of Slavery in the North, West, and South of Saint-Domingue," *The Americas*, 41, no. 3 (January 1985): 47–55; Dubois, *Avengers*, 154–166; Popkin, *You Are All Free*, 327–374.
85. Charles-Joseph Pancoucke, ed., *Gazette nationale ou Le Moniteur universel*, no. 137, 17 Pluviôse Year II (5 February 1794), 554.
86. Wanquet, *Révolution*, 2:336–341; Wanquet, *Abolition*, 306–307.
87. Wanquet, *Révolution*, 2:356–357.
88. Wanquet, *Révolution*, 2:349–350, quoting ADR L 449.
89. "Every individual is free as soon as he has entered France." Assemblée nationale constituante, 28 September 1791, ratified 16 October 1791. Wanquet, *Révolution*, 2:459–463, 3:104–105, 3:114; 3:129, 3:372, 3:390–392.
90. Wanquet, *Révolution*, 2:459–460, quoting ADR L 325/14.
91. Wanquet, *Révolution*, 2:353–354, quoting ADR L 307/2 and L 325.
92. Wanquet, *Révolution*, 2:353–354, and 2:463, quoting ADR L29, L 307/2, and L 325. In addition to Pierre Louis's charges of sedition, he and his mother were accused of using witchcraft against both blacks and whites.
93. Wanquet, *Révolution*, 2:339.
94. The Isle de France resolution was adopted on 24 Ventôse (March 14); Wanquet, *Révolution*, 2:449.
95. Some families placed their domestic servants in chains; the widow Herbert beat one of her female slaves furiously for having lost her dog. Wanquet suggests that such abuse was the exception, not the rule (Wanquet, *Révolution*, 2:439, 2:453).
96. "Relation anonyme de l'arrivée des agents du Directoire," reprinted in *La revue historique et littéraire de l'Ile Maurice* 4, nos. 48 and 49 (1891), quoted in Wanquet, *Abolition*, 307.
97. Compte de Villèle, *Mémoires et correspondance* (Paris, 1888), 1:146–147, quoted in Wanquet, *Abolition*, 308.
98. Wanquet, *Abolition*, 279–310.
99. Census, Isle Bourbon, Saint-Denis, la Citoyenne Veuve Routier Year IV (1796) (ADR L142.1). Maque's sex is apparent in the subsequent census record of 1799 (ADR L142.2).
100. Census, Isle Bourbon, Saint-Denis, la Citoyenne Veuve Routier, Year IV (1796) (ADR L142.1). The fifth member of the household was a young white woman, Claudine Mancèl[l]e (19), the youngest of eleven children, born in 1777 to Vincent Mancel and Marguerite Dulauroy. According to Augustin Routier's later census, she moved in with the Routier family as a toddler on 20 January 1779, presumably out of charity, though she never appears on a census until the widow's in 1796. Both of her parents died in 1786; perhaps she served the widow Routier as a lady's maid. By 1804, Claudine Mancel, "orphan," age 25, would move in with Augustin Routier's family, perhaps assisting with the care of their five children. She would die at the age of thirty in 1817. Census, Réunion, Sainte-Marie, Routier Year XIII (1804)(ADR L168). Ricquebourg, *Dictionnaire généalogique*, 2:1826–1827.
101. Historians Laurent Dubois, Rebecca Scott, and Jean Hébrard have identified individuals' efforts to create "freedom papers" in the chaotic era of competing state authorities in

revolutionary Guadeloupe, Saint-Domingue, and Louisiana. Dubois, *Colony of Citizens*, 348, 374–378; Scott and Hébrard, *Freedom Papers*, 38–39, 44–47, 54–55, 63, 101–102. See also "*la nommée* Thérèse" who asked a notary to record a letter modeled on an act of manumission, stating that her master, Vanovre Bazin et Bazin, "desists from this moment all the rights that I had or could have on the person and the services of the said Thérèse." ADG Notoriat Castet, Minutes of 2 Vendémaire Year X (24 September 1801), quoted in Régent, *Esclavage, métissage, liberté*, 327. The original letter was signed 17 Germinal Year IX (6 April 1801).

102. Sue Peabody, "Free Upon Higher Ground: Saint-Domingue Slaves' Suits for Freedom in U.S. Courts, 1794–1827," in *The World of the Haitian Revolution*, ed. David Geggus and Norman Fiering (Bloomington: Indiana University Press, 2009), 261–283; Martha S. Jones, "Time, Space, and Jurisdiction in Atlantic World Slavery: The Volunbrun Household in Gradual Emancipation New York," *Law and History Review* 29, no. 4 (2011): 1031–1060; Rebecca J. Scott, "Paper Thin: Freedom and Re-Enslavement in the Diaspora of the Haitian Revolution," *Law and History Review* 29, no. 4 (2011): 1061–1087.

103. Wanquet, *Abolition*, 279–315.

104. Census, Isle Bourbon, Saint-Denis, Citoyenne Veuve Routier, Year VIII (1799) (ADR L 142.2), Year IX (1800) (ADR L 143), and Year X (1801) (ADR L 144). The elderly slave Maque apparently died before 1800; Madeleine and Constance continue to be listed as "libre" in 1807; Census, Isle Bourbon, Saint-Denis, Dame Ursule Desblottières Veuve Routier, 1807 (ADR L 151.2).

105. Rosemary Brana-Shute, "Sex and Gender in Surinamese Manumissions," in *Paths to Freedom: Manumission in the Atlantic World*, ed. Rosemary Brana-Shute and Randy J. Sparks (Charleston: University of South Carolina Press, 2009), 175–196.

106. A striking contrast between European slavery and African or Arab slavery was European colonists' marked preference for male over female slaves, at least in part because of distinct gender roles in each society's agriculture. John Thornton, "Sexual Demography: The Impact of the Slave Trade on Family Structure," in *Women and Slavery in Africa*, ed. Martin Klein and Claire Robertson (Madison: University of Wisconsin Press, 1983), 39–48; Thornton, *Africa and Africans*, 107.

107. Census Isle Bonaparte, Saint-Denis, Dame Ursule Desblottières, Veuve Routier, Year XIII (1805) (ADR L168) and 1806 (ADR L151.2).

108. In Year X (1801), the widow Routier filed two identical census returns (ADR L143 and ADR L144); both state that Madeleine and Constance lived with her, as well as Claudine Mancèle, in Saint-Denis. Two years later, in 1803, Madeleine, Constance, and Constance's son, Auguste, are all living with the widow Routier in Saint-Denis, but no slaves are listed on the census form (ADR L147). Furcy does not appear in any of the Sainte-Marie census returns of the widow's oldest son, Augustin, in 1804 (ADR L168), 1805 (ADR L170), or 1806 (ADR L171), nor is he listed among the slaves of the widow Routier on her Sainte-Marie plantation in 1805 (ADR L170). Furcy appears for the first time since 1787 on the widow's 1806 Saint-Denis census return, completed on her behalf by Joseph Lory on 31 December 1806 (ADR L151.2).

CHAPTER 5

1. Wanquet, *Révolution*, 3:348–351, 369–380; 418–427.
2. Wanquet, *Révolution*, 3:375–399.
3. Wanquet, *Révolution*, 3:484–485.
4. "The assembly has exhausted all means of persuasion . . . to invite you to meet at the primary assemblies in greater numbers. Its paternal exhortations have made no impression. It announces to you that if you persist in your culpable apathy, the reign of anarchy establishes itself, the political machine breaks for lack of support to sustain it and the social contract is torn up." Assembly Proclamation of 27 Ventôse Year VIII (16 March 1800) (ADR L 46), quoted in Wanquet, *Révolution*, 3:322.
5. The Treaty of Amiens was concluded 25 March 1802; Decree of 30 Floréal Year X (20 May 1802).
6. Heuer, *Family and the Nation*, 127–157.
7. Rachel G. Fuchs, "Magistrates and Mothers, Paternity and Property in Nineteenth-Century French Courts," *Crime, Histoire, Sociétés/Crime, History and Societies* 13, no. 2 (August 2009): 13–26. Fuchs nevertheless demonstrates how women and magistrates in the metropole managed to hold men responsible for paternity through tort suits, especially in the second half of the nineteenth century.
8. B. Fortier, "1799–1830: Ruptures et continuités du régime législatif des quatre vieilles colonies françaises," in *Rétablissement de l'esclavage dans les colonies françaises aux origines de Haïti*, ed. Marcel Dorigny and Yves Bénot (Paris: Maisonneuve & Larose, 2003), 505–522.
9. Albert Jauze, *Notaires et notariat: Notariat français et les hommes dans une colonie à l'est du cap de Bonne-Espérance: Bourbon—La Réunion, 1668–milieu du XIXe siècle*, Sciences Humaines et Sociales, Histoire (Paris: Éditions Publibook, 2009), 190, n. 450. This gesture was ratified by the emperor with the imperial decree of 2 February 1809, *Bulletin des lois de l'Empire français*, 4th ser., 2 (1809): 20–21.
10. Arreté 47, 1er Pluviôse Year XII (22 January 1804), esp. art. 15–16, in *Recueil des lois publiées à Maurice depuis la dissolution de l'Assemblée Coloniale en 1803, sous le Gouvernement du Général Decaen, jusques à la fin de l'administration de son Exc. Sir R. T. Farquhar en 1823* (Maurice: Mallac Frères, 1822–1824), 50–54.
11. In the Saint-Denis parish, for example, although entries for slaves were increasingly recorded in a separate section or register book, the church's baptism, marriage, and burial records for free people were maintained together, with the exception of a brief period in 1785–1786. Separate registers for whites and free people of color would continue until new legislation of the July Monarchy in 1832. Paul Carrère and André Scherer, *Répertoire des registres paroissiaux et d'état civil antérieurs à 1849* (Nérac, France: Impr. G. Couderc, 1963), 27–38.
12. Arreté 48, 3 Pluviôse Year XII (24 January 1804), in *Recueil des lois publiées à Maurice*, 54.
13. Arreté 85, 19 Brumaire Year XIII (31 October 1804), and Arreté 96, du 1er Messidor Year XIII (20 June 1805), in *Recueil des lois publiées à Maurice*, 114–116 and 123. For example, unless the slave had committed some extraordinary feat, such as saving a master's life or killing an enemy in combat, slaves had to be owned by the same master for at least five years before they could be freed.

14. "A master cannot free his slave through self-purchase using his peculium; it is especially recommended to citizens and the public ministry to oppose any manumission that has a motive of this nature." Article 6, Arrêté 96, 1er Messidor Year XIII (20 June 1805), *Recueil des lois publiées à Maurice*, 123.

15. "[The master] will present himself before the judge of [the court of] first instance to ask that his slave be named a guardian [*patron*], who will be charged with all the necessary tasks for the confirmation of the manumission, to receive the sum given by the master and to deposit it with the Charity Bureau, and to reclaim it for the freedman when the condition imposed for this purpose has been fulfilled." Article 10, Arrêté 85, 19 Brumaire Year XIII (10 November 1804), *Recueil des lois publiées à Maurice*, 115.

16. "Children under the age of seven years, born of a female slave who shall obtain her freedom, will follow the condition of their mother. In this case, the master will be required to add to the sum allocated for her manumission a sum of five hundred francs for each child." Article 4, Arrêté 30, 1 Messidor Year XIII (20 June 1805), *Recueil des lois publiées à Maurice*, 123.

17. Saint-Denis censuses of Year XVIII (1799) (ADR L142.2), Year IX (1800) (L 143), Year X (1801) (L144), Year XII (1803) (L147), and Year XIII (1804) (L170). These censuses do not give street addresses, but this was very likely the family property where Eugénie and Joseph Lory lived after the widow's death at the corner of Grand Chemin and the rue du Barachois. "Dépot du procès verbal d'expertise de deux meubles, dépendant de succession en communauté de feu M. Joseph Lory par M. Antoine Pitel, 24 aout 1846" (ADR 3 E692, no. 284); Census, Isle de la Réunion, Sainte-Marie, Augustin Routier, 1806 (ADR L170); Ricquebourg, *Dictionnaire généalogique*, 2:1827.

18. The year and month of Auguste's birth is deduced from the unusually precise 1811 census return, filed 7 May 1811, giving his age as "nine years, nine months." Census, Isle Bourbon, Saint-André, Jenptiste Eufemie [*sic*], 1811 (ADR L195). Neither of the annual returns of 1800 or 1801 mention Auguste's existence; he first appears at the age of three in the widow Routier's entry on the 1803 Saint-Denis census, living with his mother and his grandmother, Madeleine; Saint-Denis census of Year XII (1803) (L147). Conceivably, he was put out to nurse with another woman for the first two years of his life. The registry of Auguste's death, on 23 March 1823 in Saint-André parish, gives his age as 21 (ANOM Etat-Civil online: http://anom.archivesnationales.culture. gouv.fr, Réunion, Saint-André, 1823). Constance herself seems unsure about the ages of her children; her 1819 census return does not correspond to the baptism acts of her youngest children.

19. Census, Isle Bourbon, Saint-Denis, Dame Ursule Desblottières Vᶜ Routier, 1806 (ADR L151.2). On the other hand, Constance's young age and the ambiguity surrounding Auguste's year of birth may suggest a hidden, presumably white, father, probably a resident of Saint-Denis. The discrepancy regarding Auguste's age—the 1803 census had him born in 1800, so he would have been six years old—is puzzling. When a child died in the eighteenth and nineteenth centuries, it was not uncommon to recycle the name to a later child; perhaps an original "Auguste" had died, only to be replaced a few years later by this boy. Or perhaps Lory was unclear about the boy's age and just wrote down a number without confirming the year of his out-of-wedlock birth, a not uncommon phenomenon in his

census returns. For example, Lory catalogued one Paul (*cafre, pioche*) as 38 in 1805, then 50 in 1807 (ADR L169 and L171). Nothing can be ascertained about Eugène's paternity.

20. The widow Routier owned 27,000 *gaulettes*, and Augustin Routier owned 4,900 *gaulettes* in the parish of Sainte-Marie, where the *gaulette* measured 15 *pieds* by 15 *pieds*; Cyrille Augustin owned 20,992 *gaulettes* in Sainte-Suzanne, where the *gaulette* measured 12 *pieds* by 12 *pieds*. The French pied (literally "foot") is equal to the American or English 12.8 inches.Totaling the three rural properties yields 3,442,688 square feet of farmland, or about 266 acres.

21. Census, Réunion, Sainte-Marie, Joseph Lory, Year XII (1804) (ADR L169).

22. This is undoubtedly a portion of Augustin Panon's original 1697 concession. Forty-three names appearing in the widow's 1787 census (ADR 71C) also appear in her returns of 1805 and 1806 (ADR L170).

23. The rest of the widow's pre-revolutionary slaves cannot be accounted for. While some may have escaped or died, it seems likely that she sold most of her imported African and Malagasy slaves. Of course, it's also possible that Augustin and Cyrille simply gave their mother's imported slaves new names. However, there are some clear continuities in names and ages of the other slaves that she gave her children, suggesting that this was not the case.

24. The widow's workforce now consisted of 49 creoles, of whom nineteen (seven boys and twelve girls) were under the age of eighteen, born since the last census. By contrast, she held only eight Africans and ten Malagasy slaves.

25. Census, Réunion, Sainte-Marie, [Augustin] Routier, Year XIII (1805) and Sainte-Suzanne, Cyrille Routier, n.d [1805] (ADR L183.2). Augustin's plantation was located between the Rivière des Pluies and the Ruisseau Qui Vit.

26. Mauritius saw devastating storms between 1806 and 1808 as well; Garnier and Desarthe, "Cyclones and Societies," 8.

27. Ève, *Le corps des esclaves*, 67, 70.

28. Conveyance (*transport*), Anne Luce to Joseph Lory, 2 April 1806, Notariat Michault d'Emery, no. 250 (ANOM DPPC NOT REU1800). Lory paid her through her proxy Denis Holland le Clos, a resident of Saint-André. The size of the land is not described in this transaction, only its general location.

29. Ève, *Le corps des esclaves*, 70.

30. Commandant of Saint-Suzanne to the governor, 6 March 1807 (ADR L 109), quoted in Ève, *Le corps des esclaves*, 72.

31. Ève, *Le corps des esclaves*, 67, 70–72; Cheke and Hume, *Lost Land of the Dodo*, 109–110, 138; Garnier and Desarthe, "Cyclones and Societies," 8.

32. Census, Isle Bonaparte, Sainte-Suzanne, Cyrille Routier, 1807 (ADR L186.1). Of his 39 slaves, three had escaped over the last decade, all of them young men in their late teens: Gaspar since 1797, Fidèle since November 1804, and Jacques since May 1805.

33. Ève, *Le corps des esclaves*, 72; Ève, *Naître et mourir à l'Île Bourbon*, 140–163.

34. Census, Isle Bonaparte, Sainte-Marie, Widow Routier, 1807 (ADR L171).

35. Census, Isle Bourbon, Sainte-Marie, Augustin Routier, 1812 (ADR L172.1).

36. Census, Isle Bourbon, Sainte-Suzanne, Cyrille Routier, 1811 (ADR L178).

37. Census, Isle Bonaparte, Sainte-Marie, Widow Routier, 1807 (ADR L171).

38. Census, Isle Bonaparte, Sainte-Marie, Widow Routier, 1807 (ADR L171); Receipt (*quittance*), *le nommé* Jeannot to the Routier heirs, 5 January 1809, Notariat Michault d'Emery, no. 664 (ANOM DPPC NOT REU1802).

39. Census, Isle Bonaparte, Saint-Denis, Ursule Desblottières, Widow Routier, 1806 (ADR L151.2). Joseph's residence in Saint-Denis appeared in notarized transactions, e.g., Conveyance, Anne Luce to Joseph Lory, 2 April 1806 (ANOM DPPC NOT REU1800).

40. Montesquieu makes this distinction, though not specifically in relation to colonial slavery, in his *Esprit des loix*, Book 12, "Des loix qui forment la liberté politique dans son rapport avec le citoyen," *Oeuvres de Monsieur de Montesquieu*, rev. ed. (Amsterdam: Arkstée & Merkus, 1764), 2:2. In France's Caribbean colonies, the informally manumitted were also sometimes called "savannah freedmen" (*libres de savane*), since their masters sometimes allowed them to settle on uncultivated land of the plantation; Gabriel Debien, *Les eslaves aux Antilles françaises* (Basse-terre, Guadeloupe: Société d'Histoire de la Guadeloupe, 1974), 374. However, this terminology tends to be more common after 1832 legislation removed many of the restrictions on manumission. It is not quite clear when the term *libre de savanne* entered the lexicon or whether it was used in Isle Bourbon. Bernard Moitt, "In the Shadow of the Plantation: Women of Color and the *Libres de Fait* of Martinique and Guadeloupe, 1685–1848," in *Beyond Bondage: Free Women of Color in the Americas*, ed. David Barry Gaspar, Darlene Clark Hine (Urbana: University of Illinois, 2004) 37–59.

41. Census, Isle Bourbon, Saint-Denis, Citizenness Widow (*citoyenne veuve*) Routier, Year IV (1796) (ADR L142.1); Census, Isle Bourbon, Saint-Denis, Citizenness Widow Routier, Year VIII (1799) (ADR L142.2); Census, Isle Bonaparte, Sainte-Marie, Ursule Desblottières, Widow Routier, Year XIII (1806) (ADR L170), 1807 (ADR L171).

42. Census, Isle Bonaparte, Saint-Denis, Ursule Desblottières, Widow Routier, 1806 (ADR L151.2).

43. "Notes écrites sous la dictée de Furcy," n.d., after 1830 (ADR 1Jp2007/1, no. 51).

44. "Notes écrites sous la dictée de Furcy," n.d., (ADR 1Jp2007/1, no. 51).

45. Census, Isle Bonaparte, Saint-Denis, Ursule Desblottières, Widow Routier, 1806 (ADR L151.2).

46. Élie's new wife was a distant cousin of Montendre Jams Adam, for whom Lory held the mortgage; both were grandchildren of a Belgian settler of Isle Bourbon, Adam Jams (1701–1769). Marirage, Routier and Dame Adam Jams, 13 February 1808, Notariat Michault d'Emery, no. 520 (FR ANOM DPPC NOT REU1801).

47. Lawyer Antoine Prospère Douyère stood in for the absent father of the bride. Antoine Prospère Douyère was, incidentally, Matthieu Vetter's father-in-law, another example of the tight familial networks of the colonial community.

48. As her dowry, the bride brought seven slaves, a house in Saint-Denis, five silver eating utensils, and diverse furnishings, including a bed and bedding, a commode, several armoires, chairs, 1,436 piasters (about $25,000) in cash, and fifty balls of coffee. Élie matched these with 4,000 piasters cash (about $70,000), of which a quarter would belong to her outright, but three-quarters would remain in usufruct for her lifetime, then pass to any future child, unless Élie predeceased her, childless, which is in fact what transpired.

49. Sale, Montalant to Sieur Lory, 18 January 1808, Notariat Michault d'Emery, no. 518 (ANOM DPPC NOT REU1801). The deal was completed 4 January 1809, when Lory acknowledged that he had received all the boats of Montalant; Receipt, Joseph Lory to Montalant, 4 January 1809, Notariat Michault d'Emery, no. 661 (ANOM DPPC NOT REU1801).

50. Sale, Montendre Adam to Lorry [*sic*], 31 May 1808, Notariat Michault d'Emery, no. 532 (ANOM DPPC NOT REU1801).

51. Sale, Boyer to sieurs Gamin and Lorry [*sic*], 19 September 1808, Notariat Michault d'Emery, no. 600 (ANOM DPPC NOT REU1801).

52. A note regarding the origin of one of his slaves in Joseph Lory's 1814 census return refers to "my bakery [*ma boulangérie*]." Census, Isle Bourbon, Saint-Denis, Joseph Lory, 1814 (ADR L165).

53. Census, Isle Bonaparte, Saint-Denis, Widow Routier, 1808 (ADR L 141).

54. Marriage, Jean Batiste [*sic*] and Constance, 30 May 1808, Notariat Michault d'Emery, no. 556 (ANOM DPPC NOT REU1801).

55. Marriage, Jean Batiste [*sic*] and Constance, 30 May 1808, Notariat Michault d'Emery, no. 556 (ANOM DPPC NOT REU1801). This would place his birth around November 1784, so about the same age as Constance. Other documents, however, imply that he was born around 1783. For example, the 1815 census gives his age as 34 and his birthplace as Sainte-Marie, which places his birth around 1781 (Census, Isle Bourbon, Saint-André, Jean B^te Euphémie, 1815, ADR L191). His baptismal record has not been found in either parish (ANOM IREL, État Civil, Réunion, Saint-André, 1779–1783, or Sainte-Marie, 1779–1783). His surname, Euphémie, suggests a possible relationship to the youngest Routier daughter, born in 1774, who died in 1799, but Jean Baptiste does not appear among the Routier's slaves in the 1780, 1784, or 1787 censuses (ADR 71C and 74C).

56. These consisted of one-third of a 400 square foot (thirty-*gaulette*) plantation in Sainte-Suzanne, near the Rivière du Mât, bordering the plantations of the widow Dumeurier to the north and west, the Ravine of Vincendo to the east, and the summit of the mountains to the south; one-third of a second, wooded plantation of about 700 square feet (fifty *gaulettes*) near the Bras de Lianne in Sainte-Suzanne; and one-third interest in three *caffre* slaves: Paul (25), Jean Marie (22), and Henriette (18). The slaves were received from Jean Baptiste's maternal uncle, Zacarie.

57. Almost a decade later, in 1817, an Adolphe Duperier, described as a "cousin" to Furcy and Constance's "son-in-law," would play an important role when Furcy began his long legal challenge for freedom; it is conceivable that the Duperier who sold Constance one of her slaves is the same or a relative.

58. Census, Isle Bonaparte, Saint-Denis, Constance *libre*, 1808 (ADR L153). Euphrosine, *caffre*, 27, and Georges, *créol*, seven (probably a mother and son), are designated as manual laborers (*pioches*) and were both purchased within the last year from a "M. Duperier." Eliza, *malgache*, eighteen, was purchased from Mattieu Vetter. By 1805, Vetter had become a distiller and may have supported himself as a minor slave trader. He eventually died on 29 March 1834 at the age of 77. Ricquebourg, *Dictionnaire généalogique*, 3:2815.

59. Brana-Shute, "Sex and Gender," 175–196.

60. "The said Jean Batiste [*sic*] declares and recognizes that *le nommé* Auguste, creole of about six years in age, natural son of the said Constance, is also his natural son, as having been

procreated by his works [*oeuvres*] with the said Constance, who likewise declares it, for which reason they intend to legitimize the said Auguste by the celebration of marriage that they will contract and will reaffirm [*nouvella*] the prescribed declaration by the act of celebration, to serve *le nommé*Auguste as may reasonably be needed in conformity with the law." Marriage, Jean Batiste [*sic*] and Constance, 30 May 1808, Notariat Michault d'Emery, no. 556 (ANOM DPPC NOT REU1801), f. 2v-3.

61. The other two signatories are Petitpas (possibly the man later assigned as Furcy's *patron*), the notary, Michault d'Emery, and an indecipherable signature: FMittle (?).

62. Census, Isle Bonaparte, Saint-Denis, Constance *libre*, 1808 (ADR L153).

63. She sent a power of attorney to Françoise Marguerite Routier, her dead husband's child by his first marriage, now residing in Isle de France, received on 26 August 1808; Sale, Routier heirs to Sieur Augustin Routier, 16 February 1809, Notariat Michault d'Emery, no. 685 (ANOM DPPC NOT REU1802).

64. Affranchissements, no. 727 (ANOM 6DPPC 3742).

65. Copies, Manumission act of *la nommée* Madeleine, *indienne*, 6 July 1789, registered by the clerk of the Tribunal of First Instance of Isle Bonaparte, 30 June 1808 (ADR 1Jp2007-1, nos. 38 and 39).

66. Arrêté 48, 3 Pluviôse Year XII (24 January 1804), *Recueil des lois publiées à Maurice*, 54.

67. Ricquebourg, *Dictionnaire*, 1:691. Furcy would later mistakenly suggest that this occurred in 1810. "Notes écrites sous la dictée de Furcy," n.d. (ADR 1Jp2007/1, no. 51).

68. An inventory of the widow Routier's belongings was made by Michault d'Emery on October 14 and the following days. Then, on 27 October 1808, the family met before the notary for an "act of distribution" (*acte de partage*), in which the slaves and moveable property were distributed to each of the widow's heirs. The latter act is mentioned in Sale, Routier heirs to Sieur Augustin Routier, 16 February 1809, Notariat Michault d'Emery, no. 685 (ANOM DPPC NOT REU1802). Both dates are cited in [Émile] Moreau, [Alphonse] Paillet, and Huart, *Mémoire pour la dame veuve Lory, et les sieurs Adolphe Lory, Henry Lory, Thomas Lory, Arthur Lory, Jules Lory, et Edouard Lory, demeurant tous à l'Ile-Bourbon, intimés; contre le sieur Furcy, homme de couleur, demeurant à l'Île de France, appelant* (Paris: Guyot, 1843), 5 (ANOM FM GEN 158/1307). The (undated) *partage* was also mentioned in "Notes écrites sous la dictée de Furcy," n.d. (ADR 1Jp2007/1, no. 51), 1.

69. The original inventory has not been found; this is a quotation from the legal brief, Moreau, Paillet, and Huart, *Mémoire pour la dame veuve Lory* (ANOM FM GEN 158/1307), 5.

70. Here spelled "Jeannot." Receipt, *le nommé* Jeannot to the Routier heirs, 5 January 1809, Notary Michault d'Emery, no. 664 (ANOM DPPC NOT REU1802). Rôle d'équipage, *La Brune* (1772–1775), Archives de la Compagnie des Indes, 2P 46–I.9 (communicated in private correspondence by Chantal Plévert, Les Amis du Service Historique de la Défense à Lorient, 25 January 2013). Affranchissements, nos. 725 and 727 (ANOM 6DPPC 3742).

71. Receipt, *le nommé* Jeannot to the Routier heirs, 5 January 1809, Notariat Michault d'Emery, no. 664 (ANOM DPPC NOT REU1802).

72. Sale, Routier heirs to Sieur Augustin Routier, 16 February 1809, Notariat Michault d'Emery, no. 685 (ANOM DPPC NOT REU1802). The youngest son, Élie Routier, had died in January 1809 of unknown causes; Ricquebourg, *Dictionnaire généalogique*, 3:2590.

He was survived by his wife, Marie Anne Vincente Calixtine Jams, but the couple had not produced any child in their marriage of less than a year. On 6 July 1809, a representative for Charles Élie Routier's widow, Marie Anne Vincente Callistine Jams Adam, transferred her rights to the share of 4,000 livres that she had received from her husband at the time of their wedding to Auguste Evaniste François de Lanux and his wife, residents of Saint-Jean in the parish of Sainte-Marie. This included 1,000 livres that she owned outright and 3,000 livres in usufruct during her lifetime, but which would return to the widow Routier's heirs when the widow Jams Adam died. The instrument essentially became a loan, since the entirety, plus interest, would come due 1 July 1813, and she offered as security for the loan her plantation house and outbuildings in Saint-Jean. Conveyance Dame Widow Charles Routier to Sieur and Dame Auguste de Lanux, 6 July 1809, Notariat Michault d'Emery, no. 717 (ANOM DPPC NOT REU1803).

73. The property was divided into 108 shares and distributed as follows: 25 shares apiece to each of the widow's surviving children and four each to the two daughters of Charles Routier's earlier marriage. Such consolidating of the property in the hands of the eldest son was a common practice in the French Atlantic as well; Palmer, *Intimate Bonds*, 22.

74. Eugénie was due to receive 41,287 livres, from "the said Sieur Desbassayns," according to the following timetable: 12,087 livres on 20 November 1809, 2,500 livres on the same date in each of the following three years (1810, 1811, and 1812), and a final payment of 32,500 livres on 20 November 1813. As the total payments came to 52,087 livres, the Lorys were essentially receiving 10,800 livres in interest (or about 4.7 percent, compounded annually). The bulk of this (41,287 livres, or $118,000) was to go to Eugénie Lory, with a small amount (2,500 livres, $7,160) accorded to her brother Cyrille, who may have already received his share of inheritance at the time of his wedding.

75. Thirty-three slaves belonging to the widow months before her death show up on the later censuses of Augustin (15), Joseph Lory (9), and Cyrille (9). Census, Isle Bonaparte, Sainte-Marie, Widow Routier, 1807 (ADR L171); Census, Isle Bourbon, Sainte-Marie, Augustin Routier, 1812 (ADR L172.1); Census, Isle Bonaparte, Saint-Denis, Joseph Lory, 1810 (ADR L157); and Census, Isle Bourbon, Sainte-Suzanne, Cyrille Routier, 1811 (ADR L178).

76. Maurice never appears among Cyrille's censused slaves, because Cyrille's only surviving census returns date from before the distribution (1807) and after Maurice's death (1810). There is another Maurice, an African, who is listed by Cyrille on the 1805 and 1807 Sainte-Suzanne censuses (ADR L183.2 and L186.1), when Furcy's brother was listed as the widow's property in Saint-Denis (ADR L151.2). I don't believe these are the same man.

77. Furcy was supposedly distributed to Joseph Lory on 27 October 1808. This date of the prior distribution, though not the specific assignment of Furcy, is mentioned a month later in Receipt, sieurs Routier and Mademoiselle Mansel to Joseph Lorry [*sic*], 30 November 1808, Notariat Michault d'Emery, no. 652 (ANOM DPPC NOT REU1802), and as the receipt of the *acte du partage* in Sale, Routier heirs to Sieur Augustin Routier, 16 February 1809, Notariat Michault d'Emery, no. 685 (ANOM DPPC NOT REU1802). I say "supposedly" because there is contradictory evidence as to whether Furcy immediately passed to Joseph Lory or whether he first became the property of Augustin Routier and was only later claimed by Joseph Lory at the final distribution of the widow's property, allegedly occurring in 1812 (and for which I have not found notarial evidence). Citing a direct

transfer to Lory is Furcy's own testimony, ca. 1830 ("Notes écrites," ADR 1Jp2007/1, no. 51), and Lory's repeated claim of Furcy as his own property on census forms, from at least 1810 (Census, Isle Bonaparte, Saint-Denis, Joseph Lory, 1810, ADR L 157). For the opposite argument, see the statement of Eugénie Lory's lawyer in 1843, who misnames Augustin Lory as Charles (Moreau, Paillet, and Huart, *Mémoire pour la dame veuve Lory*, 1, ANOM FM GEN 158/1307), repeated by a British journalist in the *Law Times* (London), December 23, 1843, 256. Unless corroborating evidence can be found, it seems simplest to assume that Furcy remained in Lory's service in Saint-Denis continuously from before the widow's death through 1817, though he may technically have belonged to Augustin until the estate was fully disposed. No extant account of this period mentions the Sainte-Marie planter Augustin Routier's stake in Furcy. Madeleine's conflict is always described as a direct conflict with Joseph Lory in Saint-Denis.

78. Receipt, Madeleine to the Routier heirs, 7 August 1809, Notariat Michault d'Emery, no. 731 (ANOM DPPC NOT REU 1803).

79. There are two nearly identical versions of Constance's petition: Copy "Mémoire de Constance en faveur de Furcy," 9 November 1817 (ADR 1Jp2007-1, no. 3), and "Extrait d'une mémoire déposé au greffe de la Cour Royale de l'Ile de Bourbon le trois Décembre 1817 par M. le Procureur général pour servir s'il y a lieu, à intenter toute procédure criminelle ou correctionnelle" (ADR 1Jp2007-1, no. 36). The latter is more complete, with some new marginalia, and in a hand that is much easier to read; I quote from the latter.

80. "Notes écrites sous la dictée de Furcy," n.d. (ADR 1Jp2007/1, no. 51).

81. "Notes écrites . . ." was found among the papers collected by Louis Gilbert Boucher (ADR 1Jp2007/1–3); it is probable that he was the one to collect Furcy's testimony, but it was also clearly framed as grounds for an appeal, rather than during Furcy's initial 1817 lawsuit.

82. "Extrait d'une mémoire déposé au greffe de la Cour Royale de l'Ile de Bourbon le trois Décembre 1817 par M. le Procureur général pour servir s'il y a lieu, à intenter toute procédure criminelle ou correctionnelle" (ADR 1Jp2007-1, no. 36). Madeleine learned of her manumission in the presence of "Monsieur Motais de Narbonne and Lory, brother-in-law of the deceased, and also of Michault d'Emmery, then notary of the succession" (emphasis in the original). The former was Augustin François Motais de Narbonne, husband of Marie Adélaide Desblottières, who was Madame Routier's younger sister; see Ricquebourg, *Dictionnaire généalogique*, 2:1994, n. 1, and 1:691. According to the lawyers representing Joseph Lory in 1838, it wasn't until 1808 that Madeleine's manumission was recorded in the *état civil*. Moreau, *Mémoire pour le Sieur Lory*, 3 (ANOM FM GEN/ 158/1307).

83. Petition (*requête*), quoted in Thureau, *Plaidoyer pour le sieur Furcy*, 4. The figure of 600 livres comes from Madeleine (ADR 1Jp2007-1, no. 36); 300 livres and 500 livres are mentioned in "Notes écrites sous la dictée de Furcy," n.d. (ADR 1Jp2007/1, no. 51). Strangely, the register containing a copy of the original manumission decree omits the clause about being a burden to the colony and the pension entirely; Affranchissement, no. 727 (ANOM 6DPPC 3742). The quittance that she eventually signed (see below) recognizes the annual rate of 600 livres. Quittance Madelaine aux h[ers] Routier, 7 aoust 1809, Notariat Michault d'Emery, no. 731 (ANOM DPPC NOT REU 1803).

84. Furcy, for example, was evaluated at 3,700 livres. *Law Times*, December 23, 1843, 256.

85. "Extrait d'une mémoire déposé au greffe de la Cour Royale de l'Ile de Bourbon le trois Décembre 1817 par M. le Procureur général pour servir s'il y a lieu, à intenter toute procédure criminelle ou correctionnelle" (ADR 1Jp2007-1, no. 36).

86. Article 6 of Arrêté 96, "Dispositions additionnelles à l'arrêter sur les affranchissements," 1 Messidor Year XIII (20 June 1805); *Recueil des lois publiées à Maurice*, 123.

87. "Extrait d'une mémoire déposé au greffe de la Cour Royale de l'Ile de Bourbon le trois Décembre 1817 par M. le Procureur général pour servir s'il y a lieu, à intenter toute procédure criminelle ou correctionnelle" (ADR 1Jp2007-1, no. 36).

88. "Notes écrites sous la dictée de Furcy," n.d. (ADR 1Jp2007/1, no. 51), 1.

89. According to Desbassayns, Constance had turned over to Boucher a copy of her mother's manumission, a *mémoire* composed on Madeleine's behalf by the lawyer Tourgouillet, to seek Furcy's freedom in 1809; "Procès Verbal des déclarations de Constance & Adolphe," 10 December 1817 (ANOM FM SG REU 97/684, no. 16). This *mémoire* has not been found, nor any reference to a lawyer by that name.

90. "Extrait d'une mémoire déposé au greffe de la Cour Royale de l'Ile de Bourbon le trois Décembre 1817 par M. le Procureur général pour servir s'il y a lieu, à intenter toute procédure criminelle ou correctionnelle" (ADR 1Jp2007-1, no. 36).

91. "Notes écrites sous la dictée de Furcy," n.d. (ADR 1Jp2007/1, no. 51), 1–2.

92. "Notes écrites sous la dictée de Furcy," n.d. (ADR 1Jp2007/1, no. 51), 2.

93. "Notes écrites sous la dictée de Furcy," n.d. (ADR 1Jp2007/1, no. 51), 2. Antoine François Hyrne was a notary in Saint-Denis, 1791–1808 (ANOM DPPC NOT REU REP 12).

94. "Notes écrites sous la dictée de Furcy," n.d. (ADR 1Jp2007/1, no. 51), 3.

95. "Notes écrites sous la dictée de Furcy," n.d. (ADR 1Jp2007/1, no. 51), 3.

96. Receipt, Madeleine to the Routier heirs, 7 August 1809, Notariat Michault d'Emery, no. 731 (ANOM DPPC NOT REU1803).

97. "Extrait d'une mémoire déposé au greffe de la Cour Royale de l'Ile de Bourbon le trois Décembre 1817 par M. le Procureur général pour servir s'il y a lieu, à intenter toute procédure criminelle ou correctionnelle" (ADR 1Jp2007-1, no. 36).

98. "Notes écrites sous la dictée de Furcy," n.d. (ADR 1Jp2007/1, no. 51).

99. Receipt, Madeleine to the Routier heirs, 7 August 1809, Notariat Michault d'Emery, no. 731 (ANOM DPPC NOT REU1803).

100. "Notes écrites sous la dictée de Furcy," n.d. (ADR 1Jp2007/1, no. 51), 3.

101. "Notes écrites sous la dictée de Furcy," n.d. (ADR 1Jp2007/1, no. 51).

102. Furcy suggests that Lory put a statement in his will that Furcy would be freed upon Lory's death or when he left for France. But this was not communicated to him until much later. Furcy insisted that "during the little time that he belonged to M. Lory, he never provided him with any service which would merit his freedom in case of death or departure." "Notes écrites sous la dictée de Furcy," n.d. (ADR 1Jp2007/1, no. 51), 4.

103. According to Constance's future *mémoire*, she tried to use the reserves to obtain Furcy's liberty on 19 December 1811; "Extrait d'une mémoire déposé au greffe de la Cour Royale de l'Ile de Bourbon le trois Décembre 1817 par M. le Procureur général pour servir s'il y a lieu, à intenter toute procédure criminelle ou correctionnelle" (ADR 1Jp2007-1, no. 36). Another later account corroborates her memory, dating this lawsuit to 1809. Desbassayns de Richemont references a "mémoire fait en 1809, et qui avait fait pour objet de réclamer

la liberté de Furcy"; Letter to the Minister, 21 December 1817 (ANOM 3201 COL REU/22/132). The fact that this is cited by the commissioner general, a fierce opponent of Furcy, gives it some credibility, but I have not been able to find independent evidence of the suit.

104. "Extrait d'une mémoire déposé au greffe de la Cour Royale de l'Ile de Bourbon le trois Décembre 1817 par M. le Procureur général pour servir s'il y a lieu, à intenter toute procédure criminelle ou correctionnelle" (ADR 1Jp2007-1, no. 36).

105. Moreau, *Mémoire pour le Sieur Lory*, 3 (ANOM FM GEN/158/1307).

106. The earlier, 1838, *mémoire* claimed that Furcy became Lory's slave sometime after 1808 (Moreau, *Mémoire pour le Sieur Lory*, 3); it was not until the "partage de la succession de Madame Routier, constaté par acte notarié, enregistré le 29 octobre 1812, que Furcy faisait partie du premier lot qui échut à M. Routier fils aîné. Mais [Furcy] désirait avoir pour maître M. Lory, beau-frère de M. Routier, et cédant à ses instances, M. Lory l'avait acquis de M. Routier immédiatement après le partage." Moreau, Paillet, and Huart, *Mémoire pour la dame veuve Lory*, 5. The second legal brief gave the precise date of 29 October 1812 when Furcy formally became Joseph Lory's slave; Moreau, Paillet, and Huart, *Mémoire pour la dame veuve Lory*, 1 and 5 (ANOM FM GEN 158/1307).

107. Census, Isle Bonaparte, Saint-Denis, Joseph Lory, 1810 (ADR L157).

CHAPTER 6

1. Copy, "Mémoire de Constance en faveur de Furcy," 9 November 1817 (ADR 1Jp2007-1, no. 3).

2. On the other hand, Constance may have simply remembered her brother's death as one of the calamities that befell the island that month.

3. Héloïse Finch, "Comprendre la traite illégale d'esclaves pendant l'occupation Britannique de La Réunion à travers les archives britanniques," in *Identité et société réunion-naise: Nouvelles perspectives et nouvelles approches*, ed. Lucette Labache, Laurent Médéa, and Françoise Vergès (Paris: Karthala, 2005), 74.

4. The British Act for the Abolition of the Slave Trade (United Kingdom, 47 Geo 3 Sess 1 c 36) followed closely on the United States' passage of the Act Prohibiting Importation of Slaves of 1807 (United States, 2 Stat. 426, enacted March 2, 1807); the latter took effect on 1 January 1808, the first date permitted by the U.S. Constitution. The Slave Trade Felony Act (1811) extended the ban to prohibit the transport of slaves "from any Part of Africa, or from any other Country, Territory or Place whatsoever," thereby effectively extending the ban to all sources in the Indian Ocean world. Finch, "Comprendre la traite illégale," 74.

5. Between 1804 and 1818, the island's recorded slave population increased from 50,350 to 54,259, or by about 8 percent, with most of the expansion occurring in the rural parishes. Ève, *Naître et mourir à l'Île Bourbon*, 25 and 29.

6. Census, Isle Bourbon, Saint-Denis, Joseph Lory, 1814 (ADR L165). Lory states that he had acquired the two African slaves (*cafres*) from "M. Guillmiand" and "my bakery." Cyrille's census shows his recent acquisition of five African slaves in 1814 and an additional eighteen Africans and eight Malagasies in 1819, including many under the age of fifteen; Census, Isle Bourbon, Sainte-Suzanne, Cyrille Routier, 1814 (ADR L190.2) and 1817 (ADR 6M422).

7. Jennings, *French Anti-Slavery*, 25.

8. Jean-François Géraud, "Des habitations-sucreries aux usines sucrières: la 'mise en sucre' de l'Isle Bourbon, 1783–1848" (thesis, Université de la Réunion, 2002), 25–29.

9. Géraud, "Des habitations-sucreries aux usines sucrières," 129, 277.

10. In order to get the most efficient use of their workforces, large plantations planted the cane—which took twelve months to ripen—in two crops, so that the slaves could be utilized year-round.

11. Hubert Gerbeau, "Quelques aspects de la traite illégale des esclaves à l'île Bourbon au XIXe siècle," in *Mouvements de populations dans l'Océan Indien*, 274.

12. The land is described as "a plantation situated between the River (or Ravine) of Mat and that of [blank]; having a length of 27 ½ *gaulettes* and . . . a height of 60 *gaulettes* . . . acquired from Madame Widow Dioré, another separate plot [une autre terain aindivi (*sic*)] at the River of Mât, in the Saint-Benoît district." Census, Saint-André, Jenptiste Eufemie [*sic*], 1811 (ADR L195). A later return will specify the Saint-André location of Champ Borne, but the size of the property, "acquired from Madame Widow Dioré," remains virtually the same; the second property is located at "the quarter of Saint-Benoît in the parish Saint-[illegible] André measuring 19 *pieds* by 12 *pieds* [about 20 feet by 13 feet] "; Census, Saint-André, J^en Batiste Euphemie, 1813 (ADR L201). In 1811, the four children are Auguste, 9, Eugène, 4, Madeleine, 2, and Judithe, 3 months; the four slaves are Euphrosine *cafrine*, 30; Eliza, *malgache*, 20; "Gorge," *creole*, 9, recently sold (*vandu*), and Dauphine, *creole*, 38).

13. Census, Saint-André, J^en Batiste Euphemie, 1813 (ADR L201). In addition to helping with the crops, the couple's slaves were probably instrumental in building a house and a store on the smaller plot, newly declared in the 1813 census. These are not the properties mentioned in their marriage contract, so presumably they had sold those and purchased these in the meantime.

14. In the earliest extant form of 1811, he spells his name "Jenptiste Eufemie," then "J^n Baptiste Euphemie," and similar variations after 1812. In 1811, he signs his name "Jenbaptiste Euphemie"; Census, Isle Bourbon, Saint-André, 1811, Jenptiste Eufemie (ADR L195). Jean Baptiste Euphémie signs his full name with a clear signature in 1812; Census, Isle Bourbon, Saint-André, 1812, J^n Baptiste Euphemie (ADR L197.1).

15. Census, Isle Bourbon, Saint-André, 1813, J^en Batiste Euphemie (ADR L201). However, the following year he declares himself a farmer again; Census, Isle Bourbon, Saint-André, 1814, J. B^te Ephemie (ADR L202.1).

16. Census, Isle Bourbon, Saint-André, Jenptisite Eufimie, 1811 (ADR L195).

17. "I declare to have given freedom to *la nommée* Dauphine, creole, age 39 years, my slave, since the month of December 1811." Census, Isle Bourbon, Saint-André, J^n Baptiste Euphemie [1812] (ADR L197.1; an almost identical return for the same year, with no substantive differences, is also filed in ADR L198).

18. Garnier and Desarthe, "Mascarene Cyclones," 5.

19. Gilles Gérard, '*La Guerre' de 1811: ou la révolution de Saint-Leu, Isle Bourbon (La Réunion)* (Paris: L'Harmattan, 2015).

20. In 1814, their children numbered five, including an unnamed boy of eight months (appearing in the subsequent 1815 census as Jean Baptiste, 20 months); Census, Isle Bourbon, Saint-André, 1814, J. B^te Ephemie (ADR L202.1) and 1815 (ADR L191.1, no. 137). They

registered his birth among the "libres" (ANOM IREL, État-civil, Réunion, Saint-André, 15 January 1815). He apparently died before 1817, when he is missing from the census. Birth of Joséphine Jean Baptiste, born October 8 (ANOM IREL, État-civil, Réunion, Saint-André, recorded 14 October 1817, Libres).

21. Furcy is listed first among the Lorys' slaves, a declaration Lory will repeat for many years; Census, Isle Bonaparte, Saint-Denis, Joseph Lory, 1810 (ADR L157).

22. Census, Isle Bourbon, Saint-Denis, Joseph Lory, 1824 (ADR 6M 201.1).

23. Pauline first appears in Census, Isle Bourbon, Saint-Denis, Joseph Lory, 1814 (ADR L165). Her designation as mulatto will appear in 1840 (ADR 6M 300). Joseph Lory's slaveholding over the next decade or so shows a fairly consistent pattern of retaining most of the same individuals year after year, with gradual, steady growth mainly through purchase, from nineteen slaves in 1810 to twenty-four in 1818. Though Lory's investment pattern shows an equal balance of male and female slaves, this arrangement did not seem to produce many offspring, or he did not declare them.

24. Desrieux filed two censuses on Lory's behalf in 1815; they are virtually identical. Census, Isle Bourbon, Saint-Denis, Joseph Lory, 1815 (ADR L167.2, nos. 571 and 1043).

25. Census, Isle Bourbon, Saint-Denis, Joseph Lory, 1814 (ADR L165).

26. Census, Isle Bourbon, Saint-Denis, Joseph Lory, 1815 (ADR L167.2, nos. 571 and 1043).

27. Renoyal de Lescouble worked with his slave Noël on the chair from August 1812 through April 1813; Jean-Baptiste Renoyal de Lescouble, *Journal d'un colon de l'Île Bourbon*, 3 vols., ed. Norbert Dodille (Paris: L'Harmattan, 1990), 60, 72–75, 99–115.

28. In this context, the French word *brave* could also mean honest, good, or hard-working. Sully Brunet, "A mon Fils," 131, 187, 190–191, 193–195.

29. Death of Madeleine, 18 January 1814 (ANOM État-civil, Saint-Denis, 1814, Libres de couleur, 14). This was the north-south street to the east of the rue des Ramparts. Emile Trouette, *L'île Bourbon pendant la période révolutionnaire de 1789 à 1803* (Paris: Challamel, 1888), 30–31.

30. "Madelaine," death, 18 January 1814 (ANOM État-civil, Saint-Denis, 1814, Libres de couleur, 14). Here Lory estimated her age; if born in 1759, as suggested in her manumission act, she would have been 55 years old. There is no indication of her burial in the civil status records.

31. "Notes [écrites sous la dictée] de Furcy," n.d., 4 (ADR 1Jp2007/1, no. 51). Furcy remembered the death as having occurred eight months after the end of Madeleine's battle with Joseph Lory for her son's freedom.

32. Gilles Gérard's painstaking work has recreated Célerine's family history: "L'esclave Furcy," . Célerine will play a key role in helping Constance and Furcy in 1817. There is no indication of Célerine's father, but at her death she had taken the last name Duverger; this is where we find the name of her mother, Bondi. Death of Célerine Duverger, 9 February 1835 (ANOM IREL, État Civil, Réunion, Saint-Denis, 1835). She was 69 at her death, so born around 1774. Several of her children, including Virginie, took the family name Béga, probably after Paul Béga, a large property holder in Isle Bourbon.

33. On 5 October 1826, after the death of Virginie, the grandmother Célerine requested that Virginie's two daughters be entered into the *état civil*. ANOM IREL, État Civil, Réunion, Saint-Denis, *Libres*, 5 October 1826 (images 311–312). Gilles Gérard has suggested this

link between Virginie and Furcy, but the relationship is uncertain. Virginie, who is first listed in the 1811 manumission document, does not appear on Célerine's census returns of 1817 (Denis 6M152) or 1819 (ADR 6M163), but reappears in 1827 (ADR 6M230), where she is specifically listed as "dead," suggesting that during the interim she had been living elsewhere to raise her daughters. As a mother, but without property, she would not have been required to fill out a census return, but it is not clear where she lived, or whether these were in fact Furcy's daughters.

34. Furcy would later lament his separation from his children after he was arrested in 1817, after which time he would not have had the opportunity to sire a child in Isle Bourbon before he was displaced to Mauritius in 1818. Furcy, Port Louis, Isle Maurice, to Boucher, 15 May 1826 (ADR 1Jp2007-1, no. 71).

35. Gérard, "L'esclave Furcy."

36. "Notes écrites sous la dictée de Furcy," n.d. (ADR 1Jp2007/1, no. 51), 7.

37. "Notes écrites sous la dictée de Furcy," n.d. (ADR 1Jp2007/1, no. 51), 7–8.

38. Ghachem, *Old Regime and the Haitian Revolution*, 62–63, 133–141, 158–159, 176–182, 199. Article 37 of the Mascarene Code Noir prohibited masters and overseers from torturing or mutilating slaves, though whipping was permitted. If a master or overseer killed a slave, they could be condemned to death, but such a sentence was never issued in Isle Bourbon. Delaleu, *Code des îles de France et de Bourbon*, IF, 250.

39. "Letters patent in the form of edict" of December 1723, article 22.

40. Furcy to Boucher, 15 May 1826 (ADR 1Jp2007-1, no. 71).

41. Napoleon had already issued such a decree as a condition of resuming power during the Hundred Days: "Décret impérial qui abolit la Traite des Noirs, 29 mars 1815," France, *Bulletin des lois de la République française*, série 6, no. 1 (Paris: Imprimerie de la république, 1815), 55. The new laws were: "Ordonnance du Roi qui pourvoit au cas où il serait contrevenu aux ordres de Sa Majesté concernant l'Abolition de la Traite des Noirs, 8 janv. 1817," France, *Bulletin des lois du royaume de France*, série 7, no. 136 (Paris: Imprimerie royale, 1817), 105–106; followed by the "Ordonnance du Roi qui prononce des peines contre les individus qui se livreraient à la traite des noirs, 15 avr. 1818," France, *Bulletin des Lois du royaume de France*, série 7, no. 206 (Paris: Imprimerie royale, 1818), 234–235.

42. Gerbeau, "Quelques aspects de la traite illégale," 275–276.

43. "Arrêté du 13 Messidor an X [2 July 1802] portant défense aux noirs, mulâtres, et autres gens de couleur de l'un ou l'autre sexe d'entrer sans autorisation sur le territoire continental de la République," France, *Bulletin de lois de la République française*, série 3, no. 219 (Paris: Imprimerie de la république, 1802), 815–816; "Circulaire du Grand Juge Claude Ambrose Regnier, ministre de la Justice, aux préfets," 18 Nivôse Year XI (8 January 1803) (AN, Pierrefitte, F/7/8444, dos. 5697–P, BB/15/208, dos. 5397–B5). See also Boulle and Peabody, *Le droit des noirs en France*, 166–170,178–179.

44. "Lettre du ministre de la marine à MM. les Administrateurs des colonies, sur les dispositions de la déclaration du Roi, du 9 août 1777, qui défend l'introduction des hommes de couleur en France," 17 October 1817 in *Annales maritimes et coloniales, 2ᵉ année, 1817, 1ʳᵉ partie: lois et ordonnances,* (Paris, Imprimerie royale, 1817), 385–386; Heuer, "One-Drop Rule," 538–539; Boulle and Peabody, *Le droit des noirs en France*, 186–187, 199–200.

45. Copy, Pierre Barthélémy Portal d'Albarèdes to Boucher, 14 October 1816 (ADR 1Jp2007-2, no. 214). Louis Boucher was the eldest son of Charles Louis Boucher,

an honorary notary in Luzarches. Mariage, Monsieur Boucher et Mademoiselle Sonthonax, 29 January 1817; AN Pierrefitte MC/ET/IV/1054. During the empire he served in Arezzo, Arno, and Rome, followed by positions in Orléans, Paris, Joigny, and Auxerre after 1814. Louis Boucher, resumé [ca. 1830] (ADR 1Jp2007-1, no. 117). His subsequent appointments were: Procureur Générale, Cour Royale, Bastia, 4–14 March 1819 and the Cour Royale de Poitiers, 16–19 August 1830. See also Copy, Boucher to the Minister of the Navy and the Colonies, 17 June 1818 (ADR 1Jp2007-1, no. 114).

46. Dubouchage, Minister of the Navy and the Colonies, Instructions to the Administrators of Bourbon, 30 November 1816 (ADR 1Jp2007-2, no. 215). For a concise overview of the historical reform of courts of Isle Bourbon, see Auguste La Barre de Nanteuil, "Regime Judiciaire," in *Législation de l'Île de la Réunion*, 2nd ed., 5 vols. (Paris: E. Donnaud, 1861–1863), 4:543–616. Similar reforms were initiated for France's other slaveholding colonies. Schloss, *Sweet Liberty*, 74.

47. The civil marriage record was destroyed in the Tuileries fire set by the Paris Commune in 1871, but the notarized contract survives, dated 29 January 1817 (A.N. MC/ET/IV/1054). Marie Sonthonax was the daughter of Pierre Louis Sonthonax, deceased, and Jeanne Marie Moulin, who had remarried Joseph Julien Le Gonidec de Kerdaniel.

48. For details of his life, see Robert Louis Stein, *Léger Félicité Sonthonax: The Lost Sentinel of the Republic* (London: Associated University Presses, 1985).

49. Her birth record was destroyed in the same fire that destroyed that of her marriage, and while a Marie Joséphine Louise Sonthonax, baptized 8 December 1791, appears in the Parisian reconstituted état-civil (Archives numérisées de Paris, "Fichiers alphabétiques de l'état civil reconstitute," V3E/N 2072, http://canadp-archivesenligne.paris.fr/archives_etat_civil/index.php), the entry doesn't name the father. Léger Félicité Sonthonax's grandfather was Pierre Sonthonax; he died in 1771 (Stein, *Léger Félicité Sonthonax*, 17). A Pierre Louis Sonthonax was sent to Lyon (Commune-Afranchie) on 12 July 1794 to survey the status of manufacturing in that city following its surrender to revolutionary forces the previous year; "Arrêté approuvant l'envoi de Pierre Louis Sonothonax à Commune Affranchie," 24 Messidor Year II (12 July 1794) (AN AF/II/76, 47). He certainly was not the famous emancipator, since the testament of the latter gives the name of his daughter as Marie Julie Félicitée.

50. Belonging to a noble Breton family, Joseph Julien Le Gonidec de Kerdaniel practiced law in Saint-Domingue from 1789 through the 1791 slave revolt and was promoted to attorney general in Port-au-Prince, where he witnessed emerging tensions between white planters and free men of color; he likely met Léger Félicité Sonthonax there. The British invasion in 1793 propelled Le Gonidec to flee to the United States and then home to Brittany, where he remained in seclusion until Napoleon came to power. Under Bonaparte, Le Gonidec was appointed appeals court judge in Hières, near Lyon, and then justice commissioner for the colonies of Isle Bourbon and Isle de France (Mauritius) until the English invasion in 1810. Fleeing the British once more, Le Gonidec went on to serve the empire as attorney general for Rome, where he met Boucher, who was assistant attorney general (*avocat general*) there, until 1814. Upon return to Paris, Le Gonidec was appointed to the Cour de Cassation in 1815, where he served until his death in 1844. Vieille de Boisjolin, Alphonse Rabbe, and Charles Augustin Sainte-Beuve, *Biographie universelle et portative*

des Contemporains: ou Dictionnaire historique des hommes vivants et des hommes morts (de 1788 à 1828) (Paris: Chez l'Éditeur, 1836), 3:138.

51. Passengers, Saint-Denis, Arrivals, 28 June 1817, *La Normande* (ANOM COL F/5B/7); Copy, Boucher to the Minister of the Navy and the Colonies, 17 June 1818 (ADR 1Jp2007-1, no. 114). Between the 1770s and the 1820s, the duration of voyages from Europe to the Indian Ocean decreased markedly, at least on British ships. Peter M. Solar, "Opening to the East: Shipping between Europe and Asia, 1770–1830," paper presented at the meeting of the Economic History Society, 5 April 2013, http://www.ehs.org.uk/events/assets/SolarFullPaperIID.pdf, 44.

52. Adolphe Robert and Gaston Cougny, "Philippe Panon Desbassayns de Richemont," in *Dictionnaire des Parlementaires française de 1789 à 1889* (Paris: Bourloton, 1889), 2:346, http://www2.assemblee-nationale.fr/sycomore/fiche/(num_dept)/16915. He would become deputy to the Assemblée Nationale in 1824–1830.

53. Georges Azéma, *Histoire de l'Isle Bourbon depuis 1643 jusqu'au 20 décembre 1848* (Paris: H. Plon, 1859), 272.

54. Personnel judiciaire: matricule des officiers de justice 1814/1830 (ANOM COL D/2C/341, fol. 26).

55. A series of documents collected between 12 and 19 December 1817 reveals an attempt to document Sully Brunet's legitimate (and white) origins in Bourbon parish records (ADR 1Jp2007-2, nos. 252–258). Yet they also include an unsigned family tree, n.d., which traces his ancestry back five generations to a ship captain, one François Noisy, who recognized his illegitimate daughter Henriette Noisy, "approximately when the colony was founded," as a note indicates (no. 252), suggesting strongly that Noisy's concubine was in all probability Malagasy.

56. Jérémy Boutier, "L'ordre public: Sully Brunet et les contradictions de la justice et de la politique dans l'Affaire Furcy (Isle Bourbon, 1817–1818)," *French Colonial History* 15 (2014): 135–163; Jérémy Boutier, "Quelques remarques sur le transfert de l'idéologie libérale française à Bourbon de 1830 à 1833," *Revue historique de l'océan Indien* 5 (2009): 68–69. Sully Brunet claimed that he owned one hundred slaves in his letter to the minister, 16 December 1817 (ADR 1Jp2007-1, no. 22). He would later publish a plan for the gradual abolition of slavery in 1840: Jacques Sully Brunet, *Considérations sur le système colonial, et plan d'abolition de l'esclavage* (Paris: Impr. de F. Locquin, 1840).

57. Or "Tétard"; Passengers, Saint-Denis, Arrivals, 28 June 1817, *La Normande* (ANOM COL F/5B/7). Bussy was here spelled "Bussé." Testard's appointment as Boucher's secretary is discussed in Portal to Boucher, 24 January 1817 (ADR 1Jp2007-2, no. 220), and Dubouchage to Boucher, 25 January 1817 (ADR 1Jp2007-2, no. 221).

58. The larger city, Saint-Paul, settled first next to the island's only natural harbor, held 11,186 residents. Ève, *Naître et mourir à l'Île Bourbon*, 28.

59. In 1810, the free nonwhite population of Saint-Denis was only 615; by 1815, it was 1,429. Ève, *Naître et mourir à l'Île Bourbon*, 28.

60. Billiard, *Voyage aux colonies orientales*, 115. Similar comments were expressed by the new commander general: "There exists in this colony a mass of indigent and lazy population, devoid of any property. The individuals of this class who have retained some principles of integrity subsist on the products of fishing and hunting, but the major portion lives at the expense of the landholders or resort to the theft of slaves." Lafitte du Courteil, *mémoire* to

the Minister, 1 September 1817, quoted in Honoré Lacaze, *L'Île Bourbon, l'Île de France, Madagascar: Recherches historiques* (Paris: A. Parent, 1880), 248–249.

61. Billiard, *Voyage aux colonies orientales*, 119–120.

62. Billiard, *Voyage aux colonies orientales*, 194.

63. Billiard, *Voyage aux colonies orientales*, 194.

64. Lafitte du Courteil, mémoire au ministre, 1 September 1817, quoted in Lacaze, *L'Île Bourbon*, 248–249.

65. Ricquebourg, *Dictionnaire généalogique*, 2:1049–1050.

66. Gillot de l'Étang entered the Tribunal of First Instance under Napoleon in 1803, then advanced to *procureur impérial* in 1807 until 1810, when he was promoted to *procureur impérial* of the appeals court, where he continued to serve under British occupation. From 1813 to 1814 Gillot de l'Étang served as president of the appeals court. With Napoleon's fall, he was provisionally installed as attorney general to the Superior Council of Isle Bourbon, pending authorization by the king and the minister, but on 2 July 1817 the minister reassigned him as assistant public prosecutor (*avocat general*). Extrait des Registres du Greffe de la Cour Royale de l'Isle de Bourbon, 18 October 1817 (ADR 1Jp2007-2, no. 204). Gillot de l'Étang would later be reappointed as attorney general (*procureur general*) to the Royal Court of Isle Bourbon in 1827. Ricquebourg, *Dictionnaire généalogique*, 2:1049–1050.

67. Of the five *conseillers* attached to the Royal Court, the future Lory family notary, Guy Desrieux and Second President Pajot repeatedly and publicly denounced Boucher.

68. Michault d'Emery had been born in Paris in 1759. He came to Saint-Denis in 1786, immediately married a local girl and advanced to the office of royal notary in 1789. Ricquebourg, *Dictionnaire généalogique*, 2:1937. Boucher, Copy, Second Report to the Minister of the Navy and of the Colonies, 17 April 1818 (ADR 1Jp2007-1, no. 2). Joseph Lory had loaned money to Philippe August Pajot, husband of Sophie Panon Desbassayns, in 1809; Obligation, Auguste Pajot to Joseph Lorry [sic], 5 January 1809, Notariat Michault D'Emery, no. 665 (ANOM DPPC NOT REU1802).

69. "Energetic" was Sully Brunet's later characterization; "A mon Fils," 187. Boucher's speech, delivered on 2 July 1817, promised to call the judiciary to righteous judgment: "Today, the completely liberated Royal Court has no other witness, no other accuser, and no other intermediary between itself and its conscience, than divinity. . . . No one can force a magistrate to let slip through his hands the sword and the scales." Reprinted in Nanteuil, *Législation de l'Île de la Réunion*, 4:554.

70. "Permit me to observe to you that on page 7, line 26, the word *title* would perhaps be better than that of *virtue*, which would not weaken in the slightest the merited elegy that you have given the first president." Panon Desbassayns de Richemont to Boucher, 30 July 1817 (ADR 1Jp2007-2, no. 189). Whether the speech was published in its original or revised form is not known, as the collection of original periodicals held on microfilm at the Archives Départementales de la Réunion does not contain any issue of the *Gazette de l'Isle Bourbon* from 1817, nor does the journal appear in the collections of the Bibliothèque Nationale de France.

71. Boucher kept copies of his correspondence, which documents escalating hostilities through the year 1817 and over a variety of differences, including the appointment of various judicial officers, Panon Desbassayns de Richemont to Boucher, 27 August

(ADR 1Jp2007-2, no. 190); Gillot L'Étang to Boucher, 14 September (ADR 1Jp2007-2, no. 208); Extrait des régistres du greffier de la Cour Royale de l'Isle Bourbon, 9 October (ADR 1Jp2007-2, no. 169); Gillot L'Étang to [Boucher?], 9 October [December?] (ADR 1Jp2007-2, no. 205); Panon Desbassayns de Richemont to the Avocat Général of the Cour Royal [Gillot L'Étang], 12 October (ADR 1Jp2007-2, no. 191); Panon Desbassayns de Richemont to Boucher, 14 October (ADR 1Jp2007-2, no. 192).

72. Boucher to the Minister, 7 and 9 October 1817 (ANOM 3201 COL REU/22/133); Bussy de Saint-Romain to the Minister, 3 September 1817 (ANOM EE 352).

73. Boucher to the Minister, 1 September 1817 (ANOM 3201 COL REU/22/133).

74. Bussy de Saint-Romain to the Minister, 3 September and 25 October 1817 (ANOM 3201 COL REU/22/134).

75. Panon Desbassayns de Richemont to Boucher, 25 October 1817 (ADR 1Jp2007-2, no. 193).

76. These letters include Panon Desbassayns de Richemont to Boucher, 5 November 1817 (ADR 1Jp2007-2, no. 194); Panon Desbassayns de Richemont to Boucher, 6 November 1817 (ADR 1Jp2007-2, no. 195), in which Panon Desbassayns writes: "I only knew of a printed song that was shown to me in a packet; as it only attacks myself and my family and I am convinced that it's prepared a triumph to the authors of these satires to attach importance to it, I have made no effort to discover its author and even if his name became known to me scorn would be my only vengeance"; and that of Panon Desbassayns de Richemont to Boucher, 7 November 1817 (ADR 1Jp2007-2, no. 196), in which Panon Desbassayns, reviewing the proofs of the forthcoming *Gazette*, writes: "You will see here under the title Politics an article extracted from the French papers, which appears to me to make allusion to the songs and anonymous writings that circulate here and against which you are proposed to publish an opinion." An extract from the registers of the Royal Court indicates that during a public audience Boucher insisted that extracts of a letter from the minister of the navy and the colonies, addressed to the administrators, and a series of acts regulating the reorganization of the colonial judiciary and lines of authority be read aloud and recorded in the register of the court. Extrait des régistres du Greffe de la Cour Royale de l'Isle Bourbon, 6 November 1817 (ADR 1Jp2007-2, no. 223).

77. I have not been able to figure out exactly what was at stake. The Royal Court's decision of 4 September 1817 in *Ball v. Desrieux*, based on the public hearings officer Sully Brunet's opinion, mentions Joseph Panon Desbassayns as an ancillary to the losing party, Guy Desrieux, but this does not seem to be the decision that prompted the Desbassayns clan's outrage. Isle Bourbon Cour d'Appel, Jugements Civils 1798–1911 (ANOM 6DPPC 2726).

78. Fédière to Boucher, 31 October 1817 (ADR 1Jp2007-1, no. 59).

79. Sully Brunet was dismissed by a joint letter from the administrators, Panon Desbassayns and Lafitte du Courteil, on 1 December 1817. "Ordonnance des Administrateurs Généraux qui suspend de ses fonctions, le Sr. Sully Brunet, conseiller auditeur de seconde classe à la Cour Royale," 1 December 1817 (ADR 1Jp2007-2, no. 251). On December 16, Sully Brunet wrote to the minister of the navy and the colonies from his exile on his plantation in Saint-Benoît, "where I have few friends," complaining that he was being held under constant surveillance and protesting his expulsion from his position. According to Sully Brunet, "My only fault, if I had committed any, would appear to be to have sacrificed

ten minutes of my time to render services to these unfortunates who came to hassle me daily, employing prayers and their tears to harness my generosity, coming to see me in the name of humanity." Behind his persecution, according to Sully Brunet, lurked the commissioner general, Panon Desbassayns, who sought vengeance for the position he had taken in a prior dispute between the Panon Desbassayns's brother, Joseph, and Bouvet. "I have therefore become the victim of intrigue and of individual vengeance of an insatiable and vain man, whose brother I had to crack down on [*sévir*] in performing my duties." Sully Brunet to the Minister of the Navy and the Colonies, 16 December 1817 (ADR 1Jp2007-1, no. 22).

80. According to Sully Brunet, Furcy's dispute with Lory was well known in the community. Sully Brunet argued that it was the reorganization of the judiciary, with the arrival of the new *procureur général*, that prompted Constance to seek his assistance. Sully Brunet to the Minister of the Navy and the Colonies, 16 December 1817 (ADR 1Jp2007-1, no. 22).

81. Olympe Joséphine Augustin was born 27 July 1817; ANOM IREL, État Civil, Réunion, Saint-Denis, *Libres*, 5 October 1826 (images 311–312).

82. Jean Baptiste Euphémie filed his last census return in 1815; Census, Isle Bourbon, Saint-André, Jean B^te Euphémie, 1815 (ADR L191.1). The birth record for Joséphine describes her as the "legitimate daughter of deceased Jean Baptiste and of *la nommée* Constance, the father and mother, this latter domiciled in this quarter"; Birth of Joséphine Jean Baptiste, 14 October 1817 (ANOM IREL, État-civil, Réunion, Saint-André, 1817, *Libres*, Births). I have searched for Jean Baptiste's death record in Saint-André between 1816 and 1817 but without success. In general, there are only a scattered few death records in the sections devoted to *libres* (free people of color)—only one or two per year between 1814 and 1817. Perhaps free people of color had little incentive to officially record these events, whereas slave owners might need proof of the death of their slaves to stop paying the head taxes.

83. Constance is referred to as "the widow Jean Baptiste" in legal records from Furcy's 1817 lawsuit; e.g., Copy, "Mémoire de Constance en faveur de Furcy," 9 November 1817 (ADR 1Jp2007-1, no. 3), and in and all censuses from 1818 forward; e.g., Census, Isle Bourbon, Saint-André, Widow Jean Baptiste, 1818 (ADR 6M5).

84. Panon Desbassayns de Richemont to the Minister, 21 December 1817 (ANOM 3201 COL REU/22/132), fol. 22. Constance had inherited some of her husband's property between the Rivière du Mât and the Ravine. The property is variously spelled in different records: "Vincent d'O," "Vincudeo," "Vincehndaux," "Vinsanh-Diau," or "Vinsen Daux"; Marriage, Jean Batiste [*sic*] and Constance, 30 May 1808, Notariat Michault D'Emery, no. 556 (ANOM DPPC NOT * REU1801); Census, Isle Bourbon, Saint-André, Widow Jean Baptiste, 1819 (ADR 6M10).

85. Boucher, Copy of the Report to the Minister of the Navy and the Colonies, 25 November 1817 (ADR 1Jp2007-1, nos. 2 and 101), Report no. 3; Huard, Statement to the Cour de Saint-Denis, 22 November 1817 (ADR 1Jp2007-1, no. 23). The 1817 census lists "Célerine, *libre*, age 41," as living on the rue des Prêtres in Saint-Denis with eight of her children and a slave; Census, Saint-Denis, 1817, Célerine (ADR L161.7). Commissioner General Panon Desbassayns, whose charges must be taken with a grain of salt, claimed that Célerine was at the time the concubine of a lawyer (*avoué*), Dominique Arnoux, a native of Marseille, but this was probably just the commissioner's attempt to defame the lawyer, whom he suspected of giving Furcy legal advice; Panon Desbassayns de Richemont

to the Minister, 21 December 1817 (ANOM 3201 COL REU/22/132, fol. 20v). Rather, many of Célerine's children, including Furcy's companion, Virginie, took the surname of a prominent planter family, Béga, which may imply that he was their father. The commissioner further records Célerine as living "at the home of Duverger, a schoolteacher," but this conflicts with the census records, which show Célerine as a head of household. Nevertheless, some of her children did later take the surname Duverger, suggesting that the two eventually married. Gérard, "L'esclave Furcy."

86. "Notes [écrites sous la dictée] de Furcy," n.d., 4–5 (ADR 1Jp2007/1, no. 51).

87. Panon Desbassayns was at a meeting of the mayors in Sainte-Suzanne, to the east of Saint-André, where Constance lived; she must have realized that this was an opportune moment to approach Sully Brunet in Saint-Denis. Panon Desbassayns de Richemont to the Minister, 21 December 1817 (ANOM 3201 COL REU/22/132), fol. 3.

88. "Procès-verbal des déclarations de Constance & Adolphe," 10 December 1817 (ANOM FM SG REU 97/684, no. 16).

89. Panon Desbassayns claimed that Célerine had moved into Duperier's house much earlier, but, if so, she filed census returns as an independent head of household in Saint-Denis between 1812 and 1817, citing her profession as "seamstress" or "hat maker" and declaring one or two slaves (ADR L160, L 167.1, 6M152).

90. Sully Brunet, "A mon Fils," 190.

91. Report of the Commissioner General Ordinator to the Commandant General for the King, "Rapport du Commissaire Gal Ordonnateur au Commandant Général pour le Roi, Saint-Denis," 29 November 1817, Attachment no. 5 to Panon Desbassayns de Richemont to the Minister, 21 December 1817 (ANOM 3201 COL REU/22/132).

92. Report of the Commissioner General Ordinator to the Commandant General for the King, "Rapport du Commissaire Gal Ordonnateur au Commandant Général pour le Roi, Saint-Denis," 29 November 1817, Attachment no. 5 to Panon Desbassayns de Richemont to the Minister, 21 December 1817 (ANOM 3201 COL REU/22/132).

93. Boucher, Copy of the Report to the Minister of the Navy and the Colonies, 25 November 1817 (ADR 1Jp2007-1, nos. 2 and 101).

94. Panon Desbassayns de Richemont to the Minister, 21 December 1817 (ANOM 3201 COL REU/22/132), fol. 22. Boucher claimed that he feared for his wife's health, so he could not take the time to read the "rather lengthy petition" that Constance set before him. Boucher, Copy of the Report to the Minister of the Navy and the Colonies, 25 November 1817 (ADR 1Jp2007-1, nos. 2 and 101).

95. A wet nurse named Marie Jeanne would accompany the couple to France in December; Passengers, Saint-Paul, Departures, 23 December 1817, *Le Télémaque* (ANOM COL F/5B/7).

96. Constance's request for the certificate of indigence was rejected by Mayor Pitois, who told her that "he could not certify anything but that Furcy was the slave of M. Lory and that no one had ever made a similar demand for a slave"; "Procès-verbal des déclarations de Constance & Adolphe," 10 December 1817 (ANOM FM SG REU 97/684, no. 16).

97. Panon Desbassayns de Richemont to the Minister, 21 December 1817 (ANOM 3201 COL REU/22/132), fol. 22v.

98. "Procès-verbal des déclarations de Constance & Adolphe," 10 December 1817 (ANOM FM SG REU 97/684, no. 16).

99. Sully Brunet's later self-exculpatory account argues that he was obliged, as "protector of the unfortunate and of the liberty of citizens," to review Constance's petition "to make known whether the case was of a nature to be sustained; after the examination of the affair, I decided in the affirmative." Sully Brunet to the Minister of the Navy and the Colonies, 16 December 1817 (ADR 1Jp2007-1, no. 22).

100. Boucher, Copy of the Report to the Minister of the Navy and the Colonies, 25 November 1817 (ADR 1Jp2007-1, nos. 2 and 101).

101. "Procès-verbal des déclarations de Constance & Adolphe," 10 December 1817 (ANOM FM SG REU 97/684, no. 16).

102. Indeed, when he recalled the events many years later in a memoir written for his son, Sully Brunet omitted Constance's role entirely, referencing only Adolphe and presenting the events solely as actions between men. Sully Brunet, "A mon Fils," 131, 187, 190–191, 193–195.

103. Likewise Célerine risked arrest for harboring a fugitive slave. Arreté 47, du 1er Pluviôse an XII (22 January 1804), esp. art. 15–16, in *Recueil des lois publiées à Maurice*, 51.

CHAPTER 7

1. Article 19 of the 1723 code stated: "Slaves who are not fed, clothed, or maintained by their masters, as we have ordained by the present [articles], will be able to give notice to our attorney general [*procureur général*] of the said councils, our representative [*procureur pour nous*], and put their petitions into his hands, upon which, and by the same office, if the notices come from elsewhere, the masters will be pursued at [the attorney general's] request and without cost, such as we wish to be observed for crimes and barbarous and inhumane treatment by the masters toward their slaves." Similar language appears in Article 16 of the 1767 ordinance; Delaleu, *Code des îles de France et de Bourbon*, IF, 248–249, IB, 62. These provisions originate in the 1685 Code Noir for the Antilles (art. 26 and 42).

2. Article 24. "Neither will slaves be party nor be in judgment in civil matters, neither as plaintiff nor defendant, nor be civil party in a criminal matter, except against their masters to act and defend in civil matters and to pursue in criminal matters reparation for outrages and excesses that they shall have committed against their slaves"; Delaleu, *Code des îles de France et de Bourbon*, IF, 249.

3. In Paris, slaves suing for their freedom petitioned the court directly, but there was no legislation or procedural guidance stating explicitly how a person wrongly enslaved should seek confirmation of their freedom in a colonial court. Peabody, *"There Are No Slaves,"* 88–92.

4. The Code Decaen's procedures for naming a *patron* were solely for the purpose of manumission, but it raised questions about whether a slave or even a free person of color, legally subsumed under this system of *patronage*, was entitled to legal personhood in other matters. Arrêté, 19 Brumaire Year XIII (10 November 1804), art. 10, 13, 14, 15, 18, and 20, in *Recueil des lois publiées à Maurice*, 114–116.

5. There are several extant versions of Constance's petition: Copy, "Mémoire de Constance en faveur de Furcy," 9 November 1817 (ADR 1Jp2007-1, no. 3), hereafter Constance, Petition; "Extrait d'une Mémoire déposé au greffe de la Cour Royale de l'Ile de Bourbon

le trois Décembre 1817 par M. le Procureur général pour servir s'il y a lieu, à intenter toute procédure criminelle ou correctionnelle" (ADR 1Jp2007-1, no. 36) and an identically titled extract (ADR 1Jp2007-1, no. 103).

6. Panon Desbassayns to the Minister, 21 December 1817 (ANOM 3201 COL REU/22/132), fol. 5r.

7. "In the arrangements made with the Sieur and Dame Routier, the Demoiselle Dispense [*sic*] had taken care to stipulate this condition, that at their arrival in Isle Bourbon, they would petition for the manumission of Magdelaine [*sic*], would assure her a lifetime annuity [*une pension viagère*] of six hundred *livres* per year, supplies necessary for her food, and would procure for her, if possible, an arrangement [*établissement*] for marriage"; Constance, Petition.

8. "... it was only a little time after the death of this last [Madame Routier], which happened in October 1808, nineteen years after her manumission, that Madeleine was made aware of her condition. During this long interval it was hidden from her"; Constance, Petition.

9. Constance, Petition.

10. Constance, Petition.

11. "A man cannot have achieved freedom to be indirectly held as a slave." Constance, Petition.

12. Justinian, *Digest* D.1.5.4, as quoted in Alan Watson, *Slave Law in the Americas* (Athens, GA: University of Georgia Press, 1989), 116.

13. Joseph Schacht, *An Introduction to Islamic Law* (New York: Clarendon, 1964), 127; Hallaq, *Shari'a*, 307, esp. n. 59.

14. Siete Partidas, 4.22, quoted in Alan Watson, *Roman Law and Comparative Law* (Athens, GA: University of Georgia Press, 1991), 216.

15. Emphasis in original. Constance, Petition.

16. The relevant decree from the Code Decaen is: "Children under the age of seven, born of a female slave who is manumitted, will follow the condition of their mother. In this case, the master will be held to add to the sum determined for the manumission a sum of five hundred francs for each child." Arrêté 96, "Dispositions additionnelles à l'arrêter sur les affranchissements," 1 Messidor Year XIII (20 June 1805), in *Recueil des lois publiées à Maurice*, 123. For the 1723 edict prohibiting the separation of mother and children through sale, see Delaleu, *Code des îles de France et de Bourbon*, IF, 250, art. 43.

17. Copy of Furcy's writ (*signification*) to the Saint-Denis Tribunal of First Instance, 22 November 1817 (ADR 1Jp2007-1, no. 23). Célerine's address, given here, is not found on any contemporary map of Saint-Denis, but was probably a small passage near the church or the presbytery.

18. Sully Brunet, "A mon Fils," 190. No doubt Sully Brunet's memory embellished the words of the petition.

19. Minutes of the Declarations of Constance and Adolphe, 10 December 1817 (ANOM FM SG REU 97/684, no. 16).

20. Copy of Furcy's writ (*signification*) to the Saint-Denis Tribunal of First Instance, 22 November 1817 (ADR 1Jp2007-1, no. 23). Alphonse was creole, 28, and listed as a field hand (*pioche*) in the census. Census, Isle Bourbon, Saint-Denis, Joseph Lory, 1817 (ADR 6M154).

21. Copy of Furcy's writ (*signification*) to the Saint-Denis Tribunal of First Instance, 22 November 1817 (ADR 1Jp2007-1, no. 23).

22. Panon Desbassayns, Report for the King, 29 November 1817" (ANOM 3201 COL REU/22/132, attachment no. 5); Minutes of the Declarations of Constance and Adolphe, 10 December 1817 (ANOM FM SG REU 97/684, no. 16).

23. Copy of Furcy's writ (*signification*) to the Saint-Denis Tribunal of First Instance, 22 November 1817 (ADR 1Jp2007-1, no. 23). Boucher would later blame the bailiff Huard for introducing the argument that Indians could not be enslaved; Boucher, Second Report to the Minister, 17 April 1818 (ADR 1Jp2007-1, no. 2). But as we have seen, the argument against the enslavement of Indians had already been voiced in Constance's petition.

24. Peabody, "Alternative Genealogy," 341–362. As a maxim, rather than a statute issued by the monarch, it was respected by French jurists, though its wording evolved over time.

25. Peabody, "*There Are No Slaves*," 16–18, and Boulle and Peabody, *Le droit des Noirs en France*, 33–36, 43–46, 57–58, 64–67.

26. Déclaration du Roi pour la Police des noirs, 9 August 1777; Peabody, "*There Are No Slaves*," 114–115, and Boulle and Peabody, *Le droit des Noirs en France*, 97, 99–102.

27. "Décret du 28 septembre 1791 [loi du 16 oct. 1791]," *Archives Parlementaires de 1787 à 1860*, 442–443.

28. Arrêté, 13 Messidor Year X (2 July 1802), France, *Bulletin de lois de la République française*, série 3, no. 219, 163, 176.

29. Matthieu Louis, Comte Molé, Minister of the Navy, 17 October 1817, Instructions to metropolitan port and colonial administrators *Annales maritimes et coloniales, 2e année, 1817, 1re partie: lois et ordonnances,* (Paris, Imprimerie royale, 1817); Boulle and Peabody, *Le droit des Noirs en France* 185, 195–196.

30. *Copy of Furcy's* writ (signification) to the Saint-Denis Tribunal of First Instance, 22 November 1817 (ADR 1Jp2007-1, no. 23).

31. Boucher, Report to the Minister, 25 November 1817 (ADR 1Jp2007-1, nos. 2 and 101).

32. Boucher, Report to the Minister, 25 November 1817 (ADR 1Jp2007-1, nos. 2 and 101).

33. In "three hours" (as claimed by Lory), "Extrait d'une pièce déposée [par Lory] au Greffe de la Cour Royale par M. Le Procureur général par acte du huit Décembre 1817 inséré au registre des Dépôts," 7 December 1817 (ADR 1Jp2007-1, nos. 4 and 50; there are two copies of this extract), or "within eight hours," according to Boucher (ADR 1Jp2007-1, nos. 2 and 101).

34. Panon Desbassayns to the Minister, 21 December 1817 (ANOM 3201 COL REU/22/132), fol. 4r.

35. Boucher to Michault d'Emery, 25 November 1817 (ADR 1Jp2007-1, no. 46).

36. Sully Brunet, omitting references to all women, recalled that Furcy was staying with his relative Adolphe; "A mon Fils," 131, 187, 190.

37. Constance, Widow Jean Baptiste, Statement, 25 November 1817 (ADR 1Jp2007-1, no. 20).

38. Sully Brunet, "A mon Fils," 191.

39. Minutes of the Declarations of Constance and Adolphe, 10 December 1817 (ANOM FM SG REU 97/684, no. 16).

40. This was likely Jacques Marie Hyacinthe de Launay de la Perrière, born in Vannes, France, but the son of a colonist who had arrived in Saint-Denis before the Revolution; he was sworn to the bar in 1815 and served as justice of the peace until he was decommissioned on

1 December 1817, perhaps because of his peripheral involvement in Furcy's case (ANOM COL D2C 341, fol. 151).

41. Minutes of the Declarations of Constance and Adolphe, 10 December 1817 (ANOM FM SG REU 97/684, no. 16). This was Eugène François Stanislas Prévost de la Croix, one of a large creole family, born in Sainte-Marie, Isle Bourbon. It's not clear why he was receptive to Constance's request.

42. Minutes of the Declarations of Constance and Adolphe, 10 December 1817 (ANOM FM SG REU 97/684, no. 16).

43. Boucher, Report to the Minister, 25 November 1817 (ADR 1Jp2007-1, nos. 2 and 101).

44. Boucher to Michault d'Emery, 25 November 1817 (ADR 1Jp2007-1, no. 46).

45. Boucher, Report to the Minister, 25 November 1817 (ADR 1Jp2007-1, nos. 2 and 101).

46. Boucher to Michault d'Emery, 25 November 1817 (ADR 1Jp2007-1, no. 46).

47. Boucher, Report to the Minister, 25 November 1817 (ADR 1Jp2007-1, nos. 2 and 101).

48. Minutes, Judicial Meeting of 16 November 1817 (ADR 1Jp2007-1, no. 49), hereafter cited only by the archival code. When he learned of it, Panon Desbassayns questioned the very legality of this extra-procedural discussion; Panon Desbassayns to the Minister, 21 December 1817 (ANOM 3201 COL REU/22/132), fol. 5v).

49. The textual basis included Constance's original petition of November 9 and Furcy's writ of November 22. The court also reviewed three letters by Boucher, one to Delaunay Laparrière, one to Michault d'Emery, also dated November 25, and the letter from the administrators of the Windward Islands (i.e., the Lesser Antilles), dated 7 January 1767, regarding the status of the black and Indian races there (ADR 1Jp2007-1, no. 49).

50. Peabody, "Furcy, la question raciale," 1305–1334.

51. ADR 1Jp2007-1, no. 49.

52. Ève, *Naître et mourir à l'Île Bourbon*, 29 and 18. The 1818 census figures reported by Ève are not itemized by ethnicity or race.

53. Boulle and Peabody, *Le droit des noirs en France*, 43–47, 63–67, 99–103. Of course, the phrase "other people of color" could be (and was) interpreted by French officials as including East Indians and Amerindians from New France, since some appear in the various eighteenth-century declarations; see, for example: Thomas, "Indien ou nègre" (298), Fany, "Indienne" (5767), and Palmore, "Indien" (8282), in Erick Noël, *Dictionnaire des gens de couleur dans la France moderne*, vol. 2, *La Bretagne, Entrée par année, début XVIe siècle– 1792* (Geneva: Droz, 2013), 2:651, 711.

54. ADR 1Jp2007-1, no. 49.

55. ADR 1Jp2007-1, no. 49.

56. ADR 1Jp2007-1, no. 49. It is interesting that Gillot de l'Étang, the former attorney general of the colony, was unaware of, or somewhat confused by, the provisions of Napoleon's restoration of the 1777 legislation.

57. ADR 1Jp2007-1, no. 49.

58. Jérôme de Pontchartrain, minister of the navy, stated on 10 June 1707 that slaves who returned voluntarily to the colonies would lose "the privilege of French soil" (*le privilège de la terre de France*); this issue would be resurrected by the French ministry after the 1836 Free Soil ordinance. Boulle and Peabody, *Le droit des Noirs en France*, 39, 219, 231–232.

59. ADR 1Jp2007-1, no. 49.

60. No such contract or deed was never offered as evidence in the dispute and may have been simply an oral agreement.

61. ADR 1Jp2007-1, no. 49.

62. ADR 1Jp2007-1, no. 49.

63. In fact, as we have seen, the 1723 Code Noir prohibited slaves from being parties in either civil or criminal affairs. Article 24. Delaleu, *Code des îles de France et de Bourbon*, IF, 249.

64. ADR 1Jp2007-1, no. 49.

65. Boucher to Michault d'Emery, 25 November 1817 (ADR 1Jp2007-1, no. 46).

66. Prévost de la Croix to Boucher, 2 December 1817 (ADR 1Jp2007-1, no. 77). Prévost Delacroix was a creole lawyer (*avoué*); his older brother, Toussaint, was *greffier* at the *cour de première instance*. Ricquebourg, *Dictionnaire généalogique*, 3:2347.

67. Boucher to Michault d'Emery, 30 November 1817 (ADR 1Jp2007-1, nos. 47 and 48, letter no. 4).

68. Fedière to Magistrates of the Tribunal of First Instance, 28 November 1817 (ADR 1Jp2007-1, no. 61).

69. Boucher to Michault d'Emery, 30 November 1817 (ADR 1Jp2007-1, nos. 47 and 48, letter no. 4).

70. Panon Desbassayns to the Minister, 21 December 1817 (ANOM 3201 COL REU/22/132), fol. 10r.

71. Panon Desbassayns to Pitois, 29 November 1817 (ADR 1Jp2007-1, no. 65).

72. Panon Desbassayns, Report for the King, 29 November 1817" (ANOM 3201 COL REU/22/132, attachment no. 5).

73. Boucher, Second Report to the Minister, 17 April 1818 (ADR 1Jp2007-1, no. 2). Boucher is clearly trying to imply that it was Panon Desbassayns's arbitrary arrest that threatened the colonial order. If he is correct, it suggests that things were, indeed, starting to heat up.

74. Constance, Widow Jean Baptiste, Statement of 29 November 1817 (ADR 1Jp2007-1, no. 19). In the corrected version, the original date of her sworn statement (Wednesday, December 8) is corrected to Wednesday, December 10, along with her original spelling. See also Alphonse Duperier to Boucher's 29 November 1817 (ADR 1Jp2007-1, no. 20). The words of Constance and Duperier's statements are verbatim, with only the slightest variations. A third copy of Constance's statement was enclosed in Boucher's 29 November 1817 letter to Michault d'Emery (ADR 1Jp2007-1, nos. 47 and 48, letter no. 3).

75. Panon Desbassayns, Report for the King, 29 November 1817" (ANOM 3201 COL REU/22/132, attachment no. 5).

76. Constance, Widow Jean Baptiste, Statement of 29 November 1817 (ADR 1Jp2007-1, no. 19).

77. Constance, Widow Jean Baptiste, to Jacques Sully Brunet, n.d., ca. November 1817 (ADR 1Jp2007-1, no. 21).

78. Constance, Widow Jean Baptiste, to Jacques Sully Brunet, n.d., ca. November 1817 (ADR 1Jp2007-1, no. 21).

79. Panon Desbassayns, Report for the King, 29 November 1817" (ANOM 3201 COL REU/22/132, attachment no. 5).

80. Boucher, Second Report to the Minister, 17 April 1818 (ADR 1Jp2007-1, no. 2).

81. According to Panon Desbassayns, "Once more, Constance threw herself at my feet to thank me, and, before leaving, she told me that she recognized well (however truly

ignorant) that the writ that she had been advised to serve [to Lory] was very dangerous, because it tended to provoke rebellion amongst the entire class of Indian Blacks." Panon Desbassayns, Report for the King, 29 November 1817" (ANOM 3201 COL REU/22/132, attachment no. 5).

82. Constance, Widow Jean Baptiste, Statement of 29 November 1817 (ADR 1Jp2007-1, no. 19). Alphonse was likewise interrogated and threatened with deportation; he also concluded his statement by confessing that Sully Brunet had dictated the writ to him. Alphonse Duperier to Boucher, 29 November 1817 (ADR 1Jp2007-1, no. 20); Boucher, Second Report to the Minister, 17 April 1818 (ADR 1Jp2007-1, no. 2); Panon Desbassayns, Report for the King, 29 November 1817" (ANOM 3201 COL REU/22/132, attachment no. 5); Minutes of the Declarations of Constance and Adolphe, 10 December 1817 (ANOM FM SG REU 97/684, no. 16).

83. Constance, Widow Jean Baptiste, Statement of 29 November 1817 (ADR 1Jp2007-1, no. 19).

84. Constance, Widow Jean Baptiste, Statement of 29 November 1817 (ADR 1Jp2007-1, no. 19). Or, as Boucher later put it in his official report: "He exhibited, by contrast, an animosity so powerful that Constance's intellectual faculties ran the risk of a dreadful alteration." Boucher, Second Report to the Minister, 17 April 1818 (ADR 1Jp2007-1, no. 2).

85. Constance, Widow Jean Baptiste, Statement of 29 November 1817 (ADR 1Jp2007-1, no. 19).

86. "Ordonnance des Administrateurs Généraux qui suspend de ses fonctions, le Sr. Sully Brunet, conseiller auditeur de seconde classe à la Cour Royale," 1 December 1817 (ADR 1Jp2007-2, no. 251). Panon Desbassayns notified Boucher of the suspension of Sully Brunet on December 2 and asked that it be recorded in the court's register; ADR 1Jp2007-2, no. 198.

87. Sully Brunet says that he was exiled to "Rivière des Roches," which traverses Saint-Benoit and Bras Panon; Sully Brunet, "À mon Fils," 191; Boutier, "L'ordre public," 153. Boucher was more successful in protecting the bailiff Huard from suspension for having accepted, recorded, and delivered Furcy's writ in the first place. "Extrait des Registres du Greffe de la Cour Royale de l'Isle de Bourbon," 3 December 1817 (ADR 1Jp2007-1, no. 6).

88. Boucher, Second Report to the Minister, 17 April 1818 (ADR 1Jp2007-1, no. 2); Mayor of Sainte-Marie to Létard, n.d. (ADR 1Jp2007-1, no. 50).

89. Constance, Petition, 9 November 1817, recorded by the clerk 3 December 1817 (ADR 1Jp2007-1, nos. 36 and 103).

90. Excerpt from the Registers of the Clerk of the Royal Court of Isle Bourbon, 6 December 1817 (ADR 1Jp2007-1, nos. 8 and 9).

91. Boucher to the Isle Bourbon Administrators, 6 December 1817 (ADR 1Jp2007-1, no. 104).

92. The arrest took place on 10 December 1817; Minutes of the Declarations of Constance and Adolphe, 10 December 1817 (ANOM FM SG REU 97/684, no. 16).

93. Constance doesn't mention the baby, but Panon Desbassayns says that he offered to let Constance and her baby stay in a room at the Intendancy overnight; he also claims that he told her that she was perfectly free to leave at 9:00 p.m. and to talk with anyone she might like; Minutes of the Declarations of Constance and Adolphe, 10 December 1817 (ANOM FM SG REU 97/684, no. 16).

94. Constance, Widow Jean Baptiste, Statement, 18 December 1817 (ADR 1Jp2007-1, no. 19). The sworn statement from the second interrogation shows that it began at 5:00 p.m., lasted until 3:00 a.m., then recommenced the next morning at 7:00; Minutes of the Declarations of Constance and Adolphe, 10 December 1817 (ANOM FM SG REU 97/684, no. 16).

95. Boucher, Second Report to the Minister, 17 April 1818 (ADR 1Jp2007-1, no. 2); see also: ADR 1Jp2007-1, nos. 47 and 48, letters no. 12, 13, 14, 16, 17, and 18.

96. Boucher to Gillot de l'Étang, 12 December 1817 (ADR 1Jp2007-1, nos. 47 and 48, letter no. 15).

97. Boucher to Fédière, 12 December 1817 (ADR 1Jp2007-1, nos. 47 and 48, letter no. 17).

98. Boucher to the Mayor of Saint-André, 12 December 1817 (ADR 1Jp2007-1, nos. 47 and 48, letter no. 18).

99. Lafitte du Courteil, orders to Boucher, n.d. (ADR 1Jp2007-1, nos. 47 and 48, letter no. 19).

100. Boucher to the mayor of Saint-André, 12 December 1817 (ADR 1Jp2007-1, nos. 47 and 48, letters no. 20).

101. Boucher solicited letters of support from sympathetic mayors and commandants throughout the colony, many of whom responded sympathetically, expressing dismay at his imminent departure. Boucher to the Commandants de Quartier and the Mayors, 14 December 1817 (ADR 1Jp2007-1, no. 47, letter no. 24). The supportive responses came from all over the colony: Saint-Pierre, Sainte-Suzanne, Saint-Paul, Saint-Leu, Sainte-Marie, and Saint-Louis, as well as from various lawyers. "Lettres Diverses reçues par le Procureur Général au moment de son départ" (ADR 1Jp2007-1, nos. 84 and 146).

102. Gillot de l'Étang to Boucher, 13 December 1817 (ADR 1Jp2007-2, nos. 110 and 206); Boucher to the Isle Bourbon Administrators (Panon Desbassayns and Lafitte du Courteil), 13 December 1817 (ADR 1Jp2007-1, nos. 47 and 48, letters no. 21, 22, and 111) and 15 December 1817 (ADR 1Jp2007-1, no. 47, letter no. 25); Boucher to Lafitte du Courteil, 14 December 1817 (ADR 1Jp2007-1, no. 47, letter no. 23); and to Michault d'Emery, 16 December 1817 (ADR 1Jp2007-1, no. 47, letter no. 27).

Boucher took Constance's sworn statement regarding her arrest on December 10 as well as testimony by Célerine's landlord and companion, Duvergé (also "Duverger"), teacher (*instituteur*) to Sr. Arnoux, the solicitor (*avoué*), who had witnessed a scene at the Intendancy; (ADR 1Jp2007-1, no. 19), and Constance, Widow Jean Baptiste, to Boucher, 15 December 1817 (ADR 1Jp2007-1, no. 50); "Extrait des registres du Greffe de la Cour Royale de l'Isle de Bourbon," 18 December 1817 (ADR 1Jp2007-1, nos. 15 and 30).

103. Panon Desbassayns to Boucher, 12 November 1817 (ADR 1Jp2007-2, no. 197). Boucher made formal statements denouncing Constance's arrest and justifying his position vis-à-vis the administrators into the official register of the Royal Court on 17 December 1817 (ADR 1Jp2007-1, nos. 14, 15, 30, 32, and 113).

104. Boucher] to the Isle Bourbon Administrators, 16 December 1817 (ADR 1Jp2007-1, no. 47, letter no. 26).

105. Boucher to the Isle Bourbon Administrators, 16 December 1817 (ADR 1Jp2007-1, no. 47, letter no. 26). He added, "If, against my request, you think, *Messieurs*, that the

law must be rigorously enforced in my regard, I am ready to give the example of obedience and of the greatest sacrifices."

106. Two years later, Panon Desbassayns's successor as governor, Bernard Milius, would call out Boucher's lack of deposit in a report to the minister on deposits paid for blacks traveling to France: "There is [another] who, in December 1817, left this island with Madame Boucher, recently delivered, and for whom she nursed the child. Commissioner [Panon Desbassayns] . . . had asked for the execution of the King's declaration. But M. Boucher . . . did not judge it appropriate to comply and left without having left any deposit for the return of this slave, who has effectively not yet returned." Milius, Commander and Administrator for the King, Saint-Denis, to the Minister, Paris, 9 November 1819 (ANOM GEN 629/ 2735). I don't know what happened to Marie Jeanne after she accompanied the Boucher family to France; there is no evidence that Boucher was punished for failing to leave a deposit.

107. Panon Desbassayns to Boucher, 18 December 1817 (ADR 1Jp2007-1, no. 54); Gillot de L'Étang to Boucher, 19 December 1817 (ADR 1Jp2007-2, no. 209).

108. Passengers, Isle Bourbon, Saint-Paul, Departures, 23 December 1817, *Le Télémaque* (ANOM Col., F/5B/7).

109. On 12 December 1817, Boucher had received a letter from Petitpas, who identified himself as Furcy's legal representative (ADR 1Jp2007-1, no. 79). Furcy later explained that it was because of the death of Prévost's wife that the new patron, Petitpas, had been assigned to Furcy. "Notes écrites sous la dictée de Furcy," n.d. (ADR 1Jp2007-1, no. 51), 9. However, Prévost's wife died in 1819, well after the Royal Court of Bourbon supposedly rendered its February 1818 decision (and, given future developments, it's not clear how Furcy would have learned of her death); perhaps this is what Petitpas told Furcy when he visited him in his cell. That Petitpas was hostile to Furcy is clear; supposedly he went to the prison following the tribunal's decision against Furcy and told him that by his petition for freedom in his own name "he had ruined his case, and menaced him with his fist."

    The identity of "M. Petitpas" is unclear. Sometime in November in the midst of the emerging story (but without a specific date of departure), Lory's brother-in-law, Augustin Routier, sent his fifteen-year-old son, Charles Etienne Auguste, described as "the governor's student," to Brest, accompanied by one Gaspard Charles Louis Petitpas; Passengers, Isle Bourbon, Saint-Denis, Departures, [n.d.] November 1817, *Le Solo* (ANOM, COL, F/5B/7). Perhaps they carried word to officials in France of the affair. If so, it was presumably another Petitpas who remained in contact with Furcy.

110. The date "17 May 1817" appears in the 6 May 1840 decision of the Cour de Cassation (ANOM FM GEN/158/1307). "17 October 1817" appears in Moreau, Paillet, and Huart, *Mémoire pour la dame veuve Lory*, 6, 8 (ANOM FM GEN 158/1307), with the date corrected to 17 December on p. 10. "17 December" appears in [Émile] Moreau, *Mémoire pour le Sieur Lory, Propriétaire, demeurant à Saint-Denis (Île Bourbon), défendeur, contre le Sieur Furcy, Homme de Couleur, Demeurant à l'île de France, demandeur* ([Saint-Denis]: Imp. de Pollet, Soupe et Guillois, 1838), 4, 5 (ANOM FM GEN/158/1307). Furcy also told his legal advisors that he lost his case by a decision of the Tribunal of First Instance, judged by "Duparc, cousin of M. Lory and on the conclusions of the royal prosecutor, Michault d'Emery, the same who had as notary drafted Madeleine's

act," but he gives no date for the decision; "Notes écrites sous la dictée de Furcy," n.d. (ADR 1Jp2007-1, no. 51), 9.

111. If the Tribunal of First Instance did indeed rule on Furcy's case, as was later alleged, Michault d'Emery's court came to the conclusion that Furcy remained the slave of Joseph Lory on the grounds that Madeleine's 1789 manumission did not include Furcy. None of the other arguments that appeared in Constance's petition or Huard's statement— the Routiers' negligence in delaying Madeleine's promised manumission, the illegality of sale or gifting of slaves in the metropole, natural law, Free Soil, or, least of all, Indian Freedom—were cited in the subsequent quotation of the 1817 decision by the Tribunal of First Instance.

112. *Gazette des Tribunaux*, 22 December 1843, 1; Thureau, *Plaidoyer pour le sieur Furcy*, 5–6.

113. The Saint-Denis prison compound is the subject of recent historical and archeological research. Bruno Maillard, "Les noirs des geôles: La répression pénale des esclaves à l'Île Bourbon, entre puissance publique et pouvoir despotique des maîtres 1815–1848" (Ph.D. thesis, Université de La Réunion, 2010); Thomas Romon and Édouard Jacquot, "Archéologie de l'ancienne prison Juliette-Dodu à Saint-Denis de la Réunion," *Les nouvelles de l'archéologie* 143 (2018): 34–38, http://nda.revues.org/3379.

114. Furcy's later account states that the second decision was rendered by the judges Major General Pajot, "cousin of Madame Lory, Dureau [?], intimate friend of the family, Deville first cousin of M. Mercan Marcau ou Marcan?]," but the date of the decision is left blank in Furcy's account; "Notes écrites sous la dictée de Furcy," n.d. (ADR 1Jp2007-1, no. 51), 10.

115. The date "12 February 1818" is cited in André-Marie-Jean-Jacques Dupin, *Réquisitoires, plaidoyers et discours de rentrée*, vol. 2 (Paris: Joubert, 1836), 422; France, *Annales maritimes et coloniales, 26ᵉ année, 1841, 2ᵉ série, 1ʳᵉ partie: partie officielle* (Paris: Imprimerie Royale, 1841), 324; Thureau, *Plaidoyer pour le sieur Furcy*, 6–8; and *Gazette des Tribunaux*, 21 December 1843, 1; and Moreau, Paillet, and Huart, *Mémoire pour la Dame veuve Lory*, 7 (ANOM FM GEN 158/1307). "18 February" appears in Moreau, *Mémoire pour le Sieur Lory*, 4; no doubt Moreau's *mémoire* was the source of the date cited in Minister to the Governor of Isle Bourbon, 29 May 1838 (ANOM FM GEN/ 158/1307).

116. Moreau, *Mémoire pour le Sieur Lory*, 4–5; Moreau, Paillet, and Huart, *Mémoire pour la dame veuve Lory*, 7–8.

117. Cour royale de Bourbon, Arrêts Civils, 1817–1824 (ANOM, 6DPPC 2726).

118. "Sʳ M. Conil délégué—B[ure]au de M. Mestro sur l'arrêt de la Cour Royale de l'île Bourbon du 12 février 1818. Furcy et M. Lory," undated (ANOM FM GEN/158/1307).

119. Alternatively, either the colonial records in the period following Boucher's departure were subject to negligence (a distinct possibility) or the record of the appeals decision was deliberately excised. A third possibility—that ministerial and colonial officers, independently or in collusion, retroactively fabricated the text of the colonial court's decision so that Furcy would have something to appeal—must also be considered.

120. "Notes écrites sous la dictée de Furcy," n.d., after 1830 (ADR, 1Jp2007-1, no. 51), 10.

121. *Gazette de l'Isle Bourbon*, 28 February 1818 (ADR 4 Mi502); Gerbeau, "L'Esclavage et son ombre," 212. When Furcy's imprisonment made him "gravely ill," the military doctor M. Labronté had him "removed from the hospital and placed at the home of . . . the

company pharmacist, at Monsieur Lory's expense, where he stayed for 43 days, after which he was returned to the prison." "Notes écrites sous la dictée de Furcy," n.d., after 1830 (ADR, 1Jp2007-1, no. 51), 10.

122. "Notes écrites sous la dictée de Furcy," n.d., after 1830 (ADR, 1Jp2007-1, no. 51), 10.

CHAPTER 8

1. Isle Bourbon Passenger lists show that "Furcy noir à M. Lory" departed from Isle Bourbon the 26 of October 1818 on the *Clélie* (ANOM COL F/5B/7). In his complaint to Governor Lowry Cole, Mauritius (copy, undated, but late in 1826), Furcy claimed to have arrived in Port Louis 10 November 1818 (NAUK, CO 415/4, fol. 2v). The subsequent 1826 investigation showed that Furcy was not among the passengers or crew declared to colonial authorities when he arrived in Port Louis but that the Maurice *Gazette* of 7 November 1818 declared Furcy, "creole slave of Monsieur Lory," as having arrived on or before that date (NAUK CO 415/11). Furcy's much later account (which might recall the time of day correctly, but probably not the dates) states that Furcy "left prison on the second [inserted: "Monday"] of November 1818, 5:30 p.m., and embarked immediately for Mauritius, on the ship *Le Clélie*, Captain Floris. Disembarked on the twelfth of the same month at Port Louis"; "Notes écrites sous la dictée de Furcy," n.d., after 1830 (ADR 1Jp2007/1, no. 51), 13.

2. "Notes écrites sous la dictée de Furcy," n.d. (ADR 1Jp2007/1, no. 51), 13–14. Furcy mentions this location again in his letter to Governor Lowry Cole, Mauritius, n.d. (NAUK CO 415/4). This is probably the Belle Mare plantation, where the widow Lory consistently censused her slaves from 1817 to 1834 (NAUK T 71/573, pp. 1248–1254; T 71/596, pp. 1103–1109; T 71/616, n.p.). On the rise of sugar production in Flacq, see Teelock, *Bitter Sugar*, 43–45; Barker, *Slavery and Antislavery*, 73.

3. "Notes écrites sous la dictée de Furcy," n.d., after 1830 (ADR 1Jp2007/1, no. 51), 13.

4. Joseph Lory's eldest brother, André Lory Jr. (*fils*) (b. Amédée Lory, Rennes, ca. 1757) had married the creole woman Jeanne Marguerite Malvezy on 9 October 1792 in Flacq (ANOM 85MIOM 1173). Adolphe was the first of their eight children. Following André's death at Joseph's home in Saint-Denis on 6 November 1813, Joseph and the widow Lory inherited the family plantation in Trois Ilôts (ANOM IREL, État Civil, Saint-Denis, 1813).

Adolphe's full name was Jean Joseph André Adolphe Lory. To distinguish him from his father, I use the name "Adolphe," which is how he is listed in the 1826 and 1830 Mauritius Slave Registers; in the Isle Bourbon census records, he is listed as "Lory, the elder" (*l'aîné*). His birthday, 7 September 1793, is given in the census of 1845. Census, Isle Bourbon, Saint-Denis, Lory aîné, 1845 (ADR 6M321). The Flacq birth register for the year 1793 is missing (NARM KJ1), and he is not found in the Port Louis register for September to December 1793 (NARM KA106). Adolphe Lory would marry Thérèse Charlotte Genève, daughter of a planter, on 22 December 1819, in the parish of Rivière Noire, on the southwestern side of Mauritius. Gaston Sarre *Recueil de reseignements sur les familles de L'Île Maurice* (National Library of Australia, Papers of Edward Duyker, Box 6).

5. Joseph Lory's father, André Lory *père* (b. ca. 1715–1717 in Nantes), had purchased the largest portion of this land (526 *arpents*, or 444 acres) in 1791, supplemented by a

smaller plot (30 *arpents*, 25 acres) abandoned by Jean Pinal (NARM LC 22, pp. 132–137). At his father's death (ca. 1805), Joseph Lory had inherited this portion of this plantation, while his elder brother, André *fils*, owned the larger portion of 918 arpents (776 acres). The Lory family built a sugar refinery there called La Louise or Lorry during the first half of the nineteenth century. Guy Rouillard, *Histoire des domains sucriers de l'Isle Maurice* (Les Pailles, Isle Maurice: General Printing and Stationery Company, Henry & Cie, 1964–1979), 133, 135, 150, 185.

6. "Notes écrites sous la dictée de Furcy," n.d., after 1830 (ADR 1Jp2007/1, no. 51), 13–14. The original manuscript states that the sugar factory was "*2 mille*" (*sic*) from the plantation, which might mean two miles or 2,000 meters (about one mile).

7. "Notes écrites sous la dictée de Furcy," n.d., after 1830 (ADR 1Jp2007/1, no. 51), 14.

8. Evidence of their real estate, lending, and wholesale trading ventures is strewn throughout the notarial archives of both islands. For Isle Bourbon, see especially the minutes of Pierre Hippolyte Michault d'Emery, 1789–1811 (ANOM DPPC NOT REU/REP/19) and Maurice Desrieux (ANOM DPPC NOT REU/REP/6). For Joseph Lory's ventures in Mauritius see the records of Jean François Arnaud, 1800–1821 (NARM ND10–11), Julien François Guérin and Marie Onésime Guérin, 1791–1824 (NARM ND14), and the office of Dubor, Maignard, and Levieux, 1829–1848 (NARM ND 24). On nineteenth-century smuggling to Isle Bourbon more generally, see Marina Carter and Hubert Gerbeau, "Covert Slaves and Coveted Coolies in the Early 19th Century Mascareignes," *Slavery and Abolition* 9, no. 3 (1988): 194–208.

9. "Compte Des Dépenses du Navire Le Succès Cap^ne Bertrand depuis son arrive à Bourbon jusqu'à son depart le 7 Juin 1820" (NAUK CO 167/92). Frederick Cooper, *Plantation Slavery on the East Coast of Africa* (New Haven, CT: Yale University Press, 1977); Abdul Sheriff, *Slaves, Spices, and Ivory in Zanzibar: Integration of an East African Commercial Empire into the World Economy, 1770–1873* (London: J. Currey, 1987).

10. "Compte de vente et net produit de la cargaison du brick *Le Succès*, Cap^ne Bertrand, vendu à Bourbon pour compte des intéressées à l'armement dudit navire" (NAUK CO 167/ 92); "Procès-verbal d'arrestation du Sieur Mourgue et de 30 noirs," 14 October 1820, and "Extrait des registres des déclarations consignés dans les archives de la mairie de Sainte-Rose & lettre de transmission du maire (arrestation du Sieur Mourgue)" (ADR U1495). Mourgue would later be incarcerated in Mauritius for his traffic in slaves in Madagascar. Great Britain, *British and Foreign State Papers*, vol. 12, 324–326. The French governor of Isle Bourbon, Freycinet, protested Mourgue's innocence; Hubert Gerbeau, "Quelques aspects de la traite illégale," in *Mouvements de Populations dans l'Océan Indien*, 279.

11. "Compte de vente et net produit de la cargaison du brick *Le Succès*, Cap^ne Bertrand, vendu à Bourbon pour compte des intéressées à l'armement dudit navire" (NAUK CO 167/ 92); Gerbeau, "Quelques aspects de la traite illégale," 279, citing (ADR 174 M1); Milius to the Minister of the Navy, 19 November 1820; [Le Torzec, supercargo] to Michaud [ship owner] 27 October 1820 (NA CO 167/ 92).

12. [Le Torzec] to Michaud, 27 October 1820 (NAUK CO 167/92).

13. "Journal de Traitte [*sic*] du deuxième voyage à Zanzibart [*sic*] commencé le 9 Février 1821 & fini le 5 mars" (NAUK CO 167/92).

14. Sheriff, *Slaves, Spices*, 47.

15. Copy of the minutes of the Instance Court of Vice Admiralty, Mauritius, 17 April 1821 (NAUK CO 167/92). The papers concerning the capture of the *Succès* consist of about 165 pages, mostly copies of documents dating from 1820 and 1821 and presented as evidence in (or created as summary for) the Vice Admiralty Court of Mauritius in the trial of the ship *Succès* for slave smuggling. Subsequently, copies of the documents were sent by the Governor Cole of Mauritius to the Earl of Bathhurst, 4 April 1827.

16. Farquhar reported this to London on June 11, "Sentence of the Admiralty Court Condemning the Success French Slave Ship & 340 Slaves to the King" (NAUK CO 714/95). It is not clear whether Bertrand suffered a personal fine or punishment, or whether he was free to depart after his conviction.

17. "Doit. Le navire le Succès, Cap^ne Bertrand son compte courant avec Lory & Gamin" (NAUK CO 167/92).

18. Drescher, *Abolition*, 85–86, 99–104.

19. Drescher, *Abolition*, 248–252.

20. Seymour Drescher, "British Way, French Way: Opinion Building and Revolution in the Second French Slave Emancipation," *American Historical Review* 96, no. 3 (June 1991): 709–734.

21. His mother, Elizabeth Mélaine Bellaine, was the illegitimate daughter of Joseph Tascher de la Pelagerie, father of Empress Josephine.

22. Lawrence C. Jennings, "Cyrille Bissette, Radical Black French Abolitionist," *French History* 9, no. 1 (March 1995): 48–66; Stella Pâme, *Cyrille Bissette, un martyr de la liberté* (Martinique: Éditions Désormeaux, 1999); Schmidt, *Abolitionnistes de l'esclavage*, 185–186.

23. Boulle and Peabody, *Le droit des noirs en France*, 186–193, 205.

24. Anthony J. Barker, *Slavery and Antislavery in Mauritius, 1810–1833: The Conflict between Economic Expansion and Humanitarian Reform under British Rule* (London: Macmillan, 1996), 16–23; Moses D. E. Nwulia, *The History of Slavery in Mauritius and the Seychelles, 1810–1875* (Rutherford, NJ: Fairleigh Dickinson University Press, 1981), 88–143.

25. Jean Fouchard has identified several surviving letters in French from the colony that became Haiti: *Les marrons du syllabaire, quelques aspects du problème de l'instruction et de l'éducation des esclaves et affranchis de Saint-Domingue* (Port-au-Prince, Haiti: Imp. Deschamps, 1953), 106, 115. More recently, Christopher Hager has offered an extraordinarily nuanced analysis of the literacy and writings of slaves and free people in the United States: *Word by Word: Emancipation and the Act of Writing* (Cambridge, MA: Harvard University Press, 2014), 44–47, 60–62.

26. Hager, *Word by Word*, 45–47.

27. Huard, Statement to the Cour de Saint-Denis, 29 November 1817 (ADR 1Jp2007-1, no. 23).

28. Furcy to the Commissioners of Enquiry into the Slave Trade in Mauritius, 9 December 1826 (NAUK CO 415/4).

29. Furcy to Boucher, n.d., 1822 (ADR 1Jp2007-1, no. 69).

30. Passengers, Bourbon, Saint-Denis, Departures, 13 June 1821, *L'Evelina* (ANOM COL F/5B/34). Lory was accompanied by an unnamed domestic.

In mid-July, Gillot de l'Étang, *avocat général* (who had argued forcefully against Furcy's freedom in 1817), traveled to Mauritius with Emile Rudelle, an English lawyer (*avocat anglais*), and his wife—one may surmise that they were called to deal with the legal repercussions of the capture of the *Succès*. Passengers, Saint-Denis, Departures, 20 July 1821, *L'Anne Marie* (ANOM COL F/5B/34). However, also listed on board the *Anne Marie* was "Furcy, and his family (free)" (*et sa famille (libre)*)." The designation "free" (*libre*) indicates that this was a free person of color, not a white person. Of all the surviving documentation that has come to light, this passage between the islands is the most mysterious. If this is Madeleine's son, Furcy, with Virginie Béga and their children, how and when had he returned to Isle Bourbon as a free man, and why was he traveling back to Mauritius on the same boat as Gillot de l'Étang and the English lawyer? It is more likely, then, that this is a case of mistaken identity, another man of color named Furcy traveling between the islands.

31. Furcy, Isle Maurice, letter to Boucher, Corsica, 1 July 1821 (ADR 1Jp2007-1, no. 70). Perhaps Lory, or one of his servants, brought word to Furcy of Boucher's new appointment.

32. Furcy to Boucher, 1 July 1821 (ADR 1Jp2007-1, no. 70). The letter has clearly been written slowly and painstakingly for the best penmanship; penciled lines are traced along the page to preserve the rows, and each letter is neatly shaped.

33. All of Jeanne Marguerite Malvezy Lory's children had been baptized in Port Louis, and several of the baptismal records give their address as "rue de la Corderie." État civil, Isle de France, Port Louis, Baptism, Louis Eugène Lory, 27 Messidor Year VII (3 July 1799) (NARM, KA 128, 69) and Louis Edouard Lory, 24 Germinal Year IX (14 April 1801) (NARM KA 134, 76).

34. I have not been able to identify Monsieur Rougevin with certainty. Passenger records mention a Jacques Hubert Rougevin, storekeeper (*commerçant*) (Isle Bourbon, Saint-Denis, Departure for Mauritius, 4 August 1820, ANOM COL F/5B/34), and a Monsieur Rougevin, officer of the merchant navy (Isle Bourbon, Saint-Denis, Arrival from Mauritius, 26 August 1821, ANOM COL F/5B/111). Perhaps the latter trip was related to Furcy's letter.

35. Furcy to Boucher, 1 July 1821 (ADR 1Jp2007-1, no. 70). The letter was forwarded to 23 rue de Bondy, Paris, today rue René Boulanger, in the 10th arrondissement.

36. This one was also addressed to Boucher in Corsica. The document we have is likely a copy, since the date is (strangely) unspecified in the year 1822, and the exterior, which normally includes the address, seal, and postal registration marks, merely reads "To Monsieur Gilbert Boucher." The signature is quite different from the first.

37. Furcy to Boucher, 1822 (ADR 1Jp2007-1, no. 69).

38. Furcy to Boucher, 1822 (ADR 1Jp2007-1, no. 69).

39. Furcy to Boucher, 1822 (ADR 1Jp2007-1, no. 69).

40. Which raises the question: did Joseph Lory pen the 1822 letter to Boucher, trying to trick him into delivering the papers he needed from Lorient? While the signature of this letter has an especially elegant flourish that is not inconsistent with Joseph Lory's signature, I think Lory would have been more likely to go through business or family contacts in France. Furcy's 1822 letter seems genuine, particularly since later ones are confirmed.

41. Furcy to Boucher, 1822 (ADR 1Jp2007-1, no. 69).

42. "Notes écrites sous la dictée de Furcy," n.d., after 1830 (ADR 1Jp2007/1, no. 51).

43. "Notes écrites sous la dictée de Furcy," n.d., after 1830 (ADR 1Jp2007/1, no. 51), 14.

44. W. Reid, *An Attempt to Develop the Law of Storms by Means of Facts*, 3rd ed. (London: John Weale, 1850), 161–163; Garnier and Desarthe, "Cyclones and Societies"; Jean-Baptiste Pipon, Lyon, to M. P. Marragon, Rodriguès, 16 February 1819, in Auguste Toussaint, *Le mirage des îles: Le négoce français aux Mascareignes au XVIIIe siècle, suivi de la correspondance du négociant lyonnais Jean-Baptiste Pipon* (Aix-en-Provence, France: Institut des Pays d'Outre-mer, 1977), 289.

45. Slave Registers of former British Colonial Dependencies, 1826 and 1830 (NAUK T 71/596, 1103–1109 and 71/612, 3556–3562)), via Ancestry database, http://www.Ancestry.co.uk.

46. Furcy to Boucher, 15 May 1826 (ADR 1Jp2007-1, no. 71).

47. On 4 September 1822, Thomy Lory arrived from Mauritius aboard *L'Edouard*. Just a week later, the widow Lory arrived from Mauritius aboard *Le Bourbon*. Then on 12 December 1822, Alfred Routier arrived from Mauritius aboard *Le Bellier*. Finally, on 20 December 1822, Thomy Lory returned to Bourbon with "Veuve Lory" aboard *La Colombe*; Passengers, Isle Bourbon, Arrivals, 1823 (ANOM COL F/5B/112). Arthur Lory traveled from Saint-Denis to Mauritius aboard *La Marie*, 17 July 1823 (ANOM COL F/5B/35). Lory (presumably Joseph) plus Dame Lory (presumably Eugénie) and Mademoiselle Lory (presumably Marie Charlette Augustine Euphémie, age 20) all traveled via *Le Philo* from Mauritius to Saint-Denis on 1 August 1824 (ANOM COL F/5B/35). In May 1825, Arthur was dining at the home of Joseph Desbassayns; see Renoyal de Lescouble, *Journal d'un colon*, 407.

48. Renoyal de Lescouble, *Journal d'un colon*, 315. Renoyal de Lescouble was invited to the funeral service.

49. Aboard the Philo, arriving 1 August 1824 (ANOM COL F/5B/34).

50. ANOM IREL, État Civil, Réunion, Sainte-Suzanne, Death, 7 August 1824.

51. "Mademoiselle Lori de Maurice morte jeudy"; Renoyal de Lescouble, *Journal d'un colon*, 329.

52. Cyrille was survived by his 48-year-old widow, Anne Adelaide Routier-Duvergé, three sons (the eldest of whom was Cyrille, now 24), and six daughters, ages six to thirty. Census, Isle Bourbon, Sainte-Marie, Marie Adeline Cyrille Router, 1822 (ADR 6M364) and 1823 (ADR 6M366); Ricquebourg, *Dictionnaire généalogique*, 2591–2592.

53. The widow André Lory does not appear in the Isle Bourbon censuses until 1840, but this record states that she had arrived in the colony in 1824; Census, Isle Bourbon, Saint-Denis, Made Veuve André Lory, 1840 (ADR 6M300). Arthur Lory had moved to Saint-Denis in either 1820 or 1821, having married a girl from Saint-Paul; Census, Isle Bourbon, Saint-Denis, Arthur Lory, 1825 (ADR 6M212) and 1828 (6M240).

54. Justine Siahime was separated from her Malagasy mother, Félité Siahime, at the age of sixteen; she would continue to be listed as the widow's slave on Mauritius censuses in 1826 and 1830; Slave Register, Mauritius, Flacq, Veuve Lory, 1826 (NAUK T 71/596, pp. 1103–1109) and Slave Register, Mauritius, Rivière de Rampart, "Lory, Mme Ve, repté par Geo. Elliott," 1830 (NAUK T 71/612, pp. 3556–3562). By 1840, Justine Siahime is listed as a free servant receiving wages at the widow's Saint-Denis home; Census, Isle Bourbon, Saint-Denis, Widow André Lory, 1840 (ADR 6M300).

55. The record of this transfer is clearest in the widow's 1840 census in Saint-Denis (ADR 6M300). By comparing these names with her Mauritius slave registers of 1817 (NAUK

T 71/573, 1248–1254), 1826 (NAUK T 71/596, 1103–1109), and 1830 (NAUK T 71/612, 3556–3562 and NAUK T 71/616, n.p.), it is possible to see how families were broken up by the move.

56. The 1828 Saint-Denis census states that Lory the eldest (*aîné*), i.e., Adolphe, 34, arrived in Isle Bourbon in 1825 (ADR 6M240), but passenger records show that the family relocated in 1826. Jules Lory, 21, moved to Isle Bourbon on 29 June 1825; he would eventually become the manager of his Uncle Joseph's plantation in Saint-Benoît, marrying in 1829. The date of his arrival in the colony appears on the later census: Census, Isle Bourbon, Commune de Saint-Benoît, Joseph Lory, 1835 (ADR 6M 97). He married the Mauritian *créole*, Elise Merlo, 21 December 1829 in Saint-Denis. Henry Lory, seventeen, likewise arrived in 1825, would eventually marry Joséphine Pajot, nine years his junior. Census, Isle Bourbon, Sainte-Marie, Henry Lory, 1836 (ADR 6M377).

57. Census, Isle Bourbon, Saint-Denis, Joseph Lory, 1822 (ADR 6M179), 1825 (ADR 6M212), 1827 (ADR 6M232), 1828 (ADR 6M240), 1831 (ADR 6M259), 1832 (ADR 6M263), 1833 (ADR 6M268).

58. Edouard Lory, single, age 23 in 1825, moved temporarily to Sainte-Marie parish of Isle Bourbon, employing a free man of color named Mauduit, charioteer, age 30, and twelve slaves, including a domestic, a cook, and four carters. Census, Isle Bourbon, Sainte-Marie, Edouard Lory, 1825 (ADR 6M370). He is missing from future Isle Bourbon censuses until 1844, having moved back to Mauritius to manage his mother's properties there (ADR 6M315).

59. Many of those no longer appearing in the census were families of skilled slaves, such as the d'Amboise family, consisting of two carpenters (the brothers Charlot and Julien, 29 and 24, respectively, in 1817), their blacksmith brothers (Martiel, 22, and Jean Baptiste, 17), and two younger siblings doing lighter labor on the plantation (*la petite bande*, Silvain, 13, and Jeannette, 11). "M^c Vve Lory, pour l'habitation dite Belle Mare, Flacq," *Slave Registers of former British Colonial Dependencies, 1812–1834*, Mauritius (NAUK T 71/573, pp. 1248–1254), via Ancestry database, http://www.Ancestry.co.uk. Two other such families of skilled slaves, departed by 1826, were the team of Front Philibert (60) and his son, Thomas (19), the former identified as *baccardier* and the latter as a domestic servant in 1817, and the Joyeux family: Zéphir (*cuisinier*, 38) and Charles (7).

60. The approximate timing of Virginie's death can be discerned from Célerine's entry of Virginie's daughters as free people of color in the État Civil (ANOM IREL, État civil, Réunion, Saint-Denis, 7 October 1826) and Célerine's 1827 census return, the only one to mention Virginie, which says "Virginie morte," at the top of the list of her daughters; Census, Isle Bourbon, Saint-Denis, Célerine Duverger, 1827 (ADR 6M24).

61. "Notes écrites sous la dictée de Furcy," n.d., after 1830 (ADR 1Jp2007/1, no. 51), 14.

62. The passenger list records only "Monsieur et Madame Lory et un enfant, Mademoiselle Lory," along with eight unnamed domestics; it is not clear whether they served the Lorys or other passengers; Passengers, Isle Bourbon, Saint-Denis, Arrivals, 4 September 1826, *L'Avance* (?) (ANOM COL F/5B/7). The year of Adolphe's arrival in Isle Bourbon is confirmed in later censuses: Census, Isle Bourbon, Saint-Denis, [Adolphe] Lory *aîné*, 182[8] (ADR 6M240) and 1847 (ADR 6M345). I deduce that Zéphir and Martial accompanied them, because they remained with Adolphe through the 1840s. Census, Isle Bourbon, Commune de Saint-[Denis], M. Lory, 1845 (ADR 6M345). Adolphe freed both of them

before general emancipation in Réunion; Census, Isle Bourbon, Commune de Saint-[Denis], Adolphe Lory, 1848 (ADR 6M356).

63. Census Returns, Rivière Noire, Génève, 1827 (NARM KK17) and 1828 (NARM KK18.1).

64. The case was decided 27 October 1819. Although Boucher was considered to have received his salary at the rate of 10,000 francs per annum through his departure from Isle Bourbon on 23 December 1817 and charged with the cost of transporting his child, the court awarded him restitution of his salary between 24 December 1817 and 14 March 1819, when the ministry formally discharged him of his position of *procureur général*. Charles D'Aubigny, *Recueil de jurisprudence coloniale en matière administrative, civile et criminelle: Contenant les décisions du Conseil d'État et les arrêts de la Cour de Cassation* (Paris: Imprimerie impériale, 1861), 223–226.

65. Louis-Gabriel Michaud, *Biographie universelle, ancienne et moderne: histoire par ordre alphabétique de la vie publique et privée de tous les hommes*, new edition, 45 vols. (Paris: A. Thoisnier Desplaces, 1843), 5:171–172.

66. Furcy to Boucher, 15 May 1826 (ADR 1Jp2007-1, no. 71).

67. It was through Le Gonidec that Furcy would eventually win the opportunity to appeal his case to Paris in 1835. Boucher had married his step-daughter, Marie Sonthonax, in 1817. Furcy was aware of the relationship. In his letter to Boucher, Furcy refers to Boucher's "father-in-law, Monsieur Legonidec" (*votre beau-père M. Legonidec*) (ADR 1Jp2007-1, no. 71), and in the cover letter to Le Gonidec he refers to Boucher as Le Gonidec's "son-in-law" (*gendre*) (ADR 1Jp2007-1, no. 72).

68. Furcy to Boucher, 15 May 1826 (ADR 1Jp2007-1, no. 71).

69. Furcy to Boucher, 15 May 1826 (ADR 1Jp2007-1, no. 71).

70. Furcy to Boucher, 15 May 1826 (ADR 1Jp2007-1, no. 71).

71. In addition to Cyrille Bissette, discussed in this chapter, there were similar political efforts by the *métis* of North America, sons of Frenchmen and Indian women. See Jacqueline Peterson and Jennifer S. H. Brown, eds., *The New Peoples: Being and Becoming Métis in North America* (Minneapolis: Minnesota Historical Society Press, 2001); Susan Sleeper-Smith, *Indian Women and French Men: Rethinking Cultural Encounter in the Western Great Lakes* (Amherst: University of Massachusetts Press, 2001); and White, *Wild Frenchmen and Frenchified Indians*, chs. 2 and 3.

72. Furcy to Boucher, 15 May 1826 (ADR 1Jp2007-1, no. 71).

73. Sue Peabody, "L'affaire Furcy," in *Français? La nation en débat entre colonies et métropole, XVIe–XIXe siècle*, ed. Cécile Vidal (Paris: Editions de l'EHESS, 2014).

74. Furcy to Boucher, 15 May 1826 (ADR 1Jp2007-1, no. 71).

75. Zoë Laidlaw, "Investigating Empire: Humanitarians, Reform and the Commission of Eastern Inquiry," *Journal of Imperial and Commonwealth History* 40, no. 5 (2012): 749–768; Zoë Laidlaw, *Colonial Connections 1815–1845: Patronage, the Information Revolution and Colonial Government* (Manchester, UK: Manchester University Press, 2005), 47; Richard B. Allen, *Slaves, Freedmen and Indentured Laborers in Colonial Mauritius*, African Studies (Cambridge, U.K.: Cambridge University Press, 1999), 15; Allen, "Licentious and Unbridled Proceedings," 101.

76. Commissioners of Enquiry, West Indies, Cape of Good Hope, Mauritius, Ceylon, 1821–1831 (NAUK CO 326/84 and CO 167/117–118).

77. Slave Registers of Former British Colonial Dependencies, 1826 (NAUK T 71/596, pp. 1103–1109), filed 15 October 1826.

78. A French proverb, roughly equivalent to the English "Once burnt, twice shy."

79. "Notes écrites sous la dictée de Furcy," n.d., after 1830 (ADR 1Jp2007/1, no. 51), 14–15.

80. Census, Isle Bourbon, Saint-Denis, Joseph Lory, 1822 (ADR 6M179), 1824 (ADR 6M202.1), 1825 (ADR 6M212), 1827 (ADR 6M232), 1828 (ADR 6M240), 1831 (ADR 6M259), 1832 (ADR 6M263), 1833 (ADR 6M268). Lory's widow, Eugénie, was omitted Furcy from the 1840 census (ADR 6M300).

81. The person who copied this letter made minor corrections in the text (e.g., "enfans" becomes "enfants"; "d'être maitre de mon temps" becomes "d'être maitre de son temps"). But sometimes the copyist introduced errors as well (e.g., "mon" becomes "m'on"; "honoré" becomes "honnoré"). Instead of exclamation points, it uses periods. The handwriting is more regular. The salutation adds the traditional respectful gesture of obeisance: "I am, with the deepest respect, your very grateful and very devoted servant." Furcy to Boucher, 3 November 1826 (ADR 1Jp2007-1, no. 73).

82. Furcy Lory to Boucher, 3 November 1826 (ADR 1Jp2007-1, no. 73). This is the first time that Furcy's name appears with a surname; he will later adopt the family name "Madeleine," but only in Mauritius. All future French records refer to him simply as "Furcy" or "le sieur Furcy."

83. On the exterior of Furcy's cover letter, in a different handwriting, someone (perhaps a member of the commission) has written: "Received 9 Dec. 1826, Lives at Monsieur Micoin—Rue de la Corderie." Furcy to the Commissioners of Enquiry into the Slave Trade in Mauritius, 9 December 1826 (NAUK CO 415/4). Recall that André Lory lived at rue de la Corderie (see NAM KA 128, 69 and KA 134, 76). I was not able to find Micoin listed in the extant censuses of Port Louis of 1823 or 1828.

84. Furcy, Petition to Governor Lowry Cole, Mauritius (copy), n.d., 1826 (NAUK, CO 415/4). Among the new elements is that his mother, Madeleine, was ten years old when she entered the service of Mademoiselle Despense in Chandernagor and that Madeleine had entered the Lorient convent together with her mistress, which is where they had met Madame Routier in 1772. Furcy incorrectly recalls many dates and occasionally confuses the names of the island colonies. The date of Madeleine's manumission is correctly listed as 6 July 1789, "passed at Isle Bonaparte, today 'Isle Bourbon,'" when in fact the island was known as Isle Bourbon in 1789 as well. Furcy quotes from it verbatim, suggesting that he retained a copy. Furcy erroneously mentions Madame Routier's arrival "in Mauritius," ca. 1773, when he means "Isle Bourbon," and he also states, "Madame Routier died in 1811 [it was 1808] and my mother in 1813 [instead of 1812]." See also: Marina Carter, "Wrongful Enslavement: The Heartfelt Plea of Furcy," *Mauritius Mag*, 4 July 2011, http://www.mauritiusmag.com/?p=373.

85. Copy, Furcy, petition to Governor Lowry Cole, Mauritius, n.d. (NAUK CO 415/4). Joseph Lory's lawyer would later claim, disingenuously, that Lory's decision not to list Furcy on census returns in Mauritius was deliberate, evidence of an "implicit consent to his emancipation" (*assentissement implicite de son emancipation*); Moreau, *Mémoire pour le Sieur Lory*, 5.

86. Manumission, Port Louis, Florancia, 22 December 1826 (NARM IE 31 p. 565–73).

87. Both were censused among the widow's slaves in 1826, and Florence noted as manumitted in the 1830 census; Mauritius, Slave Register, widow Lory, 1826 and 1830 (NAUK T 71/596, 1103–1109 and T 71/616, n.p.), via Ancestry database, http://www.Ancestry.co.uk.

88. The 1826 census listed Rosa and Félix as "absent, à Bourbon"; Slave Register, Widow Lory, 1826 (NAUK T 71/596, pp. 1103–1109). Rosa, Félix, and Florentia all appear on the widow's censuses fourteen years later as free people; Census, Isle Bourbon, Saint-Denis, Widow André Lory, 1840 (ADR 6M300).

89. Manumission, Port Louis, Florancia, 22 December 1826 (NARM IE 31 p. 565–573).

90. Furcy, petition to Governor Lowry Cole (copy), Mauritius, n.d. (NAUK, CO 415/4).

91. Furcy, petition to Governor Lowry Cole (copy), Mauritius, n.d. (NAUK, CO 415/4).

92. While the copy of Furcy's petition concludes with his signature, the cover letter to the Commissioners on Eastern Inquiry is signed with an X, concluding, "Not knowing how to sign, I made my ordinary cross, replacing my name of Furcy." Furcy to the Commissioners of Enquiry into the Slave Trade in Mauritius, 9 December 1826 (NAUK CO 415/4).

93. "The governor sent the case back to the grand judge to have a *patron* named for him. Actually he was given to M. Brusseau [*sic*]"; "Notes écrites sous la dictée de Furcy," n.d., after 1830 (ADR 1Jp2007/1, no. 51), 14. The name is spelled "Brusard" in Furcy's letter of 9 December 1826 (NAUK CO 415/4). Raymond Brusaud was sworn in as public defender on 22 March 1826 (NARM Z3A 52). He lived with a free domestic servant named Jersey on Government Street in 1828; Census Returns, Port Louis, 1828–1829 (NARM KK20). I have not found any record of a hearing before the "grand judge."

94. This omission refers to the records of arrival in Port Louis. As we have seen, "Furcy, noir à M. Lory" can be found on the passenger list of *La Clélie* departing Isle Bourbon on 26 October 1818 (ANOM COL F/5B/7).

95. "Notes écrites sous la dictée de Furcy," n.d., after 1830 (ADR 1Jp2007/1, no. 51), 14–15.

96. According to the sentence rendered by the Cour de Cassation in 1840, Furcy began to enjoy his freedom in Mauritius in 1825 ("It was not until 1825 that [he] became free"), but this does not jibe with Furcy's dated letters. Arrêt de la Cour de Cassation, Paris, 6 May 1840, "Bourbon, Affaire Furcy, Ordonnance royale du 29 avril 1836 (1838–1844)" (ANOM FM GEN 158, dos. 1307).

97. Furcy does not appear in the reports of the slave protector, established by the British as a result of the Commission on Inquiry, the first of which began in March 1829. Great Britain, *British Parliamentary Papers . . . Slave Trade*, vol. 78, orig. published by the House of Commons, 10 March 1831 (Shannon: Irish University Press, 1969), 57. As Barker and Nwulia make clear, Furcy's chances before the slave protector would not have been very good; most slaves' charges against their masters were dismissed. Barker, *Slavery and Antislavery*, 83–84; Nwulia, *History of Slavery in Mauritius*, 111–133.

98. All future references to Furcy's achieving freedom in Mauritius are vague about the date when this occurred. For example, the 1843 *mémoire* on behalf of Lory's heirs stated that Furcy formally achieved his freedom at the age of 44 (Moreau, Paillet, and Huart, *Mémoire pour la dame veuve Lory*, 10), which would have placed any such decision in 1830 or 1831.

99. Teelock, *Bitter Sugar*, 269.

100. Alain Romaine, *Les souliers de l'abolition, ile Maurice, 1830–1840: Quand les esclaves chaussèrent la liberté* (Beau-Bassin, Mauritius: Éditions Marye-pike, 2007), 23–44.

101. "Souliers faraud, mes domaz zaute manz lipie!" translated in Teelock, *Bitter Sugar*, 285.

102. Port Louis Census Returns, 1835 (NARM KK 25B). For "le sieur" Furcy, see Dupin, *Réquisitoires, plaidoyers*, 422; Moreau, *Mémoire pour le Sieur Lory*; Desaponay [sic], *Mémoire pour le sieur Furcy*; and Moreau, Paillet, and Huart, *Mémoire pour la dame veuve Lory*.

103. Moreau, Paillet, and Huart, *Mémoire pour la dame veuve Lory*, 8; *Gazette des tribunaux*, 22 December 1843, 1. Census Returns, Port Louis, 1835 (NARM KK 25B).

104. At the top of the "Notes écrites sous la dictée de Furcy" is written, "First envelope to Monsieur Joseph Dioré, proprietor at Port Louis Isle Maurice, second envelope to remit to Furcy" (ADR 1Jp2007-1, no. 51). There are three different census returns within this register for Joseph Dioré, all bakers, all white. One appears to be the business address and Dioré's age is given as 27, born in "Krigure [?]." The second, in the Faubourg-Ouest section of the register, gives his age as 37, origin Maurice. The third, on rue de la Corderie, perhaps the father of the former, lists the age as 53, origin Maurice. Census, Mauritius, Port Louis, Joseph Dioré, 1828–1829 (NARM KK20).

105. Drescher, *Abolition*, 245–270.

106. In the midst of this economic and social turmoil, Joseph Lory and his sister-in-law, the widow Lory, sold their property in Trois Îlôts, Flacq, Mauritius, to a Madame Cottry, perhaps to raise cash, at a significant loss of its original value at inheritance. According to the division of Joseph Lory's property after his death, his portion of the Mauritius plantation, which had been evaluated at 90,000 francs (about $375,000) in 1794, at the time of his wedding to Eugénie, was worth only 31,875 francs ($164,000) at the time of the sale. "Dépot du process verbal d'expertise de deux meubles, dépendant de succession en communauté de feu M. Joseph Lory par M. Antoine Pitel, 24 aout 1846" (ADR 3 E692, no. 284).

   In April 1834, on the eve of general emancipation, they re-purchased the land. At least, that is what the Mauritian Pierre Regnard wrote to his correspondent Eugène Leclézio: "I plan to go sleep tonight near Trois Îlôts, the better to arrive early at the home of Madame Cottry, tomorrow to render into the possession of Monsieur E. Malvezy, who had purchased for Madame Lory the property that had been sold by her to the said Dame Cottry. I wait today for the paperwork necessary for this operation. This will be a quick job." Pierre Regnard, *Lettres de Pierre Regnard à Eugène Leclézio (1830–1840)*, annotated by Noël Regnard, (n.p. [Mauritius]: chez l'auteur, n.d [199-?]), 267. It's hard to make sense of this transaction without more information.

107. Nwulia, *History of Slavery in Mauritius*, 144–149.

108. The widow André Lory was successful, receiving over £2,791 (around $351,000) in 1836 for 93 slaves held in Rivière de Rampart (Mauritius claim 6654a); "Slavery Abolition Act: An Account of All Sums of Money Awarded by the Commissioners of Slavery Compensation," *Parliamentary Papers*, 1837–1838, vol. 48 (215), accessed via *Legacies of British Slave-Ownership*, https://www.ucl.ac.uk/lbs/search/. So did her oldest son, Adolphe, who received £25.9s.9d (about $3,200) for a single slave in 1837 (Mauritius claim 1034A).

109. Adolphe, Edouard, and Jules Lory, residents of Isle Bourbon for almost a decade, sent Julien Malvezy, a relative on their mother's side, as a proxy to claim reimbursement for a handful of slaves; Mauritius Government *Gazette* 38 (19 September 1835), supplement (NAUK CO 171). Their claims (1034A, 1035, and 1036, and in 6645B), were disallowed under the 28 August 1833 Abolition Act (3 & 4 W[illiam] Cap. 73), probably because of previous failure to register the enslaved people in Mauritius.

110. "Furcy alias Magdeleine" was awarded £84.18s.2d (about $10,677) for two slaves on 6 January 1837; Mauritius Claim 3523; "Slavery Abolition Act, accessed via *Legacies of British Slave-ownership*, https://www.ucl.ac.uk/lbs/search/, and Mauritius Government *Gazette* 36 (5 September 1835), supplement (NAUK CO 171). Although there were many people with the first or last name "Furcy" living in Isle de France, his use of the last name "Magdeleine," as it was spelled in English records, makes this identification certain.

111. Herbert S. Klein and Clotilde Andrad Paiva, "Freedmen in a Slave Economy: Minas Gerais in 1831," *Journal of Social History* 29, no. 4 (Summer 1996): 934; Michael P. Johnson and James L. Roark, *Black Masters: A Free Family of Color in the Old South* (New York: Norton, 1986), 63. As noted by Larry Koger, urban free people of color in Charleston, South Carolina, the heart of free black society in the South, ownership of slaves was more common and often undercounted in the censuses; *Black Slaveowners: Free Black Slave Masters in South Carolina, 1790–1860* (Columbia: South Carolina University Press, 1994), 9. In some societies, free women of color owned more slaves than their male counterparts, Melanie J. Newton, *The Children of Africa in the Colonies: Free People of Color in Barbados*, Antislavery, Abolition, and the Atlantic World (Baton Rouge: Louisiana State University Press, 2008), 48–52. Based on his study of pre-revolutionary Saint-Domingue notarial records, Stewart R. King suggests that free people of color owned 30 percent of all slaves in the colony, and these formed an important portion of their capital, even when individuals were of very modest means *Blue Coat or Powdered Wig: Free People of Color in Pre-revolutionary Saint-Domingue* (Athens, GA: University of Georgia Press, 2001), 84–86. By contrast, in the same era, free people of color in Guadeloupe held only 5 percent of the enslaved population; Régent, *Esclavage, métissage, liberté*, 6.

   Richard B. Allen's detailed accounting of slave ownership amongst those labeled "free people of color" in Mauritius shows that by 1806, 50 percent owned at least one slave. His analysis for 1826 is limited to the Plaines Wilhems district, but there he found that three-quarters of these households owned slaves, with 30 percent owning five or more individuals. Allen, *Slaves, Freedmen and Indentured Laborers in Colonial Mauritius* (Cambridge, U.K.: Cambridge University Press, 1999), 90; Allen, "Free Women of Colour and Socio-economic Marginality in Mauritius, 1767–1830," *Slavery and Abolition*, 26, no. 2 (August 2005): 186.

112. Teelock, *Bitter Sugar*, 269; Allen, "Free Women of Colour," 193.

113. "Grace, a Slave" (1827), reported in John Haggard, *Reports of Cases Argued and Determined in the High Court of Admiralty*, vol. 2, *1825–1832* (London: Saunders & Benning, 1833), 117.

CHAPTER 9

1. Prizes were awarded to a wide variety of sugar-based confections and preserves, including pineapple jam and "liquor of perfect love" (*liqueur du parfait amour*) from Mauritius and Isle Bourbon at the 1855 Universal Exposition. *Rapports du jury mixte international . . ., Tome 1* (Paris: Imprimerie Impériale, 1856), 656–659.

2. A Chinese mercantile community had established itself in Port Louis in the sale of candy and spices. Jill Moore, "Community Values in Multicultural Mauritius: A View from Britain," *Journal of Mauritian Studies* 1, no. 1 (1986): 33.

3. These were the words of the Lorys' lawyer as quoted in *Gazette des Tribunaux*, 22 December 1843, 1.

4. Philip Mansel, *Paris between Empires: Monarchy and Revolution 1814–1852* (New York: Saint-Martin's, 2001), 231–261.

5. Law of August 23, 1830, in Jennings, *French Anti-Slavery*, 31.

6. Renoyal de Lescouble, *Journal d'un colon*, 969; *Annales Maritimes et Coloniales, 18ᵉ année, 1833, 2e série, 1ʳᵉ partie: partie officielle* (Paris: Imprimerie Royale, 1833), 39. Azéma was succeeded by Pierre Conil in 1833.

7. Jacques Sully Brunet and fellow delegate Pierre Conil became co-signatories to *Lettre à M. Isambert . . . 23 avril 1835* (Paris: impr. de Guiraudet et Jouaust, 1835). Sully Brunet began to promote the lowering of sugar tariffs and debate legislation to gradually abolish slavery in 1832; [Jacques] Sully Brunet, *Considérations sur le système colonial, et la tarification des sucres* (Paris: Selligue, 1832).

8. Louis Philippe was a member of an elite humanitarian association, the Society for Christian Morals (1821–1830), which had explored various antislavery measures without leaving much of a tangible impact on colonial slavery.

9. Jennings, *French Reaction*, esp. 96–106, 178–193; Jennings, *French Anti-Slavery*, 30–36, 67–71; Schmidt, *Abolitionnistes de l'esclavage*, 83; Serge Daget, "Abolition de la traite des noirs en France de 1814 à 1831," *Cahiers d'études africaines* 11, no. 41 (1971): 53–58.

10. Many were the so-called "free of the savanna" (*libres de savane*), whose masters no longer held them as slaves but had not paid the fees and filed the paperwork to formalize their freedom. Léo Elisabeth, "The French Antilles," in *Neither Slave nor Free: the Freedmen of African Descent in the Slave Societies of the New World*, ed. David W. Cohen and Jack P. Green (Baltimore: Johns Hopkins University Press, 1972), 146.

11. Death of Auguste, fils de Constance, 23 March 1823 (ANOM État-civil, Saint-André, 1823, Libres de couleur, 14).

12. Her children were Eugène (26), Marie Madeleine (23), Judith (21), Jean Baptiste (18), and Josephine (16). Census, Isle Bourbon, Saint-André, Widow Jean Baptiste Euphémie, 1832 (ADR 6M42).

13. Two of Constance's slaves had remained with her since her wedding: the African woman "Irogine," now 57, and the younger Malagasy woman Eliza, now 26. Her two purchases from Mathieu Vetter, in 1820 and 1822, are noted in the 1822 census. Shortly after the death of her son, Constance had purchased a young African man, La Fortune (by now 24), to help with the farm work. By 1832, Constance had lost (whether through sale, liberation, or death is unclear) Eliza, but had welcomed the elderly, infirm, and eventually paralyzed creole Olivette (now 77). Census, Isle Bourbon, Saint-André, Widow Jean

Baptiste Euphémie, 1819 (ADR 6M10), 1822 (ADR 6M18), 1830 (ADR 6M35), 1832 (ADR 6M42).

14. Around 1825 Joseph Lory went into business with a retailer (*marchand*), Pierre Adolphe Nau. Their enterprise was staffed by seven male slaves: an Indian hat maker (*chapellier*) named César (43), a Malagasy domestic named François (18), and five unskilled African and Malagasy laborers (*manoeuvres*). Census, Isle Bourbon, Saint-Denis, Nau et Lory, 1826 (ADR 6M223 and 6M259). There Renoyal de Lescouble purchased tar (*goudron*), resin, and "two balls of cardboard" (*carton*) in exchange for sugar on 21 February 1830; Renoyal de Lescouble, *Journal d'un colon*, 876, 880. Joseph Martial Wetzell mentions giving instructions to Lory and Nau's workshop crew (*atelier*). "Résumé des travaux," 14 and 17 May 1831, quoted in Géraud, "Des habitations sucreries," 391, 400.

15. "Business goes from bad to worse: Gamin, the pillar of commerce, is lost. The government gave him a loan of eighty thousand piasters in cash, but that's just putting off the evil day (*cela ne le fera recculer* [*sic*] *que pour mieux sauter*)." (Renoyal de Lescouble, *Journal d'un colon*, 942).

16. The purchase and the name of one plantation, "Belle-Vue," is referenced by Joseph Martial Wetzell, "Résumé des travaux," 30 April, 8 May and 6 June 1831, quoted in Geraud, "Des habitations sucreries," 527, 528, 531.

17. The first, "between the Rivière du Mât and that of Vincendo," was 2,063 feet (137.5 *gaulettes*) in width, while the second, "between the Rivière du Bras Panon and that of Vincendo," was 2,475 feet (165 *gaulettes*) in width. Census, Isle Bourbon, Saint-Benoît, Joseph Lory, 1835 (ADR 6M97). The census records prior to 1835 for Saint-Benoît have not survived.

18. Census, Isle Bourbon, Commune de Saint-Benoît, Joseph Lory, 1835 (ADR 6M 97).

19. The 1831 census lists Lory's daughter as "Marie Charlotte Augustine," but the subsequent year adds "Euphémie"; Census, Isle Bourbon, Saint-Denis, Lory, 1831 (ADR 6M259) and 1832 (ADR 6M263). There was relatively little turnover on Lory's staff.

20. Death of Marie Charlette Augustine Euphémie Lory, 1 December 1832 (ANOM IREL État Civil, Réunion, Saint-Denis). The diarist Renoyal de Lescouble mentions an epidemic fever raging through the colony that he eventually survived, but it took his invalid daughter. Renoyal de Lescouble, *Journal d'un colon*, 1117–1120.

21. Louis Nicias Gaillard, *Discours prononcé aux funérailles de M. Gilbert-Boucher, Procureur général près la Cour royale de Poitiers, le 7 mars 1841,* ([Poitiers ?]: Imprimerie de F.-A. Saurin, 1841), 12.

22. Isambert, who had represented Cyrille Bissette in appealing Martinique's conviction of treason for pamphlets asserting equal rights for free men of color, was a founding member of the French Society for the Abolition of Slavery, organized with members of the French lower legislative body, the Chamber of Deputies, in August 1834. Jennings, *French Anti-Slavery*, 48–75. In 1835 Isambert represented a mulatto music teacher who was accused of fomenting slave revolt in Isle Bourbon and who owned copies of Bissette's *Revue des colonies*. Shelby McCloy, *The Negro in France* (Lexington: University of Kentucky Press, 1961), 140–141. *Revue des colonies*, 3 (1836): 8–12 and 3 (1837): 3–6. Louis T. Houat, *Un proscrit de l'île de Bourbon à Paris* (Paris: F. Malteste, 1838), 3–6. Auguste Billiard, who was resident in Isle Bourbon during Furcy's 1817 lawsuit, joined the society by June 1835. Jennings, *French Anti-Slavery*, 61.

23. Serving as *procureur général* to the Court of Cassation from 1830, Dupin, a liberal econo-
mist and confidant of the king, held a simultaneous appointment as a deputy for Nevers
since 1824 (and until 1848). His brother, Baron Charles Dupin, favored liberal policies
regarding child labor but would succumb to the influence of the colonial lobbyists, employing a "system of trials and temporization" to resist antislavery measures during his tenure in
the Chamber of Peers (1837–1848). Jennings, *French-Anti-Slavery*, 77, 129, 223. André
Dupin's friendship with Boucher was celebrated in the latter's funeral discourse: Gaillard,
Discours prononcé aux funérailles, 8. André Dupin ("Dupin the elder") was president of
the Society for Elementary Instruction (Société pour l'instruction élémentaire), founded
in 1831, in 1836, 1838, 1841, 1845, and 1850; active from at least the late 1830s, Furcy's
lawyer Camille Godard de Saponay likewise served as president in 1852 and 1857.

24. *Gazette des tribunaux*, 21 December 1843, 1.

25. Ships now traveled directly to Europe, making the voyage in two to three months; *Asiatic
Journal and Monthly Register* 18 (September-December 1835): 39, 142. Unfortunately,
the surviving commercial ship manifests do not list passengers who might have traveled on
board the ships, laden primarily with sugar, bound for England; "Customs Department-
Copies of manifests of outgoing ships (1821–1900)" (NARM Z/7F/12 and Z/7F/13,
1835), http://www1.gov.mu/.

26. Godard de Saponay's address is mentioned in the *Gazette des Tribunaux*, 22 August
1841, 1113.

27. It is likely in 1835 that the new delegate, Pierre Conil, reported that he could not find any
record of either decision to the ministry. The terse note reads:

> Act of the Royal Court of Isle Bourbon of 12 February 1818. Furcy & Monsieur
> Lory. Monsieur Conil, delegate—Office of Monsieur Maestro. It does not exist at
> all in the collection of the acts of the Royal Court of Bourbon for 1818; there is
> not even an act of this date. As there is no directory for the first semester of 1818, it
> is impossible to know if this act was actually rendered in the colony and would be
> [among] those for which the double minutes were not sent, although such exists for
> the second semester of 1818, after examination and comparison with the directories
> of the said collection. (ANOM FM GEN/158/1307)

28. Dupin, *Réquisitoires, plaidoyers*, 2:422. The original text of Godard de Saponay's arguments has not been found, but the gist of it can be gleaned in the court reporter's summary,
included in Dupin's collection.

29. Dupin, *Réquisitoires, plaidoyers*, 422–423.

30. Dupin, *Réquisitoires, plaidoyers*, 422.

31. "The plaintiff, who attended the audience, had mulatto coloring but very regular features
and black hair similar to that of the Europeans"; Dupin, *Réquisitoires, plaidoyers*, 423.

32. Furcy to Boucher, 15 May 1826 (ADR 1Jp2007-1, no. 71).

33. *Gazette des Tribunaux*, 13 August 1835, 1.

34. Capitalized in the original. Dupin was closely following the Free Soil arguments laid out
by the celebrated attorney general Henrion de Pansey following the 1770 parliamentary
strike against the crown's "despotic" rule. Pierre Paul Nicholas Henrion de Pansey, *Discours
prononcé à la rentrée de la Conférence publique des messieurs les avocats au Parlement de*

Paris, le 13 janvier 1775 (Lausanne, Switzerland: n.p., 1775). Dupin cites Henrion de Pansey explicitly; *Réquisitoires, plaidoyers*, 426.

35. Dupin, *Réquisitoires, plaidoyers*, 426.

36. *Gazette des Tribunaux*, 29 August 1835, 1044.

37. Joseph Louis E. Ortolan, *Notice biographique sur m. [A. M. J. J.] Dupin* (Paris: Imprimerie du Fain & Thunot, 1840), 90–91.

38. Gaillard, *Discours prononcé aux funérailles*, 11.

39. Passengers, Bordeaux, Departures, 23 October 1835, *La Camille* (ANOM COL F/5B/62).

40. *Bulletin des lois du royaume français*, 9th ser., 12, no. 419 (1st semester 1836): 172–173; Boulle and Peabody, *Le droit des noirs en France*, 218, 226.

41. Honoré Pontois, *La conspiration du Général Berton: Étude politique et judiciaire sur la Restauration Honoré Pontois* (Paris: E. Dentu, 1877), 217–219; Dupin, *Réquisitoires, plaidoyers*, 422. Dupin, who would later advocate for Furcy before the same court, took Boucher's side, finding no evidence of the defamation with which he was charged.

42. Furcy to Boucher, 1 October 1836 (ADR 1Jp2007-1, no. 74).

43. Furcy to Boucher, 1 October 1836 (ADR 1Jp2007-1, no. 74).

44. Census, Isle Bourbon, Saint-André, Widow Jean Baptiste Euphémie, 1836 (ADR 6M50) and 1837 (ADR 6M53). Her eldest daughter, Madeleine, 27 in 1837, was also listed as absent that year.

45. Furcy to Boucher, 1 October 1836 (ADR 1Jp2007-1, no. 74).

46. Furcy to Boucher, 1 October 1836 (ADR 1Jp2007-1, no. 74). This was the new Isle Bourbon governor, Jacques-Philippe Cuvillier, appointed in 1832.

47. Copy of Governor Cuvillier to Furcy, 17 September 1836, in Furcy to Boucher, 1 October 1836 (ADR 1Jp2007-1, no. 74).

48. Furcy to Boucher, 1 October 1836 (ADR 1Jp2007-1, no. 74).

49. Census, Isle Bourbon, Saint-Denis, Joseph Lory, 1833 (ADR 6M268). Lory did not file census records for Saint-Denis between 1835 and 1839; the next would be filed by his widow in 1840.

50. This was probably Simon Julien Galdemar, who had married locally in Rivière des Remparts, where he lived for a number of years, siring a daughter, but the family would soon move back to Nantes. Perhaps he was selling the property in anticipation of his departure. Sale, Galdemar to Furcy Madeleine, Notariat Desroullade, 13 October 1836 (ADR 10J128).

51. It was different in Mauritius, where masters such as the widow Lory selected surnames for their slaves, apparently on a whim. She, or her husband or father-in-law, chose the following family names for their slaves: Olive, Ravoul, Tortoni, Calle, La Fleur, Alentouc, Mavac, Siahime, Pacotté, Manuel, Scillie/Sally, D'Amboise, Antoinette, Sylvie, Eraste, Samson, Philibert, Fande, Bétif, Mathère, Joyeux, Le Laid, and many others; Slave Register, Mauritius, Flacq, Madame Ve Lory. 1817 (NAUK T 71/573, 1248–1254).

52. Sale, Galdemar to Furcy Madeleine, Notariat Desroullade, 13 October 1836 (ADR 10J128).

53. Included in the sale were "shelves, counters, and miscellaneous items"; Sale, Galdemar to Furcy Madeleine, Notariat Desroullade, 13 October 1836 (ADR 10J128). The Rue des Limites was renamed Remy Ollier Street in 1903; Piggott and Thibaud, *Consolidated Laws of Mauritius*, 132, 133.

54. Sale, Furcy to Richard, Notariat Jollivet, 11 April 1838 (ADR 10J42).

55. Sale, Madame Labat to Furcy Madelaine, Notariat Jollivet, 28 April 1838 (ADR 10J42).

56. Sale, Furcy to Richard, Notariat Jollivet, 11 April 1838 (ADR 10J42).

57. Marie Anne Nelcine would now be 23, and Olympe Joséphine Augustine 21 (ANOM IREL État Civil, Saint-Denis, 1826).

58. As usual, there was no cause of death recorded. Two witnesses, Charles David de Floris, police commissioner, 29, and Pierre Français, "town hall secretary and neighbor of the deceased," 27, reported the death of "Dame Marie Constance, widow of Sir Jean Baptiste Euphémie," age 55, the following day, Bastille Day (ANOM IREL État Civil, Saint-André, Réunion, Death, 13 July 1838).

59. The eldest two, Eugène (31) and Madeleine (28), were listed as "absent"; Census, Isle Bourbon, Saint-André, Widow Jean Baptiste Euphémie, 1838 (ADR 6M57).

60. In Constance's census returns from 1808 through 1838, one female slave, an African (*caffre*) laborer, is consistently listed first amongst her slaves, but the spelling of her name varies tremendously as Euphronine, Eufronine, Eufrogine, Irogène, and Irogine. Because this slave's age advances consistently from record to record, it is likely the same person. Irogine's death is reported in Census, Isle Bourbon, Saint-André, Widow J. Baptiste Euphémie, 1837 (ADR 6M53).

61. Census, Isle Bourbon, Saint-André, Widow Jean Baptiste Euphémie, 1838 (ADR 6M57).

62. Deposit of Items, Joseph Lory, 21 February 1837, Notariat, Saint-Denis, Desrieux (ADR 3E 678).

63. France, Ministry of the Navy and the Colonies, "Commission consultative pour les affaires des colonies instituée par décision royale du 14 janvier 1834," *Annales maritimes et coloniales, 24ᵉ année, 1839, 2e série, 1ʳᵉ partie: partie officielle* (Paris: Imprimerie Royale, 1839), 105.

64. Moreau, *Mémoire pour le sieur Lory.*

65. Moreau, *Mémoire pour le sieur Lory*, 1.

66. Moreau, *Mémoire pour le sieur Lory*, 2.

67. Minutes, Judicial Meeting of 16 November 1817 (ADR 1Jp2007-1, no. 49). The precipitant drop in the estimated number of slaves to be freed by Furcy's case is probably the function of more precise calculations than Gillot de l'Étang or Desbassayns's wild estimates rather than a real drop in number of Indian slaves.

68. Minister to the Keeper of the Seals (Garde des Sceaux), 29 May 1838 (ANOM FM GEN/158/1307).

69. Minister to the Governor of Isle Bourbon, 29 May 1838 (ANOM FM GEN/158/1307).

70. Desaponay [sic], *Mémoire pour le sieur Furcy* (ADR 1Jp2007-1, no. 275), 8. The factum is undated but mentions the beginning of 1838, so it must have been composed sometime thereafter. One of Lory's nephews, a W. Terrasson, resident in Paris, wrote to the ministry with a copy of the new *mémoire* composed on Furcy's behalf by Godard de Saponay. W. Terrasson, letter to the ministry, 19 February 1839 (ANOM FM GEN/158/1307).

71. Desaponay [sic], *Mémoire pour le sieur Furcy* (ADR 1Jp2007-1, no. 275), 4–5.

72. Desaponay [sic], *Mémoire pour le sieur Furcy* (ADR 1Jp2007-1, no. 275), 6, 31.

73. Desaponay [sic], *Mémoire pour le sieur Furcy* (ADR 1Jp2007-1, no. 275), 51.

74. ANOM IREL, État Civil, Réunion, Saint-Benoît, Death, 20 April 1839. The notice mentioned his wife, Eugénie, but left a blank space for the name of his father, unknown to the two witnesses certifying his death.

75. "Dépot du procès-verbal d'expertise de deux meubles, dépendant de succession en communauté de feu M. Joseph Lory par M. Antoine Pitel, 24 aout 1846" (ADR 3 E692, no. 284).

76. Marriage, F. Madeleine and Zulmé Maugué, "Contrat de marriage de M. F. Madelaine avec Dlle Zulmé Maugué," Notariat Trebuchet, 14 October 1839 (ADR 10J174). Monsieur "Maulguée" also resided on the Moka road.

77. The marriage contract stipulates the property of each party. Furcy brought his land in Pamplemousses, 35 *arpents* of land, plus the usufruct of another adjoining property, also 35 *arpents*, adjoining the two properties of the Arlanda men and the Bay of the Arsenal.

78. Curiously, the register that should contain the decisions of the Court of Cassation, 1837–1841 (*Enregistrement au ministère de la justice, des arrêts de la cour de cassation*, vol. 46), does not appear in the Archives Nationales inventory and, if it ever existed, apparently disappeared from the collections long ago. Instead, I have consulted: Copy, Decision of the Court of Cassation, 6 May 1840 (ANOM FM GEN//158/1307, dos. 1). Public hearings had been held 29 April, 4 and 6 May 1840. The case rendered its decision against Joseph Lory, not the heirs, suggesting that news had not yet formally reached Paris of his death. The decision was covered in the judicial newspaper, *Gazette des tribunaux*, 13 May 1840, 1.

79. This date is impossible, since Boucher did not arrive in the colony until July.

80. Copy, Decision of the Court of Cassation, 6 May 1840 (ANOM FM GEN//158/1307, dos. 1).

81. "Déclaration du Roi, concernant les nègres esclaves des colonies," 15 December 1738, in Boulle and Peabody, *Le droit des noirs en France*, 64.

82. Like the Parisian judges of the eighteenth century, they insisted on the perpetual application of the "ancient" tradition of Free Soil. Peabody, "Alternative Genealogy," 341–362; Peabody, "*There Are No Slaves*," 11–15.

83. Copy, Decision of the Court of Cassation, 6 May 1840 (ANOM FM GEN//158/1307, dos. 1); *Bulletin des arrêts de la Cour de cassation rendus en matière civile, 1840* (Paris: Imprimerie Royale, 1841), 42, no. 5 (1841): 202–204.

84. Copy, Decision of the Court of Cassation, 6 May 1840 (ANOM FM GEN//158/1307, dos. 1).

85. The estimate of the number of slaves accompanying their masters to the metropole annually is based on figures recorded for 1817–1819. "Note," n.d. (ca. 1820) (ANOM GEN 629, dos. 2735).

CHAPTER 10

1. Godard de Saponay to Furcy, 28 October 1840 (ADR 1Jp2007-1, no. 136). This copy was among the documents belonging to Louis Gilbert Boucher; it contains some curious errors, including the transcription of Furcy's name as "Monsieur Farry à Paris."

2. Godard de Saponay to Furcy, 28 October 1840 (ADR 1Jp2007-1, No. 136).

3. Godard de Saponay to Furcy, 28 October 1840 (ADR 1Jp2007-1, No. 136).

4. Godard de Saponay to Furcy, 28 October 1840 (ADR 1Jp2007-1, No. 136).

5. Godard de Saponay to Furcy, 28 October 1840 (ADR 1Jp2007-1, No. 136).

6. Godard de Saponay also advised Furcy to arrange for two official copies of the decision of the Court of Cassation and to deposit one with a notary. Furcy's further legal disputations regarding his marriage in Mauritius have not yet been discovered.

7. The 6 November 1863 marriage contract for Marie Euridice Madeleine specifies her parents' names—Furcy Madeleine, deceased, and Amélie Zulmée Maulgué—but not her date of birth, Notariat Victor Barry, Mauritius (ADR). A mortgage contract mentions that Thélécourt Félix, divorced, married Louise Furcy Madeleine, without mentioning the date of her birth or the marriage; "Affectation hypothécaire par M^r. et Mad^e. Th. Félix au profit de M^r. C. M. Barle," 14 September 1876, Notariat Victor Barry (ADR). Thanks to Gilles Gérard for making copies of these documents available to me.

8. Their subsequent legitimization is inferred from the records declaring Furcy Madeleine as their father.

9. Sale, Mademoiselle Barry to Furcy Madeleine, 24 June 1841, Notariat Yves Isidor Jollivet, Mauritius (ADR 10J 50). The 1880 Descubes map labels one piece of property "Con[cession] Barry or Bois bellau," at the base of Paille Hill; A. Descubes, *Map of the Island of Mauritius* (Mauritius Public Works Department, 1880), available online at http://www.depalmas-france.com/MAURITIUS/MAPS/CartesDescubes1880.html. The description of Furcy's purchase states that it bordered the "Great Road of Moka" perhaps the spur known as Bonnefin Street.

10. Four years later he was described as a "shopkeeper" (*commerçant*) living in Port Louis; Receipt, Furcy Madeleine to Widow Joseph Lory, 9 December 1845 (ADR 3E690).

11. "Procuration pour M. Furcy Madeleine," Notariat Yves Isidor Jollivet, Mauritius, 24 July 1841 (ADR 3 E690). Pierre Gabriel Toussaint de Quièvrecourt was born in upper Normandy and arrived in Isle Bourbon as a lawyer in 1835. He eventually was elected president of the bar in Saint-Denis. Ricquebourg, *Dictionnaire généalogique*, 3:2575.

12. Michaud, *Biographie universelle*, 5:171–172.

13. Gaillard, *Discours prononcé aux funérailles*, 13.

14. Acts proceeding from their lives, including marriages, land transactions, receipts, and others, are scattered throughout the Saint-Denis Isle Bourbon notarial records of Maurice Desrieux, 1829–1852 (ANOM DPPC NOT REU/REP/6).

15. Since 1835, Jules had left his position as manager and his replacement took charge of the 260 slaves, producing some 21,583 tons of sugar in the water-run mill in the previous year. Census, Isle Bourbon, Saint-Benoît, Widow Joseph Lory, 1840 (ADR 6M113). Geraud mentions the testing of a steam-driven mill by Joseph Lory at "Bellevue" in 1839, but perhaps he is confusing Joseph with one of his nephews. Geraud, "Des habitations sucreries," 246.

16. Geraud, "Des habitations sucreries," 379.

17. "Rapport au Roi sur les recensements dans les colonies," 11 June 1839, *Annales maritimes*, 2nd ser., 68 (1839): 550. The resultant "Ordonnance du Roi sur les recensements dans les colonies," 11 June 1839, *Annales maritimes*, 2nd ser., 68 (1839): 552–600, implemented these directives beginning with the 1840 census.

18. Census, Isle Bourbon, Saint-Denis, Charles Lory, 1840 (ADR 6M300).

19. Frédérick and Eugène were first recorded in Joseph Lory's 1833 Saint-Denis census as six-month-old "twins" (*jumeaux*) (ADR 6M268), but when Charles Routier filled out the census for the widow Routier in 1840, he apparently did not realize they were twins (they

were probably fraternal), and so recorded them (incorrectly) as three and a half and four years old on the basis of observation (ADR 6M300).

20. By 1847, this couple would be married and have three more children, all living on the Lory's Saint-Benoît plantation; Census, Saint-Benoît, 1847, E. R. Lory (ADR 6M142).

21. One house, at the intersection of the rue du Grand Chemin, was purchased at an unspecified date from Madame de Lafosse, the second in 1839 from the notary Dubois. Census, Isle Bourbon, Saint-Denis, Widow André Lory (ADR 6M300).

22. These include: her lady's maid, Justine Siahime (35); the domestic Martial Egiste (49); the cook, Valentin Calle (39); the gardener, Jean Bétif (38); the laundress, Rosa Sylvie (46) and her four children, Florentia (18), Félix (14), and the twins, Alphonse and Alphonsine (10); and Florentia's daughter, Rasquia (three months). These were assisted in their tasks around the building and grounds by five laborers: Jeannette (16), Gertrude (29), Malais (31), Pierre Georges (16), Paul (31), and Joseph (23).

23. Adolphe partnered with Jean François Pitel to invest in skilled slaves and a light industrial workshop to create the essential components for sugar factories; he now employed five enslaved tinsmiths, five blacksmiths, three boilermakers, two lathe operators, two locksmiths, and a foundry worker. He lived with his wife and four daughters, served by two of the slaves they had brought over from Mauritius, now listed as free, plus four enslaved servants and their three children (two of whom were listed as "mulatto"); Census, Isle Bourbon, Saint-Denis, Lory ainé, 1840 (ADRL300),1845 (ADR L321), 1847 (ADR 6M345), 1848 (ADR 6M 356).

Thomy Lory went into business with three men outside the family to purchase a plantation in Sainte-Rose, already outfitted with a sugar factory, in 1831; Census, Isle Bourbon, Saint-Denis, Thomy Lory, 1840 (ADRL300), 1845 (ADR L321), and 1848 (ADR 6M 356), and Geraud, "Des habitations sucreries," 122, 136, 334, 391.

Arthur had married another sugar scion, the widow Heloïse Bellier de Villentroy, with a sugar plantation and factory in Saint-Benoît; Census, Isle Bourbon, Saint-Denis, Arthur Lory, 1840 (ADR 6M300). Madame Bellier de Villentroy's sugar factory was one of the earliest built on the island, in 1820; Geraud, "Des habitations sucreries," 136.

Thomy, Edouard, and Jules ("Lory *frères*") jointly owned another sugar plantation in Sainte-Rose called Piton near the three sugar mills owned by Pierre Gamin (the business associate of Joseph Lory), Claude Lenoir, and Paul Richemont Desbassayns (son of Philippe); "Résumé des travaux," 4, 6, 17, 19, 21 and 22 May 1831, quoted in Geraud, "Des habitations sucreries," 391–392.

After serving his uncle briefly as a plantation manager in 1835, Jules purchased a small sugar plantation in Sainte-Marie and became involved in a water dispute with his neighbors over access to the Rivière des Pluies; Census, Isle Bourbon, Commune de Saint-Benoît, Joseph Lory, 1835 (ADR 6M 97); Census, Isle Bourbon, Sainte-Marie, Jules Lory, 1840 (ADR 6M385); Geraud, "Des habitations sucreries," 174. He married the Mauritian creole Elise Merlo on 21 December 1829, in Saint-Denis.

Henry Lory, married to Josephine Pajot, was a "merchant, first class" in Saint-Denis; Census, Isle Bourbon, Saint-Denis, Henry Lory, 1840 (ADR 6M300). The youngest son, Charles, 27, still unmarried, was an assistant merchant in Saint-Denis; Census, Isle Bourbon, Saint-Denis, Charles Lory, 1840 (ADR 6M300).

24. Quoted in Géraud, "Des habitations sucreries," 386. Founding members included many of Furcy and Boucher's opponents: the sugar barons Charles Desbassayns, Paul de Richemont Desbassayns, Xavier Gillot de L'Étang, and Testard, with Jules and Edouard Lory participating as "correspondents."

25. Moreau, Paillet, and Huart, *Mémoire pour la dame veuve Lory*, 10 (ANOM FM GEN 158/1307).

26. The famous painting of the 1840 World Anti-Slavery Convention, by Benjamin Robert Haydon, can be viewed at the National Portrait Gallery in London and on the gallery's excellent interactive website: http://images.npg.org.uk/800_800/2/8/mw00028.jpg (NPG 599). François Isambert, the secretary and prime mover of the French Society for the Abolition of Slavery, is seated by the black Haitian lawyer Jean-Baptiste Symphor Linstant de Pradine. Schmidt, *Abolitionnistes de l'esclavage*, 152–161; Jennings, *French Antislavery*, 152–154; Boulle and Peabody, *Le droit des noirs en France*, 222, 235.

27. Jennings, *French Antislavery*, 148–186, 170–172, 192, 237–244.

28. Schœlcher was an anticlerical autodidact and supporter of a variety of progressive causes, especially the abolition of colonial slavery. See Nelly Schmidt, *Victor Schœlcher et l'abolition de l'esclavage* (Paris: Fayard, 1994); Victor Schœlcher, *La correspondance de Victor Schœlcher*, ed. Nelly Schmidt (Paris: Maisonneuve & Larose, 1995); Anne Girollet, *Victor Schœlcher abolitionniste et républicain* (Paris: Karthala, 1999); Schmidt, *Abolitionnistes de l'esclavage*, 229–246; Jennings, *French Anti-Slavery*, 161.

29. Albin Roussin, Minister of the Navy, to Nicolas Martin du Nord, Minister of Justice, 8 December 1843 (ANOM FM GEN/158/1307).

30. *Gazette des tribunaux*, 21 December 1843, 1; Cyrille Bissette, "Affaire Furcy: Les esclaves qui touchent le sol de la France sont libre," *L'abolitioniste français* 1 (1844): 58; Thureau, *Plaidoyer pour le sieur Furcy*, 44. The current Palais de Justice is a replacement, which opened in 1868; the Sainte-Chappelle and the Conciergerie prison, once the royal residence, are part of the original structures.

31. Edmond Rousse, *Édouard Thureau, avocat à la Cour d'appel de Paris, doyen de l'ordre, 1830–1893: Notice lue à l'Assemblée générale de l'Association amicale des secrétaires et anciens secrétaires de la Conférence des avocats le 18 décembre 1893* (Paris: Typographie de E. Plon, Nourrit & Cie, [1893/1894?]), 9–10, 21.

32. "Discours prononcé le 21 janvier 1893 aux obsèques de M. Thureau par M. le battonier du Buit," in Rousse, *Édouard Thureau*, 35.

33. Thureau, *Plaidoyer pour le sieur Furcy*, 2. For more detailed analysis of Thureau's legal arguments, see Peabody, "La question racial et le 'sol libre de France.'"

34. *Gazette des tribunaux*, 21 December 1843, 1.

35. Thureau, *Plaidoyer pour le sieur Furcy*, 42.

36. The 1817 decision was first referenced (but not quoted) in 1838, in Moreau, *Mémoire pour le Sieur Lory*, 4.

37. Thureau, *Plaidoyer pour le sieur Furcy*, 6.

38. Thureau, *Plaidoyer pour le sieur Furcy*, 6.

39. Thureau, *Plaidoyer pour le sieur Furcy*, 44.

40. *Gazette des tribunaux*, 22 December 1843, 1. Like Thureau, Paillet, 47, came from a provincial bourgeois family and had studied law in Paris. Paillet initially made a name for himself by defending (unsuccessfully, but apparently quite eloquently) a notorious murderer

of two children in the Bois de Vincennes outside Paris. By now he was president (*bâton-nier*) of the Paris bar. M.E. Pascallet, *Notice biographique sur M. Paillet (A.-G.-V.)*, 2nd ed. (Paris: Bureau central de la Revue générale biographique et nécrologique, 1845), 4–5.

41. Moreau, *Mémoire pour le Sieur Lory*; Moreau, Paillet, and Huart, *Mémoire pour la dame veuve Lory*, 22–23; *Gazette des tribunaux*, 22 December 1843, 1, makes it clear that it was Paillet who delivered the arguments orally.

42. Moreau, Paillet, and Huart, *Mémoire pour la dame veuve Lory*, 28. No doubt this is because someone had scoured the appropriate records and found no trace of her.

43. Although this law was never registered in Isle Bourbon, Paillet emphasized, it was certainly registered by the Parlement de Bretagne, in whose jurisdiction Madeleine resided during her residence in France. Moreau, Paillet, and Huart, *Mémoire pour la dame veuve Lory*, 22; *Gazette des tribunaux*, 22 December 1843, 1.

44. He claimed, incorrectly, that this resulted from "French sympathies for the Indians of this part of the world in which slavery of the natives did not exist and had never existed," *Gazette des tribunaux*, 22 December 1843, 1.

45. Moreau, Paillet, and Huart, *Mémoire pour la dame veuve Lory*, 11–21; *Gazette des tribunaux*, 22 December 1843, 1.

46. Moreau, Paillet, and Huart, *Mémoire pour la dame veuve Lory*, 34, n. 1. There Moreau had argued that the 1723 Code Noir's article 42 prohibiting the separation of families through sale did not result in the freedom of the slaves in question, only that the purchaser could by rights claim the remaining family members from the seller; and that the 1805 Code Decaen decree, which explicitly freed mother and child under the age of seven, was not yet in effect.

47. Moreau, Paillet, and Huart, *Mémoire pour la dame veuve Lory*, 33–36.

48. "There will not be formed [*formé*], in cause of appeal, any new demand, unless it does not concern compensation, or that the new petition is not part of the principle action. The parties will be able to ask for interest, unpaid wages [*arrérages*], rents, and other incidentals owed between the decision of the [court of] first instance and the damages and interest for the wrong suffered since the said judgment"; quoted in Moreau, Paillet, and Huart, *Mémoire pour la dame veuve Lory*, 34.

49. Moreau, Paillet, and Huart, *Mémoire pour la dame veuve Lory*, 35.

50. Moreau, Paillet, and Huart, *Mémoire pour la dame veuve Lory*, 35.

51. Moreau, Paillet, and Huart, *Mémoire pour la dame veuve Lory*, 36.

52. *Gazette des tribunaux*, 24 December 1843, 1.

53. *Gazette des tribunaux*, 24 December 1843, 1; *Journal du Palais* 1, no. 6 (1844): 223; Bissette, "Affaire Furcy," 58. Hébert's assistant was Nouguier. *Gazette des tribunaux*, 21 December 1843, 1.

54. Hébert was a child of the July Monarchy. Studying law not in Paris but in Rouen, he advanced rapidly in his career. As a member of the Chamber of Deputies, he was architect of the reform of the French judiciary and would eventually advance to minister of justice in 1847, only to fall with the government during the 1848 Revolution and flee into exile in England; he returned to Paris and practiced law privately until his retirement. Adolphe Robert and Gaston Cougny, *Dictionnaire des Parlementaires français*, 5 vols. (Paris: Dourloton, 1889–1891), 3:327.

55. *Gazette des tribunaux*, 24 December 1843, 1; *Journal du Palais* 1, no. 6 (1844): 223.

56. *Gazette des tribunaux*, 24 December 1843, 1; *Journal du Palais* 1, no. 6 (1844): 223.

57. Hébert cited a host of colonial regulations emanating from French Pondichéry (dated 20 July 1778, 1 April 1788, "a regulation of 1786," 17 December 1790, and 16 October 1792) that had been offered in the Lorys' lawyers' two *mémoires*. He also quoted statistics of the number of "Indian slaves" in Isle Bourbon published by the French ministry in 1839 and cited two British laws "relative to Industan"; the first, of 1833, affirmed the maintenance of slavery in British India, including Ceylon and Saint-Helena, and the second, from 1843, abolishing slavery in Bengal. *Gazette des tribunaux*, 24 December 1843, 1; Bissette, "Affaire Furcy," 59; *Journal du Palais* 1, no. 6 (1844): 223.

   The term "Indian," in the 1739 royal order prohibiting the enslavement of Indians and Caribs, applied solely to "residents of the American continent" and "the West Indies." Moreover, according to Hébert, the 1739 order applied only to the *Îles du Vent*, i.e., Lesser Antilles islands of Saint-Martin, Saint-Barthélémy, Guadeloupe, Martinique, La Désirade, Les Galantes, Isles des Saintes) and not to the *Îles sous le Vent*, i.e.,the smaller islands off the coast of modern Venezuela, such as Aruba and Curaçao). Bissette, "Affaire Furcy," 59; *Gazette des tribunaux*, 24 December 1843, 1; *Journal du Palais* 1, no. 6 (1844): 223.

58. Bissette, "Affaire Furcy," 59.

59. *Gazette des tribunaux*, 24 December 1843, 1; *Journal du Palais* 1, no. 6 (1844): 224.

60. *Gazette des tribunaux*, 24 December 1843, 1.

61. *Gazette des tribunaux*, 24 December 1843, 1.

62. As passenger records show, she never passed through Isle Bourbon on the outward passage from India. The correct places to look would have been passenger records of Pondichéry and Isle de France.

63. *Gazette des tribunaux*, 24 December 1843, 1.

64. *Gazette des tribunaux*, 24 December 1843, 1.

65. *Gazette des tribunaux*, 24 December 1843, 1.

66. *Gazette des tribunaux*, 21 December 1843, 1; *Gazette des tribunaux*, 22 December 1843, 1.

67. These included the royal ordinance of 2 March 1739, which prohibited the trade in "Caribs and Indians of nations with whom the French are not at war" (ANOM, COL, B68, f° 15v°) and the 7 January 1767 directive of the minister of the navy, which insisted upon a fundamental distinction between "Indiens" and "Nègres," for the purpose of granting titles of nobility (Moreau de Saint-Méry, *Loix et constitutions*, 5:80–81). Curiously, no eighteenth- or nineteenth-century French legal professionals mentioned the 1727 East India Company ban on trading Indian slaves or the 1712 Martinique legal decision freeing "Matthieu de Surat," which the creole lawyer Pierre François Régis Dessalles considered evidence for the ban on trading East Indian slaves. B. Vonglis, ed., *Les annals du Conseil souverain de la Martinique*, 2 vols. in 4, originally published in 1786 (Paris: L'Harmattan. 1995), 1:363–364.

68. Isle Bourbon, Correspondance générale 1727, ANOM C3/5 fol. 206.

69. Thureau, *Plaidoyer pour le sieur Furcy*, 45–46; *Journal du Palais* 1, no. 6 (1844): 224.

70. Galignoni [*sic*], "Curious Trial," *Law Times* 2 (23 December 1843): 256–257. The author was one of two brothers—Jean Antoine or Guillaume—Galignani, who published the journal founded by their father, *Galignani's Messenger*, dedicated to the furthering of Anglo-French relations. William Lloyd Garrison, *The Letters of William Lloyd Garrison*, ed. William M. Merrill (Cambridge, MA: Harvard University Press, 1979), 5:537, n.5;

"Galignani," in *Oxford National Dictionary of Biography* (Oxford: Oxford University Press, 2004–2009), http://www.oxforddnb.com/view/article/10301.

71. *British and Foreign Anti-Slavery Reporter* 5, no. 1 (10 January 1844): 7.

72. Jennings, *French Anti-Slavery*, 72–73.

73. Bissette, "Affaire Furcy," 59. Bissette's two-page summary contains a few errors, especially regarding dates.

74. This paper was published in Boston from 1831 to 1865; *Liberator*, available online at http://www.theliberatorfiles.com/. In a letter from a much later period (4 September 1867), Garrison barely hides his contempt for the French, whose language he doesn't understand, lamenting that the French antislavery organizers were remiss in "not having had a competent reporter present" to cover the 1867 Paris conference (Garrison to Helen E. Garrison, 4 September 1867, in *Letters*, 536).

75. Their master had taken them to free soil of Illinois and the Northwest Territory, and their lawyers argued that this made them and their subsequent children free. Don E. Fehrenbacher, *The Dred Scott Case: Its Significance in American Law and Politics* (New York: Oxford University Press, 1978); Lea VanderVelde, *Mrs. Dred Scott: A Life on Slavery's Frontier* (New York: Oxford University Press, 2009). VanderVelde's study offers some fascinating parallels and counterpoints to the life stories of Madeleine, Constance, and Furcy, including the question of slaves gifted on free soil and the role of women in taking the initiative to sue for freedom for the men in their lives (husband or brother).

76. Missouri jurisprudence traditionally upheld the capcity of residence to free slaves if the term of residence was long enough; see Lea VanderVelde, *Redemption Songs: Suing for Freedom before Dred Scott* (New York: Oxford University Press, 2014). The Saint Louis Circuit Court and the Missouri Supreme Court initially ruled in favor of the Scotts' freedom, only to have those decisions overruled by the U.S. Supreme Court in 1857.

77. Beginning in 1788, British antislavery activists had initiated petition drives aimed at ending the slave trade, culminating with the slave trade ban of 1807. Women activists may have provided the tipping point by organizing independent petition drives and contributing to each successive drive. In 1833, on the immediate eve of the passage of the British general emancipation bill, English activists collected 1.3 million signatures, including those of perhaps 400,000 women, to pressure Parliament to end colonial slavery; Drescher, *Abolition*, 250.

78. Jennings, *French Antislavery*, 239–240. Schmidt reproduces the text of these petitions in *Abolitionnistes de l'esclavage*, 845–872.

79. Seymour Drescher, "Two Variants of Antislavery: Religious Organization and Social Mobilization in Britain and France, 1780–1870," in *From Slavery to Freedom: Comparative Studies in the Rise and Fall of Atlantic Slavery* (New York: New York University Press, 1999), 43–63.

80. Jennings, *French Antislavery*, 204–228; Schmidt, *Abolitionnistes de l'esclavage*, 128–137.

81. The date of his petition appears in Receipt, Furcy Madeleine to Widow Joseph Lory, 9 December 1845, Notariat Desrieux (ADR 3E 690).

82. Delabarre de Nanteuil had just completed his comprehensive catalogue, *Législation de l' Île Bourbon*.

83. It was Terrasson who had supplied the ministry in Paris with a copy of Furcy's (1838–1839) *mémoire* composed by Godard de Saponay on 19 February 1839 (ANOM FM GEN/158/

1307). I have not been able to find a copy of Joseph Lory's testament, but they are heirs named in Furcy's lawsuit. Terrason's full name appears in "Partage des biens dépendant des consignements et succession de feu M. Marie Joseph Lory," 21 February 1848, Notariat Desrieux (ADR 3E397).

84. An interim decision permitted the concatenation of two separate lawsuits (presumably aimed at the different heirs); Decisions of 13 February and 13 March 1845, mentioned in the Decision of the Royal Court of Bourbon, 30 August 1845 (ADR U483 and ANOM DPPC 2895).

85. Decision of the Royal Court of Bourbon, 30 August 1845 (ANOM COL D2C 341, fol. 95v and 1COL10).

86. The decision describes the dates of these notarized acts, dated 7 August 1809 and 7 January 1811, as those notarized by "Villeprié," dated "10 August 1809, 76, n. 1653, 8th register, and 8 January 1811, no. 522, fol. 24, 9th register"; Decision of the Royal Court of Bourbon, 30 August 1845 (ADR U483 et ANOM DPPC 2895). These are not the same receipt (*quittance*) as the one Madeleine affirmed before Michault d'Emery, when she received a year's worth of corn and less than $200 (in today's value) as her food allowance, and they have not been found in the archives; Receipt, Madeleine to the Routier heirs, 7 August 1809, Notariat Michault D'Emery, no. 731 (ANOM DPPC NOT REU1803).

87. Decision of the Royal Court of Bourbon, 30 August 1845 (ADR U483 and ANOM DPPC 2895).

88. Census, Isle Bonaparte, Saint-Denis, Joseph Lory, 1810 (ADR L157).

89. The decision states that the 1818 decision was registered 19 November 1834, fol. 195, CG); Decision of the Royal Court of Bourbon, 30 August 1845 (ADR U483 et ANOM DPPC 2895).

90. Receipt, Furcy Madeleine to Widow Joseph Lory, 9 December 1845, Notariat Desrieux (ADR 3E 690).

91. Census, Isle Bourbon, Saint-Denis, Widow Joseph Lory, 1845 (ADR 6M 132).

92. "Dépot du procès-verbal d'expertise de deux meubles, dépendant de succession en communauté de feu M. Joseph Lory par M. Antoine Pitel, 24 aout 1846" (ADR 3 E692, no. 284).

93. "Dépot du procès-verbal d'expertise de deux meubles, dépendant de succession en communauté de feu M. Joseph Lory par M. Antoine Pitel, 24 aout 1846" (ADR 3 E692, no. 284).

94. Census, Isle Bourbon, Saint-Denis, Eugénie Routier Lory, 1840 (6M300), 1846 (ADR 6M330), 1848 (ADR 6M356).

95. Census, Isle Bourbon, Saint-Denis, Eugénie Routier Lory, 1848 (ADR 6M356).

96. "Partage des biens dépendant des commissions et succession de feu M. Marie Joseph Lory," 21 February 1848, Notariat Desrieux (ADR 3E397).

97. Schmidt, *Abolitionnistes de l'esclavage*, 319–386; Schmidt, *Victor Schœlcher et l'abolition de l'esclavage*, 101–148; Jennings, *French Anti-Slavery*, 273–284. The text of the decree, consisting of nine articles, can be found in Schmidt, *Abolitionnistes de l'esclavage*, 979–981. One set of laws addressed the living and working conditions for former slaves; new colonial institutions would be established to care for aged, disabled, and orphan slaves; new compulsory and tuition-free primary schools would be established to educate the children of the newly freed; a new tribunal system, based upon term-appointed juries,

would hear labor and civil disputes and punish those who resisted the new labor regime. Though slavery was abolished, labor was compulsory and wage-based; all vagabonds would be subject to arrest and required to join "national work-teams" (*ateliers nationaux*). A second group of laws prepared to address colonial debt; each colony would establish savings banks, and new detailed regulations sought to manage mortgages, foreclosures, and seizures of assets. Taxes were levied on distilled liquor and wines. A third set of laws concerned the political rights of colonists and former slaves now that universal male suffrage had been declared for France; all adult males "of French nationality" were eligible to elect representatives to the National Assembly; colonial councils were abolished; freedom of the press was declared for the colonies. Schmidt, *Abolitionnistes de l'esclavage*, 331–337; texts of these decrees can be found in 981–1003.

98. Algerian slaveholders were exempted from the government's compensation plan; Jennings, *French Anti-Slavery*, 282; Alain Buffon, "L'Indemnisation des planteurs après l'abolition de l'esclavage," *Bulletin de la Société d'histoire de la Guadeloupe* 67–68 (1986): 53–73; M. A. I. Fischer-Blanchet, "Les travaux de la commission de l'indemnité coloniale en 1848," *Espaces caraïbes* 1 (1983): 37–56; Laurent Blériot, "La loi d'indemnisation des colons du 30 avril 1849, aspects juridiques," *Revue historique des Mascareignes* 2, no. 2 (2000): 147–165.

99. Joseph André Adolphe Lory (12,602.58 francs), Jules Lory (12,602.58 francs), Louis Edmond Lory (20140.62 francs), Louis Eugène Lory (67783.35 francs), Marc Victor Thomy Lory (37,160.01 francs); Indemnité coloniale la Réunion (ANOM K14).

100. Fuma, *L'abolition de l'esclavage à La Réunion*, 75–81; Jean-Régis Ramsamy-Nadarassin, "Les travailleurs indiens sous contrat à La Réunion (1848–1948)" (Ph.D. thesis, Université de La Réunion, 2012). Recruitment of indentured laborers had begun in the 1830s. Alessandro Stanziani, "Travail, droits et immigration: Une comparaison entre l'Isle Maurice et l'Isle de La Réunion, années 1840–1880," *Le Mouvement Social*, 241, no. 4 (2012): 51.

101. Fuma, *L'abolition de l'esclavage à La Réunion*, 66–74.

102. The decree of 13 February 1852 made labor compulsory in the colonies, although it applied to both blacks and whites; it would not be repealed until 1884.

103. Stéphane Becuwe and Bertrand Blancheton, "Les colonies sucrières françaises, victimes de la libéralisation commerciale internationale des années 1860?" *Outre-Mers: Revue D'histoire* 382/383 (March 2014): 201–214.

AFTERWORD

1. Gilles Gérard's research on enslaved families, and on Madeleine's descendants, cited earlier in this book and generously shared with me, has been absolutely essential for the completion of this book.

2. Judith took the surname Jean-Baptiste, while her brother, JeanBaptiste, took the surname Euphémie, after his father, naming his eldest daughter Marie Madeleine. Census, Isle Bourbon, Saint André, 1846 (ADR 6M82). Joséphine took the surname Jean-Baptiste as well (ADR 6M83).

3. The 1817 edition of the official government publication of the *Gazette de l'Isle Bourbon*, site of the struggle between Boucher and Panon Desbassayns, is missing from both the

Archives Départementales de la Réunion and the Bibliothèque Nationale de France. Key years of Furcy's story are missing from the journal of Renoyal de Lescouble, a friend of the Routiers and Lorys and ordinarily an effusive observer of colonial scandal. Renoyal de Lescouble, *Journal d'un colon*, 155–161. One gap runs from 16 January 1815 until 14 January 1820, a period of five years, including 1817–1818, when Furcy's case created a major stir in the colony; a second gap runs from 19 March 1820 until 1 March 1822, when the *Succès* case was tried. It is really a shame not to be able to get Renoyal de Lescouble's take on these events. According to the editor, Norbert Dodille, this lacuna derives from the author's lapse—the entries late in 1815 are less frequent. It seems that he simply lost interest, then resumed in the midst of the cholera epidemic of 1820. Dodille speculates as to whether there might be missing notebooks between the two, but concludes that this is probably not the case (Renoyal de Lescouble, *Journal d'un colon*, xx–xxii).

Additional missing documents include the inventory of the widow Routier's estate and the *échut de partage* in which Furcy was transferred to Joseph Lory, both of which are missing from the double minutes of the Michault d'Emery notary in the Archives Nationales d'Outre-Mer in Aix. That these two documents once existed can be deduced from a later notarized receipt, which mentions both of them: Quittance, Sieurs Routier, and Demoiselle Mansel to Joseph Lory, 30 November 1808, Notariat Michault D'Emery, no. 652 (ANOM DPPC NOT REU1802).

There are no sentences recorded of decisions in Furcy's cases in the official register of the Tribunal of First Instance (1817) or the Royal Court of Bourbon (1818) (Isle Bourbon Cour d'Appel, Jugements Civils 1798–1911, Arrêts civils, 1817–1824 [ANOM 6DPPC2726]).

4. The inventory in the Salle des Inventaires skips over the code that should have been assigned to 1843: Enregistrement au ministère de la Justice, des arrest de la Cour de cassation, 1837–1841 (AN, BB/19/46).

5. The parish registers for Pamplemousses, Isle de France, which should contain Joseph Lory's 1770 baptism, skip from 1766 to 1775 (NARM K: Registres Paroissiaux et D'Etat-Civil: 1721–1810, C: Pamplemousses), though this is more likely due to a natural disaster than human intervention. The carton, which, according to the index in ANOM DPPC NOT REP 6, should contain three estate inventories for Joseph Lory, dated 6 May, 13 May, and 15 October 1839, is missing all but two documents from 1839 (ADR 3E680). However, another copy of the inventory appears as "Inventaire après décès de Joseph Lory" (ADR 3 E 692, no. 284).

6. Hubert Gerbeau, "Les libertés de Bourbon: d'une révolution à une autre," in Wanquet and Julien, *Révolution française et Océan Indien*, 347–360. Gerbeau's early study was popularized in Tristan Picrate, "Un procureur général favorable aux esclaves indiens," *Témoignages*, 1 December 1992, http://archive.is/tXZni. Gerbeau expanded the story in his doctoral thesis: Gerbeau, "L'Esclavage et son ombre," 211–226, 942–948.

7. Arius and Batiskaf, *Liberté plastiK*, and the website http://batiskaf.blogspot.com/2007/09/libert-plastik.html.

8. Aïssaoui, *L'Affaire de l'esclave Furcy*.

9. In addition to those mentioned in the introduction, n. 2, a new play by Francky Lauret "Fer6," was performed by Érick Isana, at Gallodrome de Primat, Saint-Denis, 26 October

2016. Kaf Malbar's song "L'Or de Furcy" ("Furcy's gold") was released in October 2014; http://www.tikreol.re/mizik-lor-de-furcy-chanson-de-kaf-malbar-paroles/.

10. Thankfully, two vibrant genealogical societies in Réunion and Mauritius are working hard to digitize and share knowledge of the islands' family trees. In Réunion especially, the Cercle Généalogique de Bourbon is systematically organizing ancestral records of thousands of slaves and free people of color, a project that—if this book is any indication—offers many blind alleys and much potential for frustration.

11. South Africa, Promotion of National Unity and Reconciliation Act 34 of 1995, available online at http://www.justice.gov.za/legislation/acts/1995-034.pdf.

12. "Libèr nout Furcy dan nout lespri / Son zistwar i fo nout tout i koné / Lès pa li sonbré, I fo pa li fini dan loubli, / Libèr nout Furcy bondié mèrsi. . . . / Marmay dwa konèt son zistwar." Kaf Malbar, "L'Or de Furcy," October 2014, http://www.tikreol.re/mizik-lor-de-furcy-chanson-de-kaf-malbar-paroles/. The lyrics on the website are posted in Réunion Kreol (Rényoné) with a French translation. Thanks to Gilles Dégras for this English translation, which I have modified slightly.

Index

abolition of slavery. *See also* free soil principle
  compensation to owners and, 154–55, 193,
    292nn109–10
  France's Second Republic (1848) and, 1, 193–94,
    305–6n97
  French Revolution (1794–1802) and, 67, 72, 76,
    79, 87, 204n6
  Great Britain's proclamation (1833) affirming,
    154–55, 159, 163, 169–70, 182, 292n110
  in Mauritius (1835), 146, 154–55, 168–70, 176,
    182, 189, 193–94
  in Isle Bourbon (1848), 193–94, 197
  in Saint-Domingue (1793), 72–73, 79, 84
Admiralty Court (France), 33
Aïssaoui, Mohammed, 197, 204n2
Alphonse (slave of Joseph Lory), 121–22
Amélina (granddaughter of Constance),
    xvii, 169
antislavery movements
  British, 140, 150–51, 187, 304n77
  French, 140, 179, 187–88, 193
  World Anti-Slavery Conventions (1840 and
    1842) and, 179
Arnold (grandson of Constance), xvii, 169
Auguste (son of Constance), xvii, 89, 93–94, 159,
    255nn18–19, 258–59n60
Augustine, Olympe Joséphine (daughter of
    Virginie Béga), 104, 114
Azéma, François Paul Étienne, 158

Baco, René Gaston, 81–82
Badale family, 21
Barry, Mademoiselle (land owner in
    Mauritius), 177
Barthe, Félix, 170
Bédier (judge at Royal Court of Isle
    Bourbon), 190
Béga, Virginie

children of, 104–5, 114, 148–49, 156, 168,
    176, 287n69
  death of, 147, 287n60
  free status of, 104–5
  Furcy and, 104–5, 114, 148–49
Bengal. *See also* Boroquichempour,
    Choknossirabat, Chandernagor
  debt bondage in, 19–20
  droughts in, 20, 28
  European colonial and trading presence in,
    12, 15–16
  famines in, 18–20, 28, 217n68
  monsoons and flooding in, 20
  sharecropping in, 20
  slave trade in, 13–14, 185
Bernardin de Saint-Pierre, Jacques-Henri
  on colonial families' "finishing" in
    France, 44–45
  on colonists in Réunion, 44–45
  Lorient described by, 33
  Paul and Virginia by, 29, 31, 42
  on Seven Years' War's impact on French
    colonial culture, 44–45
  on wet nurses, 41–42
Bernier, François, 27
Bertrand, Vincent, 139
Bigge, John Thomas, 151
Bissette, Cyrille, 140, 179, 187, 193
Blair, William, 151
Boroquichempour (Bengal), 16, 21, 24
Boucher, Louis Gilbert
  arrival in Isle Bourbon of, 109
  as attorney general in Corsica, 143, 148,
    150, 166
  as attorney general in Poitiers, 161, 166
  as attorney general in Isle Bourbon,
    107–10, 112–33
  auction of papers (2005) of, 197

Boucher, Louis Gilbert (*Cont.*)
  death and funeral of, 164–65, 177
  departure from Isle Bourbon by, 132–35, 145,
    158, 279n101, 288n64
  on the enslavement of South Asian Indians,
    127–28, 149, 275n23
  on the free soil principle, 127–28
  Furcy's court petition (1817) and, 6, 116–20
  Furcy's freedom suit (1817) and, 121–33
  Furcy's letters (1821–36) to, 136, 141, 143–52,
    162, 165–68, 285n36
  Gillot de l'Étang's conflicts with, 126, 132–34
  Lafitte de Courteuil and, 125
  marriage of, 108, 114
  Michault d'Emery's conflicts with,
    113–14, 131–33
  Panon Desbassayns's conflicts with,
    112–15, 117, 124, 132–34, 158, 197,
    269–70n71, 270n76
  question of assigning a *patron* to Furcy's legal
    proceedings and, 128–30
Boyer, Victor, 93
Brahman caste, 17
British East India Company, 14–15, 18
Brulon, Jean Baptiste, 113, 124
Brunet, Auguste, 175
Brusau, Raymond, 153
Burnel, Etienne, 81–82
Busson, Françoise, 38
Bussy de Saint-Romain, Jean Romain, 109–10,
    112, 167

Cape of Good Hope, 14, 32, 151
Caribbean, the. *See also* Guadeloupe, Martinique,
    Saint-Domingue
  Code Noir (1685) in, 7–8, 55, 236–37n35
  French Revolution and, 76, 81, 84
  manumission in, 84, 252–53n101
  racial hierarchies in, 35, 49–50
  slave revolts (1830s) in, 154
  sugar production in, 69
Catholic Church
  French Revolution and, 72
  record-keeping and, 5
  Restoration Era re-emergence of, 158
  Isle Bourbon and, 52, 54
Cécile (slave belonging to Anne Despense de la
    Loge), 28–29, 35, 46
Champ Borne (Réunion), 195–96
Chandernagor (Bengal)
  Catholic Church in, 17, 215–16n53
  census (1768) in, 24
  famines (1760s) in, 18–19, 28
  interracial marriage in, 16–17

possible existence of nuns during eighteenth
    century in, 24–25
  Seven Years' War and, 18
  slaves in, 16–18, 25
  slave trade restrictions regarding, 36, 224n38
  textile industry in, 16
  threat of British attack (1770s) on, 28
  trade networks in, 15–16
Charles X (king of France), 141, 157–58, 163
Chatelain, Françoise, 40, 52
Chevalier, Jean Baptiste (governor of
    Chandernagor), 18
Choknossirabat (Bengal, 16, 21, 24
Clive, Robert, 18
Code Decaen (French India colonies)
  free persons restricted under, 88
  fugitive slave law under, 88, 117
  inheritance restrictions under, 88, 95
  manumission restrictions under, 88–89, 97, 118
  manumission through military service
    under, 101
  patron required to represent slaves in court
    under, 118, 273n4
  separation of slave parents and children
    prohibited under, 120, 181, 274n16
Code Noir (Caribbean, 1685), 7–8, 55, 236–37n35
Code Noir (Indian Ocean islands, 1723)
  inheritance restrictions in, 57
  interracial marriage ban in, 55–56
  restrictions on disciplining of slaves in, 266n38
  separation of slave parents and children
    prohibited under, 120, 181, 302n46
  slaves' financial rights under, 88, 105
  slaves' right to appeal to court system under,
    118, 273nn1–2
Code Noir (Louisiana, 1724), 55
Coëffard, Maurice, 59
Colbert, Jean Baptiste, 15, 51–52, 233n9
Cole, Lowry, 152–53
Colebrooke, William Macbean George, 151
Commission on Eastern Inquiry (Great Britain,
    1820s), 150–52
Company of the West (*Compagnie d'Occident*), 16
Conil, Pierre, 135, 295n27
Constance (daughter of Madeleine)
  arrests and detentions (1817) of, 130–33, 277n73,
    277–78n81, 279n94, 279n103
  attempt to buy Furcy's freedom (1817) by, 114,
    262–63n103
  birth and baptism of, xvii, 1, 62, 240–41n82
  census (1796) and, 82–83
  claims regarding Madeleine's manumission by,
    70–71, 84–85, 97
  death of, xvii, 168, 297n58

Duperier's alliance with, 114, 116
estate of, 168–69
Furcy's court petition (1817) and, 116–20, 161,
    169, 261n79, 273–74n5
Furcy's freedom suit (1817) and, 121–26,
    129–34, 169
historical silences regarding, 64, 66, 70
landholdings of, 103, 159
manumission (1786) of, 10, 62–64, 66, 84, 194
marriage of, 89, 94, 113, 258n55
naming of, 63
paternity of, 62–65, 71, 89, 94
possible descendants in Champ Borne
    (Réunion) of, 195–96
Routiers as godparents of, 62, 240–41n82
slaves owned by, 62, 64, 66, 94, 99, 155, 159,
    241n91, 264n13, 293n13
testimony on behalf of Furcy by, 9, 24, 60,
    70–71, 96, 100
Vetter's ownership of, 62
widowhood of, 114, 117, 119
Corsica, 148
Court of Cassation (Paris)
Bissette affair and, 140
damages awarded to Furcy at, 174, 177,
    180, 186
Dupin as attorney general at, 161,
    163–64, 295n23
on the free soil principle, 162–63, 170,
    172–74, 185
Furcy's case (1835–40) before, 161–64, 166,
    169–75, 180, 182–83, 185
Le Gonidec as judge on, 161
Royal Court of Paris's affirmation (1843) of
    Furcy ruling of, 186
ruling in favor of Furcy (1840) at, 172–75, 180
créole (island-born) populations
elite members of, 2, 40, 100–101, 109, 113, 124,
    132, 135–36, 156
in Mauritius, 136
racial categories complicated by, 7–8,
    53–55, 70
in Isle Bourbon, 7–8, 53–55, 70
in slavery, 7, 34, 50, 54, 235n25
Cuba, 84

Dauphine (slave of Constance), 103
debt bondage, 12–13, 19–20, 183
Decaen, Charles, 88, 90
Declaration of 15 December 1738. *See under* free
    soil principle
Declaration of the Rights of Man and Citizen
    (1789), 71
deeds of sale *(cawbowla* or *kabolah),* 14, 22

de las Casas, Bartholomé, 7
Delaunay, Pierre Auguste, 125
Desblottières, Augustin Louis, captain, 29, 32, 37
Desblottières, Jean Louis Gilles, xviii
Desblottières, Marie Anne Ursule. *See* Routier,
    Marie Anne Ursule née Desblottières
Desblottières, Marie, née Panon, xviii,
    42–44, 227n65
Despense de la Loge, Anne
arrival in Chandernagor of, 17
biographical background of, 17
Catholicism of, 17–18, 26, 46, 186
census of Chandernagor (1768) and,
    24, 215n48
in France, 1, 33, 35–37
Madeleine as slave of, 1, 12, 17–18, 20, 25–32,
    35–37, 289n84
Madeleine sold, gifted, or transferred by, 1–2,
    37–38, 46–47, 70, 119, 122, 128, 135, 144–45,
    170–71, 173, 181–83, 185–86, 274n7
physical appearance of, 27
possible residence in a convent or uncloistered
    community, 24, 46–47, 144, 231n104
voyage to France (1771) by, 28–33, 48
Desrieux, Maurice, 169, 190
Dioré, Joseph, 154, 291n104
Douyère, Félicité Constance, 63
Dubouchage, Vicomte (minister of the navy), 107
Dufresne (slave owner in Isle Bourbon), 79–80
Duparc, Joseph Boulley, 124, 280–81n110
Duperier, Adolphe
arrest (1817) of, 130, 278n82
Constance's alliance with, 114, 116
education of, 114, 116
Furcy's court petition (1817) and, 114, 116–117
Furcy's freedom suit (1817) and, 121–22, 130
Dupin, André, 161, 163–66, 185, 295n23
Dupleix, Joseph François, 17
Dupont, Demoiselle (resident of Mauritius), 63
Duras, Claire de, 4
Dutch East India Company, 15
Duverger, Célerine
Constance's residence with, 114, 117
family history and biographical background of,
    265n32, 271–72n85
Furcy's freedom suit (1817) and, 121–22,
    124, 130
Virginie as daughter of, 104, 121, 147,
    265–66n33, 287n60

Edict of October 1716. *See under* free soil
    principle
Elisa (slave of Constance), 94, 103, 293n13
emancipation. *See* abolition of slavery

Eraste, Benoît, 75

Eraste, Eugène, 75–76

Eraste, Perrine, 75–76

Eugène (son of Constance), xvii, 89, 94, 166

Euphémie, Jean Baptiste

  biographical background of, 94

  Constance's marriage to, 89, 94, 113, 258n55

  death of, 114, 116, 271n82

  land and slaves owned by, 103, 159, 264n13

Euphrosine (slave of Constance), 94

Faciolle, Claude Louis, 93

famines

  in Bengal, 18–20, 28, 217n68

  in France, 19–20

  in Mauritius, 39

  in Isle Bourbon, 60, 90–91

Farquhar, General (British governor of Mauritius
    and Réunion), 102

Faustino Santiago (slave owner), 11, 23–24,
    26, 171

Fédière, Gabriel Auguste, 126–27, 129, 133

Félix (slave of Lory family), 152, 290n88, 300n22

Floriancia (slave manumitted by Lory
    family), 152

Francisque case (Parlement of Paris, 1759), 36

François, Claude, 78

free persons *(libres)*

  libre de droit (free by law) and, 92, 154,
    182, 184

  libre de fait (free in fact) and, 92, 154, 184

  in Mauritius, 8, 55, 154–55, 157, 159–60, 165–68,
    172, 177, 189–90, 194, 198–99, 292n111

  restrictions regarding, 57, 88

  in Isle Bourbon, 8, 45, 54–56, 62, 70, 81, 90, 92,
    109–10, 130, 194, 246n20, 268–69n60

  slaves owned by, 62, 64, 66, 94, 99, 155, 156, 193,
    292n111

free soil principle

  Declaration of 15 December 1738 and, 35, 123,
    128, 170, 173, 182–83, 185

  defining the terms of, 2, 33–34, 233n27

  Edict of October 1716 and, 35, 123, 170

  free persons who return to colonial territories
    and, 127–28

  French Revolution and, 80, 123

  Furcy's Court of Cassation case (1835–40) and,
    162–63, 170, 172–74, 185

  Furcy's freedom suit (1817) and, 122–24, 126–28

  Furcy's Mauritius petition (1826) and, 145,
    149, 152–53

  Furcy's Royal Court of Paris case (1841–3) and,
    180–83, 185–86

  legal cases regarding, 2, 36

Madeleine's time in France and, 120, 122, 149,
    162–63, 170, 180–83, 185

Ordinance of 29 April 1836, 165, 174, 290n96

Police des Noirs (Policing of the Blacks) Law
    (1777) and, 46, 123

Restoration Era changes regarding, 123

Somerset case (Great Britain, 1772) and, 140

French East India Company

  founding of, 15

  Madagascar and, 15

  Mauritius and, 38–39

  merger with other trading companies (1719)
    and, 16

  Isle Bourbon and, 51–54, 56–57

  slave trade and, 36, 52–55, 185, 303n67

French Revolution

  abolition of slavery (1794–1802) and, 67, 72, 76,
    79, 87, 204n6

  Catholic Church suppressed during, 72

  Code Decaen in French India colonies during,
    88–89, 95, 97, 101, 120

  Declaration of the Rights of Man and Citizen
    (1789) and, 71

  free soil principle codified (1791) during,
    80, 123

  Isle Bourbon/Réunion and, 67, 69, 72, 76–78,
    81–82, 87

  Jacobin regime during, 72

  Napoleonic Civil Code and, 8, 87–88, 118,
    176, 247n31

  Saint-Domingue Revolution and, 3, 71–73, 76,
    79–82, 102, 247n27

  slavery reintroduced (1802) during, 84, 87

  Treaty of Amiens (1802) and, 87

  voting rights extended to freeborn peoples of
    color (1791) and, 79

Furcy (son of Madeleine)

  basic literacy skills developed by, 141, 167

  birth certificate and, 176

  birth of, xvii, 1–2, 64

  Boucher as recipient of letters (1821–36) from,
    136, 143–52, 162, 165–68, 285n36

  children of Virginie Béga and, 104–5, 114, 148–49,
    156, 168, 176

  children with Zulmée Maulgué and,
    176–77, 198

  compensation during slavery's abolition for, 155,
    292n110

  confectionery businesses in Mauritius of, 154,
    157, 159, 167–68, 172, 177

  Constance's attempt to buy freedom of, 114,
    262–63n103

  Court of Cassation case (1835–40) involving,
    46, 161–64, 166, 169–75, 180, 182–83, 185

daily conditions in slavery of, 92–93, 105–6

death of, xvii, 198

freedom suit (1817) and, 1–2, 7, 121–35, 141,
161–62, 169, 174, 181, 183, 196, 281n111

as free person in Mauritius, 154–57, 159–60,
162, 165–70, 172, 177, 189–90, 194, 198–99,
290n96, 290n98

free soil principle as basis for freedom claims
by, 122–24, 126–28, 145, 149, 152–53, 162–63,
170, 172–74, 185

historical silences regarding, 196–98,
306–7n3

imprisonment (1817) of, 125, 130, 134–35,
281–82n121

land in Mauritius purchased by, 167–68, 177

as Lory family slave, 1–2, 92–93, 96–100,
103–6, 114, 119, 135–38, 141,
143–53, 151, 160, 166, 183, 188–92,
260–61n77, 282n1

Madeleine's attempts to buy freedom of, 2, 95,
97–100, 104, 112, 119, 152

marriage to Zulmé Malgué of, 172, 176

naming of, 65

paternity of, 6–7, 64–65, 71, 106, 149–50, 164

patron in the suit (1817) of, 128–29, 134

petition (1817) in Isle Bourbon of, 24, 114,
116–20, 161–62, 169, 261n79, 273–74n5

petition (1826) to governor of Mauritius of, 145,
149, 152–53, 290n92

physical appearance of, 65

popular culture portrayals of, 1, 195, 197–99,
203–4n2

return to Mauritius (1835) by, 164–65

as Routier family slave, 1, 66, 69, 86, 92, 94,
119, 183

Royal Court of Bourbon appeal case (1818)
and, 134–35, 162, 172–73, 175, 281n114,
281n119

Royal Court of Isle Bourbon appeal (1845)
by, 188–90

Royal Court of Isle Bourbon award of damages
to, 190–92

Royal Court of Paris case (1841–3) and, 2–3,
163, 174–76, 179–88, 196

settlement of Royal Court of Paris case
and, 176–78

slaves owned by, 155–56

sugar plantation work by, 145–46, 189–90

travel to France (1835) by, 161

Virginie Béga as companion of, 104–5,
114, 148–49

Galbaud-Dufort, François Thomas, 79

Galdemar, Simon Julien, 296n50

Gamin, Pierre, 93, 138–39, 159, 294n15, 300n23

Garrison, William Lloyd, 187, 304n74

Génève, Auguste, 147

Georges (slave of Constance), 94, 103

Gérard, Gilles, 195

Gerbeau, Hubert, 197

Gillot de l'Étang, Nicholas Pierre, 40

Gillot de l'Étang, François Xavier Aimé
as assistant public prosecutor in Isle Bourbon,
112, 126–29, 132–34, 269n66
Boucher's conflicts with, 126, 132–34
on the enslavement of South Asian Indians,
126, 128
on the free soil principle, 127
Furcy's freedom suit (1817) and,
126–29, 132–34
question of assigning a patron to Furcy's legal
proceedings and, 128–29

Godard de Saponay, Camille
Furcy's case at Court of Cassation and, 162–63,
170–71, 173
Furcy's case at Royal Court of Paris
and, 175–77
Isle Bourbon case precedents involving Furcy
and, 162–63

Great Britain
abolitionist movement in, 140, 150–51,
187, 304n77
Commission on Eastern Inquiry (1820s)
in, 150–52
India trading networks of, 12, 15
Napoleonic Wars and, 76, 79, 87–88, 101
Réunion and Mauritius occupied (1810–1815)
by, 76, 101–2
Seven Years' War and, 18
slavery abolished (1833) by, 154–55, 159, 163,
169–70, 182, 292n110
slave trade and, 13–14, 21
slave trade banned (1807) by, 102,
139, 263n4
Somerset case (1772) in, 140

Guadeloupe, 56, 72, 76, 84, 237n38

Guiana, 35, 56

Guizot, François Pierre Guillaume, 192

Haiti. *See* Saint-Domingue

Hébert, Michel, 184–85, 302n54, 303n57

Hector, 29–33

Hickey, William, 29

Hindus and Hinduism, 13, 17–18, 21–22, 170

Hippolyte (fugitive slave), 147

Hirne (lawyer), 98

Honoré (leader of slave appeal in
Réunion), 79–80

Huard, Étienne Toussaint
  as bailiff receiving Furcy's freedom petition,
    116, 278n87
  dismissal from job of, 130
  Furcy's freedom writ (1817) and, 121–22,
    124, 130–31
  Lory's charges against, 130

Imogène (slave of Constance), 103
India Company (Compagnie des Indes), 15, 16
Indians (of South Asian origin)
  legality of enslavement of, 2, 7, 14, 34–36, 119–
    20, 123–30, 149, 152, 170, 173, 180, 183, 185,
    224n41, 275n23, 302n44, 303n57
  residents of France, 276n53
  residents of the "black towns" of French
    India, 21
  residents of Isle Bourbon, 55, 67
Indians (of the Americas),
  banned enslavement in French colonies, 36, 183,
    185, 303n67, 224n41
  banned enslavement of in Spanish America, 7
  Code Noir and, 236n35, 276n53
  intermarriage with French men, 234n18, 237n38,
    288n71
Irogine (slave of Constance), 169, 293n13, 297n60
Isambert, François André, 158, 161, 294n22
Islam
  French colonial laws regarding, 55
  purdah and, 14–15
  Shari'a law and, 13, 17, 120
  slave ownership and, 14, 55
Isle Bonaparte (1806–10). See Isle Bourbon and
    Réunion
Isle Bourbon (Réunion). See also Réunion (1794–
    1810 and 1848 to present)
  agriculture and ecology of, 4, 49, 51–53, 58–59,
    64, 67, 69, 73, 91, 110
  British occupation (1810–15) of, 76, 101–2
  categories of slaves in, 55
  Catholic culture in, 52, 54
  census requiring skin color (1840) in, 178, 180
  Code Decaen and, 88–89, 95, 97, 101, 117, 120
  Code Noir (1724) and, 55–56
  colonial assembly's resolution against
    emancipation (1796) and, 81–82
  colonial elite in, 40, 44–45, 108, 110, 112, 124–
    25, 132, 135, 156
  créole (native-born) population in, 2, 53–55, 70,
    100–101, 109, 113, 124, 132, 135, 156
  cyclones and extreme weather in, 60–61, 78,
    90–91, 110, 196, 240n70
  droughts in, 61, 64, 75, 78, 87, 90–91

economic and agricultural crises (1790s)
    in, 77–78
  famines in, 60, 90–91
  first settlement (1662) at, 50–51
  France's abolition of slavery (1794) and,
    79, 81, 87
  free people (libres) in, 8, 45, 54–56, 62, 70, 81,
    90, 92, 109–10, 130, 194, 246n20, 268–69n60
  French citizenship laws via marriage and, 56–57
  French East India Company's role in settling,
    51–54, 56–57
  French laws regarding manumission and, 57
  French Revolution and, 67, 69, 72, 76–78,
    81–82, 87
  fugitive slave law (1804) in, 88
  gender imbalance among colonial settlers in,
    45, 51–52, 59
  gender imbalance among slaves on, 61
  geology of, 50
  interracial marriage and, 52, 54, 56–57
  judicial reform in, 101, 107, 112–13
  lack of protected harbor at, 32, 49
  La Fournaise volcanic eruption (1791)
    and, 76–77
  manumission restrictions in, 77–78, 87
  maroon (fugitive slave) communities in,
    68, 72, 87
  measles outbreak (1824) in, 146
  orders against interracial marriage
    (1689–1767) in, 56
  racial and ethnic diversity of population on,
    50–53, 55, 67
  slave revolt (1811) in, 103
  slaves and slavery in, 14, 34, 41, 43, 45, 49, 52–
    53, 55, 58–61, 64, 66–70, 72, 77–81, 85–94,
    101, 110, 112, 120, 126–27, 156, 166, 180, 263n5
  slaves' descendants in, 193
  slave smuggling in, 138–39
  slave trade and, 22, 34, 53–55, 61, 64, 66, 76, 102,
    126, 138–39
  slave trade suspended (1794) in, 77
  sugar production in, 4, 69, 73, 101–2, 110, 157,
    159–60, 179
Isle de France (1715–1810) /Isle Maurice. See
    Mauritius

Jacobin regime (French Revolution), 72
Jams, Montendre Adam, 90, 93
Jams Adam, Marie Anne Vincente Calixtine, 93,
    257n48, 259–60n72
Janot (slave belonging to Despense), 28–29, 35,
    46–47, 231n101
Jean Baptiste (son of Constance), 169, 306n2

Jeanneton (slave belonging to Routier family), 44

Jeannot (slave belonging to Routier family)
  continued residence with widow Routier of, 92
  in France, 44, 232n1
  manumission of, 69–70, 73, 92, 95, 245n18,
    246n19, 246n23
  post-manumission pension of, 95,
    97–98, 246n19

Jean Pierre (free man in Isle Bourbon), 80

Jennings, Lawrence, 179

Joséphine (daughter of Constance), xvii, 114, 116,
    169, 271n82

Judith (daughter of Constance), xvii, 169, 306n2

July Monarchies era (1830–48)
  direct elections to colonial councils established
    during, 158
  establishment of new government (1830)
    and, 158
  free soil principle expanded during, 165, 185–86
  liberal reforms and legal codes' decreasing
    emphasis on race during, 8, 158, 161
  slave trade suppressed during, 160

Justine Siahime (servant of widow Lory), 146,
    286n54, 300n22

Kaf Malbar, 197, 199

Karikal (French trading post in India), 18,
    21–23, 36

Kermorseven, Leroux, 63

Kopytoff, Igor, 6

Kshatriya caste, 17

L'Affaire de l'esclave Furcy (Aïssaoui), 197, 204n2

"L'Or de Furcy [Furcy's Gold]" (Kaf Malbar), 199

La Barre de Nanteuil, Auguste de, 188

Lafitte du Courteil, Hilaire Urbain de, 108, 110,
    125, 131–33

Landes, Matthieu des, 63

La Salle, Antoine, 43

Launay de la Perrière, Jacques Marie Hyacinthe de,
    275–76n40

Ladérouille, Chouchou (slave of Furcy), 155

Le Gonidec de Kerdaniel, Joseph Julian, 108, 148,
    161–62, 165, 267n50, 288n67

Levillin-Desrabines, Matthieu, 81

Lescouble, Renoyal de, 104

Letters patent in the form of edict (1723). *See*
    Code Noir (Indian Ocean islands, 1724)

libre de droit (free by law). *See under* free persons
    (libres)

libre de fait (free in fact). *See under* free persons
    (libres)

Lorient (France), 33

Lory, Adolphe
  compensation during slavery's abolition for, 155,
    193, 292n109
  Furcy as slave of, 137–38
  land and wealth of, 179
  marriage of, 287n56
  move to Isle Bourbon (1826) by, 146–47,
    287n56, 287n62
  sugar enterprises of, 300n23

Lory, André Jr., 74, 76, 282n4

Lory, André Sr., 74, 249n46, 249n47, 250n50,
    282n4, 282–83n6

Lory, Arthur (nephew of Joseph Lory),
    179, 300n23

Lory, Edouard
  Floriancia manumitted by, 152
  Furcy freed on legal technicality by, 153–54
  land and wealth in Isle Bourbon of, 179–80,
    287n58, 300n23
  Lory family plantation in Mauritius and, 146,
    151, 153, 287n58

Lory, Marie Charles Eugénie ("Eugénie") née
    Routier
  birth and baptism of, xviii, 48, 59, 100
  census (1784) and, 61
  damages to Furcy (1845) paid by, 190–92
  education of, 66
  Furcy as slave of, 1–2, 92–93, 96–100, 103–6,
    114, 119, 135–37, 146, 151, 160, 166, 183, 188–
    92, 260–61n77, 282n1
  Furcy's lawsuit at Royal Court of Isle Bourbon
    (1845) against, 188, 190
  inheritance of, 96, 160, 172, 191, 260n74
  marriage of, 74–76, 159, 250n51
  in Isle Bourbon, 48, 57–59
  Saint-Denis townhouse of, 191–92
  settlement of Furcy's Royal Court of Paris case
    and, 176–78
  widowhood of, 171, 178

Lory, Henry (nephew of Joseph Lory),
    179, 300n23

Lory, Jeanne Marguerite née Malvezy (sister-in-
    law of Joseph Lory)
  compensation during slavery's abolition for, 155
  land and slaveholdings of, 178–79, 291n108
  marriage to André Lory, 282n4
  move to Isle Bourbon by, 146–47, 152, 286n53

Lory, Jeanne Perrine née Bertin, 74

Lory, Jenny, 146

Lory, Joseph Marie
  birth of, xviii, 74
  Court of Cassation case by Furcy (1835–40)
    against, 164, 169–71, 174

Lory, Joseph Marie (*Cont.*)
  Court of Cassation damages (1840) assessed
    against, 174, 177, 180, 186
  death of, xviii, 171
  estate of, 171–72
  Furcy as slave of, 1–2, 92–93, 96–100, 103–6,
    114, 119, 135–37, 146, 151, 160, 166, 183, 188–
    92, 260–61n77
  Furcy's freedom petition (1817) and,
    11–12, 116–19
  Furcy's freedom suit (1817) and, 121–25,
    129–31, 175, 182
  Furcy transferred to Mauritius by, 135–36,
    188–89, 282n1
  landholdings and business dealings of, 78, 90,
    93, 98, 104, 159–60, 167, 294nn14–15
  Madeleine deceived and cheated by, 2, 96–100,
    114, 116, 119, 124, 130, 188
  Madeleine's bills of sale and, 1, 22, 24–26, 99,
    169, 171
  marriage of, 74–76, 159, 250n51
  Mauritius plantation of, 136–37, 291n106
  question of sexual relations with slaves and,
    75–76, 178
  Royal Court of Bourbon appeal of Furcy case
    (1818) and, 135
  Royal Court of Isle Bourbon verdict (1845)
    favoring, 188–90
  Royal Court of Paris appeal case (1841–3)
    involving, 183–84
  sale of Furcy to Adolphe Lory and, 137–38
  slave smuggling by, 138–39
  slaves purchased owned by, 89, 93, 102, 104,
    160, 263n6
  widow Routier and, 86, 92, 95–96
Lory, Jules (nephew of Joseph Lory), 159,
  299n15, 300n23
Lory, Marie Charlette Augustine Euphémie
  ("Euphémie"), 75, 160, 294nn19–20
Lory, Marie Charlotte Eugénie, 75
Lory, Perrine Jeanne, 65, 74, 249n47
Lory, Thomy, 179, 286n47, 300n23
Louisiana, 42, 49–50, 55–56
Louis Philippe (king of France), 158, 192, 293n8
Louis XIV (king of France), 15, 35, 51, 238n42
Louis XV (king of France), 31, 36, 55–56
Louis XVI (king of France), 72, 163
Louverture, Toussaint, 9, 79
Luce, Anne, 90, 93–94, 98

Mackau laws (1845), 187–88
Madagascar. *See also* Malagasy populations
  early failure of French settlement at, 51
  French East India Company and, 15

revolt (1662) in, 50, 232n5
  slave trade and, 34, 73
Madeleine (mother of Furcy and Constance)
  attempts to buy Furcy's freedom by, 2, 95,
    97–100, 104, 112, 119, 152
  bills of sale (1762 and 1768) for, 1, 11–12, 22,
    24–26, 169, 171
  birth of, xvii, 2, 11, 209n7
  Catholicism and, 12, 17–18, 26, 186
  childhood of, 12, 17, 25–26
  death of, xvii, 104, 119
  Despense as owner of, 1, 12, 17–18, 20, 25–32,
    35–37, 289n84
  in France, 1, 33, 35–37, 149
  free soil principle applied to case of, 120, 122,
    149, 162–63, 170, 180–83, 185
  French language skills of, 26
  illiteracy of, 25, 98, 100
  Lory's deception and cheating of, 2, 96–100,
    114, 116, 119, 124, 130, 188
  manumission (1789) of, 2, 10, 37, 67, 69–
    70, 73, 92, 95, 97, 100, 119–20, 135, 183,
    185, 188, 245–46n18, 246n19, 261n82,
    281n111, 289n84
  manumission hidden from (1789–1808), 2, 70–
    71, 85, 97, 119–20
  naming of, 12
  paternity of children of, 59–60, 62–65, 71, 89,
    94, 106
  physical appearance of, 27, 60, 65, 220n95
  possible baptism of, 12, 17–18
  as possible sexual partner to Charles Routier
    and, 47–48, 60, 62–65, 71, 89
  post-manumission pension of, 2, 70–71,
    95–97, 100, 114, 119, 188, 246n19
  reclaimed as slave (1796) and, 67, 82–85
  as Routier family slave, 38, 47–48, 58–60,
    62–66, 69, 100, 119
  sale or transfer to Routier family of, 1–2, 37–38,
    46–47, 70, 119, 122, 128, 135, 144–45,
    170–71, 173, 181–83, 185–86, 274n7
  voyage to France (1771–2) by, 28–33, 48, 162
  as wet nurse, 47, 60
Madeleine, Furcy. *See* Furcy (son of Madeleine)
Madeleine, Louise Furcy (daughter of Furcy),
  177, 299n7
Madeleine, Marie Euridice (daughter of Furcy),
  177, 299n7
Mahé
  bills of sale from, 21–23
  slave trade and, 36
  Topas community in, 24
  Treaty of Paris (1763) preserving French trading
    post at, 18

Mahé de la Bourdonnais, Bertrand François, 31

Malagasy populations
as free men, 8, 34, 50–52, 57
in Mauritius, 31
in Isle Bourbon, 34, 57, 67, 89–90, 126–27
as slaves, 34, 73, 90, 126–27

Mancel, Claudine, 252n100

Manuel (slave in Isle Bourbon), 80

manumission. *See also* abolition of slavery; free soil principle
children and, 57, 86, 89, 120, 170, 180–81, 255n16
Code Decaen restrictions regarding, 88–89, 97, 118
Constance and, 10, 62–64, 66, 84, 194
French laws regarding, 57, 158, 254n13, 255n14, 257n40
global patterns regarding, 85–86
Madeleine and, 2, 10, 37, 67, 69–70, 73, 92, 95, 97, 100, 119–20, 135, 183, 185, 188, 245–46n18, 246n19, 261n82, 281n111, 289n84
Isle Bourbon's restrictions regarding, 77–78, 87
slaves' own purchasing of, 86, 255n14
women *versus* men in, 85–86

Maque (slave of Routier family), 82

Marie Anne Nelcine (daughter of Virginie Béga), 104

Marie Jeanne (wet nurse for Boucher family), 134, 272n95

Martial Égiste (slave of Adolphe Lory), 147, 287n62, 300n22

Martinique
Bissette affair in, 140–41
French Revolution and, 76
interracial marriages and, 56
slavery formally re-established (1802) in, 87
slave trade in, 36

Mascarin Island. *See* Isle Bourbon

Maulgué, Zulmé, 172, 176–77, 198

Maurice (son of Madeleine)
birth of, xvii, 1, 59
death of, xvii, 101, 249n44, 263n2
paternity of, 59–60
as Routier family slave, 66, 69, 74, 86, 94, 96, 249n44, 260n76

Mauritius (Isle de France)
abolition of slavery (1835) in, 146, 154–55, 168–70, 176, 182, 189, 193–94
agitation against abolition of slavery (1796) in, 81–82, 85
British occupation (1810–4) of, 76, 101–2
British rule (after 1814) of, 101, 136, 139, 161, 163
Civil Status Act of 1981 and, 198

Code Noir (Indian Ocean islands, 1724) and, 55–56
colonial assembly's resolution against emancipation (1796) in, 81
Commission on Eastern Inquiry and, 151
créole elite in, 136
cyclones and extreme weather in, 60, 78, 90, 145, 147, 240n70
Dutch control (before 1710) of, 31
famine (1750s) in, 39
free persons *(libres)* in, 8, 55, 154–55, 157, 159–60, 165–68, 172, 177, 189–90, 194, 198–99, 292n111
French control established (1721) in, 31
French East India Company and, 38–39
gender imbalance in settlement at, 32
interracial sexual relationships and, 63, 75–76
Lory family holdings in, 136–38, 143, 145–47
manumissions suspended (1800) in, 87
maroon population in, 31
post-abolition apprentice system in, 155
racial and ethnic diversity of population on, 50
slaves and slavery in, 14, 31–32, 41, 63, 87, 135–38, 141, 143–49, 151–55
slaves' descendants in, 193
slave smuggling in, 136, 153
slave trade and, 77, 102, 136, 153
smallpox epidemic (1757) in, 39
sugar production in, 4, 68, 102, 135–36, 138, 145, 157, 189–90
trial of *Succès* ship owners (1821) in, 139

Michault d'Emery, Pierre Hippolyte
Boucher's conflicts with, 113–14, 131–33
Constance interrogated by, 130–32
on the enslavement of South Asian Indians, 127
on the free soil principle, 127
Furcy's freedom suit (1817) and, 125–33, 280–81n110, 281n111
Madeleine's attempt to purchase Furcy's freedom and, 98, 112, 130
question of assigning a patron to Furcy's legal proceedings and, 128–29
as royal prosecutor in Isle Bourbon, 112–13, 125–33
widow Routier's estate and, 95–96

Miers, Suzanne, 6

Milius, Pierre Bernard, 135, 280n106

Miskīn (author of slave autobiography from Afghanistan), 25

Moreau, Émile, 169–70, 182, 302n46

Moresby, Fairfax, 139

Mourgue, Jules, 11, 26, 138, 169

Mughal Empire, 15

Napoléon
blacks banned from entering France under, 107, 123
civil code (1804) and, 8, 87–88, 118, 176, 247n31
defeat (1814) of, 101
Napoléon III (emperor of France), 193
Netherlands
impressment of sailors and, 23
India trading networks of, 12, 15, 51
Mauritius and, 31, 101
slave trade and, 21
"Notes written under the dictation of Furcy" document (1830s), 96–97

Ogerdias family, 29
Ourika (Duras), 4

Paillet, Alphonse Gabriel Victor, 182–84, 188–89, 301–2n40
Pajot, Jean Baptiste, 122, 158
Panon, Augustin, 39–40, 52
Panon, Françoise, xviii, 39–40
Panon Desbassayns, Henri Paulin, 40
Panon Desbassayns, Joseph, 113
Panon Desbassayns de Richmont, Philippe
arrival in Isle Bourbon of, 109
Boucher's conflicts with, 112–15, 117, 124, 132–34, 158, 197, 269–70n71, 270n76
as commissioner general of Isle Bourbon, 26, 108, 112–13, 115, 124–25, 130–35, 167
on Constance and Duperier, 116
Constance arrested and detained on orders by, 130–32, 277–78n81, 277n73
Constance interrogated by, 132
Furcy's freedom suit (1817) and, 12, 26, 124–25, 130–35
Sully Brunet dismissed from office by, 131–32
Sully Brunet's conflict with, 113, 270n77, 270–71n79
widow Routier's estate and, 96
Panon Desbassayns, Charles, 102, 108
Panon Desblottières, Marie. *See* Desblottières, Marie, née Panon
Panon-Lamare, Joseph, 40
Paria caste, 22, 170
Paris Commune of 1871, 197
Parlement of Paris, 36
Patterson, Orlando, 6
Paul and Virginia (Saint-Pierre), 31, 42
Pauline (mulatto child born to Lory family slaves), 104, 178, 265n23
Petitpas (lawyer for Furcy), 134, 175, 181–82, 280n109

Phélypeaux, Jérôme, 35
Piccart, Antoine, 32
Pierre Louis (slave in Isle Bourbon), 80–81
Pillai, Anandaranga, 22–23
Pitois, Louis Antoine, 130, 132
Police des Noirs (Policing of the Blacks) Law (France, 1777), 46, 123
Polverel, Etienne, 79
Pondichéry
slave trade restrictions regarding, 36, 77, 224n38, 251n70
Treaty of Paris (1763) preserving French trading post at, 18
Ursuline community of nuns in, 24–25
Pontchartrain, Jérôme de, 276n58
Port Louis (capital of Mauritius), 142
Portugal
India settlements and trading networks of, 12, 15, 51
slave trade and, 11, 14, 23–25, 55, 212n22
Pouliat caste, 170
Poulichi caste, 170
Prévost de la Croix, Eugène, 125, 129, 134
purdah, 14–15

Quakers, 140

race
black (*nègre* or *noir*) and, 4, 7, 27, 35–36, 50, 54
créole category as complication for, 7–8, 53–55, 70
Enlightenment scientists and, 27
French civil laws regarding, 49–50
hierarchy reinforced through, 35–36, 56–57, 155–56
indiens and, 27, 35–36
libres (free people of color) and, 4
parish records regarding, 57
Isle Bourbon census requiring skin color (1840) and, 178, 180
white (*blanc*) and, 4, 7, 27, 50, 54, 57
Rathier-Duvergé, Anne Adélaïde, 74, 248n38
Rathier-Duvergé, Thérèse Agnès, 74, 248n38
Restoration Era France (1815–48)
abolitionist movement in, 140
Catholic Church in, 158
colonial legal reform and, 101, 107–8
constitutional monarchy in, 150
free soil principle and, 123
interracial marriage ban lifted (1818) in, 107
legal codes' decreasing emphasis on race during, 8, 118
patronage politics in, 150

restrictions on slave mobility implemented
during, 141
slave trade ban during, 106–7
Réunion (1794–1806 and 1848 to the present).
See also: Isle Bourbon
departmental archives of, 9, 25, 26, 195, 197
location and governmental organization of, x,
xiii, 1, 30, 88, 111
post-emancipation conditions (after 1848),
193–194
recent memory of Furcy in, 196–199
renamed again during France's Second Republic
(1848), 193
revolutionary events (1794–1806) in, 72,
77–82, 85, 87, 90
Revolution of 1848 (France), 192–93
Richard, Jean Daniel Renaud, 168, 172
Ricquebourg, Louis, 79–80
Rosaire, Alexandre de, 24
Rosamel, Claude Charles Marie du Campe de, 170
Rosa Sylvie (slave of Lory family), 152,
290n88, 300n22
Rougevin, Monsieur (friend of Furcy in
Mauritius), 143, 162, 285n34
Rousseau, Louis, 32
Roussette, Jean, 32
Roussin, Albin, 179–80
Routier, Charles François Augustin ("Augustin")
birth of, xviii, 41
census (1784) and, 61
damages to Furcy delivered (1845) by, 190–91
divorce and remarriage of, 74,
248n38, 249n40
in France, 44
Furcy as possible slave of, 183, 188–89,
260–61n77
inheritance of, 96, 99, 183, 188–89
landholdings and business dealings of, 66,
86, 89, 91
marriage of, 74
slaves purchased and owned by, 89–90
on Sully Brunet, 132
Routier, Charles (son of Augustin Routier),
xviii, 74
Routier, Cyrille
birth of, xviii, 41
census (1784) and, 61
death of, xviii, 146, 286n52
education of, 66
in France, 44
inheritance of, 96, 260n74
landholdings and business dealings of, 74,
78, 89, 91
marriage of, 74, 248n38

slaves purchased and owned by, 89–90,
96, 101–2
Routier, Charles Marie Élie ("Élie," son of
Charles Routier), xviii, 59–61, 93, 257n48,
259–60n72
Routier, Marie Joseph Élie Louise (daughter of
Charles Routier), xviii, 41, 44–45
Routier, Marie Charles Euphémie ("Éuphémie")
birth and baptism of, xviii, 59
census (1784) and, 61
Constance as goddaughter of, 62, 240–41n82
death of, xviii, 75
education of, 66
in Réunion, 59
Routier, Augustin Marie François ("François"),
xviii, 41
Routier, Françoise Marguerite, xviii, 40–41
Routier, Jean Nicholas (*père*), xviii, 38–39, 47, 59,
64, 226n52, 243n103
Routier, Jean Nicholas François ("Fauchin"), xviii,
45, 59, 61, 66, 230n97
Routier, Marie Anne Ursule Desblottières (widow
Routier)
death of, xviii, 2, 10, 95
dowries as means of perpetuating family wealth
of, 73–74
estate of, 95–97, 99, 160, 183
in France, 44, 46
Furcy claimed as slave of, 86
inheritances of, 43–44, 66, 73, 229–30n81
investments of, 78
Madeleine as slave of, 38, 47–48, 58–60,
62–66, 100
Madeleine manumitted by, 2, 10, 37, 67,
69–70, 73, 92, 95, 97, 100, 119–20, 135,
183, 185, 188, 245–46n18, 246n19, 261n82,
281n111, 289n84
Madeleine purchased by or transferred to, 1–2,
37–38, 46–47, 70, 119, 122, 128, 135, 144, 170–
71, 173, 181–83, 185–86, 274n7
Madeleine reclaimed as slave (1796) by,
67, 82–85
Madeleine's manumission hidden (1789–1808)
by, 2, 70–71, 85, 97, 119–20
marriage of, xviii, 39, 227–28n65
move to Saint-Denis by, 82
slaves of, 43–44, 61, 66, 89, 91
stepchildren of, 41
wet nurses of, 41, 60
Routier, Marie Élie, xviii, 39
Routier, Marie Euphrasie, xviii, 39
Routier de Granval, Charles Gabriel
birth of, xviii, 38
Constance as godchild of, 62, 240–41n82

Routier de Granval, Charles Gabriel (*Cont.*)
  death of, xviii, 2, 66, 73
  Madeleine as potential sexual partner of, 47–
    48, 60, 62–65, 71, 89
  Madeleine as slave of, 38, 47–48, 58–60, 62–65
  Madeleine purchased by or transferred to, 1–2,
    37–38, 46–47, 70, 119, 122, 128, 135, 144, 170–
    71, 173, 181–83, 185–86
  marriage of, xviii, 39, 227–28n65
  military service of, 39, 59
  slave trade and, 61, 64
  wealth and holdings of, 39, 43–44, 58, 64
  widowing and remarriage of, 39
Royal Court of Bourbon, 134–35, 162–63, 172–73,
  175, 188–90, 281n114, 281n119, 295n27
Royal Court of Paris (Cour Royale de Paris)
  damages for Furcy denied at, 183, 186
  Furcy's case (1840–3) at, 2–3, 163, 174–76,
    179–88, 196
  Tribunal of First Instance case (1817) cited at,
    181–82, 184
  verdict favoring Furcy (1843) at, 184–88

Sabino de Gomes (slave owner), 11, 23–24, 26
Saint-Denis (Réunion), 109–11, 198
Saint-Domingue
  interracial marriages in, 56
  maroon (fugitive slave) communities in, 72
  revolution (1790s) in, 3, 71–73, 76, 79–82,
    102, 247n27
  slavery abolished (1793) in, 72–73, 79, 84
  slave trade and, 71
  sugar production in, 69
Saint-Germe, Julie, 134
Samson, Paul, 147
Schœlcher, Victor, 179, 193–94, 301n28
Scott, Dred and Harriet, 187, 304nn75–76
Senegal, 35, 51
Seven Years' War, 18, 44
Shari'a law, 13, 120
Siraj ud-Daulah, Mirza Muhammad, 18
slave narratives, 3
slavery. *See also* abolition of slavery; manumission
  children born into, 14
  Code Decaen and, 88–89, 95, 97, 101, 117, 120
  corporal punishment and, 68–69, 81,
    87, 105–6
  créole (island-born) slaves and, 7, 34, 50, 61
  daily living conditions under, 4, 6, 67–69, 79–
    81, 87, 92–93, 105–7, 138, 143, 251n65
  debt bondage and, 12–13, 19–20, 183
  deference and authority in, 4, 68, 106
  escapes from, 68, 147
  fictional portrayals of, 3–4, 197, 204n2

free persons' owning of slaves and, 62, 64, 66,
    94, 99, 155, 156, 193, 292n111
  French laws regarding South Asian Indians and,
    2, 7, 36, 119–20, 122, 123, 125–28, 130, 149,
    152–53, 162–63, 170, 173, 180–81, 183–86,
    275n23, 303n57
  Islamic law regarding, 13
  Mackau laws (1845) and, 187–88
  new names conferred in, 12
  plantation colony wealth reflected
    through, 10, 43
  precolonial India and, 13
  re-enslavement of freed persons and, 84, 92
  revolts and, 50, 68, 103, 154
  Roman law and, 120, 129
  sexual relations with owners of overseers
    and, 47–48, 59–60, 62–65, 71, 75, 89,
    231–32n108, 242n93
  "social death" and, 6
  wet nursing and, 41–42, 47, 60, 116, 133
slave trade
  abductions and, 22–23, 34
  Arab slave traders and, 55
  bills of sale and, 1, 11–12, 22–26, 169,
    171, 218n74
  British ban (1807) on, 102, 139, 263n4
  British traders and, 13–14, 21
  demand for children in, 12–14, 21–22, 72–73
  Dutch traders and, 21
  French ban on, 106–7, 158
  French traders and, 14, 21, 52–55
  Mauritius and, 77, 102, 136, 153
  Portuguese traders and, 11, 14, 23–25,
    55, 212n22
  restrictions regarding, 36–37, 55, 77, 102, 120,
    136, 158, 160, 185, 224n38, 263n4
  Réunion and, 22, 34, 53–55, 61, 64, 66, 76, 102,
    126, 138–39
  smuggling after bans and, 136, 138–39, 153
  U.S. ban on, 263n4
Somerset v. Stewart (1772), 140
Sonthonax, Leger Félicité, 79, 108
Sonthonax, Marie Josephine Louise, 108,
    114, 267n49
Sophie (slave of Constance), 169
Spanish Empire
  Napoleonic Wars and, 76, 79
  slavery and, 7, 120
  wet nurses and, 41
Succès, 138–39, 143, 284n15
Sudra caste, 17
sugar production
  in the Caribbean, 69
  Furcy's work in, 145–46, 189–90

in Mauritius, 4, 68, 102, 135–36, 138, 145,
    157, 189–90
in Réunion, 4, 69, 73, 101–2, 110, 157,
    159–60, 179
Sully Brunet, Jacques
    as court hearings officer in Réunion, 109–10,
        113, 116, 118–24, 126–29, 131, 141
    dismissal from office and house arrest of, 113,
        131–32, 135, 270–71n79, 278nn86–87
    on the enslavement of South Asian
        Indians, 127–29
    on the free soil principle, 127
    Furcy's court petition (1817) and, 116,
        118–20, 273n99
    Furcy's freedom suit (1817) and, 121–24, 126–
        29, 131–33, 141
    as General Council member in Réunion, 158, 161
    Panon Desbassayns family case and, 113,
        270–71n79, 270n77
    question of assigning a patron to Furcy's legal
        proceedings and, 129
Suzanne (slave of Constance), 62, 64, 66, 241n91

Terrasson, Pierre Laurent Washington, 188
Testard, Jean Louis, 109, 113–14, 134
Thureau, Nicolas Marie Edouard, 180–82, 184
Topas (Euro-Indian Catholic community), 21, 24
Toussaint de Quièvrecourt, Pierre Gabriel, 177,
    188, 190–91, 299n11
Treaty of Amiens (1802), 87

Treaty of Paris (1763), 18–19
Treaty of Paris (1814), 101
Truth and Reconciliation Commission (South
    Africa), 199

United Kingdom. *See* Great Britain
United States, 69, 84, 140, 187, 263n4
Ursuline community of nuns, 24–25

Vaishya caste, 17
Vetter, Matthieu, 62–64, 94, 242n96, 258n58
Victor Théophile (slave of Furcy), 155
Villèle, Jean Baptiste de, 157–58
Voyage à l'Ile de France (Bernardin de Saint-Pierre), 31

Wanquet, Claude, 72
wet nursing
    Boucher family and, 133–34
    in Louisiana, 42
    Madeleine and, 47, 60
    Routier family and, 41–42
    Saint-Pierre on, 41–42
    Spanish Empire and, 41
World Anti-Slavery Conventions (1840 and
    1842), 179

Yanoan (French trading post in India), 18

Zephir Joyeux (slave of Adolphe Lory),
    147, 287n62